A HISTORY OF CRETE

A History of Crete

CHRIS MOOREY

First published in 2019 by
HAUS PUBLISHING LTD
4 Cinnamon Row
London SW11 3TW
www.hauspublishing.com

The moral rights of the authors have been asserted

A CIP catalogue record for this book is available from the British Library

ISBN: 978-1-912208-53-1
eISBN: 978-1-912208-54-8

Typeset in Garamond by MacGuru Ltd

Printed in the UK by TJ International

Contents

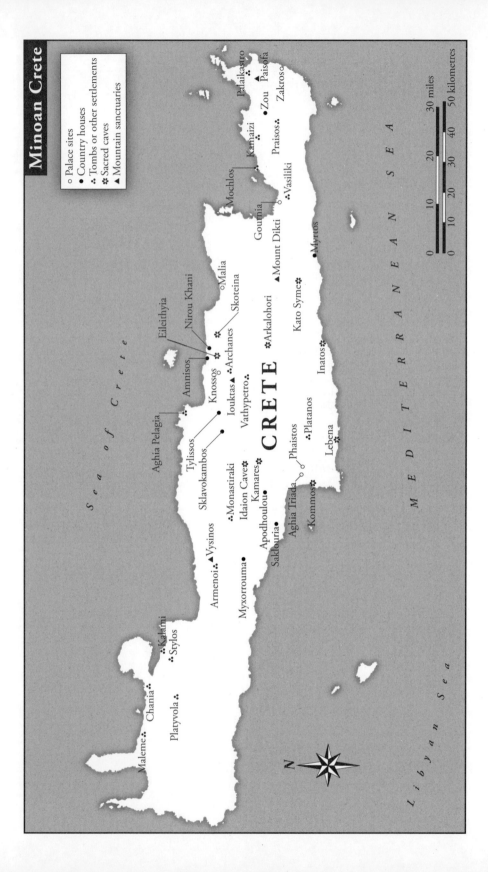

Minoan Crete

Palace sites ○
Country houses ●
Tombs or other settlements ❖
Sacred caves ✿
Mountain sanctuaries ▲

Sea of Crete

MEDITERRANEAN SEA

Libyan Sea

CRETE

N

0   10   20   30 miles
0   10   20   30   40   50 kilometres

Maleme ❖
Chania ❖
Platyvola ❖
Kalami ❖
Stylos ❖
Armenoi ❖ ▲ Vrysinos
Myxorrouma ●
Aghia Pelagia ❖
Tylissos ●
Sklavokambos ●
Monastiraki ❖
Idaion Cave ✿
Kamares ❖
Apodhoulou ●
Saklouria ●
Aghia Triada ○
Kommos ✿
Phaistos ○
Platanos ❖
Lebena ❖
Amnisos ❖
Knossos ●
Ilouktas ▲ ❖ Archanes ❖
Vathypetro ●
Arkalohori ❖
Kato Syme ✿ ❖
Inatos ✿
Myrtos ●
▲ Mount Dikti
Gournia ●
Vasiliki ❖
Mochlos ○
Kamaizi ❖
Praisos ❖
Palaikastro ○
Zou ●
Zakroso ○
Paisofa ▲
Eileithyia ✿
Nirou Khani ❖
Malia ○
Skoteina ✿

Dorian and Roman Crete

N

Sea of Crete

CRETE

MEDITERRANEAN SEA

Libyan Sea

Itanos
Siteia
Olous
Lato
Hierapytna
Chersonisos
Biannos
Lyttos
Arkades
Priansos
Inatos
Knossos
Gortyn
Axos
Phaistos
Eleutherna
Sybrita
Lappa
Phoenix
Aptera
Aradena
Kydonia
Elyros
Polyrmenia
Lissos
Kissamos
Kantanos
Gavdos

30 miles
50 kilometres

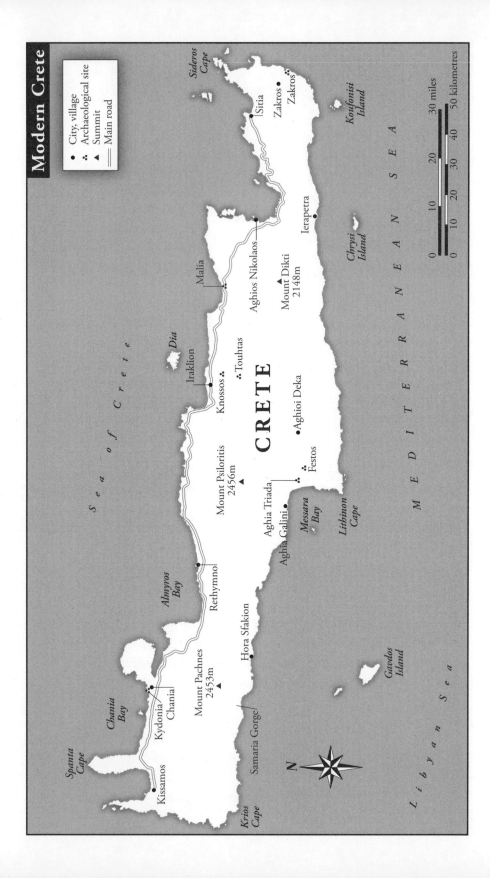

Preface

In the introduction to his excellent *History of Crete*, Professor Theocharis Detorakis writes that "one might be excused for seeing the attempt at writing a general history of Crete as a somewhat hazardous enterprise".[1]

He also refers to a third-century Roman historian's assertion that "since most of those who have written on Crete are not in accord with one another, it should be no wonder if some may disagree with what we are about to relate".[2]

To both these cautions I can only give my unqualified agreement. Military experts, when discussing tactics in battle, have sometimes made the point that there are narrow lines between courage, reckless-ness and sheer stupidity. In writing this book, I have sometimes felt I have strayed over one of these lines. So, why make the attempt?

A few years ago, it was brought to my attention that, with the exception of the book already mentioned, there is no general history of Crete written in English for the general reader. Although Detorakis' book is unique in its comprehensiveness, scholarship and readability, it is now over twenty years old and a little too academic and detailed for the average reader. I therefore felt that there was a place for a more brief and general outline of Cretan history which, while still providing a serious treatment of the subject, might attract a wider readership and encourage them to dig deeper.

To achieve this object, I have followed two strict principles. On the one hand, I have tried at all times to be true to the subject and to research thoroughly each period. I have used original sources and new research wherever possible, and in many cases I have been helped by experts in a particular field to ensure that there have been no errors of fact, misinterpretations or misleading oversimplifications.

The details of these experts' contributions can be found in the Acknowledgements.

At the same time, I have sought to create a simple and straightforward picture of the broad sweep of Cretan history from the mists of time to the present. In general, I have tried to keep names and dates to the minimum necessary to follow the story. I have also tried to avoid other details which could confuse readers or send them running to reference books or the internet. Where I have been forced to use potentially unfamiliar terms such as Byzantine or Ottoman military ranks, I have explained them briefly in the Glossary. These words are distinguished by bold type. Finally, this is not an academic work. Where I have quoted directly from another writer or used a lot of detail from a single source, I have, of course, acknowledged this, but it is perfectly possible to enjoy the book without constant referral to notes.

Two other points need to be made. Although I try at all times to be objective with the facts, I am not averse to giving my own opinion at times. One of my favourite historians is the idiosyncratic Edward Gibbon and, while I in no way approach his genius, my style has certainly been influenced by his. I trust that any personal opinions are always clearly marked. Finally, I like to include wherever possible individual tales and testimony from the period in question to give the historical facts a human face.

General Notes

1. Since most of the names of people and places in this book are Greek, we come across the age-old problem of how to spell them in English. I have tried to follow certain rules. For ancient names, I have used the standard Greek spelling, except where the Latin spelling is better known. For example, "Icarus" rather than "Ikaros", or "Homer" rather than "Omeros". Where the information is from a particular source, I have spelled personal names according to the source material or, in some cases, according to the spelling preferred by the person concerned. In all other cases, I have used my own transliteration of the original Greek, e.g. "Ioannis" or "Georgos". For place names, I have generally followed the spelling used on

Google Maps, both for consistency and for ease of location. I speak from experience when I say that some sources use such odd transliterations that it can take half an hour to identify the place they're referring to.

2. It was pointed out to me that some of the dates in my first draft manuscript were from the Old (Julian) Calendar and some were from the New (Gregorian) Calendar, which Greece did not adopt until 1923. I have tried to ensure that they are now all consistently based on the Gregorian calendar. I cannot guarantee that this is always the case – but, as Ralph Waldo Emerson once said, "A foolish consistency is the hobgoblin of little minds."

3. It could be argued that, with the union of Crete with Greece in 1913, there was no longer a separate Cretan history – but this would be an oversimplification. There were events that were either unique to the island or had distinctly Cretan aspects, which deserve attention. For this reason, I have taken the history right through to the present. The personal opinions expressed in the final chapter are based on observation and, in most cases, reflect the views of many Cretans.

4. For copyright reasons, I was unable to reproduce illustrations for chapters 3–6. Pictures of most of the items and sites mentioned in the text can easily be viewed online. In particular, at the time of writing, there are some good photographs of Minoan artefacts at https://www.ancient.eu/Minoan_Art and https://en.wikipedia.org/wiki/Minoan_civilization. A comprehensive collection of Minoan archaeological sites can be found at www.minoancrete.com.

1

Introduction

Round him spread his native country, whose lost meaning he was now experiencing for the first time. Hard of approach, rebellious, harsh was this land. She allowed not a moment of comfort, of gentleness, of repose. Crete had something inhuman about her. One could not tell whether she loved her children or hated them. One thing was certain: she scourged them till the blood flowed.[1]

In his great novel of Cretan rebellion, *Captain Michalis* (known in the UK as *Freedom and Death*), Nikos Kazantzakis thus describes in emotional terms the effect of the landscape on the Cretan soul, and it is certainly true that the geology of the island has played its part in shaping the history, society and economy of what has been called "a tiny continent".

Four mountain ranges effectively cut off much of the south from the north. From west to east, these are the Lefka Ori (White Mountains), the Psiloritis range, the Dikti range and the less formidable Siteia range. As a result, for much of the history of the island, the major cities and most of the population were concentrated on the north coast. In the south – with the exception of the Messara plain – very high summer temperatures, hot winds from Africa and stony soil meant that agriculture was limited to a subsistence level. Along much of the south coast, steep cliffs made access difficult if not impossible, and there were few natural harbours. As for the interior, even up to relatively modern times, overland transport was limited to mule paths, so that any area without good access to the sea was isolated. From the Cretans' point of view this harsh landscape had its advantages, in that many areas of the island were inaccessible to conquerors such as the Romans, Arabs, Venetians, Ottomans and the Third Reich.

Another major influence on Crete's history has been its location. Close to the junction of three continents, Crete has always been of major strategic importance. This has occasionally been to the island's advantage; for example, during the Bronze Age, it was an ideal location for a seafaring trading society. However, more often, Crete has attracted the attention of foreign invaders, not to mention pirates. For the Romans, the island was an ideal stopover for the trade routes to Africa and the Middle East; to the Third Reich, it would become an "aircraft carrier" for attacks on Egypt, Cyprus and Palestine. For at least 1,270 years, Crete was occupied by invaders, and much of its troubled history has revolved around how the Cretans dealt with these conquerors and the influence of foreign rule on their culture.

In spite of, or perhaps because of, the repeated invasions and the harshness of the landscape, Cretans have developed a unique character, which has manifested itself throughout the years. First of all, they nurture a fierce patriotism and love of their island, described by Robert Pashley in 1837:

> Distinguished as all the Greeks are by the love of their own country, this general characteristic is still more strongly developed in the Cretans than in the inhabitants of any other district, with which I am acquainted in this part of the world. In ancient times, the Cretans shewed this affection for their native island by calling it, not by the common name of fatherland (πατρίς), but by the still dearer appellation of motherland (μητρίς).[2]

Along with this love of their country, two other loves exist in the Cretan soul: a love of freedom and a love of life. Whether it be in the defiant resistance to Venetian rule or in guerrilla warfare against the Nazis, the Cretan battle cry throughout history has been that of the nineteenth-century rebellions against the Ottomans: Eleftheria i Thanatos (Freedom or Death). As for love of life, it is as visible in the colourful and joyful Bronze Age frescoes as in the dancing at any party in any village in the twenty-first century.

The geology of Crete, the circumstances of its location and the unique character of its inhabitants have all played their part in the dramatic history of the island. Their influence will be recognised time and again in the different periods described in this book.

Mythological Crete

Why Mythology?

It is, perhaps, unusual to begin a history book with mythology – which, almost by definition, is the opposite of historical fact. The relevant word here is "almost". Over the years, many stories that were always assumed to be pure myth or legend have been found to have at least a symbolic or tenuous relationship with history. Nowadays, we no longer dismiss the myths as primitive fiction but examine them to see what they can tell us about history. Perhaps the most famous example of this is Heinrich Schliemann's attempts to link the Trojan War of Homer's *Iliad* with actual historical events. In similar fashion, it was to myth that Sir Arthur Evans turned to give a name to the Bronze Age civilisation that he uncovered at Knossos. Myth and history often seem to touch and, as we shall see, it is possible that new insights into the latter may be gained by being aware of the former. Moreover, Crete held a central place in Greek mythology and was of immense importance in the religion of classical Greece right up to and including Roman times. At the very least, therefore, some knowledge of the myths and legends may help lead us to a better understanding of the culture of ancient Crete.

There are many different versions of the Greek myths – some of them contradictory – and the following stories do not represent all possible variations.

Zeus

The main reason that Crete was so important in Greek mythology was that it was the birthplace of Zeus, the king of the Olympian gods. The first gods to rule the world were the Titans, of whom Kronos was the chief. Fearful of being betrayed and overthrown by his children, he took the rather extreme step of swallowing each of them as soon as they were born. His wife, Rhea, eventually decided that this could not continue. When Zeus was born in the Diktaion Cave, in Crete, she hid him, and gave Kronos a rock wrapped in swaddling clothes. The ruse succeeded and Kronos ate the rock, but Rhea, still fearing for the safety of the baby, had Zeus moved to the Idaion Cave, where he was looked after by the nymph Amaltheia. For added protection, the cave was guarded by a group of good-natured but strong demigod giants called Kourites.[1] They were under instructions to perform noisy war dances whenever the baby cried, to prevent Kronos hearing him. Zeus grew to manhood safely, and fulfilled Kronos' prediction by killing his father and becoming king of the Olympian gods.

As is well known, Zeus wasn't exactly a faithful husband to his wife, Hera, but one particular affair had enormous ramifications for Crete and Europe. Zeus once saw the daughter of the king of Tyre, in modern Lebanon, playing on the beach, and fell madly in love with her. The girl's name was Europa. Turning himself into a gentle bull, Zeus tempted her to climb on his back, whereupon he plunged into the sea and carried her to the island of Crete. They settled into an idyllic love nest under the plane trees near where Gortyn was later built, and there Europa gave birth to three sons. When Zeus tired of her, he gave her in marriage to King Asterion of Crete, who adopted the three boys as his heirs.

King Minos

The three sons of Europa were Minos, Rhadamanthus and Sarpidon. The eldest, Minos, became ruler of Knossos and seems to have been a powerful, wise and just king. Every seven years, he visited the Idaion Cave, where he received directly from Zeus the laws that would govern

Crete. Rhadamanthus and Sarpidon also ruled their cities wisely but, eventually, Midas sent his brothers into exile, fearing competition from them. Rhadamanthus moved around the Aegean, acting as a sort of peripatetic judge, noted for the fairness of his decisions; on his death, Zeus appointed him to be judge of human souls in Hades. Sarpidon settled in Lycia, which he ruled wisely for three generations, by permission of Zeus.

Minos was married to Pasiphae, a lady from a pretty notorious family: her sister was the sorceress Circe and her niece the murderess Medea. She, however, comes across as more of a victim, having to put up with her husband's numerous affairs. The god Poseidon, protector of Crete, sent Minos a pure white bull to be sacrificed in his honour, but the king couldn't bring himself to kill the beautiful animal, and hid it to keep for himself. When Poseidon discovered this impiety, he decided on an appropriate revenge. He made Pasiphae fall passionately in love with a bull. The inventor Daedalus constructed a wooden cow, into which she could climb to consummate the relationship. (Yes, I know. I didn't write the story, I'm just the messenger.) The result of this somewhat odd affair was Asterion, known as the Minotaur, a creature with a human body and the head of a bull.

The Labyrinth

Since the Minotaur was carnivorous and particularly fond of human flesh, Minos had Daedalus build him a massive and complex maze underneath his palace at Knossos. The Minotaur was chained up at the centre. Several different versions of the labyrinth story exist, but this version is probably the best known. In classical times, the labyrinth was associated with Knossos, but other theories associate it with a complex of caves near Gortyn.

The story now shifts to Athens, where Androgeos, son of Minos and Pasiphae, went to compete in an athletic competition. He won every event, and his jealous rivals ambushed and killed him. In a fury, Minos attacked and defeated Athens and insisted on a tribute to Crete every seven years. Part of the tribute was the provision of seven brave young men and seven beautiful maidens to be fed to the Minotaur. After the second tribute, the young hero, Theseus, son of King Aegius of Athens, volunteered to be one of the victims. The group set sail in a ship with a black sail, Theseus having told his father that if they returned victorious he would hoist a white sail instead. When the group arrived in Crete, Ariadne, daughter of Minos, fell in love with Theseus and tried to find a way to help him. Daedalus suggested that she give the hero a ball of thread which he could unroll as he entered the labyrinth and thus find his way out again. Theseus went first into the maze, found his way to the centre, killed the Minotaur and escaped with the other thirteen victims, taking Ariadne with him.

The story did not have an entirely happy ending. First, Theseus abandoned the lovelorn Ariadne on the island of Naxos, where she was later found by the god Dionysos. He married her and took her to Mount Olympus, where she became a minor goddess. Meanwhile, Theseus sailed back to Athens, but forgot to hoist the white sail. Aegius was watching from a rock on Cape Sounion and, seeing the black sail, believed his son was dead. He threw himself into the sea and drowned, and the sea has been called the Aegean ever since.

Daedalus

Daedalus was an Athenian, a great inventor and a skilled craftsman. Exiled from Athens for murder, he fled to Crete, where he worked for King Minos. He was the architect and builder of the palace of Knossos and designer of the labyrinth. According to some versions of the legend, he was also the builder of Talos, the giant bronze automaton who patrolled the seas around Crete, protecting it from pirates and invaders. When Minos found out how Daedalus had helped Pasiphae and Ariadne, he flew into a rage. Fearing for his life, Daedalus decided to flee Crete with his son, Icarus – but since Minos controlled all the ports and sea routes, he had to find other means. He constructed two sets of wings from wood and feathers, the latter glued on with wax, and the pair flew off into the sky. Icarus got so excited by the speed and height at which they were flying that he flew nearer and nearer to the sun. The wax melted, the wings fell to pieces, and the boy plunged to his death in the sea, which is today still called the Icarian Sea. Daedalus made it safely to Sicily. Minos followed but, before he could capture him, was himself murdered by the daughters of King Kokalos of Sicily.

Given that the myths may have their origins in folk memories of historical facts, it has always been a source of confusion that Minos seems to have had a split personality. Sometimes he is depicted as a lawgiver and priest, the "friend of god". At other times, he appears as a cruel and vengeful tyrant. For this reason, many scholars are now of the opinion that the name Minos was, in fact, a sort of generic title for the king of Knossos, similar to the words "Caesar" and "Pharaoh". Thus, the myth of Minos could well have been a conflation of several different myths.

3

Prehistoric Crete

From the Mists of Time to 3000 BC

The Earliest Visitors

Until recently, it was generally believed that the earliest evidence of human inhabitants in Crete dated from about 6000 BC during the **Neolithic era** (New **Stone Age**, about 7000 BC to 3000 BC). Although there is speculation that there may have been earlier occupation, no convincing evidence has been found.[1] In 2008 and 2009, a group of American and Greek archaeologists directed by Thomas Strasser and Eleni Panagopoulou began looking for evidence of human artefacts dating from before 6000 BC in the area of Plakias, in south-western Crete. They did indeed find spearheads and arrowheads from the **Mesolithic era** (Middle Stone Age, about 8300 BC to 7000 BC), but what happened next was astounding. As they explored deeper, they found more stone hand-axes and tools of a much older style, buried in a geological stratum that couldn't have been less than 130,000 years old, putting this location well back into the **Palaeolithic era** (Old Stone Age, from the mists of time to 8300 BC). Curtis Runnels, one of the team, said in an interview, "We were flummoxed. These things were just not supposed to be there."[2]

About 2,000 tools were collected, and detailed geological examination of the stratum in which they were found confirmed that they were buried by seismic activity between 130,000 and 190,000 years ago. However, this was a conservative estimate as the quartz hand-axes, cleavers and scrapers were in the Acheulean style, which dates from much earlier. Estimates of the true age of the tools vary from 260,000 to 700,000 years, although archaeologists think the latter might be stretching it a bit. Since then, more evidence of pre-Neolithic occupation has been discovered at Mochlos, Loutro and Gavdos, but the finds are still being examined and results are as yet inconclusive. Investigation and further excavations are continuing, and a lively debate is taking place among academic experts.[3]

Although no final consensus has been reached, we can now say at the very least that humans or pre-human **hominins** were present in Crete much earlier than had been believed. The artefacts' minimum age of 130,000 years places them long before the time when *Homo sapiens* was believed to have appeared in Europe, about 40,000 to 60,000 years ago. This means that either *Homo sapiens* reached Europe much earlier than thought or these early tool makers were pre-human hominins. During the period we are considering, Neanderthals (*Homo neanderthalensis*) occupied most of Europe and the species *Homo erectus*, believed to have been the originator of Acheulean tools, was present in most of the Middle East. Whoever these visitors were, we can only speculate on where they came from. Up to now, the only evidence of early sea crossings in the Mediterranean is from artefacts discovered in Cyprus, some Greek islands and Sardinia, dating from 10,000 to 12,000 years ago at the earliest. Since Crete became an island about 5 million years ago, the toolmakers must have arrived by sea, either departing from Africa or island-hopping from Turkey or the **Levant**.

The general consensus among academics has always been that hominins such as *Homo erectus* or *Homo neanderthalensis* "lacked the cognitive faculties, technical abilities and linguistic capacities needed to construct watercraft to cross the open sea".[4] Now we have evidence that they must have had not only the ability to build seaworthy craft but also rudimentary navigation skills. In order to cross from the nearest land mass to Crete, they would have needed at least steering oars or paddles and simple sails, such as a wide paddle, to be held up in order to catch the wind.[5] The visits to Crete were certainly made by hunter-gatherers and must have been short stays, as there is no evidence of long-term occupation. But were these visits intentional or accidental? The prevailing winds and currents between Crete and Santorini, the nearest island, make it very likely that accidental landings occurred. On the other hand, it has been argued in a different context that, under the right conditions, Crete's chain of mountains and the cloud mass above it is visible from high ground on nearby Melos and Santorini.[6] This implies that curiosity may have led to deliberate exploration of the island by hunter-gatherers, as Strasser and Panagopoulou's team has asserted:

> These findings may push the history of seafaring in the Mediterranean back by more than 100,000 years and have implications on the colonization of Europe and beyond by early African hominins, our pre–*Homo sapiens* ancestors. The view that Europe and Asia were peopled exclusively by land needs to be rethought.[7]

These are exciting times in the field of prehistoric studies!

Neolithic Crete

We are on slightly firmer ground as we move into the Neolithic period, although hard evidence is scarce and dates are still a little vague. Up until recently, excavation of Stone Age sites has been spasmodic, partly because research has tended to focus on the more "glamorous" Minoan sites. However, in the last two decades, there have been concerted efforts to widen and deepen our knowledge of Neolithic Crete.[8]

The origins of the Neolithic settlers are unknown, but a detailed DNA analysis of Minoan remains on the Lassithi plateau, carried out in 2013, seems to confirm that the Minoans were direct descendants of Neolithic farmers. These in turn originated in the Levant, migrating from there via Anatolia to the Dodecanese and then island-hopping to Crete and the south of mainland Greece.[9] Perhaps the myth of Zeus carrying Europa from Tyre to Crete may not be as improbable as it seems!

So, how did they get to Crete? In contrast to the visits of the earlier Palaeolithic and Mesolithic hunter-gatherers, which were almost certainly short term, the colonisation of Crete by Neolithic agriculturalists has been convincingly shown to have been both purposeful and large in scale. Moreover, it is almost certain that these settlers brought animals and grain with them. There is no evidence for the existence of indigenous wild forms of any of the domesticated species reared by the Neolithic farmers, or of most of the crops grown. As previously mentioned, the existence of Crete would be known to people on neighbouring islands, and news of its fertility and potential for agriculture could easily have been brought back by hunters. The original migration would have required careful planning, both for the trip and to ensure adequate supplies to form a new colony. A fascinating study of the requirements for setting up such a community estimates that at least forty people would have been needed to set up a founder population.[10] The minimum livestock requirement would have been between ten and twenty sheep and goats, and a similar number of pigs and cattle. Finally, forty units of grain (250 kg each) would have been needed to plant and to feed the population for the first year. All this gives a total weight for the voyage of between 15,000 kg and 19,000 kg. The boats would have needed to be watertight to prevent spoilage of the grain, and big enough to transport large living cargoes. Thus, about ten to fifteen hide or log boats would have been needed to transport the settlers to their new home. My admiration for our Neolithic ancestors continues to increase.

The land that these early Cretans inhabited was very different from today's environment. Much of the island was thickly wooded, with mostly evergreen oak in the fertile valleys and plains, and pine and cypress in the more mountainous areas. Because of the way in which the island emerged from the sea as a result of seismic activity, it has not had a land link with the mainland for more than 5.5 million years. Thus, the fauna prior to human settlement was restricted to creatures that could swim, fly or "hitch-hike" on floating vegetation. These animals developed unique features due to their isolation from other members of their species. On the one hand, a lack of food resources resulted in pygmy versions of herbivores such as elephants, hippos and deer. On the other hand, the absence of carnivorous predators allowed rodents like mice to be much larger than their mainland equivalents. All the pygmy and giant species became extinct in the earliest period of Neolithic human settlement due to hunting, loss of habitat or displacement by new species introduced by the settlers.[11] However, for unknown reasons, the Cretan shrew did not develop a giant form, and has survived to the present day.

Almost all the evidence for the earliest years of the Neolithic era in

Crete comes from excavations underneath the lowest Minoan levels at Knossos and, although this is not sufficient in itself to give a clear picture of life in Stone Age Crete, it is enough to indicate that settlements followed similar patterns to those in other areas of Greece, the Balkans and the Near East, for which we have more direct evidence.

Agriculture

The arrival in Crete of a settled agricultural community changed the island dramatically and permanently. Indeed, in all areas of the world, changes in lifestyle and social structure brought about by the move to agriculture had effects that were so dramatic and far-reaching that they have been called the Neolithic Revolution. The practices of hunting, fishing and gathering wild berries and plants did not end and were still used during bad harvests or to supplement the diet. However, the primary source of food was the cultivation of cereal crops such as wheat and barley, which, together with pulses (mainly lentils) began to be cultivated very early. Later, millet, rye, oats, peas and broad beans were added, together with flax for weaving. The bones of domestic animals including goats, sheep, cattle, pigs and dogs have been found in the earliest stratum of Knossos. Apart from the dogs, these animals were reared mainly for meat, although sheep were also kept for their wool in later years. Towards the end of the period, the donkey and rabbit were introduced to Crete.

The collection of wild berries and nuts continued, and there is evidence of early cultivation of fruit and nut trees including almonds, plums, apples and pears. Charcoal evidence shows the presence of wild olive trees but, to date, there is nothing to show that olives were cultivated at all until the later years of the Neolithic era, when there is evidence of spasmodic and limited olive harvesting. Systematic farming of olives, as well as grapevines, did not begin until the Bronze Age.

Technology

Closely linked to the agricultural revolution were developments in tools. Before the Neolithic period, stone implements and weapons were made by chipping and flaking rocks. The development of grinding and polishing techniques meant that tools could be given a finer finish, increasing their strength and cutting ability. Polished stone axes could cut through wood more easily, making large-scale forest clearance possible. Sickle blades could now be manufactured, and the invention of the adze made the shaping of wood easier.

Pottery also developed, starting with the very simplest of designs baked in fires, with no handles or decoration. Throughout the Neolithic period, pottery was handmade, usually by the coiling technique familiar to many of us from primary school. Clay was rolled into long threads and then moulded by hand to form the shape of the vessel. The potter's wheel didn't appear in Crete until the Minoan era but, even so, as the period progressed, more complex and varied ceramics appeared. By about 5000 BC, there is evidence of simple decorative patterns being carved into pots. In the earliest strata at Knossos, baked clay figures have been found, and the number of these increased substantially during the period. Early finds are usually of female forms, pointing to some sort of female deity worship, fertility cults or lineage histories. Towards the end of the era, there is a much greater variety of figurines, including bulls, birds and both male and female human representations. We can only guess at whether these were religious symbols, children's toys or even teaching aids.

Jewellery in this period included bracelets, rings and amulets made of stone, clay, shells or, more rarely, silver and gold. Other technological advances included the invention of weaving and, significantly, towards the end of the era, weapons and tools made of copper. By about 3800, there is early evidence of specialisation, with the manufacture of pottery, weapons and jewellery being concentrated in separate workshops.

Architecture

No complete buildings have been found from the earliest settlements of Neolithic Crete, but we know that walls were built of unbaked mud bricks or stones held together with mud, and that houses were partly dug into the ground. Very soon, however, building techniques became more sophisticated, with generally rectangular houses made of fired mud-brick walls built on stone foundations. These walls were covered with a simple plaster, and the roofs were made of tree trunks, reeds or clay. Hearths and ovens were built between houses, indicating some sort of communal living or at least shared cooking facilities. Later, houses tended to be larger and to contain many small rooms, as shown by excavations at Knossos, Katsambas on the coast near Iraklion, and Mitropoli near Gortyn. Permanent hearths within houses became a common feature, indicating a move towards more family-oriented living.

Population

The earliest Neolithic settlements were villages of 50–100 inhabitants. By about 5000 BC, there was a noticeable increase in the size of villages, which now ranged from 100–300 people. In the later part of the Neolithic era, there is evidence of a significant population increase and a simultaneous rise in the number of settlements, which came to include Phaistos, Gortyn, Kastelli and Chania. The uplands, including the Lassithi and Siteia plateaux showed signs of habitation, as did some caves in west and central Crete. By the end of the Stone Age, human activity had spread to most of the island, and it is estimated that Knossos held up to 2,000 people.

Society

Whether Stone Age society was basically egalitarian or whether there were tribal chiefs and some sort of hierarchy is still subject to debate. In the early Neolithic period, the basic unit of society seems to have been the extended family or clan, and there is little evidence of differences of class or wealth among the members of the community. Whether the head of the family was regarded as a sort of chieftain or whether the society was matriarchal or patriarchal is unknown. Later, the nuclear family became the basic social unit and, together with increasing trade and specialisation in production, this led to the emergence of economic and social differences among community members. There is evidence that some people held more gold and silver jewellery and copper tools, and some sort of hierarchy might have been emerging.

In the early Neolithic period, there is evidence of trade in food and raw materials between neighbouring settlements, but the difficulties of sea travel initially limited trade with the mainland or other islands. Over time, however, trade expanded within the Aegean area. For example, the only sources of obsidian, a stone highly prized for its strength, were a few Aegean islands, primarily Melos. The existence of tools made from obsidian in Crete indicates some sort of trading network, while further evidence is provided by imports of copper, silver and lead from mines on the mainland (Lavrion) and the Cyclades (Siphnos). After about 3000 BC, trade with the Cyclades, Egypt and the East became widespread.

Burial customs in Crete followed normal Neolithic practices. The dead were buried under the floor within houses or very nearby, sometimes on the edge of the settlement. There is little evidence of cemeteries, although they have been found in other parts of Greece. The graves were simple pits, and the bodies were usually buried in the foetal position. Partial or complete cremation was also used. Pottery, stone tools and small animals were buried in graves, while late in the period figurines and jewellery were added. This seems to indicate some sort of belief in an afterlife, although this is an area where we can have no real certainty.

Although it is believed that Neolithic society in general had become more aggressive and warlike than in earlier periods, evidence of defensive ditches and fences like those discovered in mainland settlements has not been found in Crete earlier than about 3500 BC. During this later period, there seems to have been movement of some settlements from coastal sites to better-fortified hilltop areas further inland, while there is evidence of several new settlements on the coast. This may indicate incursions by new tribes – possibly early Bronze Age settlers from the Middle East – but whether this migration was peaceful or violent is unknown. The transition between the Neolithic era and the Bronze Age was certainly a process lasting a considerable time and, as we shall see, the exact mechanisms of progress are still subject to debate.

4

The Bronze Age

3000 BC to 1100 BC

Who Were the Minoans?

Although references to Crete and its people are common in classical Greek writing, the existence of an ancient civilisation under the rule of King Minos was assumed for centuries to have been a myth. However, in the early years of the twentieth century, the finding of an ancient coin showing a labyrinth design and the word "Knossos" led Evans to begin excavating at Knossos. Eventually, he revealed enough to show that there was indeed a thriving civilisation in Bronze Age Crete. Nobody knew, or knows, what these ancient Cretans called themselves or their country, so Evans described them as Minoan, a term first coined in the nineteenth century to describe the society found in Greek myth. Through the work of Evans and widespread later excavations throughout Crete, there can now be few who have not heard of Minoan Crete, and one cannot go far in the country without falling over a Minoan archaeological site or some reference to what was arguably the most glorious period of Crete's history.

Evans was the first to propose that the Minoans migrated to Crete from North Africa, based on similarities between the artefacts found at Knossos and those from Egypt and Libya, but this theory has been largely discredited by strong evidence for large-scale cultural exchange between these countries. More recently, it has been proposed that the Minoans' origins were more likely Turkey, the Balkans or the Middle East. In 2013, however, a major DNA analysis of prehistoric skeletons indicated that the Minoans were more likely to have been descendants of the existing Neolithic inhabitants of the island.[1] On the other hand, the previously discussed settlement patterns of the late Stone Age seem to indicate incursions from the east. It is therefore possible that the Minoans were a mixture of an indigenous Neolithic population and a new wave of settlers, the two races becoming intermingled early in the Bronze Age. DNA researchers are now working to sequence the entire **genome** of ancient remains taken from Crete, Mycenae on the Greek mainland and western Anatolia, which should help scholars better understand how homogeneous or heterogeneous Crete's ancient population was, and how it varied over time. The researchers' preliminary findings were reported in 2017:

> Minoans and Mycenaeans were genetically very similar, with about three-quarters shared ancestry with the first Neolithic farmers of western Anatolia and the Aegean and most of the remainder from ancient populations like those from the Caucasus and Iran. Unlike the Minoans, however, the Mycenaeans also showed additional ancestry related to Bronze Age inhabitants of the Eurasian steppe (the region encompassing Eastern Europe and North Eurasia). Their analyses also find that Modern Greeks share ancestry with the Mycenaeans but with some additional dilution of the early Neolithic ancestry.[2]

Unfortunately, although we know a great deal about the art, artefacts and architecture of this period, the only written records have yet to be translated, so we have little knowledge of the actual history. The bare bones of the events of Bronze Age Crete have been pieced together and there have been various attempts to define a chronology, but the terminology used by the various archaeologists is generally complex, confusing and, indeed, the subject of academic dispute.[3] A simplified version of the categories first outlined by Evans is probably the most straightforward timeline. It is based on the types of ceramics found at the various strata of Knossos. A second chronology is based on the development of the different types of palace used as the seat of government and varying over time, and can also be useful. Both of these are still generally accepted by the academic community, although some of the details have been disputed and exact dates may vary.

Evans		Palatial	
Early Minoan	3000 BC to 2000 BC	Prepalatial	3500 BC to 1900 BC
Middle Minoan	2000 BC to 1600 BC	Protopalatial	1900 BC to 1650 BC
Late Minoan	1600 BC to 1100 BC	Neopalatial	1650 BC to 1450 BC
		Creto-Mycenaean	1450 BC to 1100 BC

The Development of Minoan Society

In the earliest years, before the building of the first Minoan palaces, society seems to have been similar to that of the late Neolithic era, although the technological advances resulting from the use of copper and bronze had become much more widespread. Settlements were centred on the family or clan and were largely independent of each other. As Bronze Age technology developed and trade between the settlements increased, local hierarchies began to emerge, leading to the establishment of ruling elites in the larger settlements. The Minoan ruler seems to have been more of a judge and high priest, with the task of administration left largely to a fledgling bureaucracy. This contrasts with the Mycenaean hierarchy on mainland Greece (from 1600 BC to 1100 BC). There, the king was a warlord with absolute power. The exact nature of the administration of the Minoan cities is somewhat controversial, but the idea of a strong "king" is becoming discredited. It has been argued that Evans' description of structures as "palaces" implied that they were the residences of kings, an assumption that coloured scholarship for many years. In fact, there are no representations of a powerful "ruler" in Minoan art, and no wealthy tombs which might be called "royal" have been found until after the Neopalatial period. It is also interesting that none of the palaces contain throne rooms, except for the one at Knossos, and even in that case there is strong evidence that the throne itself was a later addition during the later Mycenaean period, when Mycenaean culture spread to Crete.

Most scholars believe that there are Prepalatial buildings and meeting areas underneath the excavated Protopalatial palaces, but it was after about 2000 BC that large-scale building of administrative centres for the local community began. A more complex and efficient bureaucracy developed, along with a class structure of nobles, artisans, merchants, peasants and, perhaps, slaves. The existence of slavery in Minoan society has still not been clearly established. If it did exist, enslaved people were either purchased by trade or captured in warfare, depending on one's view of the Pax Minoica. During this period, a paved road network was beginning to link some of the major communities, while overseas trade with Egypt and the Middle East expanded substantially.

Sometime around 1700 BC, the first palaces were destroyed, either by earthquake or invasion. Whatever the cause, the result was an even greater flourishing of Minoan culture. The palaces were quickly rebuilt on an even grander scale, and the road network expanded to connect most parts of the island. At the same time, there was a growth in settlements outside the palaces, where villages of 150–200 people carried out farming and developed cottage industries. Some of these villages developed into small towns. By the late period, an affluent upper class of landlords had gained a certain amount of secondary power, and were able to build substantial villas in the countryside, modelled on the royal palaces and, like them, acting as the administrative and ceremonial centres of the settlements. It has been estimated that, at its height, Minoan Crete had a maximum population of about 250,000, with Knossos having anything between 15,000 and 40,000. While it is clear that Knossos, Phaistos, Malia and Zakros were ruled by their own independent elites, there seems to have been an overall administrative, cultural and economic unity. Although Knossos has usually been assumed to have had overall dominance over the other palaces, many scholars now believe it to have been more of an ideological and cultural centre, exercising an influence similar to that of the Vatican in modern times.

In contrast to almost all societies at the time, there is strong evidence that women had a greater degree of equality with men, and played an important role in society, especially during the late period. While it was not unusual for early civilisations to honour women in a religious context either as goddesses or priestesses, Bronze Age Crete seems to have gone further, with women being a majority within the priesthood and possibly being in charge of religious rites. Images of women participating in ceremonies far outnumber those of men – for example, in the famous Aghia Triada sarcophagus – while the preponderance of female forms among Minoan figurines indicates an emphasis on female deities and priestesses. What is more, there is evidence that women also took an active part in other aspects of public life. In the Grandstand Fresco from Knossos, for example, it is the women who appear to have the places of honour, whereas the men merge into an anonymous mass. In contrast to Mycenaean art, there are few images of women in a domestic or child-rearing context, and the images we do have indicate that women were involved in administration and business as well as being craftswomen and priestesses. The images of women in bull-leaping frescoes do not show them participating in the leaping, but they are certainly involved in the ceremony, either as minders or judges. All in all, the little we know about this intriguing aspect of Minoan life raises more questions than it answers, whetting our appetites to know more.

Minoan civilisation was thus at its pinnacle during the two or three centuries after about 1700 BC, having reached a stage where political and economic systems worked together in unity, supported by a shared culture and religion.

Palaces – or Were They?

It was Evans who first identified the massive complexes at Knossos and other sites as palaces, with the implication of a centralised royal court governing the country, organising the economy and raising taxes. However, scholars now believe that this was either a misconception or at least an oversimplification. Although part of the typical palace may have been the living quarters of a royal family or ruling elite, by far the greater part seems to have been communal. There were areas for workshops, food processing and storage, domestic use, administration and religious rites. All in all, the palaces might be better described as court compounds, which the archaeological writer Jarrett Lobell likens to "more of a city core than the single domestic entity that the word 'palace' connotes."[4] Within this complex, trade and exchange would be organised, and the supply of staple resources controlled in order to ensure enough were available for religious celebrations, feasting and paying artisans and craftsmen for their work. It's not too outrageous to imagine Buckingham Palace, Westminster Abbey, the Houses of Parliament, Whitehall and the Bank of England all in one vast building!

We can only speculate on the precise function of the palaces, but two aspects of the structures leave no room for doubt. Firstly, even as ruined archaeological sites, the sheer scale of the palaces is striking. When complete, they must have been awe-inspiring, and in architectural terms they were certainly very advanced for their time, both in their size and in the use of advanced building materials such as ashlar (cut stone) and gypsum doorjambs. The main palaces cover areas of several thousand square metres and the largest, at Knossos, had 1,500 rooms. Even more impressive is that the palaces could be up to three storeys high in parts. With elaborate staircases, sophisticated drainage and plumbing systems and magnificent frescoes, the effect must have been stunning.[5]

Another striking feature of Minoan architecture was the distinctive column which, unlike Greek columns, was wider at the top than at the bottom. Made of wood rather than stone, the columns were generally painted a deep red or black and rested on a stone base. At the top was a round, pillow-shaped capital. The pillars were used not only to support a roof or upper storey but to create large open-plan spaces protected from the sun. It is also likely that the small pillar crypts found in most of the palaces may have had religious significance, possibly as symbolic representations of the sacred groves which formed a part of early Cretan religion.

The structure of the palaces was, in general, efficient and functional. Walls were made of sandstone or limestone blocks and rubble, packed with clay, and external walls in the late Neopalatial period had a facing of ashlar to improve their appearance. The existence of rubble and wooden crossbeams in the walls has led to speculation that the flexibility provided may have given some protection against small earthquakes. Light and ventilation were provided by open courtyards, together with the frequent use of light wells (unroofed shafts in the middle of the buildings).

Excavations

There have, of course, been numerous and extensive excavations of Minoan sites in all parts of Crete. Indeed, such is the wealth of archaeological material that many of the sites have been abandoned through lack of funds. Just a few of the main sites so far discovered and at least partially excavated are as follows.

Knossos and Phaistos are the two largest and most famous palaces, but extensive excavations at Malia have revealed a whole workshop area and a possible council chamber close to the main palace. The Kato Zakros palace is on a smaller scale but in an enchanting location. About 30 km south of Iraklion, Galatas is the most recently discovered palace, excavated between 1992 and 2005.

There are also some further possible palaces. Aghia Triada, near Phaistos, is intriguing as it seems to be a palace, but on a smaller scale and with a different design. There are also possible palaces at Gournia; Petras, near Siteia; and Monastiraki, south-east of Rethymnon.

There are a large number of excavations of settlements and towns, or parts of towns, throughout the island. Probably the most extensive is Gournia, about 20 km east of Aghios Nikolaos. Mochlos, an island east of the Gulf of Mirabello, may have been a centre for gold and silver jewellery and stone vases. On Pseira, a small island near Mochlos, over sixty buildings and a town square have been unearthed. Perhaps the most frustrating site is Kydonia, which is mostly under the city of Chania and largely inaccessible. It is interesting because it shows some evidence of central town planning. More evidence of the trade and transport network can be seen at Kommos, on the coast 6 km south-west of Phaistos, where there is a harbour and shipyard, and a paved road leading to Phaistos. Probably the best-preserved Minoan site in existence is not in Crete but on the island of Thera (Santorini), which may well have been a Minoan colony. Sometimes called "the Greek Pompeii", the recently re-opened site at Akrotiri alone makes a visit to Santorini worthwhile.

Peak sanctuaries and sacred caves have been found on Mount Iouktas, near Knossos; Simi, on the south side of Mount Dikti; and Arkalochori, 30 km south-east of Iraklion, where a massive collection of votive offerings was found in the 1930s. A possible temple or shrine at Anemospilia, on the north side of Mount Iouktas, has been used to support the human sacrifice theory. Cemeteries include Armeni, between Rethymnon and Spili, with 200 tombs, and Phourni, just south of Knossos, which apparently remained in use for over 1,000 years and has a rare Mycenaean tomb.

There are, of course many other tombs, villas and other excavations all over Crete. It is not possible to go into detail here, but information on individual sites is readily available on the internet.[6]

Language

Although we know nothing of the language spoken by the Minoans, it was actually the discovery of tablets inscribed with unknown symbols that first prompted Evans to begin his excavations at Knossos and led to the discovery of the Minoan civilisation:

> In the course of a visit to Greece in the spring of 1893 I came across some small three- and four-sided stones perforated along their axis, upon which had been engraved a series of remarkable symbols ... My inquiries succeeded in tracing these to a Cretan source ... I therefore determined to follow up my investigations on Cretan soil.[7]

And we all know what resulted from that.

The complex administration of the palaces would not have been possible without a written language with which to keep records, and it is no coincidence that the earliest scripts in the Aegean were developed in Crete. There were three systems: Cretan hieroglyphics; the script of the famous Phaistos Disc; and what Evans called Linear A. Cretan hieroglyphics were possibly based on the Egyptian or Hittite scripts, but could well have been home-grown. Linear A was a more stylised script. Neither of these two has been deciphered to date, largely because of the scarcity of examples. Clay tablets inscribed with hieroglyphs dating from about 2100 BC have been found, while Linear A emerged in the eighteenth century BC. Hieroglyphics seem to have disappeared some time during the seventeenth century BC, but for about 100 years the two systems existed side by side, and it seems likely that Linear A was a development from hieroglyphics. A clay bar from Knossos appears to show hieroglyphs alongside a few signs resembling Linear A, which may represent a transition between the two scripts.

Examples of hieroglyphics have been found in four locations in Crete and on the island of Samothrace. To date, a total of about 800 symbols have been found. The similarities and differences between the Cretan script and others from that era, including Hittite hieroglyphics and the script from Cyprus, suggest that they are related, possibly evolving from a common ancestor.

So far, Linear A has yielded about sixty symbols which appear to represent syllables, and about the same number of stylised pictograms which are thought to represent whole words, objects or abstract ideas. Thus, it seems to have been not only a development from hieroglyphics but, more importantly, a precursor of a later script called Linear B. Since the latter has been successfully decoded, one would think that it would be easy to decode Linear A by applying the same syllables to the signs. However, all attempts to do this have yielded unintelligible words, so it appears that the Linear B script was adapted by the Mycenaeans to fit their early form of Greek, while the language of Linear A was something very different – perhaps Minoan. Over 1,400 specimens of Linear A have been discovered to date, most of them in Crete but a few on other Aegean islands and in mainland Greece, southern Bulgaria, Turkey and Israel. Most of the examples from outside Crete seem to be locally produced, which might indicate use of the script beyond the area where the Minoan language was spoken. This in turn could indicate the adoption of the script by other languages.[8] In 2018, two scholars claimed to have deciphered a Linear A tablet.[9] This is an exciting development but, until the full paper is published, we will not know the details. The academic community is, for the time being, somewhat sceptical.

The Phaistos Disc is a clay disc about 6 inches in diameter, covered on both sides with hieroglyphic symbols. Discovered in 1908 at Phaistos, it can now be seen in the Heraklion Archaeological Museum. Although there are apparent similarities between the symbols on the disc and Cretan hieroglyphics, the Phaistos Disc typography is generally considered a separate script. Many of the symbols do not seem to relate to Cretan hieroglyphics, and it has been suggested that the disc may have originated outside Crete. The text remains a mystery in spite of countless attempts at deciphering it, ranging from the plausible to the more fanciful. Among the former suggestions are that it is a prayer, a call to arms or an inventory of goods. Less likely claims include the proposal that the disc is a relic from Atlantis or, inevitably, an alien artefact. With only 241 symbols and without much more information or further relevant finds, it is unlikely that the mystery will ever be solved.

Economy

The Minoans were excellent shipbuilders and sailors, and from very early days they were trading with mainland Greece, Egypt and the Middle East. Exports included olive oil, other agricultural products, timber and cloth, but it was mainly the manufactured items which were popular, especially ceramics and metalwork. A wide range of imports included raw materials like copper, tin, gold, silver, alabaster and ivory. Other imports included papyrus from Egypt and ostrich eggshells for decoration. The distribution of Minoan ware over a wide area of the Aegean, the Greek mainland and the Middle East indicates the depth of admiration for the skill and craftsmanship of the Minoans. It seems likely that the giant ceramic storage jars (**pithoi**) were, like well-made oak barrels in the Middle Ages, not just used to carry wine or oil exports but highly prized in their own right.

In Gournia on the north coast, a fully functioning harbour has been discovered, complete with a wharf, boathouses, a shipyard and a well-built cobbled road to the nearby town. The evident skill of the Minoans in shipbuilding enabled their navy to dominate the Aegean for several centuries. The ships had rounded prows, and each bore a single mast carrying a square sail. In addition to the sail, each ship was propelled by up to fifteen oars on each side, and was between 75 and 100 feet long. There is some evidence that after about 1600 BC, warships with rams were being built.

The peace and prosperity of the middle period enabled a rapid expansion of trade links with Egypt and the Middle East. Minoan artefacts have been found as far afield as Mesopotamia and the Indus valley to the east, and Sicily, Sardinia and Spain to the west, although we cannot be sure whether these were direct exports or secondary trade links. Oddly, although logic suggests that there would have been trade between Crete and Cyrenaica (Libya), extensive research and excavations have shown no evidence of this.

Technology and Science

The already-advanced technology of the Minoans was aided further by increasing specialisation, leading to an even more intensive level of production. The excavation at Gournia offers a vivid picture of a thriving industrial and trading centre. Over fifty areas which seem to have been workshops have been found. Of these, twenty produced pottery, fifteen produced stone vases, eighteen cast bronze and manufactured bronze implements, and a few showed evidence of textile production. An area of burned bedrock indicates a possible foundry, as confirmed by the archaeologist Matthew Buell:

> Here we have all sorts of scraps of bronze crucibles, bronze drips, copper scraps, and iron used for flux. Elsewhere, we also found a tin ingot, the closest known source of which is Afghanistan, and copper ingots from Cyprus, so it's clear they are making and working metal into objects on the site.[10]

Perhaps the most extraordinary aspect of Minoan technology was their innovative attitude to water supply and sanitation. Although the Romans would later develop aqueducts and drains to regulate the water supply, the sophistication of the Minoans' integrated approach to plumbing, sanitation and hygiene was probably not matched until the nineteenth century AD. Complex drainage and sewage systems were constructed from the early Minoan period onward, and these were repaired as required over the later periods. So well made were they that the main water supply ducts in Knossos, Phaistos, Zakros and Aghia Triada are still functional today. The Italian scientist Angelo Mosso, visiting Phaistos in 1907, was astounded:

All the sewers were still working! It was very interesting for me to see the water in the drainages and sewers so big that a man could enter. I doubt if there are other examples of ancient sewerages working after four thousand years.[11]

The water management system began on the roofs of the palace, where rainwater was collected in cisterns or allowed to run down the light wells for direct use or for collection in further cisterns. Pipes took the water to all parts of the palace, where it was either purified for drinking or used for baths and flushing out waste from the toilets. The water purification system used hydraulic filters: the water was forced against a porous ceramic wall which captured impurities, allowing the cleaned water to fall into jars. Sand and charcoal filters were also common. The terra cotta water pipes were themselves of an innovative design that could well have been more efficient than modern pipes. Four to six inches in diameter, each section tapered to a narrow end which fitted tightly into the broad end of the next. This created a sort of jetting action, which increased the speed of the water, thus stopping any build-up of sediment. The joints were sealed with cement. The existence of pairs of pipes lying alongside each other has raised the possibility of a hot and cold water system, but this is not certain. The means of heating the water is also unknown, except in the case of Akrotiri on Thera, where it seems likely that the volcanic hot springs could have been used. There has also been speculation that some sort of underfloor heating system existed, similar to the Roman hypocaust, but, again, this may apply only to Thera.

There seem to have been both permanent bathrooms and moveable bathtubs, both of which were filled and emptied by hand, the waste water being discarded into a hole in the floor leading to the main drain. The toilets were almost modern in design, vertical in front and sloping at the back, with a pan filled with water and a wooden or stone seat. In rainy weather they were automatically flushed by rainwater coming through a pipe from the roof. Otherwise, water was poured into a pipe located outside the door. The waste was carried off to the main sewer, well away from the living quarters. It appears that the Minoans were every bit as conscious of cleanliness as the Romans, and a caravanserai (inn for travellers) near Knossos includes a public bath and a large communal footbath, where weary travellers could sit and soak their feet.

The large drains carried all waste water away, either to the river or to be used in the irrigation system, while storm drains were built to take the overflow during heavy rain. Thus the water management system reached its conclusion. With the complex interaction of aqueducts, cisterns, filters, rainfall harvesting, fountains, baths, lavatories, drains and sewers, it is no wonder that modern sanitation engineers hold the Minoans in the highest respect.

In addition to technology, there is increasing evidence of other scientific advances made by the Minoans. Their reputation for skill in medicine is recorded in Egyptian texts, but it is their apparent development of astronomy to "a level comparable to the Egyptians and Babylonians"[12] that has caused much excitement. Researchers carried out extensive studies of the orientation of Minoan buildings in relation to the calendar positions of the sun, moon and stars in Crete. There was a very strong correlation and this, together with the Minoans' known navigational skills and some literary evidence from classical writers, points to high level of astronomical knowledge. It has been argued that the peak sanctuaries were also used as observatories, and at least some of the figurines found in them might be representations of the moon and constellations.

Agriculture

The irrigation system, coupled with technical advances in tool manufacture, resulted in great improvements in agriculture. Wooden or bone tools gave way to bronze tools with holes to take a wooden handle. At some stage, the Minoans developed the idea of oval holes and handles to prevent the tool head spinning, a small but significant advance. Ploughs were generally of wood, pulled by pairs of oxen or donkeys. The practice of growing more than one crop at a time (polyculture as opposed to monoculture) enabled a more varied diet, leading to better health and an increasing population. It also maintained soil fertility and improved productivity, all adding to the prosperity and success of the Minoan civilisation.

Generally, the animals farmed and the crops grown during this period were little different from the later agriculture of the island, and the foundations of the "Mediterranean diet" were laid. Cattle, sheep, pigs and goats were raised and bees were domesticated for the first time. Cats were imported from Egypt for hunting wildfowl. Wheat, barley, vetch and chickpeas were grown and grapes, figs and olives were cultivated, along with poppies, perhaps for opium production. Palm trees and pomegranates were introduced from the Middle East, although lemons and oranges had yet to make an appearance. In addition to all this, nature itself was bountiful, as lettuce, celery, asparagus, carrots, pear trees and quince trees grew wild. To supplement the diet, hunting yielded wild deer and boar, while edible molluscs, fish and octopus seem to have been an occasional treat.

A creature very similar to the modern wild kri-kri (also known as the Cretan goat) is depicted in Minoan art in both domesticated and wild settings, leaping around the mountains or being hunted. This implies that, at that time, there was little to distinguish between the domesticated and wild species. There is also some speculation that the wild kri-kri is descended from domesticated goats that escaped and went feral. Cattle were generally reared for their milk rather than for meat, although they were also used as draught animals and their skins were used to make shields. The bulls, of course, were also used in the famous bull-leaping events. Although they were probably domesticated, they were kept in a semi-wild state to make them more difficult to manage.

Fashion

The great amount of artwork discovered has given us a very good idea of the clothing the Minoans wore. Like almost everything they did, their costumes show a high degree of skill, both in design and manufacture. The warm Cretan climate meant that clothing was generally light. In the earlier years, men usually just wore loincloths of linen, leather or wool, with brightly coloured patterns and decorative codpieces. Later, they began to wear short-sleeved jackets and occasionally long skirts, similar to the women's, probably for more formal occasions. Women also wore loincloths underneath long skirts that were richly ornamented and sometimes flounced. A close-fitting sleeved jacket, sewn at the shoulders, was cut low at the front to leave the breasts fully exposed. A decorated apron at the front of the skirt completed the ensemble. The outer garments were discarded for sporting events like bull leaping. Slim waists were considered fashionable for both men and women, the former wearing tight metal belts, and the latter using something like a girdle.

Young people of both sexes seem to have had shaved heads with two locks, a short one at the front and a longer one at the back. Much has been written about the religious or age-related significance of various hairstyles, but nothing conclusive has been established. There seems to have been a variety of adult hairstyles including ringlets and buns, all of which indicate care for appearance and a high degree of elegance.

Art

It is fortunate that so many Minoan frescoes survive, mainly in Knossos, because, together with the beautifully preserved frescoes from Thera, they give us a wonderful picture of the Minoan lifestyle. In historical terms, they are of enormous value; in purely artistic terms, they are works of genius, pointing to a culture that valued life, beauty and colour. Minoan art has little of the religious symbolism of Egyptian, Mesopotamian or Persian art; nor does it often deal with military exploits and battles, like Mycenaean and later Greek painting. Although some of the frescoes depict religious or court ceremonies, many seem to have been composed simply to entertain and to please the eye: the original "art for art's sake".

Some Egyptian influence may be detected in the stylised depiction of people in profile with the eye at the front, but everything else is uniquely Minoan. In describing the details of the frescoes, some care is needed, as many of them have been reconstructed – not always convincingly – from a few surviving fragments. However, we can still be certain of the methods used, and about much of the style. In most cases, the pigments were applied directly onto wet plaster, as opposed to painting on already-dry plaster. This had the advantage of binding the pigments to the wall, keeping the colours bright and ensuring they would endure for a long time, but it required a great deal of skill and speed. However, this disadvantageous haste brought artistic benefits. Because the artists had to work quickly, the resulting pictures had a feeling of spontaneity and vitality that is absent from much art.

The subjects of the frescoes were varied, but usually involved nature or everyday court life. While some show scenes at court, processions, festivals or sporting events, many others depict flowers and plants without human presence – another Minoan first. Animals are usually shown in their natural habitats. Male figures are painted in dark colours, usually red, while females are depicted in white. This may follow the Egyptian convention in which the men's darker reddish brown reflects their outdoor life, while the women's lighter colour alludes to their mainly indoor domestic life. Although this theory makes interpretation of the frescoes easier, it is somewhat speculative. A rare almost-complete fresco on all four sides of a sarcophagus found at Aghia Triada shows a funeral procession, depicted with great skill and a vibrant use of colour.

Pottery

As with the frescoes, the pottery of the Minoan period demonstrates advanced technical competence coupled with great artistry. Even ordinary domestic pottery was often carefully decorated, again pointing to a culture that loved beauty. Even if, like mine, your mind tends to go blank when confronted by a room full of pottery in a museum, you will be surprised how much you enjoy a visit to the Minoan pottery exhibition at the Heraklion Archaeological Museum.

During the early Minoan period, pottery developed along more or less the same lines as in the late Neolithic era. The major development at that time was a sort of turntable which made the building up of the clay easier and more accurate. The resulting pots were somewhat clumsy round-bottomed jugs and bulbous jars, with simple linear black patterns on a red or brown base. Gradually, the designs became more adventurous, with a greater range of markings and more variety of colour decoration, which now included red, orange, yellow and white.

With the development of the potter's wheel around 2000 BC, a greater delicacy and a much wider range of designs became possible. Almost every kind of pottery was made, ranging from small cups to the giant storage jars (pithoi), often inscribed with Linear A characters. From about 1850 BC, very thin "eggshell" cups were produced. The elegant Kamares ware from this period was characterised by new colours – often red-and-white designs on a black background, decorated with abstract curves and spirals. Occasionally, stylised fish shapes were precursors of the later Marine style, and there were a few human figures, albeit in a very abstract style. By 1600 BC, there was a return to dark decoration on a light background and, for the first time, flower and shell shapes were attached to the surfaces of the pots.

Around the middle of the sixteenth century BC, several technological advances brought further improvements to Minoan pottery. Faster potters' wheels, better quality clay and the ability to increase temperatures in the kilns produced more graceful shapes and more naturalistic designs. Decoration was usually brown or dark red on a lighter background colour such as yellow. Plants and marine life were now common subjects – for example, branches with leaves, flowers, starfish, dolphins and octopuses. Bulls' heads and double axes, which may have represented religious themes, also appeared.

After 1450 BC, the influence of the Mycenaeans became apparent, with a return to more stylised and abstract designs. Bird designs were seen for the first time, as were military symbols such as helmets and shields.

Statuary

If monumental statuary existed in Minoan times, none has yet been discovered, but a host of small figurines display the artistry and technical expertise common to all Minoan artefacts. Single figures or groups were made in a variety of materials: ivory, gold, bronze and faience, a brightly coloured glass-like material. Various portrayals of the snake goddess (or priestess) are amazingly lifelike, while clay figurines of people at prayer tend to be more stylised. The famous bronze statuette of a bull leaper gives a vibrant impression of movement and fluidity, while a similar, but incomplete, ivory model is remarkable for its elegance. Perhaps the most famous – certainly the most striking – example of Minoan craftsmanship is the beautiful bull's head drinking vessel (rhyton). Although dating from about 1450 BC and possibly Mycenaean, it is of obvious Minoan origin and takes your breath away when you first see it.

Jewellery

Taking in the beauty of Minoan jewellery, one is struck by how modern much of it is. In fact, many of the more famous pieces have been copied and still sell well to visitors and Greeks alike. Some of the techniques were probably learned from the Syrians and Egyptians, including the use of gold leaf, but to this sophisticated technology the Minoans added their own exuberance and joy in natural, flowing shapes. Jewellery was mostly handmade, but rings and beads were often moulded, allowing limited mass production. Materials used included gold, silver and bronze, as well as ivory, shell and enamel. Semi-precious stones including amethyst were used to enhance the pieces. The amethyst was imported from Egypt and illustrates the individuality of the Minoans, who continued to use it long after it fell out of fashion in Egypt. As with modern jewellery, the Minoans produced a complete range of items from diadems and earrings to bracelets and anklets. Rings, of course, were extremely popular both as decorative wear and as seals. Usually gold, they were mostly engraved with detailed miniature scenes. Two of the most famous pieces of Minoan jewellery demonstrate the high point of skill and artistry: the Bee Pendant, found at Malia, and the Master of the Animals Pendant, from Aegina but certainly of Cretan origin.

Pax Minoica

As a result of his extensive excavations at Knossos, Evans developed the theory that the Minoan era was a golden age of prosperity and peace. His theory of a Pax Minoica was based on the lack of evidence for widespread fortifications and the relatively few weapons found. In recent years, this appealing and utopian vision has been the subject of much debate. (What isn't, in the world of archaeology?) Without getting too bogged down in the detail, a few interesting points can be highlighted.

Evans certainly overstated the lack of fortified defences. Mapping and cleaning operations of the excavations at Gournia have found evidence of defensive walls and a possible tower, designed to protect the town against attacks from the sea, while other sites have revealed signs of guardhouses. Moreover, tombs have been found containing people buried with swords, one particular tomb producing an entire collection of daggers, swords and other items. There have been suggestions that the weapons may have been ceremonial or symbolic, as they were not suitable for actual battle, but these are inconclusive. In fact, tests with exact replicas of some of the swords have proved them to have lethal capabilities in battle. In any case, logic suggests that a society that never uses weapons in battle would be unlikely to include them in ceremonies.

Without any further finds, the general consensus at the moment seems to be a sort of compromise. There remains no direct evidence for major warfare within the Minoan sphere of influence, but this does not mean that the cities had no defensive capabilities against external threats. An interesting parallel has been drawn with Switzerland, whose neutrality and peace are maintained by a strong citizen militia.[13] On the other hand, there remains no solid evidence for an actual Minoan army or any subjugation of cities outside Crete. Perhaps the clinching argument lies in the field of art. In most contemporaneous cultures (for example, those of Egypt, Mycenae and Babylon), paintings, sculptures and even pottery are full of images of warfare and military life. Although images of warlike activities do exist in some Minoan frescoes, they are few and ambiguous. It seems that, while they maintained a defensive capability, the Minoans relied on the goodwill generated by their prosperity and trade network, backed up by a powerful navy including warships, to ensure peaceful relations within their sphere of influence. If this was the case, Evans' idea of a golden age may not have been so far from the truth, especially when compared with other civilisations of the time.

Religion

Artwork and artefacts supply ample evidence of Minoan religious practices, but the lack of any written language renders all conclusions speculative. It seems that there were many predominantly female deities, pointing to a polytheistic religion, but it is not impossible that the goddesses represented different aspects of one deity. Some male gods certainly existed, but were greatly outnumbered by female deities. Among the goddesses for whom we have no name are:

- A Mother Goddess of fertility, depicted nursing an infant
- A goddess of animals and hunting
- A Snake Goddess of the underworld
- A goddess of sacred trees
- A goddess of the mountains, shown standing on a peak, protected by two lions
- A possible goddess of the sea or protector of sailors and voyages

As with most ancient religions, there also seem to have been protectors of cities, households and the harvest. Other probable goddesses are shown with doves, representing the heavens; with poppies, indicating sleep, peace and calm; or with sword and shield, possibly symbolising protection.

More detailed descriptions of Minoan rites and religious beliefs are usually based on logic or comparison with other early religions – but they are still largely speculative. For example, the depiction of some human figures with animal heads may indicate the existence of animal-headed gods, as in ancient Egypt, but could equally show priests or priestesses wearing masks. In either case, a half-man, half-bull creature could represent the origin of the Minotaur legend.

Whatever the details, it seems fairly clear that the Minoans were a very spiritual people, and many objects were highly charged with religious meaning. Sacred trees, springs and pillars all had their place in the religious rites, while the famous horn-topped altar is seen in countless seal impressions and was probably of religious significance, along with the bull, the double-headed axe (labrys), the serpent and the sun disc. However, some scholars have disputed that all of these were religious objects.

The significance of the well-known bull-leaping ceremony was likely to have been at least partly religious, but probably also had elements of entertainment and sport. Since both girls and boys took part, it may not be too fanciful to suppose that the events also performed the same function as Victorian balls and modern nightclubs in introducing youngsters to each other.

It appears that the priesthood was almost entirely female, although the king may well have carried out some religious functions. There were shrines, where religious rites were performed, in palaces and private residences, but there is no evidence of dedicated temples in separate buildings. However, worship also took place in remote caves and on almost-inaccessible mountaintops, the so-called "peak sanctuaries". In some of these, the large numbers of wine goblets unearthed seems to indicate a festive aspect to the religious ceremonies. Worship in some of these sanctuaries continued well into classical times. There is strong evidence of animal sacrifice, but the possibility of human sacrifice is based on a single piece of evidence and remains extremely inconclusive.

There were a variety of burial practices during the Minoan era. In the earlier years, circular tholos tombs (beehive shaped, with a dome) were common in south Crete, while "house tombs" were used in the north and east. The latter were either cut into the rock or built like small houses, and contained either members of the same family or groups from the same settlement. Later, while tholoi and rock-cut tombs continued, single burials in large pithoi became common throughout Crete, and clay or wooden sarcophagi appeared. Cremation seems to have been unusual throughout this period. Tombs were mainly individual, but a funeral complex exists at Malia. There is some evidence of social distinction in the size and type of tomb.

The Extent of Minoan Influence

From about 1600 BC, there was further expansion of Minoan cultural influence, probably spread by trade, since there is no evidence of any attempt at military conquest. Many of the Aegean islands – including

Kastri (Kythira); the islands of the Cyclades, especially Thera (San-torini); and even Messenia in the Peloponnese – could be called Minoan. There is evidence for Minoan settlements on many of the Dodecanese islands, including Karpathos, Saria, Kasos and Rhodes. The extent of Minoan domination varies between these locations, and it is not clear whether they were colonies, Cretan settlements or trading stations, or were merely within the sphere of Minoan cultural influence. It has been suggested that the Greek legend of Theseus and the Minotaur, as with so much mythology, may stem from a folk memory of a time when Minoan Crete was powerful enough to exact tribute from Mycenae. Although told from the Greek point of view and detrimental to the Cretans, it may give an inkling of the relative power of the two civilisations at one point in time. Certainly, Plato treated the legend as history:

> When Minos, once upon a time, reduced the people of Attica to a grievous payment of tribute, he was very powerful by sea, whereas they possessed no warships at that time such as they have now, nor was their country so rich in timber that they could easily supply themselves with a naval force. Hence they were unable quickly to copy the naval methods of their enemies and drive them off by becoming sailors themselves.[14]

Cultural links between the Minoans and other civilisations went beyond direct influence. Various artefacts, together with frescoes of a distinctly Minoan style, have been found as far away as the Canaanite palace at Tel Kabri in Israel. There are also paintings from fifteenth-century BC Thebes in Egypt which depict obviously Minoan-looking people carrying gifts to the pharaoh. The significance of these pictures is uncertain, but could indicate some sort of tribute, a trading transac-tion or an exchange of gifts between equals. The hieroglyphs identify the bearers as being from "Kleftiu, Islands in the Middle of the Sea". This is generally believed to be the only known reference to a name for Bronze Age Crete. In 1987, thousands of fragments of obviously Minoan frescoes were discovered near the ancient Hyksos palace of Tell el-Dab'a, in the Nile delta. These include depictions of bull leaping and a possible hunting scene.

The End of Minoan Crete

Sometime around the middle of the fifteenth century BC, most of Crete's palaces and villas were destroyed, together with the living quarters at Knossos, although the palace at Knossos remained intact until 1375 BC. For a long time, this was linked to the eruption of the volcano on Thera (Santorini), which was among the most devastating in history. The theory was that ash from the eruption and flooding by the subsequent tsunami destroyed crops and killed animals, leading to complete economic collapse. More recently, however, it has been argued that the easterly jet stream would have carried most of the ash to the east, leaving Crete largely untouched, with a maximum of 5 mm of ash anywhere on the island. Indeed, Minoan remains have been found above the level of the ash from Thera. More seriously, new analysis now sets the date of the Thera eruption much earlier, around 1645 BC. This makes nonsense of a straightforward cause and effect, since the Late Minoan period was one of great building and a flourishing society.

The arguments still rage, and there is no general consensus on the ending of Minoan society. Some still maintain that seismic activity later than the eruption on Thera may have caused devastation to the coastal areas of Crete, resulting in major losses of shipping and a decline in trade. Alternatively, drought might have led to social unrest, revolution or civil war, and a generally weakened society. Either of these events would have rendered Crete easy pickings for the more warlike Mycenaeans from the mainland. However, there is actually little evidence for a Mycenaean conquest. The famous Lion Gate at the citadel of Mycenae does seem to be a representation of Mycenaean power, with the two lions resting their feet on an obviously Minoan pillar, but this could represent cultural dominance as much as conquest. While the theory of an invasion by the Mycenaeans has not been completely dismissed, a growing number of scholars are suggesting that the development of Mycenaean culture in Crete was an extension of the widespread cultural interaction between Crete and the mainland during the Late Bronze Age. Whether this included immigration of Mycenaeans or merely the large-scale importation of Mycenaean administrative structures and culture is unknown. As with so much of Cretan history, there are plenty of PhD theses still to come.

Mycenaean Crete

The Mycenaean civilisation developed in the Peloponnese around 1650 BC, towards the end of the Middle Minoan period. Like the Minoans, the Mycenaeans were a trading culture, but they were far more aggressive in expanding their influence and defending their trade routes. Their society was based on city states, each with its own king, who was the political and religious leader. Beneath the king were local chiefs, responsible for administration. Class distinctions seem to have been much stronger than in Minoan culture: the king was at the top, supported by a powerful ruling class, and everyone else was a long way down at the bottom.

We do not know the nature of the transition, or the reasons for it, but by the second half of the fifteenth century BC Crete was largely composed of Mycenaean city states, while the Minoans were pushed out to the fringes, largely in the east. As previously noted, there had already been a fair degree of cultural interchange between the Minoans and the Mycenaeans, and this intensified, although the main direction was now from the latter to the former. Indeed, archaeological evidence suggests that Knossos now became a major centre for weapon production, and it is likely that the chariot was first introduced to Crete during this period.

Although Homer's *Iliad* was a heroic epic, written down several hundred years after the events it describes, there is significant evidence that, at least in part, it describes some historical places and people generally believed to have existed in late Mycenaean times. The term "Mycenaean" itself was coined by archaeologists but, as noted below, the Achaeans that are mentioned in *The Iliad* are almost universally accepted by academics to be Mycenaeans. In this case, a strong link seems to have existed between Mycenae and Crete. Menelaus' maternal grandfather was in fact Cretan, and Menelaus' attendance at the funeral of his grandfather in Crete was the reason for his absence while Paris was busy seducing Helen. More significantly, the king of Knossos, Idomeneus, joined the expedition against Troy, along with unnamed kings of other cities:

Leader of the Cretans was Idomeneus, renowned with spear, those who held Knossos and the walls of Gortyn, Lyktos and Miletos and white Lykastos and Phaistos and Rhytion, well-founded cities; and the others who lived in the hundred cities of Crete. These men were led by the famous spearman Idomeneus, and Meriones, a warrior equal to the god of war himself, the man-slayer. With them there followed eighty dark ships.[15]

The Mycenaean period is the first that provides us with some knowledge of the language of the people of Crete: an early form of Greek, using Linear B for writing. Linear B was a development from Linear A, learned from the Minoans as early as the seventeenth century BC. It was mainly a syllabic script with about 200 signs. The script was not deciphered until 1952, when Michael Ventris, a young English architect building on the work of the American scholar Alice Kober, proved that the script was Mycenaean Greek.[16] The bad news was that the script was only used for trade and economic records and, with the exception of a few names of deities, there were no religious or literary writings.

There have been many suggestions that there was a relationship between the Minoan religion and the Mycenaean but, although such a relationship is logical, the links are tenuous. Most of what we know about the latter comes from classical Greek sources written many centuries later, but there are intriguing links. For example, the Mycenaean goddess of childbirth, Eileithyia, born in a cave near Amnisos, was the subject of a cult from Neolithic times, which almost certainly continued through the Minoan era. There are many references to "Potnia", but this appears to be a title meaning "lady" or "mistress" rather than a name. For example, Ariadne, the daughter of King Minos, was worshipped as the Mistress of the Labyrinth in the Mycenaean pantheon. Most interesting are the cases where there was a degree of cultural imperialism by the Greeks. The goddess of mountains and hunting, Britomartis (meaning "Sweet Virgin"), continued into Greek mythology but as a mere mountain nymph (oread) and daughter of Zeus. Diktynna, goddess of Mount Dikti, who may have been the same as Britomartis, fared a little better. She became the goddess of hunting, Artemis. In Mycenaean – and possibly Minoan – mythology, Artemis nursed the god Hyakinthos, who was demoted to a hero by the Greeks and replaced by Apollo.

During the Mycenaean period, we also see the beginnings of the classical Greek pantheon. In Linear B inscriptions there is evidence of Poseidon – at this stage more related to earthquakes than the sea – and a sea goddess called Diwia. It is possible that Poseidon's name was derived from "Poteidan", the male form of Potnia. There are also early references to Zeus, Hephaestus, Hera, Ares, Hermes, Dionysos and Erinya. A single incomplete Linear B reference to "Potnia At–" may refer to Athena, but could equally mean Athens.

The strange story of the "Cretan Zeus" also emerges at this time, and may well be linked with earlier Minoan myths. Even in Greek mythology, Zeus had strong links with Crete, having been born and raised on the island, either in the Diktaion Cave on the Lassithi plateau or in the Idaion Cave on Mount Ida. He was also the father by Europa of the first three kings of Crete: Minos (Knossos), Rhadamanthus (Phaistos) and Sarpedon (Malia). While the Cretans worshipped Zeus as a minor god, however, he was regarded as mortal, dying a violent death each year and then being resurrected. The similarity of this to many early pre-Hellenic myths points to it being a remnant of an earlier, possibly Minoan, religion. Incidentally, the Greeks regarded the idea of Zeus being mortal as blasphemous, resulting in the belief that Cretans were liars, as famously quoted in Saint Paul's Epistle to Titus:

> One of the Cretans, a prophet of their own, said, "Cretans are always liars, evil beasts, lazy gluttons."[17]

The Mycenaean period in Crete lasted about 300 years. There is evidence that walls around the cities were strengthened and enlarged in about 1200 BC, but what threat was expected we do not know. There are many theories, but none of them seem entirely satisfactory on their own, and some sort of combination might offer the most logical solution. It is possible that Crete was subject to raids by the "Sea People", a loose alliance of warlike tribes responsible for large-scale depredations in Anatolia, the Levant and Egypt. These attacks would have disrupted trade, destroyed cities, displaced populations and caused famine. The economic decline could well have led to revolution and/or inter-city warfare. Alternative theories propose similar internal problems caused by environmental factors, such as drought or unusually violent seismic activity. For many years it was assumed that, thoroughly weakened by one or all of these causes, Crete could have fallen easy prey to a new wave of Greek tribes from the north – the Dorians. The idea of a Dorian invasion has recently been challenged by archaeologists, although some scholars are reluctant to throw out the theory completely, pointing to the wealth of literary evidence from ancient historians. Whether the Dorians attacked a weakened Mycenaean Greece or merely migrated into depopulated areas in an "invasion without invaders" is subject to dispute. What is certain is that, by the end of the twelfth century BC, a new Iron Age civilisation had pretty well established itself in Crete.

5

Dorian Crete

1100 BC to 69 BC

The First 600 Years

Theories about the origins of the Dorians are numerous and contradictory, and even the existence of a distinct Dorian tribal entity has been called into doubt. The literary evidence from classical historians and the linguistic evidence are inconclusive, and there is little clarity to be gained from archaeology. Nevertheless, at some stage, various communities in parts of Greece, especially Sparta, began to identify themselves as having a common Dorian identity. In Crete, the exact nature and timescale of the transition from Mycenaean to Dorian is unknown but, for the sake of simplicity, I shall refer to the whole period as Dorian.

According to Homer, there was a mixture of races existing side by side in Crete, but the history of this period is almost entirely the history of the dominant Dorians:

> Out in the wine-dark sea, there lies a land called Crete, a rich and lovely land surrounded by the sea, densely populated, with ninety cities and several different languages. First, there are the Achaeans; then the Eteocretans, proud of their native stock; next the Kydonians; the Dorians, with their three clans; and finally the noble Pelasgians.[1]

There is no reason to doubt this analysis, and, apart from the Dorians, the Achaeans can be clearly identified as the Mycenaeans. On the other hand, the other groups are by no means clear. According to Herodotus, the Kydonians may have been Syrian and Samian refugees from a failed revolt. The other two races are intriguing. The Eteocretans ("true Cretans") could well have been the remnants of the Minoans, while the identity of the Pelasgians is very unclear. They seem to have been pre-Greek, or a different early tribe of Greek speakers, but beyond that the academic arguments still rage.

Little is known of the early process of change in Crete, but it is fairly certain that there were early Spartan colonies in Lyttos (Lyktos) and Gortyn. There was steady migration from the mainland well into the ninth century BC, and there is evidence of struggles between the settlers and the Mycenaean and Minoan inhabitants. It is not clear, however, where all these immigrants came from. Strong fortifications were built at Gortyn, Prinias, Axos and Hyrtakina (and probably other locations) and, by the end of the ninth century BC, most of the cities of Crete were proclaiming their allegiance to a shared Dorian heritage. Trade still existed, though on a much-reduced scale, as the Phoenicians took over command of the seas and became the major trading nation in the eastern Mediterranean.

With the general expansion of Greek colonialism in the eighth century BC, there was a revival in trade. From about 735 BC, Crete established colonies in Sicily, Etruria and near Massalia (Marseilles). A joint colony with Thera was established in Kyrene (Libya) around 631 BC – probably the first Greek colony in North Africa. By the end of the seventh century BC, however, there seems to have been a further decline in Crete's fortunes, brought about by a combination of factors. This period saw the rise of Ionian Greek city states such as Athens and Miletus, and the Dorians of Crete – having inflexible political and social systems and being riven by internal disputes – were unable to respond to this challenge to their dominance. Whatever the reason, Crete now became largely isolated from the rest of the Greek world for about 100 years.

Although the island was largely marginalised, some trade continued, including Cretan cypress exports to Athens and Kerkyra (also known as Corfu), but the demand was usually related to specific major building projects and was intermittent. Agriculture during this period, and indeed right up to the Roman invasion, was restricted to subsistence farming, producing enough food for the cities but leaving little surplus for export. The only significant exports for most of the Dorian period were of high-quality Hadra vases, which have been shown to have originated in Crete. Recent archaeological evidence demonstrates that at least one city, Knossos, remained a major trading centre, rich in imports from all over the Mediterranean. It is also now believed that the city was at least three times bigger than earlier estimates suggest.[2]

Meanwhile, alliances were still being made between various cities and states, notably Rhodes, Argos and Lindos. These were almost certainly part of the ongoing power struggles between the cities, which continued to weaken the power of the island as a whole. With frequent wars, coups and revolts, Crete during this period resembled England during the devastating wars between King Stephen and Empress Matilda in the twelfth century AD. In his *Laws*, written in the fourth century BC, Plato has the Cretan Kleinias outline the problem:

> For what men in general term peace would be said by him [the Cretan legislator] to be only a name; in reality every city is in a natural state of war with every other, not indeed proclaimed by heralds, but everlasting.[3]

These chaotic times had a disastrous effect on the economy, leading to extreme poverty across much of the island. This in turn resulted in a trend that lasted for many centuries: emigration. Because of the rugged nature of the terrain in Crete, horse riding was practically unknown and strong and agile foot soldiers, usually equipped with bows and arrows, were the norm. So skilled did the Cretan archers become that they were highly sought after as mercenaries. There were Cretan archers in almost every army and in almost every period, from the Greek cities' war with Persia through the Peloponnesian War and Alexander's campaigns, and right up to Julius Caesar's campaigns in Gaul. A Roman historian quotes a somewhat cynical exchange between Julius Caesar and a mercenary:

> A Cretan came to the consul Julius and offered to act as a traitor. "If by my help," he said, "you defeat your enemies, what reward will you give me?" Caesar replied, "I'll make you a citizen of Rome, and you

will be in favour with me." At these words, the Cretan laughed and said, "Citizenship is considered a nonsense amongst the Cretans. We aim at gain when we shoot our arrows; we only work on land and sea to get money, and so I have come here in search of money. As for political rights, grant that to those who are fighting for it and who are buying this nonsense with their blood." The consul laughed at this and said to the man, "Well, if we are successful, I will give a reward of a thousand drachmae."[4]

The Ptolemy dynasty of Egypt also made frequent use of Cretan mercenaries, a habit which was to have interesting consequences later, when Cretans fought for both sides in the war between Octavian (later Augustus) and Cleopatra.

The Classical Period: 500 BC to 323 BC

There seems to have been a decrease in population during the classical period. This, together with its inherent instability and weak economy, resulted in Crete playing little part in mainland history. Apart from providing a continuous supply of mercenaries, the Cretan cities remained neutral during the major wars of the fifth century BC. They did not join the rest of Greece in the fight against the Persians under Xerxes in 481 BC, using a warning from the Oracle at Delphi as divine justification. This was not so much an act of cowardice as practical politics. Separated from the mainland and closer to the Levant, it was unlikely that Crete could have withstood a concerted attack by the Persians. Crete also remained neutral during the bitter Peloponnesian War (431 BC to 404 BC) between Athens and Sparta, in spite of the kinship between the two Dorian communities. A naval attack by an Athenian fleet on Kydonia in 429 BC seems to have been targeted at pro-Spartan fugitives from Aegina, rather than being a direct assault on Cretan territory. Nevertheless, in typical Dorian Cretan fashion, Gortyn and its neighbour Polichna used the occasion to join in the assault on Kydonia.

By the mid-fourth century BC, Crete began to re-emerge onto centre stage as its strategic location and usefulness in political alliances became apparent. At the same time, the perceived distinctive constitution and society of the Dorian cities became of interest to philosophers and historians. Plato and Aristotle, among others, left us with a great deal of useful description and analysis, although it is now apparent that their views were somewhat simplified, and there was less homogeneity among the cities than they believed.

Meanwhile, the struggles between the cities continued but with little resolution. An event in 346 BC is particularly illuminating: the so-called Foreign War. Knossos, not for the first (or last) time, was claiming first place among the cities and, aided by a mercenary army, besieged Lyttos, a Spartan settlement. Lyttos called on Sparta for help, and a Spartan army crushed the mercenary army and relieved the siege. The interesting thing about this is that, in spite of their willingness to engage in war, neither city had the strength to fight alone, leading them to rely on outside support.

The Hellenistic Period: 323 BC to 69 BC

After the death of Alexander the Great, his empire was divided up, creating new states such as Ptolemaic Egypt and the Seleucid Empire. Crete continued to remain independent of any of these, but as its geopolitical importance grew there were increasing attempts by various states to create alliances with Cretan cities and gain influence over the island. The quarrelling between the cities became endemic, and the shifting alliances grew more and more complex. However, there is a growing body of opinion that, in spite of the wars, there was still a fairly flourishing economy in many areas. There is evidence of a thriving fishing industry, and rural settlements grew up near the main cities, leading to an increase in population. The prosperity of the cities can also be deduced from expensive large-scale improvements to the defensive walls at Gortyn and the restoration and refurbishment of the sanctuary complex of Asklepios, both carried out during this period.[5]

There were two driving forces behind most of the changing alliances and inter-city wars of the period: the struggle for domination between Knossos and Gortyn, and attempts by other states in the region to gain power or at least influence over the island. The aims of Knossos were imperialistic; it sought complete domination of the island, as succinctly explained by one historian writing in the classical period:

> The Knossians contended for the sovereignty of the island, which they alleged belonged to them, on account of both the ancient dignity of the city, and the glory and renown of their ancestors in the heroic age.[6]

Gortyn, on the other hand, was more interested in leading the island as head of a federation. In fact, the ambitions of both cities were often curbed by Lyttos and Kydonia, sometimes allied with each other, sometimes in conflict. To complicate things further, Lyttos, Gortyn and several other cities were also heavily influenced by Sparta, which became increasingly involved in Cretan politics.

In about 270 BC, Itanos was, not for the first time, in dispute with Praisos over control of the important sanctuary of Diktaion Zeus at Palaikastro. Eventually, the city appealed for help from Ptolemy II of Egypt, who sent a military force under General Patroklos to establish a base at Itanos. Patroklos was declared a citizen of the city, with responsibility for the direct administration of Itanos, and the Egyptian garrison remained for the next century. Soon Egyptian influence spread to many other cities, and the east of Crete became a virtual protectorate of the Ptolemies, although, with the exception of Itanos, this was mainly achieved through military aid and diplomacy.

In a surprising development, the two great rivals, Knossos and Gortyn, formed an alliance to share control of the whole island – apart from Lyttos, which refused to submit to the dual rule. Knossos was not actually keen on the idea of an independent Lyttos, but wasn't strong enough to do much about it. Gortyn was, at that time, weakened by a dispute between the "Elders", who supported Knossos, and the "Young Ones", who wanted to maintain an independent Lyttos. In 220 BC, Knossos imported 1,000 Aetolian mercenaries to seize Gortyn and secure the power of the Elders. In spite of several other cities breaking ranks and supporting Lyttos, Knossos now felt confident enough to turn on the city. While its men were absent on a campaign against Hierapytna (modern Ierapetra), Lyttos was totally destroyed in an attack, vicious even by the standards of the time, vividly described by Polybius:

The Lyttians, having left with their whole force for an expedition into the enemy's country, the Knossians getting word of it seized on Lyttos which was left without defenders, and having sent off the women and children to Knossos, and burnt, demolished, and in every way they could wrecked the town, returned home. When the Lyttians came back to their city from the expedition and saw what had happened, they were so much affected that none of them had the heart even to enter his native town, but one and all, after marching round it and many times bewailing and lamenting the fate of their country and themselves, turned their backs on it and retired to Lappa ... Thus was Lyttos, a colony of the Spartans and allied to them by blood, the most ancient city in Crete, and ever, as all acknowledged, the breeding-place of her bravest men, utterly and unexpectedly made away with.[7]

One interesting result of the brief agreement between Knossos and Gortyn for joint control of the island in 221 BC was the establishment of the **Koinon** of the Cretans (loosely meaning the Cretan League). This was a sort of assembly of representatives from all the cities. Each city was deemed equal but, in practice, Knossos and Gortyn were "more equal than others", playing the leading role in organisation and control. The exact function of the koinon is not fully understood, and we don't know how frequently it met. There seem to have been two chambers: a council of delegates and a general assembly. It is likely to have been responsible for setting a basic legal code to which all the cities adhered, and it may have regulated trade relations between the cities. Perhaps the intention was to maintain the peace, although this was not entirely successful. Whatever its failings, the koinon did later come into its own as a unifying factor against external enemies, such as the Romans. Plutarch made a perceptive point when he advised his readers to emulate the practice of the Cretans, "who, being accustomed to frequent skirmishes and fights, nevertheless, as soon as they were attacked by a foreign enemy, were reconciled and went together".[8]

The continuing resistance to Knossos led to Polyrrhenia and Lappa eventually seeking help from Philip V of Macedonia, who saw the opportunity to gain Cretan support in his ambitions to control the entire Aegean. He sent an expeditionary force of 700 troops, which led to three more cities breaking from Knossos, resulting in some-thing of a stalemate. Philip now had control or influence over a large part of western Crete and, by 216 BC, a Macedonian protectorate was established. Together with other Greek states, Philip brokered a peace between the cities and set out to gain their support against his biggest rival (and supposed ally), Rhodes, a major naval power which controlled almost all sea trade in the area. He began by using Cretan pirates, supported by Nabis, the king of Sparta, to destabilise the trade routes. He then called on the Cretan cities to declare war on Rhodes. Olous (modern Elounda) and Hierapytna were the first to answer the call, but Rhodes immediately called on Rome for assistance. Rome declared war on Macedonia, leaving Rhodes free to respond to the Cretan threat. In alliance with Knossos, Rhodes attacked Hierapytna and Olous, defeating both and imposing stringent terms, including total control over all harbours and naval bases. This meant that not only did Rhodes now more or less control eastern Crete, it had bases from which it could protect its fleet from pirates.

There now seems to have arisen a slightly odd situation in which eastern Crete was a protectorate of Egypt, with at least two cities actu-ally controlled by Rhodes, while western Crete was a Macedonian protectorate, with many harbours under the control of Sparta. Com-plicated? It gets worse.

The piracy continued from bases in western Crete loyal to Nabis (who was a supporter of Rome and supplied it with 300 Cretan mer-cenaries), mainly from Gortyn. Having finally defeated Philip of Mac-edonia in 197 BC, Rome turned on its former ally, Nabis, and imposed a treaty on him which, among other things, forced him to break off all relations with the Cretan cities and give control of all ports under his control to Rome. Although the Romans did not involve them-selves directly in control of the cities, this began more than a century of increasing Roman involvement in Cretan affairs. In 189 BC, for example, there was an attempt to free thousands of Roman prisoners taken by pirates – although all the cities refused to release them except for Gortyn, which remained consistently pro-Roman.

After the defeat of **Carthage** in the Second Punic War, Hannibal sought refuge in Crete for some time. On the pretext of mediating between the cities, many important Romans – including the victor over Carthage, Scipio Africanus – travelled around the island trying to seek Hannibal out. The labyrinthine diplomacy of the day is illustrated well by events in 170 BC. Some years earlier, Gortyn and Kydonia, along with thirty other cities, had signed a treaty with Pergamum, a Greek city state on the coast of Anatolia. When yet another dispute arose between Gortyn and Kydonia, Pergamum sent 300 troops in support of Kydonia against its other ally! Again, the Romans intervened to keep the peace. A second war between some of the cities of Crete and Rhodes, caused by continuing piracy, led to a request by Rhodes for Roman support and yet another imposed peace treaty. It seemed to the Romans that something would have to be done about Crete.

Dorian Society

Throughout the complexities of 1,000 or so years of wars and alliances, Dorian society showed remarkable consistency, right up to the Roman conquest of 69 BC. Moreover, in spite of warfare and instability, there was a basic similarity in the institutions of the Cretan cities, along-side considerable variations in the details of law, customs and political systems. Inherently conservative, the Dorians brought with them not only the use of iron for tools and weapons but a more austere and martial lifestyle, closely similar to that of the Spartans. In fact, many ancient historians believed that it was from Crete that Sparta derived its laws and customs, although the two systems diverged over time:

> The Spartan regime may have adopted a Cretan "starter-kit", but its systems continued to develop thereafter towards greater complexity.[9]

In Crete, on the other hand, the Dorians quickly abandoned monarchy, replacing it with an oligarchy formed from the great Dorian families, so that the system was somewhat less rigid than that of Sparta and even had some superficially democratic elements.

The class system was simple, divided into free citizens (Dorians), free inhabitants and slaves. The Dorians were, of course, the ruling elite, with exclusive control of all military and political affairs. All land was administered by this group and held in common – and, in general, displaying private wealth and prioritising the individual at the expense of the social group were frowned upon. On the other hand, a drinking song of the fourth century BC illustrates a swaggering arrogance among the Dorians towards the hoi polloi, reminiscent of the attitude of some Norman lords towards the Saxons:

> *I have great wealth: a spear and a sword,*
> *And a fine leather shield to protect my skin.*
> *For with this I plough, with this I reap,*
> *With this I trample the sweet wine from the vines,*
> *With this I am called master of serfs.*
> *Those who do not dare to have a spear and a sword*
> *And a fine leather shield to protect their skin*
> *All cower at my knee and prostrate themselves,*
> *Calling me master and great king.*[10]

The free inhabitants were the non-Dorian original inhabitants of Crete. In Gortyn and Knossos they were called **apetairoi** (meaning "without political rights") but nothing is known for sure about their exact status in the other cities. The majority were peasants who owned land and paid taxes, but the class also included craftsmen, merchants and seamen.

Enslaved people were either native Cretans or captives from military campaigns and pirate raids, and they could either be privately owned or belong to the community. There is some uncertainty about the exact nature of slavery in Crete, as contemporary historians and inscriptions sometimes use different words to describe the slaves: "dolos" and "woikeus". On the one hand, it has been argued that there were in fact different categories of enslaved people, a dolos being more like a **serf**, tied to the land but allowed to marry and hold property, while a woikeus may have been a chattel slave in the more traditional sense of being the property of the master, his "mortal property", along with livestock. Another interpretation, and one that has growing support among scholars, is that both terms described a single legal status, although they had different nuances. For example, the words "dog" and "hound" are basically synonyms, but are used in different contexts. They were probably used inconsistently in the archaic legislation and this inconsistency was carried forward into the later Gortyn Code. There is no positive evidence of serfs who were bound to specific plots of land, and it is probable that Gortyn, like other Greek cities, had just one servile status: slaves. Each city had its own rules stipulating the obligations and legal position of enslaved people, but we only know the details of these in Gortyn. It is unlikely that these people had rights as such. Although the law codes do include protection against overly harsh and unjust treatment of enslaved people, this invariably refers to abuse at the hands of a third party. This, together with the absence of any rules limiting a master's right to inflict harm on his slave, implies that the laws were more about protecting the master's "property" from damage than protecting the interests of the enslaved. There was, however, provision for enslaved people to become free inhabitants, although the division between free citizens and free inhabitants remained absolute.[11]

One aspect of slavery in Crete which is intriguing is the absence of slave revolts there compared with other Dorian states, especially Sparta. Aristotle notes this phenomenon and offers two reasons for it. He states that the laws governing slaves in Crete were relatively mild, the Cretans allowing enslaved people everything except access to the gymnasia and the right to bear arms. He also conjectures that there was perhaps a sort of gentlemen's agreement between the cities that, even in war, there would be no attempt to incite the enslaved workers of an opposing city to revolt in order to weaken the city. This was obviously in the interests of all cities so, again, unlike in parts of the Greek mainland, there was no external influence or provocation.

In addition to Aristotle's arguments, several other factors preventing slave rebellions have been identified. Firstly, there were considerable geographical differences between Sparta and Crete. The Spartan territory was enormous: some 8,500 km², bisected by a massive mountain range. Since the citizens of Sparta lived in the city itself, they were almost entirely absent from their farms and had little direct contact with their slaves (known as "helots"). Moreover, in the early fifth century BC, it is known that the helots outnumbered the Spartan citizens by at least seven to one, and this ratio certainly increased over time. In contrast, the average Cretan city's territory was only about 120 km² and absenteeism was far less acute, while the farms in Crete were generally small, allowing closer supervision of enslaved workers. It is very unlikely that the enslaved in Crete outnumbered their masters to anything like the same degree as the helots of Sparta. Although there would undoubtedly be runaways, the size of the island offered little scope to form large colonies of people who had escaped slavery, as existed in Sparta. Finally, the safety valve of religious rites like the Hermaea (described below) may well have served to ease tensions and prevent potential conflicts.[12]

The political and social organisation of Dorian Crete varied between the cities, but the differences were largely in the detail, and there was still a great deal of homogeneity in the underlying structures and beliefs. In all the cities, one could find a preoccupation with status and a focus on military training; common meals and men's clubs; limitations on non-citizens' rights, including those of women, foreigners and artisans; entrenched conservatism; and a tendency towards petrification of social and political institutions.

> It is not so important whether Gortyn had ten **kosmoi** and another city only five. What is far more important is the fact that wherever we find kosmoi – and we do find them in almost every city – these officials represent the executive power, that the entire board of the annually elected kosmoi belonged to a single tribe and that, consequently, they must have been military leaders of the tribes.[13]

Although the titles, number and selection process varied between the cities, the main administration of a city was in the hands of the kosmoi[14], a ruling committee of between four and eleven members. These members were elected from and by the aristocracy and held office for one year, with re-election forbidden for between three and ten years. In times of war, the committee became the military high command. During peacetime, members were assigned ministries for specific purposes, such as alien affairs or religious matters. One of the kosmoi was designated protokosmos, roughly analogous to prime minister. The kosmoi were able to summon all the free citizens to assembly to ratify decisions, but were not obliged to. However, at the end of the year, they had to give an account of their policies, and any failure of duty or misuse of privileges was subject to severe penalties.

The Council of Elders was an advisory body, composed of previous kosmoi of particular experience and prestige. They were always available for advice and may have had judicial powers of appeal. In the event of the kosmoi being dismissed for misbehaviour or cowardice, the council could act as an interim administration. The third element, the Ekklesia (Assembly) had only one function, to ratify the decisions of the kosmoi. It was called on certain specific days or for emergency sessions and was, of course, composed only of free citizens.

The Great Gortyn Law Code

We know a fair bit about the laws of Dorian Crete, partly through the works of classical Greek writers like Plato and Aristotle, but we are also fortunate to have about seventy inscriptions of some of the laws of Gortyn, dating from the late sixth or early fifth century BC. Early fragments relate to loans, mortgages, funerals, use of water resources, purification and the status of freedmen, but the most famous is the Great Gortyn Law Code. Written in the ancient Dorian dialect of Crete, the greater part of it still survives on a wall in the Odeon at Gortyn. It is extremely likely that similar laws existed in other Cretan cities, and the laws probably date back to much earlier than the date of the inscription, making the Gortyn Code one of the earliest examples of a written legal system in Greece. Like many inscriptions of the time, it reads alternately from left to right, then right to left.

There is no logical sequence to the laws, but the code covers many aspects of personal liberty (of free citizens), clear distinctions between the classes, civil and criminal offences and family law. In spite of the strictness and austerity of Dorian society, punishments were rarely severe and always had to be sanctioned by the Council of Elders. It has been suggested that the difference between the Cretan legal system and that of other Dorian states may stem from its incorporation of earlier Minoan and Mycenaean law codes. There is no mention of a death penalty, although the existing code doesn't cover crimes such as murder or treason.

A few examples will give some idea of the nature of the Gortyn Code.[15] The most serious crime mentioned is rape, which is punishable by a fine, varying according to the relative status of rapist and victim:

If one commits rape on a free man or woman, he shall pay 100 staters, and if on the son or daughter of an **apetairos** ten, and if a slave on a free man or woman, he shall pay double, and if a free man on a male or female slave five drachmas, and if a slave on a male or female slave, five staters.[16]

Although the status of women was not high in Dorian society, they did have some legal protection:

If a husband and wife be divorced, she shall have her own property that she came with to her husband, and the half of the income if it be from her own property, and whatever she has woven, the half, whatever it may be, and five staters, if her husband be the cause of her dismissal; but if the husband deny that he was the cause, the judge shall decide on oath.

There is some evidence that enslaved people here had more rights than those in other parts of Greece, including Athens. The enslaved were able to possess and inherit property; marriage between enslaved and free people was possible; and the children of such a marriage could, in certain circumstances, be free:

If a slave, going to [live with] a free woman, shall wed her, the children shall be free; but if the free woman [goes to live with] a slave, the children shall be slaves; and if from the same mother free and slave children be born, if the mother die and there be property, the free children shall have it; otherwise her free relatives shall succeed to it.

Because of the difficulty in making unambiguous translations of the early Dorian language, there has been recent debate about the exact meaning of this section, and it has been argued that the status of enslaved people may not have been as liberal as suggested.

The Andreion

One of the most interesting of the Dorian institutions was the Andreion (men's hall), which also existed in Sparta. Every city had this public mess hall in which the male free citizens ate communally. All adult citizens were organised into groups called hetaireiai, each group having its own table in the Andreion. In addition, there were two guest tables, where guests were treated with great hospitality. Indeed, the hospitality of the Cretans was noted by several contemporary historians, who compared it favourably with the Spartans' reputed xenophobia. The public mess tables were paid for from a citizens' tax, based on a fixed proportion of citizens' income and the income from publicly owned land. This was different from the Spartan system of a poll tax that was fixed, regardless of income, which could lead to impoverishment of citizens during economic downturns:

> Now the Cretan arrangements for the public mess-tables are better than the Spartan; for at Sparta each citizen pays a fixed poll-tax, failing which he is prevented by law from taking part in the government, as has been said before; but in Crete the system is more communal, for out of all the crops and cattle produced from the public lands, and the tributes paid by the serfs, one part is assigned for the worship of the gods and the maintenance of the public services, and the other for the public mess-tables, so that all the citizens are maintained from the common funds, women and children as well as men.[17]

The food was prepared by women, assisted by enslaved workers. Although women and girls didn't eat in the Andreion, portions of the food were distributed to their homes. The size of each person's portion depended on their status, ordinary citizens receiving a normal portion, male children a half portion and the ruling aristocracy a quadruple portion. The separation of men and women was noted by Aristotle as a deliberate policy for population control, although it is not clear whether the sexes lived completely separately for most of the time.

The Andreion was a very important element in the political affairs of the Cretan city. Somewhat like a gentlemen's club in England, it was a place where city affairs could be discussed in a relaxed way, while social cohesion was strengthened through battle songs and tales of worthy citizens, and young men could learn the customs and values of Dorian society.

Education

Aristotle described how the education of the young (boys only) in Dorian Crete was dedicated to the single aim of creating brave warriors to serve the military system:

> In Sparta and Crete both the system of education and the mass of the laws are framed in the main with a view to war.[18]

Up to the age of eighteen, boys were educated within the family. They learned to read and write and, when ready, were taught other subjects necessary for their future life, as described by a Roman author:

> In Crete, the children of free citizens were firstly taught the laws by means of song, so that they might more easily retain them in the memory, and so that if they were ever to infringe the laws they could not plead ignorance of them. Secondly, they had to learn hymns to the gods. And thirdly, they learned eulogies on great men.[19]

At the age of eighteen, the young men joined groups called agelai for military training. Each group was led by the father of one of the members and the emphasis was on strict discipline, austerity and gruelling exercise. Lessons involved physical training, hunting training and weapons training, especially archery and javelin. In war games, they practised real combat to the extent that genuine injuries often resulted:

> With a view that courage, and not fear, should predominate, they were accustomed from childhood to the use of arms, and to endure fatigue. Hence they disregarded heat and cold, rugged and steep roads, blows received in gymnastic exercises and in set battles.[20]

Intriguingly, in addition to all this martial training, each member of the group had to plant an olive tree at the beginning of his training and cultivate it until it had reached a specific size. Failure in this task resulted in a fine of fifty gold pieces. At the end of training, the members swore an oath of allegiance to the homeland – presumably the city – and the group was disbanded. All young men were obliged to marry on completion of their training, and it is likely that mass weddings were organised for the purpose. This system of education remained virtually unchanged until well into the second century BC.

It could be argued that a form of education devoted exclusively to the creation of a military elite may have been a contributing factor in the continuous warfare between the cities. After being trained in the arts of war, it is not surprising that the young men looked for some adventure and, in the absence of a common external enemy, either became mercenaries or fought against other cities.

Art and Culture

There is little evidence of cultural activity in the early years of Dorian Crete. Dorian society was geared towards the arts of war and, apart from martial songs, there was little time for the "finer things in life". Plato's description of Spartan education in his work *Hippias Major* probably applies equally to Crete. In Plato's dialogue, when asked what the Spartans enjoy listening to most, the character Hippias scorns astronomy, geometry, logic, poetry and music, but says:

> They are very fond of hearing about the genealogies of heroes and men and the foundations of cities in ancient times and, in short, about antiquity in general.[21]

The attractive Geometric style of pottery was probably imported from the East, but there was some Dorian Cretan activity in the architectural field. The first actual temples were built during this period, and the one at Kommos (near Pitsidia in Messara) may be the oldest in Greece. In the eighth century BC, there was a brief renaissance, also influenced by the East, and beautifully decorated bronze weapons and shields have been discovered. However, the most important development of this period was in sculpture. A sculptor called Daidalos (not the probably mythical Minoan) invented new instruments for sculptural carving, which enabled him to produce the first large-scale statues in marble and earthenware. He is also reputed to have developed the use of hammered bronze for statues, and the first examples of such work have been found in Dreros. Daidalos and his pupils set up a workshop in the Peloponnese, and there is a lot of evidence that other Cretan artists could be found in Athens and other parts of Greece during the seventh century BC. It is therefore possible that Crete was, at this time, an important artistic centre, acting as a link between the artistic world of the East and mainland Greece.

The general opinion, even among contemporary writers, is that for most of the classical and Hellenistic periods Crete itself was something of a cultural wasteland. Plato has his Cretan character Kleinias admit, "We Cretans do not indulge much in foreign poetry." In spite of such comments, this does not mean that talented writers, sculptors and architects did not exist in Crete. Not for the last time, the lack of scope in Crete led to a brain drain as, like the mercenaries previously mentioned, people emigrated to areas with better conditions and opportunities.

On the other hand, at least three eminent philosophers were of Cretan origin. Possibly the most important was Epimenides, who was a contemporary and friend of Solon, the great Athenian statesman and lawgiver. As well as being a philosopher, he was a poet, prophet, historian and healer, especially learned in herbs and their medicinal value. Certainly, Pythagoras is believed to have gained his knowledge of herbs from Epimenides, when he stayed with the seer in the Idaion Cave. Epimenides' contemporaries regarded him as the originator of some of the purification rites, and such was his fame that, in 612 BC, he was invited to Athens to conduct the purification ceremonies of the city after a sacrilegious murder in the Temple of Athena. He is also reputed to have given Solon advice on sacrifices and funeral rites, and was later put in charge of all religious affairs and festivals in Crete. He was regarded as one of the seven sages of ancient Greece and, upon his death at a very advanced age, was worshipped as a god in Crete. Epimenides is probably best known for saying that all Cretans are liars, as quoted by Saint Paul from a poem Epimenides wrote, in which Minos addresses Zeus to refute the Cretan belief that Zeus had died:

> *They fashioned a tomb for you, holy and high one,*
> *Cretans, always liars, evil beasts, idle bellies.*
> *But you are not dead: you live and abide forever,*
> *For in you we live and move and have our being.*[22]

Although there is no indication that anything ironic is intended in the poem, the so-called Epimenides paradox has become an example of the liar paradox: since Epimenides is a Cretan, his statement that Cretans are always liars must be itself a lie. Therefore, Cretans are not liars. (Stop there, or it might blow your mind.)

There is some argument over whether the fifth-century-BC philosopher Diogenes of Apollonia was from the Cretan city of that name or from Thrace, but he was a major figure in pre-Socratic philosophy. In some ways very modern in his thinking, Diogenes made the first attempt to describe in scientific detail the structure and organisation of the physical world in his great work *On Nature*. Although his basic assertion that air is the principal element from which all other matter is formed might have been superseded, it was definitely a starting point. His detailed description of the blood and its circulation, on the other hand, was considered by Aristotle worthy of quoting in full,[23] and was not improved on until William Harvey's work in the seventeenth century AD. Another first achieved by Diogenes was his suggestion that meteorites came from outer space:

> Along with the visible bodies are carried around invisible stones which, being invisible, have gone unrecognized. They often fall to the earth and are extinguished, as happened to the rocky heavenly body that fell in a blaze of fire at Aegospotami.[24]

The Cretan philosopher Ainesidimos of Knossos lived in Alexandria in the first century BC and was responsible for a revival of the Sceptic school of philosophy, but only fragments of his work remain. Briefly, in reaction against Plato's somewhat dogmatic approach, he claimed that humans are in no position to affirm or deny anything categorically.

Little is known of the three Cretan poets who can be identified from the period, although there is evidence from contemporary sources that they were influential. The first, Thaletas (or Thales) of Gortyn, was a seventh-century-BC poet and musician who introduced Cretan music and dance to Sparta:

> Thales (Thaletas) passed as a lyric poet, and screened himself behind this art, but in reality he did the work of one of the mightiest law-givers. For his odes were so many exhortations to obedience and harmony, and their measured rhythms were permeated with ordered tranquillity, so that those who listened to them were insensibly softened in their dispositions, insomuch that they renounced the mutual hatreds which were so rife at that time, and dwelt together in a common pursuit of what was high and noble.[25]

Thaletas was the inventor of the Cretan metre, a particular kind of poetry accompanied by music. According to at least one early historian, he was also the originator of many Cretan customs, such as the giving of gifts of weapons and the wearing of military-style dress.

The second, Rhianos, was a third-century-BC epic and love poet. He seems to have produced a vast output, but only forty-four verses remain.

The third and most interesting of the poets was Sotades of Maroneia, a third-century-BC writer of coarse satirical verses, who lived in Alexandria. He seems to have made a habit of abusing and mocking kings in various cities. His most famous poem attacked Ptolemy II for his incestuous marriage to his sister (something of a habit among the Ptolemies): "He pierced forbidden fruit with deadly sting." For this, Sotades was sentenced to death, but he escaped to the island of Kaunos in south-west Anatolia. There, he was captured by Ptolemy's general, who sealed him up in a lead pot, carried him out to the open sea and drowned him. Unfortunately, with the exception of the somewhat sanitised quotation given here, the only examples of his work I have been able to find are utterly obscene and not suitable for quoting.

In the field of the plastic arts, sculptors from Crete also joined the emigrants. Two sixth-century-BC sculptors, Aristokles of Kydonia and Cheirisophos, produced fine bronzes at Olympia and Tegea in

Arcadia. Pliny reports seeing four works by Kresilas of Kydonia at Olympia, including a statue of Perikles and a self-portrait. Kresilas was a contemporary of the great fifth-century-BC Athenian sculptor Pheidias. A father-and-son team of architects, Chersiphron and Metagenes of Knossos, were responsible for the famous temple of Artemis at Ephesus, while in Crete itself the ruins of some interesting buildings can still be seen. These include the superb temple of Asclepius at Lebena; temples dedicated to Apollo at Knossos (the Delphinium) and Gortyn (the Pythium); and the temple of Athene at Lyttos.

Religion

During the Dorian period, the Greek Olympian deities became firmly established as the primary focus of Cretan religion, but with local variations based on earlier Minoan and Mycenaean beliefs. As noted in the previous chapter, Britomartis and Diktynna found a place in Greek mythology, while, as the birthplace of Zeus Kretagenes (meaning "Zeus born in Crete") and much of the Greek pantheon, Crete was regarded as a place worthy of particular reverence. In a possible echo of Minoan religion, Zeus Kretagenes was worshipped as a young man who died and was reborn each year, a belief regarded as blasphemous by many Greeks.

There were major temples to Apollo at Knossos and Gortyn, and a temple to Athene at Itanos, while the Idaion Cave continued to be a major religious sanctuary. One intriguing and plausible theory is that the Cretan caves acted as religious academies where priests and holy men could pass on their knowledge to pupils, as in the case of Epimenides and Pythagoras. In the sanctuary of Diktaion Zeus at Palaikastro (near Siteia), a largely intact inscription found in 1904 turned out to be a hymn to Zeus. It began:

> *Hail! Supreme Son of Kronos, master of all gone below ground,*
> *You stand at the head of the gods.*
> *Come back to Dikti at the turn of the year*
> *And take pleasure in our happy song,*
> *Which we blend with harps and pipes,*
> *And sing having taken our places around your well-walled altar.*

An important temple to Asclepius, including an impressive mosaic floor and several almost-intact pillars, can still be seen at Lebena. The worship of Asclepius, god of medicine and healing, together with his daughter Hygeia, goddess of health, cleanliness and hygiene, was a major cult in both Hellenistic and Roman times. The procedure was for the patient, after purification rites, to sleep in the temple; from his or her dreams the priests would devise the correct treatment. This would be based largely on herbal remedies, including hibiscus, cardamom, bay, quince and figs, together with water from sacred springs. It was also common for people to leave dedicatory statues of their children to ensure good health and protection.

The sanctuaries, whether temples or cave sanctuaries, were operated jointly by priests, who were responsible for the performance of rituals, and by magistrates, who administered the holy places. The latter organised the sacrifices, dedications and festivals; distributed war booty; and, more practically, repaired and erected statues, temples and altars. The mountain sanctuaries also played a significant role in coming-of-age rituals. We know of one example from the sanctuary of Hermes Kedrites in Simi, but the pattern was almost certainly repeated elsewhere. Under strict regulation, a young man would be "abducted" by an adult of high social rank and taken to the sanctuary, where they would live together in the mountains for two months. They would hunt together, and the young man would receive instruction in religious rites and beliefs. When they returned, the boy would be introduced to the citizen community, receiving gifts of a cup, a warrior's dress and an animal, which would later be sacrificed during a festival of Zeus.

Another interesting aspect of the sanctuaries is their possible political role. Most of them seem to have been outside the cities, often on the border between two, possibly indicating territorial claims to an area. They would often attract worshippers from the wider region, and there is evidence that at least three were not part of the territory of any one city but sacred land dedicated to a particular god. What we don't know is who was responsible for the administration of these "independent" sanctuaries: a single city, several cities in rotation, or a combination of cities? However they were run, there is a strong possibility that these neutral holy places were used as meeting places for informal discussions and the formation of alliances. On the other hand, the presence of citizens from different, sometimes opposing, cities could also have created flashpoints for the beginning of yet more wars.[26]

In Crete as in other Greek areas, the Hellenistic period saw the introduction of exotic deities from Egypt and the East. Temples to Isis and Serapis have been found at Gortyn. It was also at this time that Jewish immigration to Crete began, probably from Alexandria. There was a large Jewish community in Gortyn, as well as a Samaritan community in Knossos. There may well have been other communities in Crete, but we have no clear evidence.

There were a large number of religious festivals during the year, which usually followed the practices in other parts of Greece. Of particular interest was the Hermaea, a festival in celebration of Hermes. Normally, this involved fairly rowdy and rough athletic contests of various kinds, but in Kydonia the festival bore more resemblance to the later Roman Saturnalia or Christian Carnival. The enslaved workers were allowed to take over the city, while the freemen had to serve them at meals. The slaves were even allowed to whip the citizens if they "misbehaved". We have little information about this custom, but this opportunity for minor retribution once a year, together with the previously mentioned laws affording some level of protection to enslaved people, could explain the relative lack of slave revolts in Crete compared with Sparta.

6

Roman Rule

69 BC to AD 365

Conquest

By the second century BC, the Hellenic world was in decline and Rome was steadily growing in power. It wasn't long before very little of the Greek mainland remained unconquered, and Crete's location close to North Africa, Europe and the near East meant that its strategic importance was becoming enormous. It was inevitable that the eyes of the new superpower would turn towards the island. As we have seen, the Romans had intervened several times to mediate in the recurring wars between the Cretan city states, but it was not until 74 BC that serious thought was given to invasion. The rebellion of Mithridates VI, the king of **Pontus**, gave the Romans exactly the excuse they needed for an attack.

At this time, pirates from Cilicia, on the south coast of Asia Minor, virtually controlled the Mediterranean. They had an efficient and sophisticated navy and were even attracting wealthy and high-born recruits in search of adventure:

> So that now there embarked with these pirates, men of wealth and noble birth and superior abilities, as if it had been a natural occupation to gain distinction in. They had divers arsenals, or piratic harbours, as likewise watch-towers and beacons, all along the seacoast; and fleets were here received that were well manned with the finest mariners, and well served with the expertest pilots, and composed of swift-sailing and light-built vessels adapted for their special purpose.[1]

It is not certain that Cretans were directly involved in the piracy, but there was certainly an informal alliance with the Cilicians, and the pirate ships were offered safe haven in all the harbours of Crete. Thus, Mithridates was able to rely on the pirates using Crete as a base to disrupt Roman shipping and supply routes. When he also began to recruit experienced Cretan mercenaries into his army, the Romans felt they had justification for action. Of course, knowledge of the immense wealth accumulated by the pirates in the coastal cities might also have influenced their decision. Indeed, modern historians generally regard economic motives as the main force behind the invasion, especially in view of the desperate financial situation in Rome at the time. Even the second-century-BC Roman historian Florus commented, somewhat cynically: "The Cretan war, if the truth is to be told, was due solely to our desire to conquer and enslave that famous island."[2]

In 74 BC, Marcus Antonius (father of the famous Mark Antony) was appointed commander of the Roman fleet, with the specific task of invading Crete. Marcus Antonius was from an eminent and well-respected family, and set out with such confidence that, according to Florus, his ships carried more chains for the expected prisoners than weapons. In spite of his high hopes, the expedition was a disaster. He initially sent an ultimatum to the Cretan cities to annul their alliance with the pirates, but this was refused, and the Cretan assembly appointed two commanders, Panares of Kydonia and Lasthenes of Knossos, to lead a unified defence. On its way to attack the island, the Roman fleet was ambushed between Iraklion and the island of Dia, and was virtually annihilated. Many of the sailors were hung in the very chains they had brought with them, and Marcus Antonius was forced to sign a humiliating treaty with the Cretans. Because of the continuing war with Mithridates and the slave revolt under Spartacus, Rome was not in a position to retaliate for the defeat – yet. As for Marcus Antonius, in a parody of the Roman tradition of giving generals names based on their victories, people awarded him the sardonic title Creticus, which means in Latin both "conqueror of Crete" and "man of chalk". He died in Crete a few years later.[3]

In spite of the treaty, the Cretans realised that Rome would be seeking revenge at some stage, and attempted to negotiate a more permanent peace. The Roman senate agreed to a new treaty, but the terms they set were so harsh that they obviously expected (or hoped) that they would be rejected, a tactic not unknown in more modern times. All prisoners of war were to be released; the whole Cretan fleet was to be placed under Roman control, even down to the smallest four-oared skiff; 300 hostages from the top Cretan families, including the military commanders, Panares and Lasthenes, were to be sent to Rome; and 4,000 silver talents were to be paid as reparations. The last was an enormous amount of money, equivalent to about half the annual tribute of all the eastern provinces combined, and gives some indication of the vast wealth the Romans were expecting to find in Crete. Although some moderates advised that the Cretan cities should comply with all the conditions, Panares and Lasthenes "stirred up the people and urged them to maintain those liberties that they had enjoyed ever since time immemorial".[4] The hawks succeeded in uniting the majority of the quarrelsome Cretan cities, except for Gortyn and Polyrrhenia, which remained loyal to Rome, or at least neutral. The treaty was rejected, and the Cretans prepared a combined army of between 24,000 and 26,000 soldiers to meet the expected invasion.

Quintus Caecilius Metellus was given command of three Roman legions – about 15,000 men – which landed in western Crete in 69 BC. The subjugation of Crete was by no means a short war but a long process of attrition, with the Cretan army putting up strong resistance at every stage. For three years, the Romans advanced city by city, harried by the experienced and fast-moving defenders, especially the famous archers. The city of Phalasarna, one of the main havens for pirates, was the first to be besieged, captured and totally destroyed, the inhabitants being dispersed inland to Polyrrhenia or along the coast. The invading army then moved on to Kydonia, where the Cretans were again defeated. Panares surrendered Kydonia to Metellus in exchange for his life, while Lasthenes fled to Knossos. A further siege at Eleutherna ended after Roman loyalists within the city poured gallons of vinegar on the mud-brick walls of a vital defensive tower, making them brittle and easy to burn. Knossos was next to be besieged. When the Romans were about to take the city, Lasthenes set fire to his own house and as many of his valuables as possible, fled and took refuge in Lyttos. He eventually surrendered to Metellus on the same terms as Panares. The last city, Hierapytna, fell in 67 BC after the destruction of most of its fleet in a storm, and all serious resistance was at an end, apart from mopping-up exercises. The historian Dio Cassius wrote: "In this way the Cretans, who had been free through all preceding ages and had never had a foreign master, became enslaved."[5] It is worth noting that, in spite of considerable damage to the resisting cities, there is no evidence of any large-scale massacres or enslavement of the populations, as there had often been in the conquest of mainland Greece. The reasons for this are not entirely clear, as the Romans were not noted for their mercy towards conquered peoples, but it could be that they were aware that the value of Crete as a future resource meant that the bitterness engendered by brutality could be counterproductive. Another possibility, for which there is some evidence from Roman historians, is that the war was in fact limited to battles with the Cretan army, and the majority of the population was more or less neutral, or even pro-Roman.

Meanwhile, Gnaeus Pompeius Magnus (Pompey the Great), in overall command of the eastern campaigns, was busy clearing the seas of pirates, and meeting with considerable success. He had been given "absolute power and authority in all the seas within the Pillars of Hercules, and in the adjacent mainland for the space of 400 furlongs [about 80 km] from the sea", which put him technically in charge of the whole of Crete, at least in his opinion.[6] Thus, when the Cretans eventually sued for peace, they showed typical fiery independence by refusing to surrender to Metellus and agreeing to submit only to Pompey. Pompey considered the war virtually won, and commanded Metellus to withdraw from the island, pending his arrival to receive the Cretans' surrender. Although Metellus refused to comply, and continued the war until the final defeat of the Cretans, Pompey, not for the first time, was quite happy to receive much of the credit for subduing Crete. Although the leaders, Panares and Lasthenes, had surrendered to Metellus, Pompey secretly sent them to Rome so that they could appear in his own triumphal ceremony, awarded for defeating the pirates. However, after the complete pacification of the island, it was Metellus who was awarded the title "Creticus" – this time not ironically. The implications of this victory were enormous:

> The coming of Rome was the most significant turning point in the history of Crete since the destruction of the Minoan palaces. It not

only meant the subjugation of Crete under foreign rule – for the first time since the coming of the Mycenaean Greeks; it not only meant the establishment of a political government. It also meant the extinction of a social and political order that had existed for almost a millennium ... Crete was now an island not on the periphery of the Aegean, a sea troubled by wars and raids, but an island in the middle of a pacified Eastern Mediterranean, entirely integrated into the Roman system of rule and the economic networks of the Roman Empire.[7]

Administration

After 63 BC, there was little further resistance, and Crete became de facto a Roman province. Gortyn, which had remained pro-Roman, was rewarded by being made capital of the province, and it remained the administrative and commercial centre of the island until the Arab invasion of AD 828.

Little is known of the early years of Roman rule, but it is revealing that the governor in 50 BC was an agricultural expert, implying that the Romans regarded this as the island's primary value at that time. The skill of Cretan archers remained widely respected, and Julius Caesar is known to have recruited them for his campaign in Gaul. During the period of joint rule by Octavian and Mark Antony after Caesar's assassination, Crete came under Antony's jurisdiction, and he used it to build up his personal power base, possibly with his eye on eventual supremacy. To increase his popularity and influence, he granted tax concessions and Roman citizenship rights to cities like Knossos which were friendly towards him. After his marriage to Cleopatra, he actually appointed her ruler of eastern Crete and Cyprus as well as Egypt, an action which so enraged the Roman Senate that it helped to precipitate the civil war with Octavian. Antony was defeated at the Battle of Actium in 31 BC, whereupon Octavian punished those cities that had supported Antony and rewarded Lappa and Kydonia, which had opposed him.

When he became the emperor Augustus, Octavian completed his revenge on Knossos by making it a full Roman colony in about 25 BC, renaming it Colonia Julia Nobilis Cnossus. Earlier, in his war against Antony, he had recruited soldiers from Sicily, rewarding the veterans with land in Capua. Now, as compensation, he awarded the displaced Capuans valuable land in Knossos.

At about the same time, Crete and Cyrenaica (modern eastern Libya) were combined into a single province, called (in Latin) Creta et Cyrenaica. This made both strategic and commercial sense. Cyrenaica was a small but fertile area, with a population speaking the same Dorian dialect as the Cretans. With harbours on both sides of the Libyan Sea, the new province would find it much easier to continue the fight against piracy in the south Mediterranean. Moreover, Cyrenaica was actually closer to Crete than it was to the two nearest cities in North Africa, Alexandria to the east and Leptis Magna to the west.[8] This meant that trade could more easily flourish between the two halves of the province. The arrangement seems to have worked well, and the dual province remained until Diocletian's reorganisation of the empire in AD 298 split Crete from Cyrenaica and joined it to the province of Asia.

The new province was declared a senatorial province, governed by a **proconsul** of high rank, with Gortyn remaining the capital. This now made even more sense: not only was Gortyn a wealthy city in a fertile area, but it had two harbours on the south coast, Lebena and Matala, ideally placed for trade with North Africa and government of the dual province. The decision to make Creta et Cyrenaica a senatorial province as opposed to an imperial one is interesting because it implied that the province was of secondary importance. The emperor generally retained control of the most important and strategic provinces, while senatorial provinces were those well away from sensitive outer frontiers, holding little threat of rebellion and needing very few legions to control. Apart from sporadic raids by Goths in AD 269, there was little military activity within Crete, although the governor of the joint province may well have had his hands full with a Jewish uprising in Cyrenaica in AD 115 to AD 117. Thus, politically and militarily, Crete had little further impact on the wider imperial history of Rome, and became a bit of a backwater – a remote outpost, useful as a place of exile for political and military figures fallen from grace. The historian Edward Gibbon makes a telling comment when he describes the punishment of a mutinous commander of the Praetorian Guard as being "gently degraded to the government of Crete", which sounds a bit like a modern British civil servant being posted to the Falkland Islands.[9]

With the exception of the colony of Knossos, local administration was generally left to the Cretan koinon, a revival from Hellenistic times, based in Gortyn. The koinon was presided over by a high priest and was responsible for the day-to-day administration of the cities as well as the organisation of annual music festivals, and athletic games in Gortyn every five years. As the cult of divine emperors developed, the koinon was also responsible for implementing it in Crete. Most cities (not including Knossos) had the right to issue their own brass coinage, and the koinon had the right to appeal to the senate over unfair and arbitrary decisions by the Roman administration. In spite of this devolution, Rome kept the cities firmly in their place. In AD 62, for example, a Cretan governor was put on trial by the senate for refusing to offer the formal thanks of the province to a proconsul at the end of his term of office. He claimed that this was within his rights, but the prosecution clearly set out the limits of provincial rights:

> And therefore, to meet the new insolence of provincials, let us adopt a measure worthy of Roman good faith and resolution, whereby our allies may lose nothing of our protection, while public opinion may cease to say of us, that the estimate of a man's character is to be found anywhere rather than in the judgment of our citizens.[10]

Rome was equally intolerant of any renewal of friction between the cities, and a dispute between Kissamos and Polyrrhenia early in the second century was quickly sat upon by the imperial authorities.

Trade

The loss of all military and political power by the Cretan states was not matched by economic and cultural decline, and the following centuries saw many changes – some dramatic, others more subtle. With the ending of civil wars, and after centuries of instability, the Cretans seemed to welcome the **Pax Romana** and the peace and prosperity it brought. Instead of pirates and mercenaries, Crete now produced olive oil and wine for export to Rome, while importing fine marble and high-quality ceramics. The Romans abolished the communal meals in the Andreion, and land was no longer held in common by the warrior class. Thus, there was increasing private ownership of land and the beginnings of a market economy. Internally, there was considerable restoration and upgrading of the road network, begun by the emperor Claudius but continued by Nero and Trajan. For financial reasons, these developments were restricted to the areas controlled by a single town and were somewhat piecemeal. According to some inscriptions and literary evidence, however, the emperor Hadrian instructed the extremely wealthy sanctuary of Diktynna near Gortyn to pay for a major road that benefitted more than one city. It is likely that this practice became the norm.[11] Hadrian seems to have taken a great interest in Crete, but it is not clear whether he actually visited the island. The evidence for a purported visit in AD 122 is inconclusive.

The growth in trade and the shift to a market economy brought on a minor but far-reaching agricultural revolution, with much more systematic exploitation of the land. Crete's climate at the time was somewhat different from that of today and, for most of this period, it was characterised by wet summers and warm winters. This led to increased fertility and lengthened growing seasons, and meant that olives and vines could be grown at higher altitudes, thus expanding the cultivable area. Five product groups formed the basis for the increasingly prosperous Cretan economy: wine, olive oil, honey, medicinal and aromatic herbs and purple dye.

Wine was by far the most widely exported product, and during this period there was a gradual but steady transformation of Cretan wine production from small-scale vineyards to intensive commercial production, especially of staphidites, also known as passum, a sweet wine high in alcohol. This seems to have been particularly popular with the Roman army, and there is evidence of its use all around the Mediterranean and even as far afield as Wales and Switzerland. Other types of wine exported were an aromatic wine; a light white wine; wine flavoured with myrtle berries, pepper, saffron or honey; and, curiously, wine mixed with seawater. The wine from Kissamos was also reputed to have medicinal properties and was highly valued. Wine was usually shipped to Italy in grain ships from Alexandria, making Crete an important stopover and hub for the eastern Mediterranean trade routes.

Olive oil had been produced in Crete from the early Bronze Age but, as with wine, production increased substantially during the Roman period. It was of high quality and was used in cooking and religious rites, in perfumes and cosmetics and for lamps. Honey and beeswax production continued; thyme honey and pine honey were especially popular, and were exported throughout the empire, mainly for medicinal purposes. Medicinal and aromatic herbs were also exported in quantity, particularly dictamnus, alternatively known as dittany. This was used in the treatment of wounds, digestive problems and arthritis. It was also believed to have aphrodisiac properties. Other plants and herbs exported include oregano, thyme, Cretan birthwort, marshmallow, anise, yellow gentian and myrtle. The small island of Leuke (now called Koufonisi) off the south-east coast was a major centre for fishing for the murex sea snails from which the rare and expensive Tyrian or imperial purple dye was extracted. This became another important export, as cloth of this colour was highly valued in Rome.

The list of exports from Roman Crete is impressive. In addition to those already mentioned, the heavily forested island produced excellent timber, including oak especially suited to building warships, and cypress useful for building and decorative purposes. This timber was exported to all parts of the empire and, as a result, there was extensive deforestation.[12] Cretan lamps were exported all over the Mediterranean, as were whetstones from the quarry at Olous.[13] At the same time, although traditional sheep herding and production of milk and cheese continued, these products were less suitable for export, and this sector became marginalised, mainly serving the local population. For the first time, cattle were bred extensively on the Messara plain. It is worth noting here that a major source of revenue for Crete was tourism, especially to the mythical and religious sites.

The increasing emphasis on trade can be illustrated by the rise of the town of Kissamos, although a similar pattern could probably be seen in other parts of Crete. In the Hellenistic period, Kissamos, in north-western Crete, was merely the smaller and less important of the two harbours serving the city of Polyrrhenia about 6.5 km away. The other harbour, Phalasarna, was a major pirate stronghold and was the first town to be captured by Metellus in 69 BC. It was razed to the ground, probably as a warning to the rest of Crete. After the war, the minor harbour at Kissamos was expanded, and a town was founded there in about 27 BC. With the new safety from piracy and increasing trade, the town grew rapidly, while Polyrrhenia declined in importance until it became little more than a suburb of Kissamos. By the fourth century AD, Kissamos was one of the four most important independent cities in Crete, along with Kydonia, Gortyn and Hierapytna.[14]

The shift of population from Polyrrhenia to Kissamos also illustrates another general trend, which had actually started in the Hellenistic period but sped up under the more peaceful conditions of Roman rule. In all parts of Crete, people were moving away from inland hillside sites to the coast, with results that can still be seen in the modern map of Crete. The town of Lato pros Kamara (modern Aghios Nikolaos) was founded by the inhabitants of the hill fortress Lato when defensive concerns became less paramount. The move from inland Vrocastro and Oleros to Istron and Hierapytna respectively are further examples. At the same time, the citizens of the new coastal towns often retained property in the hills to which they could escape the rush and dust of city life, especially in the hot summers – a practice that continues to this day.

By the second century AD, the 100 cities of Crete had decreased to about 20, although the area controlled by each had grown larger, often incorporating smaller towns. Of these, Gortyn and Hierapytna were by far the largest, with an estimated population of 22,500 each. The population of Kydonia was about half that, while Kissamos had by then nearly reached 9,000. Phaistos had a population of 7,500 and Knossos, having declined in both importance and population, had fallen to under 7,000. [15]

Culture

Within the overarching rules of Roman government and total loyalty to the emperor, the empire tolerated a high degree of cultural diversity, and the lifestyle in Crete followed the pattern of most provinces in the Roman Empire. On the one hand, there was no deliberate attempt to "Romanise" the island and, for most ordinary Cretans, culture and language remained mainly Cretan Greek. Customs and traditions continued as they had done for centuries, including worship of the old Greek gods. On the other hand, the upper classes and, of course, the Roman colonists seem to have increasingly followed the typical Roman lifestyle, although there were variations between the cities. In the colony of Knossos, for example, people seem to have generally chosen to accept the economic benefits of Roman culture, while rejecting the use of Latin except for administrative purposes. In other cities, there was more willingness to adopt Roman culture, including the language and the imperial cult. Although there are few records showing the development of Roman Crete, recent research has indicated a general process of slow "self-Romanization". Just as in other colonial situations – British India, for example – the social trappings of the conquerors became status symbols among the Cretan elite, and a degree of "keeping up with the Claudiuses" ensured the further spread of Roman culture. The elite was composed of landowners, often Roman citizens with a classical education, and usually holding political power in the community. Later, as trade expanded, wealthy merchants increasingly became members of the elite and, since there is little benefit in being an elite if nobody knows it, outward symbols of power and wealth spread through the island.

Excavations have shown an increasing trend towards large houses built around an open central courtyard (**atrium**) with a shallow pool (impluvium) in the middle. This was a typical Roman feature, which, by demonstrating that the owner had an adequate supply of water, was a status symbol in the hot, dry Cretan summer. The popularity of this type of building has other implications. During the Hellenistic period, Cretan social life was largely communal, with the men doing military training and eating together in the Andreion, only going home to sleep in their relatively small private houses. The Romans brought a shift away from this militaristic culture based on collective ownership of land and communal life, and moved Crete towards a more individualistic society based on trade and private ownership. This in turn resulted in a fashion for large houses, in which the master of the house could entertain and show off his possessions. In domestic life, a detailed study of the import of fine Roman ceramics to Crete indicates that Roman products were fashionable in many parts of Crete, perhaps suggesting that the Cretan elite "set the table like Romans, even if they did not speak Latin at the dinner table".[16] There is, as yet, no evidence of major artistic activity during the Roman period, although mosaic work of high quality has been found, and it is likely that skilled mosaic artists immigrated to Crete to fulfil the demand for this form of decoration. Examples of some magnificent mosaics can be seen in the museum at Kissamos.

Such evidence as we have to date, therefore, seems to point to deliberate attempts among the wealthier Cretan aristocracy and merchants to Romanise their lifestyles and their buildings, both public and private. By the second century AD, however, it seems that Roman fashions had become integrated into Cretan elite society, and the wealthy were less concerned with emulating the Romans than with emulating each other and showing a clear distinction between themselves and the lower classes. For example, the popularity of houses with atria continued in Crete well into the fourth century AD, long after they had fallen out of fashion in Italy, indicating that the style had become fully integrated into Cretan life.

Public architecture saw perhaps an even greater Roman influence. The *Monty Python* question "What have the Romans ever done for us?" is easily answered. Aqueducts were almost unknown during the Hellenistic period but, by the second century AD, every major city had at least one. Remains of aqueducts can still be seen at Lyttos and Chersonisos, while the latter has an impressive fountain dating from the second or third century AD. As in other parts of the empire, the building of new roads began across the island, while theatres, amphitheatres and temples to foreign gods proliferated. The largest theatre discovered to date was at Lyttos but, sadly, a reputedly well-preserved theatre in Kydonia was destroyed by the Venetians, who looted the site for stone to build a castle. Nearly every Roman site shows evidence of the use of high-quality decorative marble, which was almost certainly imported. Some of the marble columns in the Venetian Basilica of Saint Mark in Iraklion (now the Municipal Art Gallery) were almost certainly taken from a Roman site, and were probably imported from North Africa. It has been suggested that the very existence of quantities of such marble indicates a vast trade system importing luxuries from a huge distance and at great expense.

We have little record of literary activity in Roman Crete, but the island did produce one major poet: Mesomedes. A freedman of Emperor Hadrian, Mesomedes wrote a large number of poems and hymns in Greek, fifteen of which survive. Four of the hymns also include the original musical notation, enabling reconstruction of the music as it would have been performed. Although best known for his hymns to the sun, to Nemesis and to his Muse, it is Mesomedes' smaller-scale poems that can still delight most, with their multiple meanings, mild eroticism and appreciation of the miraculous in everyday life. The writer Dianne Skafte notes that "While other poets were praising the glories of war and the feats of heroes, Mesomedes wrote little odes to a mosquito, a sundial and a sea sponge."[17] A sample from the poem about the sea sponge gives a flavour of his style:

This flower I bring to you in my hands
With many holes from the deep rocks of the sea,
The very image of a beehive, like honeycomb
On Hymettus from the crags of Attica,
Which gives Glaucus pleasure in his waters.[18]

Religious Life

Roman rule was tolerant of a wide range of religious beliefs and, as mentioned above, worship of the old Greek gods continued, as well as worship of their Roman equivalents, especially among poorer people. Indeed, there was an upsurge of interest in the Cretan sanctuaries of Zeus on Mount Ida and Mount Dikti, while there is evidence for a steady stream of pilgrims from Cyrenaica visiting the sanctuary of Asclepius at Lebena, famous throughout the Mediterranean. As in other parts of the empire, colonists and traders from Italy brought with them new religions and cults, such as mystery religions, cults of healing and worship of the emperor, but it is not known how far the popularity of these extended outside the aristocracy. At the same time, as trade with the eastern provinces expanded, Egyptian religions began to spread, while the large Jewish population in Crete may well have helped Christianity to gain a foothold.

The archaeological site at Gortyn contains a group of temples that almost represent a library of religions and cults. The Temple of Pythian Apollo represents continuity between the old Greek gods and the Roman pantheon. It is interesting that Apollo was one of the few Greek gods not renamed by the Romans. Nearby, the Temple of the Augustan Gods provides a place of worship for the imperial cult. By the time it was built, Julius Caesar, Augustus, his wife Livia and Claudius had been officially deified, although more were to be added later. Another temple is dedicated to the Egyptian gods, primarily Isis but also Serapis and Hermanubis, a composite of the Egyptian Anubis and the Greek Hermes. The cult of Isis was popular in many parts of the empire, appealing to all ages and social classes – but especially to women. Followers developed an almost personal relationship with the goddess, who offered healing for the sick and eventual resurrection for all. Perhaps the most intriguing place in the complex is the altar to The Most High God (Theos Hypsistos), an unnamed deity originating in Egypt and Palestine and popular throughout the Mediterranean. This was a monotheistic religion in which believers would gather around an outdoor altar to worship a god of light, represented by the flames of lamps.

The Coming of Christianity

One cultural event in Roman Crete was probably barely noticed at the time, but was to have far-reaching consequences for the future of the island: the arrival of Christianity. We know very little about how and when this occurred, and what we do know is often contradictory and vague, based mainly on a few lines in the Acts of the Apostles, together with local tradition. Nevertheless, it is certainly worth outlining the few details we do have.

The roots of the conversion of Crete may well lie in the sizeable Jewish community that existed on the island in the first century AD. Many Cretan Jews were present in Jerusalem on the day of **Pentecost** (about AD 33) and were among those converted by Saint Peter's address. It seems likely, therefore, that at least some of them returned to Crete and began to spread the new Christian message. Some years later (AD 60), Saint Paul is believed to have visited Crete on his way to imprisonment in Rome, but it is unclear from the Acts of the Apostles whether he actually landed.[19] A storm forced the ship to shelter at Kaloi Limenes (meaning "Fair Havens") near Lasea on the south coast. Paul recommended that the ship stay there for three weeks, but the captain decided to sail to a safer anchorage at Phoenix (Loutro). According to very ancient local lore, after they landed at Phoenix, Saint Paul spent the winter there and baptised the first Christian converts. The next event on record seems to have been a mission to Crete by Saint Paul in about AD 63 after his release from prison in Rome. According to his Epistle to Titus in the New Testament, he left Saint Titus in charge of organising the young Church. Certainly, Saint Titus is generally regarded as the first bishop of Crete and is revered as such in the Orthodox Church. His head is preserved as a relic in the Church of Aghios Titos in Iraklion. The remains of a basilica dedicated to Saint Titus are still at Gortyn, but this basilica was not built until the sixth or seventh century AD.

Although the early days of Christianity in Crete are shadowy, it seems likely that the growth of the Church was steady, with the bishops of Gortyn quickly establishing themselves as leaders. The historian Eusebius mentions a letter from Dionysios, bishop of Corinth, to Philip, bishop of Gortyn commending his fortitude and warning him against heresies prevalent at the time. Indeed, Philip had written a strong and detailed refutation of the heretic Marcion, which is sadly no longer existent. Eusebius also mentions Pinytos, bishop of Knossos, as one of the early fathers from whom "has come down to us in writing the [solid] and orthodox faith received from apostolic tradition".[20]

The few other details of Christian activity in Roman Crete come from early mentions in liturgies and church dedications. These indicate that Crete had its fair share of Christian martyrs during the two-centuries-long period of persecutions by the Roman state and local authorities, and there is evidence of monastic life even before the legalisation of Christianity. By the end of the second century AD, Christianity had spread beyond the areas of Gortyn and Knossos to other towns in the west and centre of Crete, but there is no evidence of any general spread of Christianity in the east of the island by this time.[21]

The Earthquake of AD 365

While there is little doubt concerning the beginning of Roman Crete, the date of its ending is more problematic. The change from Roman Empire to **Byzantine Empire** was not a single event but a long process. Indeed, the very term "Byzantine" was not used until the fifteenth century AD, and the people of Byzantium still referred to themselves as the Roman Empire until the fall of Constantinople in AD 1453. Thus, any choice of date for the end of this chapter is arbitrary and subject to dispute. I have decided to follow a recent suggestion that the earthquake of AD 365 was the turning point, for reasons that will become apparent.[22] At the very least, it makes a suitably dramatic ending to the chapter!

Crete, sitting on two active geological faults, is at the centre of an area of major seismic activity, and there were at least three serious earthquakes during the Roman period. The first, during the reign of Nero in about AD 66, was charmingly described by an eyewitness:

> Here Apollonius was haranguing on one occasion about midday, and was addressing quite a number of people who were worshipping at the shrine [of Asclepius at Lebena near Gortyn], when an earthquake shook the whole of Crete at once, and a roar of thunder was heard to issue not from the clouds but from the earth, and the sea receded about seven stadia [1.3 km]. And most of them were afraid that the sea by receding in this way would drag the temple after it, so that they would be carried away. But Apollonius said: "Be of good courage, for the sea has given birth and brought forth land."
>
> And they thought that he was alluding to the harmony of the elements, and was urging that the sea would never wreak any violence upon the land; but after a few days some travellers arrived from Kydonia and announced that on the very day on which this portent occurred and just at the same hour of midday, an island rose out of the sea between Thera and Crete.[23]

There is also a reference by a historian in the fourth century AD to tombs at Knossos being damaged by this earthquake. Intriguingly, one of the tombs contained a piece of bark inscribed with an unknown alphabet and language. Scholars at the time could make little sense of it, but more recently it has been suggested that this was in fact an early discovery of a Linear B text.

There is little information about an earthquake in AD 262, but it is believed to have been the same as one that destroyed the Sanctuary of Demeter and Persephone in Cyrene at about the same time. Archaeological evidence from Ptolemais in Cyrenaica and Kissamos in Crete attest to its suddenness and severity, with crushed skeletons being found in excavated buildings in both locations.

In contrast, the earthquake of AD 365 was widely reported in contemporary histories, although there is some confusion in the various reports. There is evidence that it was the worst of a string of earthquakes during a period of heightened seismic activity lasting several years. Geological and archaeological evidence points to a megaquake of about 8.5 or more on the Richter scale, exceeding all modern earthquakes in the region. With its epicentre 40–70 km under the sea south-west of Crete, it caused extensive damage in central and southern Greece, northern Libya, Egypt, Cyprus and Sicily, and as far as Spain. The resulting tsunami continued the destruction, devastating the coasts of Libya, Egypt and the Levant. The effect on Alexandria was vividly and accurately described by a contemporary historian:

A little before sunrise there was a terrible earthquake, preceded by incessant and furious lightning. The sea was driven backwards, so as to recede from the land, and the very depths were uncovered, so that many marine animals were left sticking in the mud. And the depths of its valleys and the recesses of the hills, which from the very first origin of all things had been lying beneath the boundless waters, now beheld the beams of the sun.

Many ships were stranded on the dry shore, while people straggling about the shoal water picked up fishes and things of that kind in their hands. In another quarter the waves, as if raging against the violence with which they had been driven back, rose, and swelling over the boiling shallows, beat upon the islands and the extended coasts of the mainland, levelling cities and houses wherever they encountered them. All the elements were in furious discord, and the whole face of the world seemed turned upside down, revealing the most extraordinary sights.

For the vast waves subsided when it was least expected, and thus drowned many thousand men. Even ships were swallowed up in the furious currents of the returning tide, and were seen to sink when the fury of the sea was exhausted; and the bodies of those who perished by shipwreck floated about on their backs or faces.

Other vessels of great size were driven on shore by the violence of the wind, and cast upon the house-tops, as happened at Alexandria; and some were even driven two miles inland, of which we ourselves saw one in Laconia, near the town of Mothone, which was lying and rotting where it had been driven.[24]

In Crete itself, even the inland towns were extensively damaged, while most of the coastal towns were totally destroyed. Athanasius of Alexandria wrote that more than 100 cities in Crete were destroyed and, even if we assume that he was including small towns in his estimate, it seems likely that Crete suffered total devastation. The violence of the earthquake was such that on the west coast of the island the ground level actually lifted by about 6–9 m. At Phalasarna, a jetty containing the remains of marine creatures has been found 6.5 m above sea level, while the Roman harbour of Kissamos now lies several metres inland. Excavations of Roman houses have revealed some of the damage caused by the earthquake. At Eleutherna, six crushed skeletons were found, while a site at Aptera revealed fallen columns dating from the fourth century AD. The governor's residence (praetorium) at Gortyn was completely destroyed, and Knossos suffered such damage that extensive rebuilding had to be undertaken. Part of the Roman town of Chersonisos was submerged by 1–2 m.

All in all, it is apparent that the destruction of harbours, the need for large-scale rebuilding and, in some cases, the movement of populations to new locations had a major impact on Cretan economic activity and social life, which signalled a clear break in continuity with the Roman period.

7

The First Byzantine Period

365 to 824

Administration

As the centre of the Roman Empire gradually shifted from Rome to Byzantium, Crete continued as a quiet provincial backwater, peaceful and prosperous and flourishing in its trade with the rest of the empire. It remained a predominantly agricultural economy, but its products were widely sought after.

After Diocletian's brief amalgamation of Crete with Mysia in Asia Minor, Constantine the Great linked the island with the large prefecture of Illyricum, which covered most of the Balkans and the mainland of Greece. Thus, with the final split into the Eastern Roman Empire and Western Roman Empire under Theodosius in 395, Crete was firmly within the Eastern Roman Empire. During most of this period, the concerns of Byzantium were mainly directed towards threats from the east and north, leaving Crete largely to its own devices, a policy that was to have disastrous consequences later. The Dorian koinon seems to have survived up to the end of the fourth century, but little is known of its responsibilities, and it is likely to have withered away as the Byzantine administration became more entrenched. By this time, it is probable that the inhabitants of the island began to regard themselves as Cretans, rather than identifying with a particular city or clan.

Up until the sixth century, the imperial provincial system followed the Roman model of separation of political and military power and administration. With the major reforms of the emperor Justinian, however, a new system of "themes" was instituted whereby the governor of the province had both military and civil jurisdiction. Although it is not certain, many scholars believe that Crete was set up as a separate theme sometime in the eighth century, with a governor based in Gortyn, which remained the capital of the island until the Arab invasion.

During the first Byzantine period, Crete is believed to have had twenty-two cities, with a total population of about 250,000, almost entirely Christian. Several areas had much larger populations than in later times. For example, the island of Gavdos, south of Crete, which now has very few inhabitants, had a population of about 8,000 in the year 900, and probably constituted a diocese in its own right. Similarly, the excavation of only a small part of what must have been a massive sixth-century basilica on the site of Olous (near Elounda) indicates the existence of a large and wealthy community.

Events

For a long time, Crete was spared major attacks by pirates, and a single attack by Vandals in 457 was followed by nearly 200 years of peace. This raid was part of an ongoing campaign against the Western Roman Empire by the Vandal leader Gaiseric, based in North Africa, and was little more than a sideshow to the main war. In 623, the newly built Slavic fleet raided Crete as part of a united Slavic and Persian attack on Constantinople, but this was also of minor importance.

Of greater long-term significance were the increasing attacks by Arab forces from the middle of the seventh century, which indicated the shape of things to come. An Arab fleet plundered the coast of Crete in about 654, and, only two years later, another major attack was launched on the island. Further raids occurred in 671 and 674, and the Arab raiders felt confident enough to spend the winter of 674 in Crete. For a long time, these raids were sporadic and of limited success, but the frequency and severity of the attacks increased during the eighth century. The islanders, especially in the coastal towns, must have felt as vulnerable as the Anglo-Saxons during the period of Viking raids, which began in 789. Many of the Cretan inscriptions of the period contain heartfelt pleas to God or the saints for protection against the "barbarians" or "enemies". We know something of these raids from the sermons of Saint Andrew of Crete, who often attempted to use his sermons to give comfort to his flock and boost their morale in the face of attacks. He is also believed to have helped in the resistance to a concerted attack on the fort of Drimeos, which was defeated by the Byzantine forces. A Byzantine historian describes the battle with a degree of bias, but with a colourful use of metaphor:

> The wicked sons of Agar [Arabs] organised their raid on the sea and with a large number of ships and made a rabid attack on the island of the Christ-beloved Cretans ... For the barbarians laid siege to the stronghold called Drimeos, to which, according to custom, the man of God [Andrew, Archbishop of Gortyn] went with the most Christian people shepherded by him because of hostile attacks. And the barbarians displayed many machines of war against it in a surrounding fortification, but they made the enterprise ineffective for themselves, suffering as loss their own destruction instead of the reward of a large body of captives, after being fought off by the missiles of the prayers of the bishop, who extended his eye to God like a bow.[1]

More serious in their effects were several major earthquakes and frequent outbreaks of plague. We have little information about the earthquakes apart from the dates, but one in 415 destroyed Gortyn, while another, only thirty-three years later, caused significant damage to the metropolis of Gortyn. Further quakes in 531 and 795 also caused damage across the island. Given the apparent prosperity of the island, it is likely that rebuilding was quick and widespread.

The so-called Justinian Plague of 542, which swept across North Africa and much of Europe, was described vividly by Procopius, a contemporary Byzantine historian:

> During these times there was a pestilence, by which the whole human race came near to being annihilated.[2]

It was probably as devastating as the better-known Black Death of the fourteenth century, and recent research has shown that it was, in fact, an early outbreak of the same disease, caused by the *Yersinia pestis* bacterium. As far as can be established, the outbreak halved the population of Europe, weakening the Byzantine Empire to such an extent that later Arab incursions met with little resistance. Even the emperor, Justinian, caught it – but he survived, and it is to his biographer, Procopius, that we owe a remarkable account of the plague. He describes, in clinical but harrowing detail, the symptoms and progress of the disease, various methods of dealing with the enormous numbers of deaths, and the social, economic and political results of the disaster. Although we know little of the plague's effects in Crete, it is likely that they followed a similar pattern to that described by Procopius in Constantinople. He set out the sheer scale and horror of the events vividly:

> Now the disease in Byzantium ran a course of four months, and its greatest virulence lasted about three. And at first, the deaths were a little more than the normal, then the mortality rose still higher, and afterwards the tally of dead reached five thousand each day, and again it even came to ten thousand and still more than that. Now in the beginning, each man attended to the burial of the dead of his own house, and these they threw even into the tombs of others, either escaping detection or using violence; but afterwards confusion and disorder everywhere became complete. For slaves remained destitute of masters, and men, who in former times were very prosperous, were deprived of the service of their domestics, who were either sick or dead, and many houses became completely destitute of human inhabitants. For this reason it came about that some of the notable men of the city, because of the universal destitution, remained unburied for many days.[3]

A further outbreak of the plague in 746 was followed by a severe drought and famine, which caused even further devastation.

Religion

After Christianity was brought to Crete by Saint Paul and Saint Titus, and legalised by Constantine the Great in 313, the new faith spread to all parts of the island until, by the late fourth century, it was almost entirely Christian – with a few small Jewish communities, mainly in the cities. At the beginning, the Church of Crete was an archdiocese of the province of Illyricum and thus under the jurisdiction of the pope as the bishop of Rome. Apart from a short time after Rome fell to the Visigoths in 476, this situation continued, until the iconoclast emperor Constantine V brought the whole province of Illyricum under the control of the **Patriarch** of Constantinople in 754. This was partly due to the politics of the Iconoclast Controversy (see later in this chapter) and partly to remove what was essentially an Eastern province from the ecclesiastical control of a Roman Church, increasingly dominated by the Western kingdom of the Franks under Charlemagne.

Whether under Rome or Constantinople, Crete seems to have been a thriving religious community, with about ten to twelve dioceses and many beautiful and imposing churches. The remains of over forty churches have been discovered to date. These include the fifth-century church at Panormos near Mylopotamos, the largest early Christian basilica in Crete and one of the largest in Greece. The sixth-century Church of Saint Titus in Gortyn became an important place of pilgrimage and is still, even in its ruined state, a magnificent sight. Some idea of the quality of the mosaic work in the churches at the time can still be seen in the remains of splendid mosaic floors at the Basilica of Sougia, near Selino, and on the island of Kolokytha near Elounda. Mosaic floors were decorated either with geometric shapes or with animals and birds, as no human representation could be shown on the floor. Nor could a cross be depicted, in case people walked on it by mistake. Unfortunately, our knowledge of the artistry of this early period is restricted to such mosaics; although frescoes certainly existed, none have survived.

As well as great buildings, the Church of Crete gave the island several outstanding clerics. Although no Cretan bishops seem to have participated in the First Ecumenical Council in Nicaea in 325, they took part in all of the other six such councils, which established the foundations of Christianity. In the fourth century the charismatic figure Myron became bishop of Gortyn. He came from a farming background, but was so renowned for his goodness that, after the death of his wife, he was chosen by the local people to be their bishop. A delightful story is told of him. When he was still a farmer, he came across a group of thieves stealing grain from his barn. Instead of attacking them, he helped them fill their sacks, and sent them on their way. It is said that the thieves were shamed by his generosity, and went straight from then on. Myron died in about 350, at the age of 100, and is venerated as a saint in the Orthodox Church.

Other prominent churchmen of the period include Saint Eumenios, another bishop of Gortyn, and Saint Kosmas the Hermit. Although little is known of the life of Saint Eumenios, he is reputed to have been a powerful bishop and author. Much of his tenure of 668 to 680 was devoted to combatting the Monothelite heresy, which questioned the human nature of Christ in relation to his divine nature. It gained a lot of ground among some patriarchs and, for a time, had the support of the emperor. Because of his strong opposition to the heresy, Saint Eumenios was exiled to Thebes in Egypt, where he died in 680, just before the heresy was condemned by the Sixth Ecumenical Council at Chalcedon. Even less is known of Saint Kosmas the Hermit, who died in about 658. According to an ancient manuscript, he was a monk who opposed the Monothelite bishops in the area, and was forced to leave the monastery. He settled in a cave in southern Crete, where he lived in seclusion until his death. The Cave of Saint Kosmas is near the Koudoumas monastery, where his life is still celebrated annually on 2nd September, although his relics were stolen by Venetian merchants in 1058 and transported to Venice.

Perhaps the most outstanding figure of the early Byzantine Church in Crete was Saint Andrew the Archbishop of Crete, who is thought to have been born in 660. Born in Damascus, he was tonsured as a monk at the age of fourteen and quickly became an exceptionally gifted preacher. After working in several important church posts, he was made Archbishop of Gortyn in 700. Revered in his lifetime for his piety, erudition and preaching, Andrew is now best known for his hymns, many of which are still used in the worship of the Ortho-dox Church. In particular, he is said to have invented a type of hymn called the canon, a highly structured hymn based on and commenting on biblical texts. The most famous of these is the Great Penitential Canon, sometimes simply called the Great Canon, which is read in sections on the first four evenings of Great Lent, and in its entirety on the Thursday of the fifth week. It goes chronologically through the whole of the Old and New Testaments, taking hundreds of examples relating to the theme of repentance. What makes it unusual and very moving is that it is largely written in the first person as a dialogue between Saint Andrew and his soul, so that the whole hymn becomes a personal quest for repentance and forgiveness. Given its subject matter, the Great Penitential Canon may be somewhat gloomy for non-religious tastes, but it is certainly powerful stuff and represents the high point in Cretan ecclesiastical poetry of the Byzantine period:

> Where shall I begin to lament the deeds of my wretched life? What first-fruit shall I offer, O Christ, for my present lamentation? But in Thy compassion grant me release from my falls.
>
> Come, wretched soul, with your flesh, confess to the Creator of all. In future refrain from your former brutishness, and offer to God tears in repentance.
>
> Having rivalled the first-created Adam by my transgression, I realize that I am stripped naked of God and of the everlasting kingdom and bliss through my sins.
>
> Alas, wretched soul! Why are you like the first Eve? For you have wickedly looked and been bitterly wounded, and you have touched the tree and rashly tasted the forbidden food ...
>
> A robber accused Thee, and a robber confessed Thee to be God, for both were hanging on a cross with Thee. But open even to me, O most compassionate Saviour, the door of Thy glorious Kingdom as to Thy faithful robber who acknowledged Thee to be God.[4]

A further twenty-four canons are attributed to Andrew, along with 111 short hymns. Andrew died on the island of Mytilene while returning from a journey to Constantinople, sometime between 712 and 740.[5]

The small Jewish community seems to have been active in various parts of Crete. Inscriptions which may relate to this community have been found near Iraklion, Kissamos, Aghioi Deka and Gortyn. An area 40 km south-east of Iraklion is known as Evraioi (meaning "Hebrews") and is believed by archaeologists to be the site of a Jewish cemetery, but no major excavation has yet taken place. The emperor

Theodosius II, who lived from 401 to 450, reinforced and extended the limitations on Jewish activity that had already begun under Constantine the Great. Despite facing political and economic disadvantages and occasional persecution, the Greek-speaking Jews of Crete, who were heavily involved in the cloth and leather industries, appear to have enjoyed more freedom to trade in Crete than in other areas of Byzantium. Nevertheless, there was considerable discontent over the restrictions they were working under. In about 430, a rabbi called Moses appeared in Crete, proclaiming that he was the same Moses who had led the Israelites from Egypt and promising to lead the Jews of Crete to the Holy Land. The power of his preaching caused nearly all the Jews in Crete to abandon their property and gather together with him on the coast, where they threw themselves off the cliffs into the sea, believing that Moses would part the waters and lead them to Palestine on dry land. It is not known what happened to Moses, but many of his followers drowned. Many others were rescued by fishermen who watched the extraordinary events. A contemporary historian, Socrates of Constantinople, writes that most of the survivors converted to Christianity. It is certainly the case that the Jews of Crete do not appear in any history of the island for several centuries after this time.[6]

Iconoclasm

Probably the most significant event in the religious life of Crete during this period was the Iconoclast Controversy. Between 726 and 843, several Byzantine emperors and bishops attempted to stamp out the use of icons in the churches. The reasons for this policy were a complex mixture of politics, early puritanism and even the influence of Islamic theology. The resulting persecutions were as brutal as those of the worst of the Roman emperors. Patriarchs and bishops were deposed and exiled; priests were imprisoned; thousands of ordinary Christians were tortured, executed or branded on the face with red-hot irons; monks had their heads shattered against icons, or were sewn into sacks and drowned. Nobody would see such savagery of Christian against Christian again until the Reformation in western Europe. The heresy was condemned at the Seventh (and final to date) Ecumenical Council at Nicaea in 787. However, it re-emerged in 814, and was not finally defeated until 843, when the empress Saint Theodora restored the icons to the churches.

Broadly speaking, most of the bishops in Crete, like many of the Western Churches under Rome, were supporters of the veneration of icons, and this had several consequences. In 727, the Cretans joined in the Helladic Uprising against the iconoclast emperor Leo III, but the rebellion was ruthlessly put down by the imperial navy, using the terrible **Greek Fire**. There followed harsh persecution by Crete's icon-oclast governor. Crete had its fair share of the multitude of martyr-doms during the period of iconoclasm. In 765, an abbot called Paul is reported to have been cruelly tortured and roasted alive for refusing to trample on an icon of Christ, but no details are known.[7] Shortly after, a man called Andronikos was killed, but we know nothing of him except brief references in early church calendars.

The most famous of the martyrs was Andrew en Krisei (the latter part of his name meaning "in judgement"). He had been taken to Constantinople in 762 and prosecuted for preaching against the icono-clasts, and was finally executed by order of Constantine V two years later. At the Seventh Ecumenical Council in 787, the Archbishop of Crete and nearly all his bishops were present, in an indication of the extent of support for the retention of icons in the Cretan Church. In spite of the ravages of iconoclasm, the Cretan Church continued to prosper until 824, when it was faced by perhaps its greatest test since the legalisation of Christianity in 313.

8

The Arab Emirate of Crete

824 to 961

The Invasion

The Arab[1] conquest of Crete was certainly one of the most traumatic events in Byzantine history. We have noted before the strategic importance of Crete; by losing it, the empire not only lost control of the eastern Mediterranean trade routes but furnished pirates with a haven from which they could ravage the area. In spite of the importance of these events, however, very little detail is known about the 140-odd years of Arab rule. Even the date and location of the invasion are not known with any certainty. What is clear is that the attack occurred at a time when Byzantium was going through a period of domestic instability coupled with external threats from Arabs to the south and east, and Bulgars and Kievan Rus from the north.

There had been Arab attacks on Crete in the seventh century, and part of the island was briefly occupied during the great expansion of Muslim territory in the early eighth century. The story of the Arab conquest of Crete, however, begins in ninth-century Spain. Most of the Iberian Peninsula was covered by an area called al-Andalus, a Muslim emirate ruled by the **emir** of Córdoba. The bulk of its population comprised Arabs, **Berbers** and Iberian converts to Islam. In 818, an alliance of Muslim clerics and **jurists** with non-Arab Muslims rebelled against the emir's rule and the harsh taxation he imposed. The revolt failed, resulting in the crucifixion of 300 clerics and the exile of 20,000 rebels. About half of these exiles settled in Fez, Morocco, but over 10,000 men, women and children in forty ships headed for

Egypt, almost certainly carrying out raids on Sicily and Crete on the way. Taking advantage of the chaos resulting from a civil war, they captured Alexandria and briefly occupied the city. It was probably here that one of their number, Abu Hafs, became their leader. The invaders were eventually besieged and defeated by a local general, but were allowed to keep their lives on the condition that they moved to a non-Muslim area.

Expelled from Alexandria, the fleet moved on to Crete. Both the events and dates are confused but, whatever the exact date, at some point about 12,000 Berbers, Arabs and non-Arab Muslims, including 3,000 fighting men, landed in Crete under the charismatic Abu Hafs, himself of mixed origin. The landing place is variously identified and may have been in Souda Bay or near Iraklion, but is most likely to have been on the south coast at the east end of the Bay of Messara, near modern Lithinon. Gibbon quotes a dramatic but probably apocryphal story based on Byzantine historians:

> They saw, they envied, they tasted the fertility of Crete, and soon returned with forty galleys to a more serious attack. The Andalusians wandered over the land fearless and unmolested; but when they descended with their plunder to the sea-shore, their vessels were in flames, and their chief, Abu Caab, confessed himself the author of the mischief.[2] Their clamours accused his madness or treachery. "Of what do you complain?" replied the crafty emir. "I have brought you to a land flowing with milk and honey. Here is your true country; repose from your toils, and forget the barren place of your nativity." "And our wives and children?" "Your beauteous captives will supply the place of your wives, and in their embraces you will soon become the fathers of a new progeny."[3]

Although a colourful story, it is more likely that the Arabs intended to settle in Crete anyway and had probably brought their families with them.[4] In any case, it seems unlikely that Abu Hafs would have destroyed his own navy, his best protection against Byzantine attacks.

Weakened by internal revolts and the capture of Sicily by the Tunisians, Emperor Michael II could do little to defend the island, but accounts vary as to the resistance met by the invaders. The earliest

Byzantine source, written in the early tenth century, refers to the siege and sacking of Gortyn, and the enslavement of twenty-eight cities, one being spared because it surrendered.[5] Some Arab historians refer to an invasion "step by step" and "fortress by fortress" but, apart from this, there is little record of serious resistance.[6] There have been interesting theories that the Cretans, who mostly supported the pro-icon movement in the bitter Iconoclast Controversy, may have welcomed the Arabs as protectors against the iconoclast emperor Michael II in Constantinople. Certainly, in some areas, Arab rulers were protective of exiles from Constantinople – for example, John of Damascus – but there is no evidence of widespread welcome of the invaders, which would certainly have been noted in Arab sources as an excellent piece of propaganda.

What is much clearer is that at some stage Abu Hafs moved his army north and set up his capital in what is now Iraklion. An apostate monk is believed to have led him to a likely area and, seeing its strategic potential, facing north and giving easy access to the Aegean, Abu Hafs fortified an existing village with a moat and palisade (or possibly a brick wall). The new fortress was nicknamed Rabdh el Khandaq ("Castle of the Moat"), Chandax or Khandax in Greek or Candia in Latin. These names were often used to refer to the whole island for many years. Chandax now became the base for the Arab conquest of the rest of Crete, although some historians believe that parts of the island were never entirely subdued.

Within ten years, Crete had become a major base for naval operations against the empire, either alone or in alliance with other emirates. Although the mighty Abbasid Caliphate, which covered most of the Islamic world, was by the ninth century reduced to exercising mainly spiritual and cultural influence, it was still a unifying force, and the various emirs frequently joined forces for major raids and expeditions. Recent research seems to confirm the view that the Cretan Emirate was more than just – as many Byzantine historians referred to it – a nest of pirates, and was in fact highly regarded as a frontier fortress in the continuing war of attrition between Islam and Byzantium. In this context, the Cretan fleet can be loosely compared with the privateers of Elizabethan England rather than with purely independent pirates.

Arab Attacks and the Byzantine Response

A little like the Hundred Years' War between England and France, the conflict between the Emirate of Crete and the Byzantine Empire was not a continuous war. There were periods of peace – or, at least, cold war – as the balance of power shifted from one side to the other. The following are the most important events during the century and a half in which the Cretan Emirate existed.

825 to 826: In spite of the difficulties facing the empire on all sides, Michael II took immediate steps to retake the island. An early expeditionary force was dispatched with a view to preventing permanent occupation by the Arabs. Led by the generals Photeinos and Damian, the army was defeated. Damian was killed.

829: Seventy ships under General Krateros landed on Crete and met with some success but, after failing to post guards, the army was defeated in a night attack. Krateros himself escaped in a merchant ship but was pursued, captured near Kos and put to death by impaling. Shortly after, while still subduing the island, Arab fleets attacked and occupied several islands in the Cyclades but were pushed back to Crete by the great Byzantine admiral Ooryphas. Later that year, the imperial fleet was destroyed off Thasos, again leaving the Aegean islands and the mainland coast open to pirate raids.

839: After further attacks on Euboea and Lesbos, the desperate emperor sent diplomatic missions to the Emir of Córdoba and King Louis the Pious, king of the Franks, begging for help against the Cretans. Although the missions improved diplomatic relations with these two Western kingdoms, they didn't result in any practical assistance.

841: In the first attack on the mainland of Asia Minor, the monastery on Mount Latros was destroyed, but the invaders were then beaten back by a local general. About this time, Abu Hafs died.

843: Much of Crete was reoccupied by General Theoktistos, and Byzantine control was briefly re-established. Following political intrigues in Constantinople, however, Theoktistos abandoned the army, which was then attacked by Arab forces and slaughtered.

Early 860s: Arab raids resumed on the Peloponnese, the Cyclades and as far as Mount Athos.

866: The raids resulted in an expeditionary force being assembled under the de facto emperor Vardas but, before they set out, Vardas was murdered by Basil the Macedonian, who was soon to seize the throne himself.

868 to 871: Cretan fleets rampaged around the Adriatic and Aegean. Brundisium (Brindisi) and Tarentum (Taranto) were captured, and Ragusa (Dubrovnik) was besieged. One of the fleets under Sa'id (son of Abu Hafs) and Photios, a Muslim convert, actually penetrated the Sea of Marmara. They unsuccessfully attacked an island only 122 km from Constantinople.

873 to 874: After further defeats, the Arabs agreed to a truce, and the Cretan emir was forced to pay tribute to Byzantium for about ten years.

884 to 904: The situation was reversed again when a Cretan fleet joined North African and Syrian fleets in new raids on the Peloponnese, Euboea and the Cyclades. Patmos and several smaller islands were occupied, and Naxos, Paros, Ios and others were forced to pay tribute. Athens itself may have been occupied from 896 to 902.

904: A Muslim convert, Leo of Tripoli, led a combined Syrian and Cretan fleet in a raid on Thessalonica. The city was sacked and 20,000 prisoners taken, many of whom were enslaved and sold or given to Crete.

911: A Byzantine fleet of over 100 ships carrying about 24,000 soldiers and 14,000 rowers launched an attack on Crete but, after several inconclusive battles, was forced to retreat within a few months. The whole armada was later destroyed by a Syrian fleet off the island of Chios.

949: Arab attacks had reached a climax in the 930s and 940s, and the emperor decided that concerted action was needed. Unfortunately, an expedition set up by Constantine VII was routed due to incompetent and inexperienced leadership.

960: Constantine's successor, Romanos II, launched a new expedition under an able general, Nikephoros Phokas. Unlike previous attempts, this was well planned and organised and better equipped, largely due to the support of Romanos' very capable minister Joseph Bringas. He and Phokas concluded that the key to success was overwhelming force, coupled with complete naval superiority in order to defeat the Arab fleet and maintain and protect lines of communication with Constantinople. The importance of the latter will be seen in due course.

Re-conquest

As always, the records of the invasion of 960 are inconclusive. Byzantine sources give the numbers as 2,000 large warships equipped with Greek Fire and holding 250 soldiers each, 1,000 fast warships (dromons) and 360 supply ships. Arab sources, on the other hand, estimate a total of 700 ships with 72,000 foot soldiers and 5,000 cavalry. Whatever its exact size, an enormous fleet and army landed at Almyros, just west of Iraklion, in June or July 960. The Arabs were caught by surprise: the innovative use of pontoon bridges and ramps allowed the troops to land directly from the warships, fully armed and mounted, much more quickly than if they had used small boats. An initial savage battle routed the Arab troops, who retreated into the fortress. After digging in outside Chandax, Phokas sent the incompetent general Pastilas out on a reconnaissance expedition, but his undisciplined troops went on a looting spree and got drunk. The raiding party was ambushed and most of the men were killed, including Pastilas. Some time later, a substantial number of Arabs attacked the Byzantine camp, but were decisively beaten. Phokas had all the attackers beheaded and impaled some of the heads on spears in sight of the defenders. The rest of the heads were put in leather sacks and fired over the walls from catapults. In spite of the demoralising effects of these tactics, the Arabs held firm.

Having surveyed the strength of the city's defences and realised that it was virtually impregnable, Phokas decided to institute a siege. He built a strong stockade all around the city, so that the defenders only had access to the sea, which was well protected by his navy. There is evidence that the emir was able to send out messengers to Egypt, Syria and North Africa seeking assistance, but it seems that no help ever reached the island.

Phokas then settled in for the winter, using the time to build siege engines, mainly catapults and towers with metal battering rams. He also carried out extensive troop training, and began work on digging tunnels under the walls. There were no further attempts by the defenders to break out, but the harsh winter conditions and shortage of provisions caused some discontent among the besieging army. Due to the efficiency of the communication links set up by Bringas, however, fresh supplies arrived quickly – in time to avert mutiny. In order to improve morale further, Phokas even asked his friend Athanasios of Mount Athos to come and address the troops. At the same time, his siege succeeded in creating famine and despair among the Arabs within the city.

Chandax was finally stormed on the night of 6th/7th March 961. The Byzantines completed the undermining of the walls, and when two defensive towers collapsed the army surged in. Even after the walls were breached, however, there was bitter fighting street by street, and even house by house, before the city was subdued.

In typical medieval fashion, the city was pillaged and the walls destroyed. Mosques were torn down or turned into churches, and all Islamic scriptures that could be found were burned. Muslim defenders were slaughtered, but Phokas restrained his men from killing those who were unarmed or who surrendered. Both Byzantine and Arab sources estimate the number killed as 200,000, with an equal number enslaved, but this is almost certainly an exaggeration. The slaughter was not without repercussions, and there were reprisals against Christian populations in some Arab countries, particularly Egypt. Since Chandax had been largely destroyed, Phokas had a massive fortress built at Temenos in an excellent defensive position about 16 km south of Iraklion. With the suppression of all resistance and the gradual conversion of the remaining Muslims to Christianity by missionaries like Nikon the Metanoeite, the island became once more a Byzantine province, many of the veterans from the invasion remaining to settle.

Phokas returned to Constantinople for the traditional triumph, although some sources claim that this was refused – possibly due to fear of his ambition – and that he merely received an ovation. As was normal in medieval warfare, the emir, Kouroupas, and his son were taken to Constantinople where they were treated with honour. In fact, the son converted to Christianity and later died in battle for the empire against the Rus. The treasure looted from Crete was vast, 300 ships being needed to transport it to Constantinople, and Phokas used a large part of it to found the Great Lavra, the first monastery on Mount Athos. The Byzantine historian Leo the Deacon, writing only thirty or forty years after the event, describes the booty vividly:

> A vast amount of gold and silver was to be seen, as well as barbarian coins of refined gold, garments shot with gold, purple carpets, and all sorts of treasures, crafted with the greatest skill, sparkling with gold and precious stones. There were also full sets of armour, helmets, swords, and breastplates, all gilded, and countless spears, shields, and back-bent bows (if someone happened by there, he would think that the entire wealth of the barbarian land had been collected at that time in the Hippodrome). The quantity was so great that it resembled an abundantly flowing river. After it came the enslaved barbarians, assembled in a numerous throng.[7]

In 963, on the death of Romanos, Phokas was crowned emperor and married his predecessor's widow.

Life in the Emirate of Crete

This period was something of a dark age for Crete, and there are not even many archaeological remains, as most physical evidence of the Arab presence was thoroughly destroyed by the victorious imperial army. The little written evidence that exists comes almost entirely from Byzantine sources that are incomplete and probably somewhat biased. For the period of Arab rule, Crete was regarded as little more than a pirates' nest, surviving on piracy and the slave trade, and contemporary writers refer to "Godless Cretans" and the "God-forsaken island".[8] However, in recent years the Emirate of Crete has been the subject of detailed research, much of it by Islamic scholars. A more balanced view of the period is beginning to emerge which, although sketchy, points to an orderly state with a strong economy based as much on trade as on piracy. The evidence that Chandax may have been an important cultural and intellectual centre is even sparser, but other Arab emirates of the time, including Córdoba, experienced a distinct flourishing of culture, and there is every reason to believe that Crete may have been similar. The jury is still out on this question, and a final verdict will probably never be reached.

The relationship between Crete and Byzantium is also far from clear cut. As previously noted, the Cretan fleet played an important role in controlling the Mediterranean, and Cretan fighters were widely admired in the Muslim world, being described by the polymath Ibn Hazm as "the staunchest and most capable people at vanquishing their enemies".[9] On the other hand, it seems that they were not in a permanent state of enmity, and diplomatic contact was not unknown. A friendly letter written in about 913 to the emir from the Patriarch of Constantinople, Nicholas Mystikos, asks for the release of the Greek prisoners captured in the 904 raid on Thessalonica. In it, he refers to the good relations that had existed between his predecessor, Saint Photios I, and the previous emir:

> The Patriarch knew well that although the barriers of religion stood between us, yet a strong intelligence, wit and character, a love of humanity, and all other qualities which adorn and dignify man's nature, arouse in the breast of good men an affection for those who love fair things. And therefore, he loved your father, who was endowed with the qualities I speak of, even though the differences of religious faith stood between them.[10]

As far as the economy was concerned, the emirate minted its own coins – gold and silver as well as copper – and these appear to have been of constant weight and composition. This means that the currency was reliable, which is the sign of a sound economy and high living standards. Evidence for the strength of the economy can be found in the few scattered Arabic sources, which point to extensive trade, not only with the Muslim world (especially Egypt) but with the Vikings and even with some of the Byzantine islands. This view has been supported by the discovery of Cretan Emirate coins not only in Egypt and Spain but in France, Greece and Scandinavia. A booming agricultural sector produced timber, wine, cheese, milk, honey, pomegranates, nuts, precious metals and medicinal herbs. Olive oil was imported from Córdoba and weapons from Egypt. The wealth of the ruling elite was apparent in their lifestyle, described in the Byzantine chronicles as luxurious, with large houses surrounded by gardens, orchards and fountains.

Moreover, various references in Islamic texts support the view that the emirate was by no means a cultural wasteland.[11] Many of the invaders were scholars and experts in Islamic law (jurists), exiled from Andalusia, and the island continued to attract educated immigrants from the Islamic world. A thirteenth-century geographer described Iqritish (Crete) as "a large island with many cities where numerous scholars gather".[12] Further indications can be found in the fact that al-Iqritishi ("of Crete") as part of a name was applied to several Muslim scholars during the period of Arab rule. Among these scholars were the authors of treatises on the Qur'an, Islamic law, religion, philosophy and an important analysis of Islamic maritime law. A contemporary biographical dictionary from al-Andalus describes the lives of scholars in Crete as "luxurious but difficult". It describes an Arab historian as owning a five-storey house, twenty enslaved girls and a large library of historical and religious books.[13]

As for the indigenous Cretans, again there are contradictory theories. There is no mention of enforced conversion, and such a policy at that time would not have made financial sense for the Arab rulers, as they were able to screw extra taxes out of Christian "infidels". The evidence from other countries where a Christian minority lived in a Muslim country points to general tolerance under certain restrictions. For example, in Palestine, Christians could repair or rebuild existing churches, but were not allowed to build new ones; they were prohibited from holding loud services or ringing bells to summon the faithful to worship; finally, they were not allowed to ride horses with saddles or wear the same clothes as Muslims. The public display of crosses was also prohibited.[14]

On the other hand, it is possible that some inhabitants converted to Islam to avoid paying the extra taxes. For whatever reasons, within a relatively short time, Muslims seemed to form a majority of the population in the cities, although there is some evidence that the countryside remained predominantly Christian. Indeed, some sources claim that, over time, there was substantial interaction between the Andalusian conquerors, the local Greek Cretans and the Arab Muslim settlers who came to the island later. This does not seem unlikely in view of the peaceful coexistence between Muslims and Christians in other emirates at that time – Córdoba, for example. It is also quite possible that some areas such as Sfakia were never subdued at all, and modern scholars are coming to the conclusion that Arab rule may in fact have been limited to the area around Chandax and some other towns of northern Crete, while the countryside was largely left to itself. This is given support by the fact that the Andalusian Arabs were mainly townspeople, scholars, merchants and sailors, who had little experience of or interest in farming. It would have been logical for the rulers to leave agriculture to the indigenous Cretans. Intriguingly, Theodosius the Deacon describes a Christian chieftain leading his people, the "inhabitants of crags and caves", down from the mountains to join the siege of Chandax.[15] However, since this is in an epic poem largely designed to glorify Emperor Romanos, it may be dubious.

Lasting cultural influence on Crete from the period of Arab rule was limited to a few words of Arabic origin and a handful of place names. The words mostly related to things popular with the Arabs like zagari (hound), psari (steed) and nerantzi (bitter orange, possibly the Seville variety). The most important surviving place name is Chania (in Arabic, Al Hanim, meaning "The Inn"). Others include Aposelemis (deriving from Abu Selim), the village of Sarakenos and a few other villages near Iraklion and Rethymnon. An intriguing linguistic oddity also originates from this period. In eastern Crete there is a dialect word, pastelas, which means "lazy and indolent". The historian Theocharis Detorakis proposes that it derives from the name of the incompetent general Pastilas at the siege of Chandax. If this is the case, the unfortunate general's failure brought him a sort of immortality.

9

The Second Byzantine Period

961 to 1204

Recovery and Reorganisation

After the reconquest of Crete and the harsh reprisals taken against its Arab defenders, the first priority was to build up the defences and administration of the island. As we have noted, Phokas himself had the fortress at Temenos built before he left, with the intention of making it the capital of Crete to replace the largely destroyed Chandax. Although this plan was abandoned, the fortress became one of a chain of defensive fortifications all around the coast. It remains an extremely impressive sight, even in its ruined state. In the end, instead of moving the capital, the defences of Chandax were rebuilt and a major naval base was established at the port. The remains of a Byzantine wall have been discovered in Iraklion, underneath the later Venetian defences.

Given that nobody on the island could remember anything other than Arab rule, the new government also needed to take steps to re-establish loyalty to the empire among the population. Phokas himself established settlements of war veterans from the imperial forces in fertile agricultural areas, which was common practice in medieval times but, in this case, had the added advantage of providing a core population with strong ties to the empire. While the efforts of missionaries like Saint Nikon and Saint Ioannis Xenos (see later in the chapter) helped to renew the Orthodox Church, the establishment of a standing garrison of 1,000 troops helped to increase morale and reduce the chances of further incursions.

Crete was re-established as a theme, with the combined office of governor and military commander based in Chandax, which now became the capital of the island, leaving Gortyn to fall into decline and obscurity. Further reforms towards the end of the eleventh century upgraded the post of governor to that of doukas (duke). The fact that the dukes often came from important aristocratic families in Constantinople, and even from the imperial family, indicates the increasing importance of the island. This makes it somewhat odd that, along with several other Aegean islands, Crete's defences again seem to have been neglected and, by the 1080s, the naval base at Chandax was severely undermanned. In 1092, the Duke of Crete, Karykes, led a revolt against the emperor, Alexios I. The cause of the revolt is not known, but it is possible that it started as a mutiny in protest at the undermining of the naval garrison. Alternatively, it could have been an attempt at secession, related to a similar revolt in Cyprus. Whatever its causes, the revolt was quickly crushed when an imperial fleet was dispatched to Crete. Even before it landed, the news of its approach panicked Karykes' supporters, who staged a coup and murdered the duke. In spite of its easy suppression, the revolt did serve as a wake-up call to the imperial authorities, and efforts were made to improve the naval base and establish stronger ties with Constantinople.

According to tradition, Alexios I attempted to consolidate imperial authority on the island by sending twelve **archontopoula** to Crete, under a **chrysovoulo**, a binding document sealed in gold by the emperor. Although there is no question about the immigration of aristocratic and royal family members to Crete at that time, doubt has been cast on the authenticity of the actual document. The only manuscript existing is a copy probably written in Venetian times, which could well be a forgery created to give historical validity to the Cretan aristocratic families in their resistance to Venetian rule. What is certain is that, between 1081 and 1185, many grants of land and posts were made to the **archons**, who developed into a powerful landowning class. Descendants of the twelve people named in the document were to play an important role in Cretan history for several hundred years, and many villages and streets are named after them. As the *Explore Crete* website delightfully puts it:

So, if during your travels around Crete you come across someone that claims to be a descendant from nobility, don't dismiss the claim, there may be some truth and a long and interesting story behind it.[1]

Generally, this remained a period of peace and stability on the island, with a strong economy and a flourishing trade in agricultural products and livestock. As far as we know, artistic achievement during this period was pretty well limited to the architecture, manuscripts and frescoes of the Church. Unfortunately, there are not many examples remaining, but those that can be found point to considerable talent in all three disciplines. About nine manuscripts have been identified as being of Cretan origin, all of them of a high quality of workmanship, including an illustrated copy of the Gospels. Although generally in a poor state of preservation, there are a few frescoes from the eleventh century, the earliest probably being in the katholikon (main church) of Ioannis Xenos' monastery at Myriokephala. Generally, the Cretan frescoes of this period are painted in a style very similar to that of Constantinople, perhaps indicating immigration of artists and builders from the imperial capital. In the early twelfth century, trade with Venice increased and, significantly, Venetian merchants began to take an interest in the island.

The Church

Although we do not know the extent of conversions to Islam during the Cretan Emirate, it is certain that the Arab occupation considerably weakened the Orthodox Church and left it leaderless and in a state of decline. In the late tenth century, a somewhat biased Byzantine historian, Leo the Deacon, described the situation forcefully:

> The Cretans are said to be addicted to divination, ribaldry and wrongful beliefs, which they learned of old from the Manichaeans and from Muhammad.[2]

Just as the primary political aim at this time was the strengthening of ties between the island and Constantinople, so it was essential to re-establish close links between the Cretan Church and the Patriarchate.

At the administrative level, the archdiocese of Crete was reinstated, but with its seat now in Chandax. The organisation of the island remained similar to that before the Arab conquest, but with some new dioceses and changes to jurisdiction to match demographic changes. A new cathedral dedicated to Saint Titus was built in Chandax, on the same site as the present-day church in Iraklion.

The restoration of morale and good practice among the faithful was a more difficult task, but there seems to have been no great effort to send missionaries from Constantinople. It is largely down to two private initiatives that the Church eventually returned to its flourishing condition of before the invasion. According to tradition, Saint Nikon Metanoeite (the latter part of his name literally meaning "Repent!") visited Crete in 962 and stayed seven years, visiting all parts of the island, founding many new churches and trying to bring back to the fold the many Christians whose faith and practice had been corrupted "by time and long fellowship with the Saracens".[3] He met quite a lot of opposition from the Cretans, who felt he was interfering in their concerns. He therefore wisely changed his tactics from passionate calls for repentance to discussion, gentle persuasion and setting his own example. In *The Life of Saint Nikon*, written not long after his death, the success of his method is described:

> Their passion quickly abated and their furious anger came to a standstill ... [He] if not through the peace of his word, but through that of virtue, was a wise fisherman and skilled in hunting souls of men.[4]

Although Saint Nikon had a well-deserved reputation for church building on mainland Greece, no churches built by him have been identified in Crete, and there are no other references to the saint's visit to the island in contemporary literature. This has led some scholars to doubt the accuracy of the story. It has been argued that *The Life of Saint Nikon* is **hagiography** rather than history, embellishments being quite common in the genre of written "lives" of saints. After the reconquest by Phokas, Crete was very much a hot topic, and the brief mention of Nikon's visit to the island may have been added to enhance the saint's importance.

There is more certainty surrounding the indefatigable and charismatic Saint Ioannis Xenos (the latter part of his name meaning
"stranger"). He is known to have been born in Messara, probably in
970. Although his natural leaning was towards solitude and the life
of a hermit, he felt inspired to participate in the revival of the Orthodox Church on the island. Besides being an intensely spiritual man,
Ioannis was extremely practical and, as well as preaching widely –
mainly in western Crete – he founded and organised many monastic
communities. His first monastery was at Myriokephala, south-west
of Rethymnon, which became the father house of eight more in
the area. With the support, either tacit or active, of the local imperial and church authorities, and helped by loyal supporters he called
philochristoi (friends of Christ), he set up support mechanisms to
ensure the survival of the monks. He seems to have been a man of
wide-ranging interests and talents: among his more practical activities
were the acquisition of land and draught animals, the construction of
water cisterns in dry areas, the planting of trees, vines and gardens, the
construction of living quarters for the monks and the setting up of
beehives. He was popular among the local people and this made it easy
for him to inspire them to provide household goods for the monks:

> The way he behaved towards local people, the way he respected
> them and the way he organised everything with clarity, integrity
> and honesty made people trust him and follow him.[5]

In order to strengthen the position of his various foundations, he
visited Constantinople in about 1025, where he obtained a chrysovoulo (a binding document sealed in gold) from the emperor, guaranteeing an annual income for Myriokephala. From the patriarch he
obtained a foundation charter granting exemption of the monastery
from ecclesiastical taxes, and independence from any lay or ecclesiastical officials. All this was a pretty substantial achievement, but the ever-
practical Ioannis also returned to Crete with gifts of monks' habits,
sacred books and vessels, and icons for distribution among the monasteries. He continued to travel and set up monasteries and churches,
until he finally seemed to have found the solitude he craved on the
west coast of the island, near Kissamos. There is some evidence that he

built with his own hands the little chapel where he found sanctuary. There he wrote his autobiography, the main source of our information. Nothing else is known but, according to tradition, he died at the monastery of Gouveneto on the Akrotiri peninsula, another institution that he founded.

It is worth noting that, since the eighth century, the Church of Crete had been under the jurisdiction of the Patriarch of Constantinople. This meant that, when the Great Schism between Rome and the four other Patriarchates occurred in 1054, Crete was securely within the Eastern Church, where it has remained ever since.

Machiavellian Machinations

Although, as we shall see, the Venetians became the legal rulers of Crete in 1204, it wasn't for another ten or so years that they could be said to be rulers in fact. European history from the late eleventh century to the early thirteenth provides a master class in intrigue, power politics and economic ambition, and it is worth looking briefly at this background.

The fate of Crete was tied up with the infamous Fourth Crusade (for which Pope John Paul II apologised to the Ecumenical Orthodox patriarch 800 years later). Without going into too much detail, it is useful to understand the broad outline of the story.[6] There had been an edgy but profitable relationship between Venice and the Byzantine Empire since the eleventh century.[7] By a treaty of 1082, Venice was given tax-exempt trade concessions with many Greek cities and islands in exchange for naval help against the Normans and their raids on the eastern Mediterranean. By this stage, Byzantium had, once again, no navy to speak of, and the Venetian fleet became the de facto imperial navy. In reality, the Venetians, while reaping enormous rewards from the trade concessions, did very little to help the empire. Indeed, their ships were still prone to raiding Byzantine merchant ships in the Aegean. As the power of Venice grew, it acted more and more independently of Byzantium, ending with open hostility in 1171, followed by a fragile truce in 1186.

When Pope Innocent III called for a crusade to capture Egypt from the Muslims, it was Venice that supplied the transport for the large army of crusaders. In return, Venice was to receive 85,000 silver marks (just under £1 million at today's silver prices) and half of the territory captured, although no specific places were mentioned. The crusaders could only pay a part of the cost, impoverishing themselves in the process, but nevertheless the fleet set sail in 1202. There is no clear evidence as to who was responsible, but at some stage the fleet diverted away from Egypt and towards Constantinople, which the crusaders attacked, captured and looted. The Byzantine Empire was now in the hands of the Frankish crusaders, and the leaders lost no time in carving it up between them. Crete was allocated to the commander, Boniface of Montferrat, but, with no naval experience and insufficient forces to control the large island, he negotiated with the Venetians to sell it to them. The far-seeing and ambitious Doge of Venice, Enrico Dandolo, jumped at the chance and bought the island for 5,000 gold ducats (just under £500,000 at today's gold prices) and a promise to support Boniface's claim on the Kingdom of Thessalonica.[8]

This treaty of 1204 meant that Venice now ruled Crete, but, since the Venetians were busy consolidating control of their other new possessions in the Peloponnese and the Aegean, they were only able to establish a small force on the Island of Spinalonga (near Elounda) to stake their claim. Unfortunately, this was not sufficient to prevent an attack by the Genoese pirate Enrico Piscatore, Count of Malta. He quickly took control of most of eastern and central Crete, meeting little resistance from the locals. He restored the fortifications in Chandax, Siteia and Rethymnon and built fourteen other fortresses around the coast, including the strong castle at Palaiokastro (9 km north-west of Chandax). The Venetians responded by sending a fleet to recapture the island in 1206, but this attempt failed. Another attempt, in 1208, met with more success and managed to establish a foothold in Crete. There followed a protracted war, which lasted four years. Eventually, in 1212, Giacomo Tiepolo defeated the Genoese, although some enclaves, including the fortress at Palaiokastro, managed to hold out for another four years. Tiepolo became the first Venetian Duke of Crete, with his capital at Chandax, now called by its Italian name, Candia (modern Iraklion).

With the final establishment of Venetian rule in Crete, Venice now controlled access to Syria, Egypt and routes through the Aegean to Constantinople and the Black Sea. It also had in its possession an extremely fertile and wealthy, but rebellious, island.

10

Venetian Rule

1204 to 1645

Administration

Once Venetian rule was firmly established, the first task of the new government was to establish a strong and permanent Venetian presence on the island, both civilian and military. From 1212, settlers from Venice were granted large estates or **fiefs** in the most fertile areas. In return for their land they were liable for military service and were obliged to provide troops and galley oarsmen from among their villagers and serfs. Estimates vary, but over the next century between 5,000 and 10,000 colonists immigrated to Crete. As we shall see, this influx significantly affected the demographics, economy and culture of the island, as well as creating a permanent source of aggravation among the Cretans. For the most part, the Venetians settled in existing towns, but the group that arrived in 1252 built the new city of Chania on the site of the deserted Kydonia, destroying in the process many Minoan and Dorian archaeological sites.

The island was a single administrative district ruled by a duke, who was elected from among the nobility of Venice for a period of two years. The Dukedom (sometimes oddly called the Kingdom) of Candia[1] also included the islands of Tinos and Cythera. Initially, the island was divided into six provinces known as sextaria, named after the six districts of the city of Venice, with the city of Candia itself being ruled directly by the city of Venice. In the fourteenth century, Crete was reorganised into four regions known as territoria, roughly coinciding with the modern prefectures. From east to west, these were: Siteia,

including Ierapetra; Candia, which included the districts of Mirabello and the Lassithi plateau; Rethymnon; and Chania. Interestingly,
the area of Sfakia was never entirely subjugated and the government
seemed content to leave it under the loose oversight of a supervisor
who was responsible, at different times, directly to Candia or Chania.
For 300 years, there was strict discrimination between the Venetian
and Cretan nobility, and nearly all administrators were appointed by
Venice. These ranged from the **rectores** (governors of the main towns)
down to magistrates and police, with treasury officials forming the
elite of the bureaucracy.

The highest military rank on the island was that of the capitano
generale de mar (naval commander), while other military affairs were
under the command of the capitano generale di Candia. In the event
of a major military crisis, a **proveditore generale** (governor-general)
was sent from Venice, with absolute power in military affairs, including defence, fortifications, mobilisation of forces and conduct of campaigns. In effect, this meant virtual control over every aspect of island
life, and the appointment of a proveditore generale was not always
welcomed by the duke. As the threat from Turkey became increasingly serious after 1569, the post was permanently established. As with
the dukes, the proveditore was elected by the nobility of Venice for a
two-year period. In spite of the wide-ranging powers they held, and
occasional abuses, the proveditori were for the most part enlightened
managers, several of whom later became **doges**.

Much of the administration was carried out in the Loggia (Lodge).
Each of the main cities was required to have one of these buildings
where the nobility could meet to discuss the affairs of the city or the
island as a whole. The Loggia was more than just an administrative
centre, however. It was also a centre of social life for the nobility, like
a gentlemen's club. It was from its balconies that heralds proclaimed
decrees of state, and dukes or other rulers watched secular or religious
parades.

As for the Cretans, the local Greek leaders were allowed to keep
their own laws and property, but they were discriminated against in
many other ways. The influx of Venetian immigrants meant that the
local Cretan archons (leaders) were bound to lose much of their best
land. Moreover, the Latin Venetian elite monopolised the higher

administrative and military posts, and received most of the income from trade. The only government professions open to Greeks were those of notaries and lawyers although, after 1500, Greeks did begin to fill more important posts. Until the end of the thirteenth century, even marriages between Greeks and Venetians were prohibited. On top of all that, as we shall see, the Roman Catholic Venetians set out to undermine the Cretan Orthodox Church in a variety of ways. Trouble loomed from the start.

The administration of justice at the basic level was, as in most societies of the time, in the hands of the local lords acting as magistrates in the rural areas. In the towns, the rectores dealt with minor criminal and civil cases, while more serious cases or appeals were heard by the duke in Candia. The lords, of course, took every opportunity to maintain their privileges, but it seems that the ducal court was fairly even handed, sometimes supporting the villagers' property rights, sometimes those of their masters. For this reason, the magistrates often went to great lengths to avoid an appeal. There are examples of them dividing a single property case into several smaller elements so that each case remained within their own jurisdiction, with no provision for appeal. The final court of appeal was the Venetian senate, but appeals to Venice were extremely costly and time consuming; a few are known to have taken twenty to thirty years to reach a conclusion.

A feature of the system in Venice and its colonies was the granting of grazie (state favours), either for payment or services rendered. Such favours included pensions, grants of land and government posts, and were offered not only to the elite but to soldiers and any other persons who had performed a service to the state. The system was not corrupt in itself, but when such grazie were allowed to be inherited, it became inefficient and open to corruption. The use of grazie was more widespread in Crete than in any other Venetian territory, and the problems created were particularly serious. There were frequent protests to Venice, and the Venetian government responded in a fairly typical way. On the one hand, they warned the Cretan government that offices should only be granted to eligible citizens on merit, and forbade the granting of grazie. At the same time, Venice itself continued to grant its own offices in Crete by grazie! There were several attempts to reform the system, but the practice continued.

Aside from the systematic use of grazie, corruption was probably no worse than in most contemporary societies. Judicial excesses or corruption could be prosecuted in Venice but, to avoid prolonged and costly investigations, most cases were put down to incompetence rather than criminality, and the decision simply overturned. From time to time, more serious cases were prosecuted, one of which stands out as particularly blatant and is worth recording in detail. In 1402, the former rectore of Chania was charged with eleven separate offences of abuse of power and corruption, remarkable in their variety:

> He had commandeered property around a fortress, endangering the defences and damaging the land.
>
> As judge, he had "illegally and dishonestly extorted" a percentage of the dowries being returned to widows of plague victims.
>
> His wife had bought many of these widows' long leases on arable land "with little money and many promises."
>
> He had taken hides from tanners and gold and silver objects from local merchants. (It is not clear whether this was theft or bribery.)
>
> He ordered the city's inhabitants to work on his palace.
>
> He had accepted a gift of meat from a local butcher, itself illegal, and then compounded the offence by reselling it.[2]

Found guilty, he was fined 600 lire di piccolo (about £22,000 at today's gold prices) and banned from Crete for life.[3]

Rebellion

It is unlikely that the Venetians foresaw just what a hornets' nest of trouble they had taken on with the purchase of Crete. The price of that purchase certainly paled into insignificance when compared with the massive investment in money and manpower needed to control the island over the next couple of hundred years. Between 1211 and 1367 alone, there were ten major revolts. The details of many of these rebellions were complex and often repetitive, so I shall stick to the broad outline of the history, with details only of the more important.[4]

Most of the major revolts were initiated by one or more of the leading Greek families for a wide variety of reasons. Many resulted from the oppressive nature of Venetian rule and the punitive taxation. Often, the spark was a seizure of family land and Church property by Venetian settlers, or a particularly cruel act by one of the governors. Underlying them all were the cultural differences between the Latin-speaking Roman Catholic Venetians and the Greek-speaking Ortho-dox Cretans, together with a desire for independence from Venetian rule. In a few cases, the aim seems to have been to restore union with the Byzantine Empire, but it has been convincingly argued that this was more for pragmatic than ideological reasons. Being further away and weaker than Venice, Byzantium would be less likely to interfere in Cretan life.

The course of the rebellions varied. Often the Cretans met with initial successes, but were finally defeated by superior forces sent from Venice, or disagreements between the leaders or even, in some cases, actual treachery. On many occasions, especially when the revolt was more to do with property or minor grievances, the Venetian rulers were magnanimous in victory, often granting extra feudal lands, fiefs, and privileges to the leaders of the rebellion. At other times, when the very existence of Venetian rule was threatened, the revolt was followed by savage reprisals, the burning of villages, torture, exile or death for the leaders and their families, and, in a few cases, the complete clear-ance and closure of whole areas.

In 1261, Constantinople was restored to the Byzantine Empire, and a revolt in 1262, incited by Emperor Michael VII Palaiologos, took on a more obviously nationalistic nature. The war lasted for four years, but the emperor's diplomatic support was not backed up by practi-cal military help, and the revolt eventually collapsed. One significant result of the failed rebellion was that the treaty signed in 1265 finally gave the empire's formal recognition of Venetian rule of Crete. This did not, of course, stop future revolts looking towards expulsion of the Venetians and reunion with Byzantium.

The revolt of Alexios Kallergis in 1282 is worth examining in a little more detail, since it was arguably the most important rebellion of the Cretan aristocracy and had significant repercussions for the future. Kallergis, a descendant of Emperor Nikephoros Phokas, had, in two previous uprisings, played the two sides against each other, supporting sometimes the Venetians, sometimes the rebels. For this reason, he had received many grants of land and honours from Venice so that he had become one of the wealthiest and most powerful of the archons, respected by Venetians and Cretans alike. When the Venetians failed to honour many of the agreements made after previous revolts and, indeed, tried to limit and reduce Kallergis' growing power, he took up arms himself. He was joined by many other families, and it wasn't long before the whole of Crete was in flames. In spite of draconian measures by the Venetians, the war dragged on for seventeen years, with neither side getting the upper hand. In 1296, the situation for the Venetians deteriorated. During one of Venice's frequent wars with Genoa, a Genoese admiral, taking advantage of the turmoil, captured and sacked Chania with a view to controlling the whole of western Crete. He offered to recognise Kallergis as hereditary governor of Crete in return for his support. Kallergis refused and, in an extraordinary development, moved towards reconciliation with Venice. War weariness on both sides, together with the usual disagreements between the Cretan leaders, led to a peace treaty in 1299. This had several important implications for future relations between the Venetians and the Cretans.

The treaty, signed by the duke and ratified by the Republic of Venice, was extensive and detailed. The main immediate beneficiary was Alexios Kallergis himself, who was restored to his pre-revolt status, granted four additional fiefdoms and, most significantly, given the right to grant fiefs, feudal privileges and honours to other Cretan nobles. He was also given control of the Orthodox monasteries to the west of Iraklion and rents from all Latin monasteries in the same area. Of wider importance were a general amnesty and restoration of all property seized by the Venetians during the war, tax exemptions for the rebels and the freeing of 100 serfs who had supported the revolt. The most significant features for the future of Venetian–Cretan relations were the granting of permission for marriage between Cretans and Venetians and the installation of an Orthodox bishop. The importance of these concessions will be examined later.

With the signing of the treaty, Kallergis became the de facto leader of the Cretan Orthodox population and a man of immense power, the undisputed "Cretarch". He seems to have remained true to the oath of allegiance sworn as part of the treaty and, as far as we know, most of his family continued to be loyal to Venice. His family name was even recorded in the Libro d'Oro (Golden Book) of the Venetian nobility, a unique privilege. Not surprisingly, he was somewhat less popular with some of the other Cretan families, who regarded him as a traitor. Although an attempt on his life failed, his son and many followers were murdered.

In spite of the treaty, abuses of power by the Venetians continued, and further insurrections occurred: two in 1319 and one each in 1333 and 1341. The first two were brought to an end relatively quickly, largely through the intervention of the Kallergis family. Interestingly, the 1333 revolt was led by Vardis Kallergis, while the 1341 rebellion was led by Leo Kallergis. We do not know what relation they were to Alexios, but we do know that his sons and grandson fought on the side of the Venetians. Both revolts failed and were brutally suppressed.

The Saint Titus Revolt

Among all the rebellions against Venice, the revolt of 1363 to 1364 was unique in that it was led by the Venetian nobles of Crete themselves. By this time, there had already been a degree of cultural assimilation among the Venetians, who were increasingly using Greek as their first language. Intermarriage became more common after the Kallergis Treaty, and the Venetian colonists were beginning to identify more with Crete than Venice. There were already rumbles of discontent among them due to the fact that their ever-increasing tax burden was only slightly less oppressive than that imposed on the Cretans. Moreover, they often felt humiliated by the aristocracy of Venice, who regarded them as second-class nobility. In 1363, when yet another new tax was imposed in order to repair and improve the harbour at Chania, vague ideas of secession coalesced into open revolt. Seventy of the Venetian feudal lords sent representatives to the duke, appealing against the new tax, but he refused to back down, threatening any who resisted with death and confiscation of property.

The next day, a crowd of lords accompanied by townspeople, servants and soldiers stormed the duke's palace and arrested him with his advisors. The initial assault was led by two of the noble families,

Gradenigo and Venier. Titus Venier declared Crete the autonomous and independent Republic of Saint Titus under the protection of the patron saint of the island. The Venetian flag of Saint Mark was torn down, the flag of Saint Titus was raised and a new governor, Marco Gradenigo, was elected from among the rebels. An almost contemporary account describes the raising of the flag and a possible ill omen for the revolt:

> In the palace, the rebels discussed whether they should raise the customary flag of San Marco, or that of San Tito. A crowd ran into the piazza crying, "Long live San Tito!" And so it was decreed that the figure of San Tito be borne on a standard, on land and sea, and be raised in public everywhere. On the same day, with an excited crowd gathered, the flag of San Tito was raised above the bell-tower, but the figure of the Saint was turned upside down, with the head below the feet. Many of those who were faithful were frightened.[5]

Within a week, the cities of Siteia, Rethymnon and Chania joined the uprising, and the Venetian rebels moved quickly to recruit the great Cretan families to their side, the first time this had happened anywhere in the Venetian colonies. They promised equal status and legal rights between the Orthodox and Catholic Churches and, true to their word, their very first proclamations revoked all previous edicts restricting the ordination of Orthodox priests and allowed freedom to those who wished to be ordained to go overseas and return freely without penalty. Many of the Venetians also converted to Orthodoxy to identify more closely with the Cretans, while many of the Cretan families joined the rebellion, including descendants of Alexios Kallergis, John, George and Alexios. There were even plans to hold Greek Orthodox services in Saint Titos Cathedral, instead of Roman Catholic ones.

Venice was in a state of shock at the speed and unexpectedness of this uprising, led by its own colonists. At first, the government tried diplomatic means to end the rebellion by sending a delegation of five envoys to the island, but they were met with defiance and had no success in restoring peace. Finally, a large army, composed mainly of Italian mercenaries, was dispatched from Venice in thirty-three galleys and twelve transport ships. Diplomatic support was received from the pope, the kings of Cyprus and Hungary, the queen of Sicily and Jerusalem, the head of the Knights Hospitaller in Rhodes, and even from Venice's old enemy, Genoa. All of them promised not to intervene.

At this point, the revolt began to falter as quarrels sprang up between the rebel groups, some of whom were beginning to doubt the wisdom of their action. The Venetian Leonardo Gradenigo, who had become an Orthodox monk, joined forces with a Greek monk, Milletos, to kill all Roman Catholics who did not support the rebellion. They incited other priests, noblemen, townspeople and peasants to go on a murderous rampage against Roman Catholics living outside Candia. They were so successful in their activities that the Venetian rebels themselves became alarmed. Apart from anything else, they feared that the rebellion would turn into a peasants' revolt, which they certainly didn't want. Gradenigo eventually allied himself with the rebel leaders, attacked and captured Milletos and returned him to Candia, where he was killed. Further rifts developed between the leaders. One faction wanted to send for help from Genoa, while another proposed surrender to Venice. The hawks, led by Gradenigo, had the leader of the other group murdered and his supporters imprisoned but, in the event, Genoa remained true to its agreement with Venice and refused to intervene.

The Venetian army landed 11 km west of Candia and immediately routed a large rebel army. Meanwhile, the fleet took control of the port of Candia, and the city itself quickly surrendered. Ten of the leaders were beheaded, and the revolt collapsed. The other three main cities – Chania, Rethymnon and Siteia – were quickly subdued without a fight. The three Kallergis family members, several members of the Gradenigo and Venier families and many other Venetian rebels escaped but were all declared outlaws, with prices on their heads. The government came down particularly hard on the Gradenigo and Venier families, which were split up and the women and children exiled from all Venetian territory in the Mediterranean. The Venetian lords who escaped execution or exile were stripped of all their original fiefdoms and privileges, and were forced to swear a solemn oath of allegiance and eternal loyalty to the Republic of Venice.

However, the story did not quite end there. Even as the purge of rebel leaders was continuing, the outlawed Venetian lords and the Kallergis family were planning another revolt. This time, it was the Byzantine flag that was raised, and the aim was reunion with the empire. The emperor gave his tacit support and persuaded Anthimos, the bishop of Athens, to move to Crete to become head of the Church of Crete and give ecclesiastical support to the rebellion. The revolt began in the Kallergis stronghold of western Crete, and met with initial success. Within a few months, the whole of western Crete was in the hands of the rebels, apart from the provincial capitals, Chania and Rethymnon, and the coastal fortresses. This set the tone for the rebellion: no pitched battles or attempts to attack the cities, but continuous harassment and guerrilla warfare. Rebel groups sprang up in other parts of Crete, and the Lassithi plateau again became the centre of resistance in the east. Support for the rebels also grew in Ierapetra, Mirabello and the area around Potami.

Venice responded quickly and sent an invasion force led by five proveditori. With great cunning, the doge persuaded the pope to declare the war on Crete to be a crusade, which meant that all soldiers who took part would receive forgiveness of their sins. Ironically, the Venetian army also included many Turkish mercenaries. With almost unlimited resources and control of the seas and harbours, the Venetians were able to virtually surround the rebel areas. Shortage of supplies and a disastrous crop failure in 1365 led to starvation and loss of morale among the rebels. One by one, the rebel leaders were hunted down and executed, and there were inevitable disagreements and splits within the leadership. Eventually, the eastern provinces declared loyalty to Venice. In Sfakia, the Kallergis brothers held out for nearly another year but, early in 1367, the insurrection was finally quelled and the Kallergis family arrested. All the rebels, except for Titus Venier who fled Crete, were tortured to death or executed, and Bishop Anthimos died in prison. The three main mountain refuges of the rebels, Lassithi, Eleutherna and Sfakia, were evacuated, and no human inhabitance or grazing of livestock were allowed for nearly 100 years.

This saw the end of major organised resistance to Venetian rule. Two conspiracies, in 1453 and 1460, came to nothing, but did result in a hardening of Venetian policy against the Orthodox Church. In 1527, an insurrection in the west of Crete was quickly and ruthlessly put down. With the fall of Constantinople to the Ottoman Turks in 1453, the Cretan nobles had generally accepted the fact that there was now no hope of help from outside. More importantly, as Turkish power in the region increased, it became clear that if the Cretans actually succeeded in expelling the Venetians, they could easily fall prey to a Turkish invasion. It must have seemed that Venetian rule was the lesser of the two evils.

Piracy

Not only did the Venetian authorities have to deal with rebellions, they also had to protect the island against continual raids by pirates. Once again, the Mediterranean was awash with pirates, mainly from the notorious Barbary Coast stretching from Morocco to Libya. However, as Detorakis wrily puts it, many Maltese, Genoese, Pisans, Catalans, Spanish, French and Greeks also "tried their hand at the art".[6] The major difference was that, while the Christian pirates tended to roam the seas singly or in small groups, attacking vulnerable ships, the Barbary pirates often set out in large fleets to attack on land and even capture whole islands. Some of them became powerful rulers in their own right, and in later years were allied with the Ottomans, practically forming part of the navy. Raids on Crete itself became a regular occurrence from as early as 1317, when, for a short time, Algerian pirates occupied Chrysi Island south of Ierapetra and used it as a base for raids along the south coast. The Venetians responded by stepping up compulsory guard duty among the population and, in 1333, used a special emergency tax to equip two galleys to patrol coastal waters. This may have helped a little, but the intermittent pirate raids continued.

By the middle of the fifteenth century, the problem became much worse as the power of the Barbary Coast pirates grew, and the attacks increased in frequency. In 1522, there was a successful raid on Ierapetra, in which many prisoners were taken and sold into slavery. Five years later, the pirates felt confident enough to seize two ships right in the middle of the harbour at Chania. As relations between Venice and Turkey deteriorated and the pirate fleets began to work with the Ottomans, the attacks became more savage. In 1537, the famous pirate

Hayreddin Barbarossa Pasha, by now an admiral in the Ottoman fleet, took eighty ships on a raiding mission, capturing many of the Aegean and Ionian islands for the Ottoman Empire. He then turned his attention to Crete and, having failed to take Chania, Rethymnon or Candia, plundered the less-protected Siteia and its surrounding villages, taking thousands into slavery. Another Barbary pirate, Dragoutis, carried out a successful raid on Rethymnon in 1562, while the notorious Algerian Uluç Ali appeared on the scene nine years later. He had been born Italian in Calabria, but was captured by Barbarossa and became enslaved in the galleys. At some stage he converted to Islam, and became a highly successful pirate himself, a not-uncommon story at that time. In 1571, he plundered the area around Mylopotamos and then attacked Rethymnon. The city was deserted as the population had fled to the countryside, but the looting was more thorough and devastating than ever.

Pirate raids either along the coast or in the seas around Crete continued right up to the Ottoman conquest of the island. It is difficult to imagine the terror inspired among the Cretans by these attacks. Not only were they in fear of death, rape or, at the very least, loss of their property, but there was a strong possibility that they would be captured and sold into slavery. The vast majority of prisoners were taken off to the slave markets of the East, where their captors could receive anything from forty ducats for an old woman or youth to 100 ducats for a beautiful woman. There was a slim chance that a slave could be tracked down and bought back by his or her family, and relatives of enslaved people are known to have practically bankrupted themselves to pay agents in the southern Peloponnese to trace and purchase a child, husband, wife or other family member. In the Ionian Islands, charitable funds were set up for the redemption of enslaved Christians, while several monastic orders were founded in other parts of the Christian world with a similar aim. In Crete, however, there was no formal financial assistance for these activities, although it did become common for wealthy and devout Christians to leave money for this purpose. A will of 1603 includes the following provision:

My inheritors and successors will undertake to give every year the sum of one hundred tzikinia[7] for the purpose of repurchasing two

Christian slaves, who desire no more and no less than to be free, from the hand of the Turks.[8]

Religious Life

As previously mentioned, there was a strong religious dimension to Cretan resistance to the Venetians. After the Great Schism of 1054, the Orthodox Church and Roman Catholic Church regarded each other as heretics. Although this was the official Church position, its impact on ordinary Christians should not be exaggerated. There is no evidence that the Venetians of this period were particularly devout in their religious observances. In fact, they often referred to themselves as "Venetians first, Christians second".[9] It was because the Orthodox Church was closely linked with Byzantium, and was a major symbol of unity for the Cretans, that the Venetian rulers saw it as a threat and deliberately set out to undermine the Church and clergy on the island. Similarly, the average Cretan probably had no great interest in doctrinal differences, but regarded Orthodoxy as part of his Greek heritage, something that set him aside from the Venetians.

For a long time, Venice was quite ruthless in its attempts to suppress Orthodoxy. This objective was approached from two sides. On the one hand, the Orthodox hierarchy was completely disbanded, with no bishops remaining on the island. Visits by Orthodox priests from outside Crete were prohibited, and relations between Crete and the Orthodox patriarch in Constantinople were largely severed. In 1418, a music teacher and cantor, Ioannis Laskaris, was exiled for life simply for including the name of the patriarch in prayers during the Liturgy. The following year, several priests were imprisoned for similar offences. These measures effectively left the local priests and even the monasteries leaderless and isolated.

At the same time, a Latin Roman Catholic hierarchy was established to control the religious life of the island. A Latin archbishop was appointed, with spiritual jurisdiction over the island, and other bishops were appointed later. To complete the attempt at suppression of Orthodoxy, a large number of Latin monasteries were founded as centres for disseminating Roman Catholic theology and practice, mainly in the cities. The highest position the Greek clergy were allowed to attain was that of **protopapas** (first priest). Although Orthodox, these protopapades had to recognise the supremacy of the pope, and were paid employees of the Venetian state. They were expected to take part in services alongside Catholic priests and show absolute support for the papacy and the government. Not surprisingly, they were generally disliked by the laity and lower clergy alike.

This situation changed little for the first 300 years of Venetian rule and, in fact, slightly deteriorated. The Council of Florence in 1439 was a serious attempt to reunite the Roman Catholic and Orthodox Churches. It failed to achieve union but, following the council, various Eastern Rite Catholic Churches developed, retaining the organisation and liturgy of the Orthodox Church while accepting the supremacy of the pope. This encouraged the Venetians to increase pressure on the Cretans to become **Uniate** as the protopapades already were. A plot by Sephes Vlastos in 1453 was largely in reaction to this and, when it was crushed, it was found that a quarter of the thirty-nine plotters were priests. As a result, there was a five-year ban on ordination of Cretan priests and a prohibition on all attempts to promote Orthodoxy on the island.

Against this historical background, the life of an Orthodox priest was, for a long time, one of poverty and often ignorance, with no spiritual and little financial support. It is therefore somewhat surprising that many young men were prepared to face the bureaucratic labyrinth necessary to be ordained a priest. First, they needed the permission of the Venetian authorities, which inevitably involved the payment of a large fee. Then, the candidate had to leave Crete and go to Venetian territories in the Peloponnese, the Ionian Islands or Asia Minor to be ordained. On returning to Crete, the new priest would undergo examination by the authorities and, finally, seek the approval of his feudal lord. He was then allowed to carry out his duties as a priest, always under the eye of his protopapas.

In general, with little guidance or supervision, there was an overall decline in the moral and religious lives of the clergy, both priests and monks, especially in the early years of this period. In 1381, a learned and highly respected monk, Joseph Bryennios, was sent from Constantinople to Crete to try to combat the decline. He certainly didn't mince his words, accusing married clergy and monks alike of impiety, avarice, debauchery and drunkenness. He managed to remain in Crete for twenty years and had some success in revitalising the Orthodox spirit on the island, but was eventually expelled by the authorities. An encyclical from the Patriarch of Constantinople in 1401 condemned the regular practice of women living with monks. In spite of the irregularities, the Orthodox monasteries did manage to keep the faith alive among ordinary Cretans, mainly away from the urban centres. There were, even in the early years of the period, men of learning and integrity, such as Neilos Damilas, the abbot of a monastery at Ierapetra, who founded a convent nearby and was the author of a set of strict rules governing convent life. He was also responsible for a well-argued treatise attacking the Latin Church.

Incidentally, it is worth mentioning that the Latin clergy did not fare much better. The higher clerics rarely visited the parishes and just enjoyed the revenues, while the priests were mainly uneducated and not known for their piety. A Scots adventurer writing in 1632 gives a hilarious account of a few weeks spent at a Catholic monastery near Chania:

> The church was little and among the four friars, there was but one mass-priest, being a Greek borne and turned to the Roman faction ... He was so free of his stomach to receive in strong liquor, that for the space of twenty days of my being there, I never saw him, nor anyone of the other three truly sober.[10]

The general situation began to improve from the early sixteenth century, with an increasing number of more moral and spiritual abbots. After the fall of Constantinople, many eminent churchmen migrated to Crete. Although some of these moved on to Venice and western Europe, there was a general improvement in the religious and cultural quality of the monasteries. As the threat from Turkey increased, the authorities sought to gain the support of their Orthodox subjects, and a more tolerant regime was established. After the great naval engagement of 1571, the Battle of Lepanto, in which the Ottomans were defeated by a combined European fleet, an Orthodox hierarchy was re-established. This improvement was short-lived, however, because the fanatical Catholic proveditore generale Foscarini revoked the decision in 1575. In fact, he went further and proposed to substantially reduce the number of Orthodox priests, all of whom he regarded as potential traitors.

The Cretan monasteries now became bastions of Byzantine Orthodoxy, organising opposition to the Latinising of the Cretan Church, and attempting to educate local people in the values of the Orthodox faith. Many produced several eminent patriarchs and bishops, including Meletios, patriarch of Alexandria, who took a strong interest in supervising the spiritual health of the island. During the sixteenth and seventeenth centuries, nearly all the abbots of the great Saint Katherine of Sinai monastery on Mount Sinai were Cretans. Schools and libraries were built, and many great theologians and artists came from among the monks. During the revival of monasticism, scores of monasteries were founded, including many that survive to this day: Toplou, Arkadi, Agarathos, Apezanes and Vrontisiou, to name but a few. Many of these were built, with encouragement from the government, in remote areas where they could be used as part of the island's defences. The monastery of Toplou, for example, was originally called Panagia Akrotiriani ("Our Lady of the Cape"), but gained its current name from the Turkish word meaning "with cannons".

Apart from Foscarini's attempt to turn back the clock, from 1550 onwards, attempts to Latinise Crete were largely abandoned. This was partly because of the threat from Turkey, but it was also a recognition that the policy had failed completely. After 350 years, not only was the Catholic population of Crete only 2% of the total, but many Venetian Catholics had converted to Orthodoxy. The patriarch of Alexandria was even able to persuade Venice to issue a decree stating that, in Crete:

> The Greek nation should be completely rid of the machinations of the Pope, and our Greek subjects, being good Christians and loyal servants of our state, should be free to live as they have always lived, according to the beliefs and practices of the Eastern Church.

From this time on, there was a much more relaxed religious life in Crete, with Catholic and Orthodox Cretans attending each other's services, especially in rural areas. The proveditore generale's report of 1602 was able to state that:

> There is no quarrel on matters of religion, since both communities live freely in their own rites, and the Greek notables and others of their rite often go to Latin churches to hear mass, and the Latins frequent the churches of the Orthodox. The clergy of both rites are respected by all. But the thing which most indicates the respect of the Greeks for the Latin rite is their general devotion to Saint Francis ... In Sfakia there are many Greeks who out of devotion to the saint give his name to the child.[11]

In the fourteenth-century Orthodox church of the Panagia Kera at Kritsa, a fresco of Saint Francis can still be seen among the Orthodox saints. There is even a small church from this period on the island of Spinalonga which has two aisles, one in Orthodox style and one in Catholic, so that the two faiths could share it.

An intriguing footnote to the religious life of Venetian Crete is the existence of a small group that attempted to spread the ideas of the Reformation. A Catholic Swiss traveller reported that, in 1568, he met an Italian schoolteacher from Lucca who was attempting to spread the doctrine of **Calvinism** to his students in Candia. He was assisted in this by two Greek Calvinists, the charismatic doctor Ioannis Kassimatis and Manousos Maras, a graduate of Padua University. His story is confirmed by the records of the local Holy Inquisition, which report that all Protestant books were burned and the local school closed. All three men were arrested, and Kassimatis was sentenced to life imprisonment in the notorious prison of the Doge's Palace in Venice, where he died in 1571. It is not clear what happened to the other two, but it is possible that they were sentenced to death. There is no record of any other reformers on the island.

During Venetian rule, there were several Jewish communities in Crete, mainly in the urban areas. In general, they suffered under the same restrictions imposed in most of Catholic Europe, including the requirement to wear a distinguishing badge in public and restrictions on where they could live. It seems, however, that they were allowed to do business outside the ghetto. It is also likely that many Jews joined in

the Saint Titus revolt of 1363 to 1364, perhaps hoping for better treatment from an independent state. Certainly, it is known that the entire
community of Jews at Castel Nuovo was killed after the suppression of
the rebellion. At the end of the fourteenth century, there was an influx
of Jews from the Iberian Peninsula, following persecution, forced conversions and expulsions. At the end of the fifteenth century, there were
400 Jewish families in Candia and four synagogues. The populations
in other cities are not known. According to the 1627 census, there were
1,160 Jews on the island in total. As well as the urban communities,
there were small groups in agricultural areas, mainly producing kosher
cheese and wine both for local use and for export, but laws were passed
to limit this competition with the Greek farmers by preventing Jews
from buying any more land. Eventually, as in many other countries,
they were limited to moneylending and trading in silk, metals, dyes
and leather. Many of the urban Jews travelled widely, especially to Italy,
and were active in the intellectual life of the island. There were often
tensions between the Christians and Jews, which occasionally resulted
in riots. The situation deteriorated as the Turkish threat increased. This
was due to a widespread belief that the Jews were favourable towards
the Ottoman Empire, and were thus liable to treason.[12]

Society

As in many colonial situations, although there was a large influx of settlers in the early days, Venetians only ever comprised about 3% of the
population of Crete. As for the total population of Crete, figures are
not reliable for the early years of the period, but it is known that there
was considerable fluctuation due to rebellions and epidemics. From
1534, there are more reliable census figures, which indicate a steady rise
from a population of about 175,000 in that year to just under 290,000
in 1644. The Greek population of the island was augmented from time
to time by refugees from Asia Minor, and after the fall of Constantinople in 1453 many Byzantine families fled to Crete.

Venetian Crete has been described as a feudal society, but, in many
respects, this is misleading. On the one hand, much of the language of
feudalism was used, especially in the early years. For example, feudal

fiefs – grants of land in return for allegiance to the state – existed, and terms like "**vassal**" and "serf" were commonplace. On the other hand, Venice was a republic, so the full system of allegiance from vassal to feudal lord to king did not exist. In fact, neither the political nor economic systems were truly feudal. Power did not stem from land ownership but from a person's status as a member of the nobility in Venice and, most importantly, his eligibility to participate in the Great Council of Venice. For much of the period, this eligibility was focused strictly on ancestry.

At the top of the tree were the Venetian nobility, Nobili Veneti, the original aristocratic colonists and their descendants. These people were usually extremely wealthy and of enormous prestige and, as noted above, were in total control of the administration of the colony. They had received land in return for their total loyalty to Venice and their participation in military service, including their provision of war-horses. Their property usually consisted of landed estates and villages, together with residences in the main coastal cities. They could not be Orthodox Christians, and if they abandoned their Catholic faith, they lost all their titles and feudal possessions. The social gap between the Nobili Veneti and Cretans of even the highest rank was enormous, which makes the promotion of Alexios Kallergis to the nobility even more extraordinary. For the most part, the Venetian nobles consti-tuted a colonial elite with significant ties to both Cretan and Venetian society. Although the Greek archons were specifically excluded from the nobility after the rebellions of the thirteenth and fourteenth cen-turies, feudal fiefs were briefly granted to a few of the Greek leaders in exchange for oaths of loyalty to Venice. After the failure of the Saint Titus revolt, most of these fiefs were withdrawn, and the rule that members of the nobility must adhere to the Roman Catholic Church was reinforced.

In the early fifteenth century, the Venetian council decided to tighten up the rules for entry into the nobility for everyone, and many of the Venetian nobles from Crete had to prove their status before the council again. Within a short time, the door was closed and it became virtually impossible for any more Venetian Cretans to claim noble status in Venice. This left some families of Venetian descent in Crete out in the cold: they considered themselves noble and held fiefs in

Crete, but they could not take up seats in the Great Council of Venice. For this reason, with the consent of Venice, a class of Cretan nobility was created: Nobili Cretesi. In spite of its name, it initially consisted of descendants of the original settlers from Venice and former nobles who had lost their Venetian titles for some reason. The Cretan nobility were able to hold council seats in Crete, but not in Venice. Very quickly, individuals of Greek Cretan descent who held fiefs were allowed to join the group and sit on Cretan governing councils. These Cretan nobles were generally not very wealthy, held little property and were mostly involved in trade. As time went by, in spite of detailed monitoring of existing members and strict rules for new entrants, membership of the Cretan nobility began to be granted to more and more indigenous Cretans – mostly Orthodox, and with little loyalty to Venice. The threat from the Ottomans made it vital for the Venetians to gain the support of the Orthodox population and, as it was with changes in religious practice, the class system became more flexible. Crete slowly became less of a colony and more of a province.

By the sixteenth century, even the partially feudal system was pretty much in tatters. Many estates were divided up, and more and more Greeks were buying fiefdoms. The majority of knights neither owned horses nor knew how to ride them. The proveditore generale, Foscarini, complained in 1575:

> When called upon to give an accounting of themselves, many would borrow a horse and stick a villager on it as the rider. The resulting demonstration was considered so hilarious that people would come from far and wide to watch and throw rotten fruit and stones at the riders.[13]

By the end of the century, only 164 out of 964 nobles in the Candia region were Venetian. In the census of 1644, there were only 82 Nobili Veneti, compared with 198 Nobili Cretesi.

The predominantly urban bourgeoisie had no titles, but consisted of the wealthy class of merchants, sailors and craftsmen. The class also included the permanent military, civil servants, doctors, lawyers and notaries, as well as somewhat poorer manual labourers. The vast majority of this group were Orthodox. As trade and seafaring developed, this class became very prosperous. In the 1590s, a report described the upper echelons of Cretan society:

> The wealth of the nobles and the bourgeoisie is apparent from their expensive clothes, festivals, feasts and funerals, which are performed with unusual lavishness.[14]

As in medieval Europe generally, almost all trades, crafts and professions were controlled by guilds responsible for training, maintenance of standards and protection of rights, and improvements in the working and living conditions of their members. They organised aid for members in difficulties, but were also engaged in general philanthropic work such as founding and maintaining hospitals and orphanages. In Venice and its colonies, each guild was led by a president and was named after its patron saint. For example, the guild of carpenters was called Saint Joseph's Guild, the guild of sailors was named for Saint Nicholas and the patron of the painters' guild was Saint Luke. The bourgeoisie were subject to limited military service, payment of a small tax and the obligation to provide accommodation for foreign mercenaries serving on the island.

At the bottom of the heap was the vast majority of the population, the rural poor. This class included free peasants, Orthodox priests and the descendants of Byzantine families, but the majority were serfs, completely owned by the feudal lords, tied to the land and with no protection or rights. Although the archon families and priests were exempt from some labour duties, all of the peasantry whether free or serf had to work on their lords' land as well as their own, especially during peak events like ploughing and harvesting. In addition, they had to give a third (often more) of their produce to their lord. As in Venice and many other Italian cities and colonies, there were also enslaved people, usually bought as household servants from the slave markets. The Venetians and Cretans generally avoided buying enslaved Christians, especially those from Roman Catholic countries, as this was specifically condemned by the pope. Since the Venetians believed that no Latin person could be of servile status, any male slave or serf who could demonstrate that his father was of Latin descent automatically gained his freedom. For example, in the late fourteenth century, a woman sued for her freedom on the grounds that she was Hungarian and therefore from a country loyal to Rome. The magistrate ruled that she was illegally enslaved and granted her immediate freedom.

Although some rights and privileges for free peasants and serfs were recognised after the Kallergis treaty, life for the rural peasantry – as in all feudal societies – was pretty grim. In addition to the hard labour of the farms and working for their lords, they were also required to undertake other compulsory unpaid work for the state. Some were set to work on the construction and repair of fortifications, while others were conscripted to man the warships. All men aged between fourteen and sixty – and, amazingly, women of all ages – were liable for conscription. In 1589, a particularly enlightened proveditore generale wrote in his report about the labourers forced into building work for the state:

> Anyone who has not seen the wretchedness of those people is unable to believe it ... These unfortunates raise with their sweat and their blood those very walls which will shut them out in time of need and they will be left to the disposal of the enemy, while the walls will protect those who made no contribution in money or labour of any kind towards their erection.[15]

Of all the work, the galleys were by far the worst. The age range for this was a little narrower than that for general conscription: men of between eighteen and fifty. While those on board chosen to be soldiers didn't have it at all easy, the lives (usually short) of the rowers were unbelievably horrible. Chained to the bench and flogged if they slowed down, exhausted by the work, malnourished and subject to illness, the poor souls also had to face sea battles, pirates and shipwreck. Even if captured by pirates or the enemy, the chances were that they would be consigned to yet another galley, in conditions unlikely to be better. Conscription to the galleys was therefore regarded as an extended death sentence. A popular song of the period illustrates the general feeling:

A widowed mother kneaded out the bread for her son;
How she kneaded with her tears, and with her laments,

How she lit the fire with the breath of a heavy sigh.
"My son, if you go to far off distant lands
And they put you to the oar ..."

The numbers involved were substantial. At various times of danger or during wars with the Ottomans, as many as 30,000 or 40,000 men were conscripted to the galleys. The fear of the galleys was such that, on news that a proveditore was due in the village, many escaped to the mountains or, in some cases, committed suicide. Gradually, a system of substitutes grew up, whereby a family would pay for somebody to enlist on the conscript's behalf. These substitutes (or "antiscari", as they were known in Italian) were, however, seldom honest. Having bled the villagers dry, they would disappear. Even the feudal lords were known to profit from the fear of the galleys. Those villagers who had no money for a substitute, or had already paid everything they had with no result, were encouraged by the lords to flee. A lord could use his influence to secure release from conscription on condition that, upon returning, the peasant would become his serf. The Venetian authorities were well aware of these abuses, but either could not or would not stamp them out, and the corruption continued until the end of Venetian rule.

As the Turkish threat increased, there were attempts to alleviate the lot of the peasantry, mainly to retain their loyalty. For example, one proveditore reported in 1639:

> They [the ordinary people] must always be treated well so that they will remain faithful and devoted. Because when they are oppressed and used too much in forced labour by the fief holders and some-times by the representatives of the state, and subject to extraordi-nary harshness, they are driven to despair. Then they abandon the kingdom and go to the Turkish territories and, enraged as they are, they devote themselves to evil doing. They incite the enemy and open the way toward attacks, which perhaps he [the enemy] would not otherwise have thought of.[16]

Nevertheless, a deep distrust of the peasantry was ingrained in the Venetian mind, to the extent that one capitane generale seriously pro-posed that, in the event of war with the Ottomans, virtually the whole male population of the island should be put to sea in the galleys. This would not only be of great military value but:

> The people [on land], each having their father, their son or their brother basically held hostage by the navy, would be very careful to remain faithful and not to engage in activities that could be harmful to themselves.[17]

Women

The position of women in Venetian Crete was socially complex. On the one hand, the life of a noblewoman, whether Venetian or Cretan, was highly regulated. Subordinate in all respects to their fathers and husbands, women's main duties were within the household. Nevertheless, unlike many of their contemporaries elsewhere, they exercised a fair degree of control over their own wealth and property and, through the Venetian laws relating to dowries and marriage contracts, had some influence on family affairs. For example, although matchmaking was common, the bride had to be present during the signing of the marriage contract, and her consent was necessary for the wedding to take place. Moreover, although a woman took her legal position from her father or husband, this did not stop her conducting business in her own right, and women were active in commerce either alongside their husbands or on their own.

Research into the records of notaries[18] has revealed many examples of women conducting business, and since there are thousands of documents not yet examined, it is likely that there were many more. Women are mentioned as being tavern keepers, shoemakers, furriers and, in one case, a physician. There is evidence that the "wifely" tasks of spinning and weaving in the home could develop into a professional textile business, including production, distribution and marketing. Many of the women describe themselves in contracts as mercatrix (female merchants) but, so far, in only one case has the phrase "with the consent of my husband" been found.[19] Since this was a legal requirement, it seems likely that most of the women concerned were widows (single women tended to enter convents at a certain age, and divorce was pretty well unheard of). Here again, the dowry laws helped, since the dowry reverted to the widow upon her husband's death, often giving her the means to set up in business. There is also fascinating evidence of women engaging in moneylending, often as part of an informal interest-free credit network but sometimes in a fully commercial contract. Some contracts show details of the use of dowries to invest in commercial trade ventures, the production and sale of wine or even long-distance trade. The extent of women's involvement in business is still unmeasured and ill defined, but it does seem to have been more substantial than previously thought.

As far as the lower classes were concerned, women fared less well. Peasant women, like all the peasantry, led lives of unremitting toil, hardship, poverty and early death. Women among the bourgeoisie, generally Greek, had few opportunities open to them and were ranked lowest in the social structure. They generally worked as servants or nurses, or in shops and taverns, and were paid significantly less than men, although there were exceptions. Wet nurses, for example, were greatly valued and earned higher wages, in some cases 20% more than a blacksmith.

Economy

Throughout the Venetian period, farming was still the primary sector, although there was a decline in production during the political unrest of the first two centuries. With restoration of peace, there was a revival of exports, primarily wine, at the expense of grain production. About half the total production of wine was exported, mainly to northern Europe, where it cost twice as much as other wines. In particular, the sweet wine called Malvazia was highly valued, because it kept much longer than the dry wines of France and Italy. It was very popular in England, where it was called malmsey.[20] An Italian priest travelling in 1494 described the wines of Rethymnon:

> There is an abundance of most excellent wines – malmseys and muscatels – in [Candia], and not only in the city but also in the whole island, especially in a city called Rethymno [sic] ... In the season

there are good melons, grapes and other good fruit. The vines are left trailing on the ground as we leave the melons and watermelons; and when they gather the grapes to make the malmseys and muscatels they crush them on chalk, because otherwise they could not extract the wine nor even preserve it; and that chalk gives them the great odour and perfume they have.[21]

During the reign of Henry VIII, from 1509 to 1547, wine exports to England became so important that an English consulate was established in Candia with the sole purpose of ensuring the wine supply. In 1512, total wine production amounted to about 100,000 metric tonnes while, in 1554, Chania alone produced 14,000 barrels. After the fall of Cyprus in 1571, wine prices rose dramatically, with English pirates visiting Crete and paying outrageous prices for the entire output. As a by-product of the wine trade, the making of wine barrels became a major industry in Candia.

The quality of Cretan grain and the resulting bread is attested by many visitors to the island, but exports of grain were strictly controlled by Venice. A quarter of the production was sent to Venice as tax, while any further exports had to be sold to the state at a fixed price, no doubt disadvantageous to the island. The extensive cultivation of land for vines resulted in less land being available for grain, which often led to hunger among the Cretans from March to early summer. The authorities tried to curtail vine cultivation, even giving orders to uproot vines on a large scale. The fact that these orders had to be repeated over many years indicates that the policy met with little success. In some years, bad harvests actually forced the government to import grain for up to four months of the year in order to prevent starvation. At first, these imports were from the Ottoman territories, but they were banned in 1555 and the situation became worse. In spite of the fertility of Crete, the possibility of crop failure was never far away. War and rebellion, drought, exhaustion of the soil, overproduction of wine, depopulation through plague and pirate raids – all contributed to the real danger of famine. A letter written in 1500 describes bands of starving villagers naked and despairing, setting out for Candia to find relief. Another chronicler wrote about a famine in 1591:

The poor lived on birdseed and weeds, where not so much as a bean was to be found. The winter was harsh and followed by torrential rains that made sowing impossible.[22]

In the early years of Venetian rule, olives were not cultivated extensively, but this situation changed gradually, as the advantages of the olive were recognised. The trees flourished in Crete, where the weather conditions were favourable, and they could be grown in the many hilly and mountainous parts of the island that were unsuitable for other forms of farming. Moreover, olives were relatively disease-resistant and required little care. Olive farming was particularly suited to small farms worked by the whole family. By 1629, about 1 million gallons of olive oil were being produced annually. This was in part the result of the attempt to curtail vine growing: when the policy was successful, the growing of vines was often replaced by the planting of more olive trees. An interesting contrast can be seen in two reports by travellers. A priest travelling in 1415 to 1417 reports seeing few olive groves in Crete. In contrast, the Scots traveller William Lithgow, writing in 1609, was able to describe the valley south-west of Souda as resembling a green sea because of the olive trees which covered the entire plain. As with vines, the Venetian authorities did not encourage olive oil production, and strictly controlled all aspects of the process, including price and trade.

Recent research has shown that, as well as the traditional Mediterranean triad of wine, oil and grain, production and export of goat and sheep cheese was of great importance to the Cretan economy, although it remained a poor fourth to the other three.[23] The two main types of cheese were the soft myzithra (still popular today) and a hard, very salty cheese more suitable for export. A lot of the cheese was sold directly to ships, aboard which it formed an important part of the sailors' diet. Another major customer was Constantinople, where cheese replaced meat for the monastic communities, except during rare festivals. The norm was a system of advance payments for cheese, whereby the merchant would pay the farmer in advance for his output. Unfortunately, the farmers often couldn't produce the required amount of cheese, and a severe problem of indebtedness developed. This was never really solved, in spite of various attempts by the authorities.

Some important exports came from specific locations in Crete. For example, the areas around Chania and Rethymnon produced citrus fruits, as they still do, mainly for export as juice. Because of its sheltered location and very high salinity, the Gulf of Mirabello became a major producer of salt during Venetian times. Salt was of tremendous importance for preserving food in the Middle Ages and, as at other times in history, the state had a monopoly on the production and sale of this essential. The Venetians built the first salt pans in Elounda as early as the thirteenth century, and by 1583 there were forty-two pans producing up to 1,400 tonnes of salt a year. Timber came mainly from Sfakia.

Wooden products were also highly prized, including carved cypress furniture such as chests and small tables. During the later years, carved wooden altar screens, crosses and altar doors were added to the list of exports. Other exports included cotton, silk, acorns for tanning, honey, wax, meat and saltpetre. Although a proportion of all exports went to Venice, the merchants were also able to export directly to European ports. However, the production, delivery and marketing of all agricultural and pastoral products were strictly controlled. Most goods were channelled towards the large urban markets, where weights-and-measures laws and taxation could be enforced more easily.

An important, but largely undocumented, element in the economy was the slave trade, which reached its height in the fourteenth and fifteenth centuries. Slave markets existed in all the port cities, and the trade was undoubtedly a major contributor to the Cretan economy.

Apart from occasional imports of grain, imports were mainly of luxury goods for the wealthy aristocrats and merchants of the cities. These included jewels, glassware and silk from Italy; spices and gum Arabic from the East; and fine Flemish woollens. Salt fish and caviar were also popular. Ironically in view of Crete's ancient history, fine ceramics were imported from Italy. With improving levels of literacy, paper also became a major import.

Natural Disasters

The people of Crete already had to endure the severity of Venetian rule,

the insecurity of rebellions and the subsequent reprisals, the depredations of pirates, and intermittent droughts and famines. To all these
can be added frequent earthquakes and outbreaks of plague during
this period. There were at least five earthquakes of varying intensity
between 1303 and 1650. In 1494, a 7.2 magnitude earthquake off the
north coast of the island mainly affected Candia. A vivid account can
be found in the diary of an Italian pilgrim:

> About the sixteenth hour, there was an earthquake of such a nature,
> that I was almost thrown from the seat on which I was sitting, to
> the ground. The friary seemed on the point of falling, the beams
> were seen to come out of their places, and made a great dust ... The
> said earthquake did much damage in the city to the bell-towers, the
> churches and also the private houses ... About the third hour of the
> night the earthquake was renewed with such violence, that people
> arose out of bed and fled to the open country.[24]

By far the most serious of the earthquakes was in 1508. It measured
5.3 in magnitude and was located 100 km directly beneath the centre
of Crete. Although lower in severity than many others, its location and
relatively small depth caused massive damage, and thousands of deaths
were reported in Candia, Siteia and Ierapetra, although the west
was largely unaffected. The first shock was a long one, described by
the Venetian governor as lasting as long as it took to recite the Lord's
Prayer in a hurry – which is probably what he was doing at the time.
Most of the houses in Candia, weakened by the first tremor, were then
demolished in the aftershock, leaving only four or five standing. In
his report, the Duke of Crete described the earthquake as "terrible,
horrendous and terrifying" and stated that "it ruined the majority of
the land, and that which remains standing is uninhabitable". Tremors
could be felt as far away as Cyprus and Asia Minor. The Cretan poet
Manolis Sklavos wrote a poem called *The Catastrophe of Crete* describing the quake and people's reactions to it. In the middle, he cries out,
*"O Crete, who could have said that you would be destroyed in this way/
And that you would lose your lofty palaces at one stroke?"*[25]

In 1629, a magnitude 7 earthquake to the north of Crete affected the
whole of the island, causing some deaths and extensive loss of property.

A witness described how "houses fell and people were crushed and the belfries of the town rang out and the earth groaned and shook and yawned wide as if it would swallow us up".[26] Then, during the siege of Candia in 1650, a submarine volcanic eruption near Santorini was followed by an earthquake and tsunami which both affected Crete. The poet Marinos Bounialis includes a dramatic description in his poem *The Cretan War*:

> *The world flared up with thunderous roars,*
> *And Crete shook and the foamless sea did move*
> *And for hours it did just swell and ever grew*
> *Until it razed the walls as if the foe were entering.*
> *It swelled and swirled without help of wind*
> *And the ships were dragged down into the abyss.*
> *Ships and galleys were washed away by force*
> *And swept and thrust across to Dia.[27]*

Because of its position as a trade crossroads of the Mediterranean, Crete was also prone to epidemics, usually the bubonic plague, which became almost endemic. There were twenty-two major outbreaks, with thousands of victims and whole villages wiped out. A demotic poem describes the epidemic of 1571 movingly and vividly:

> *Sick became the people and sick the lords,*
> *Danger there was that no one would remain.*
> *... Death himself had no time to fright them all*
> *As they fell one after another.*
> *The priest had not time to give them holy communion,*
> *And whoever fell ill was doomed to die.*
> *... It was not forty that died each day –*
> *Thirty an hour were brought out on the cart.[28]*

So serious was the problem of plague on the island that the authorities initiated a system of quarantine, based on the one used in Venice itself. Crete, like all the Venetian colonies, had its own *proveditore alla sanità* (health superintendent) backed up by a bureaucracy, sanitation police and an armed garrison. Two lazarettos, or "pest houses", were located outside the walls of Candia for the quarantine of newcomers. The officials were also helped by several monasteries, hospitals and charitable institutions in their efforts to control epidemics. The system was described by the English traveller Fynes Moryson in 1596, whose description combines admiration at the thoroughness of the measures with irritation at their practical impacts on his own convenience. In another part of the narrative, he describes the restrictions as "comfortable but irksome":

The Italians in regard of their clime, are very curious to receive strangers in a time of plague, and appoint chiefe men to the office of providing for the publike health, calling the place where they meete, the Office of Health. Also without their Cities (especially in the State of Venice) they have publike houses, called Lazaretti, and for the most part pleasantly seated, whither passengers and Merchants with their goods, must at their first arrival retire, till the Providers for Health have curiously inquired, if they come from any suspected place, or have any infectious sicknesse. And here they have all things necessary in abundance, but may not converse or talke with any man, till they obtaine the grant of free conversation (called la prattica), or if any man speake with them, he must be inclosed in the same house, and because they stay fortie dayes there, for the trial of their health, this trial is called far' la Quarantana. Moreover, they that goe by land in Italie, must bring a Testimonie of Health called Boletino, before they can passe or converse ...

In the meane time they shut us up in a garden house, where we had pleasant walkes, and store of Oranges and like fruites, and the Country people bringing us Partridges and many good things to eate ...

These Gentlemen (according to the custome), such as the state of no passenger can be hidden from them, caused ropes to be hanged acrosse our chamber, and all things we had, yea, our very shirts, to be severally taken out, and hanged thereupon, and so perfumed them with brimstone, to our great annoyance, though they well knew we had no infectious sicknesse, which done, they gave us freedome to goe into the City, and wheresoever we would.[29]

In spite of all these precautions, and because the system had become lax and complacent, the outbreak of 1592 to 1595 was possibly the worst in Cretan history. Ironically, it seems that a single case was misdiagnosed by doctors who then themselves spread the disease via their patients. Candia was the most affected, with about 200 deaths a day. Looting and other crime increased, with theft of clothing from the houses of victims spreading the disease further. A limited martial law was imposed, but the plague spread among the soldiers themselves, largely as a result of the off-duty militia inviting prostitutes into the garrison. After the nobility were given permission to leave for the country, with unkept promises to return with food from the villages, only about 1,800 citizens remained. A chronicle in the monastery of Apezonon describes some of the side effects of the epidemic, looting and possible Turkish attacks:

> They heaped up the dead unsung and without the proper rites like dogs. Fifty priests died in Candia ... And many lost all their possessions because the houses were abandoned as everyone fled the town and went to dwell in caves and in holes in the ground ... The lords were spared of this evil because they left the town and hid themselves in their villages in strong keeps so that no one would approach them there ... We were most afraid then, for we learnt that the Turk was preparing an armada to fight Crete now that we were so few, having been killed by the plague. But God blinded him and we were saved from falling into his hands.[30]

In fact, a Turkish squadron of galleys and heavy gunboats did anchor off the coast near Candia, but the capitano generale, with only six out of 100 military patrols available for defence, carried out a brilliant bluff. He got his men to organise a spectacular and highly visible and audible carnival to convince the watching Ottomans that all was well within the walls. The ruse seemed to have worked, because the fleet quietly sailed away. The plague continued to rage and, by early 1594, Candia was virtually a ghost town. Gradually, the epidemic abated until, in September 1595, the city and countryside around it were officially declared free of plague.[31] According to the proveditore generale's official report, the final death toll for the city of Candia was about 8,600

(52% of its population), plus 5,300 from the villages, plus the children under eight years old, Jews and gypsies who were not included in the official figures.

One result of the horrible events of 1592 to 1595 seems to have been a tightening up of the lazaretto system, as witnessed a year later by Fynes Moryson. Although there were further epidemics in 1611, 1630 and 1646, and between 1655 and 1661 during the siege of Candia, none of them was as devastating.

Education and Culture

In discussing Venetian Crete, the historian Monique O'Connell makes the point that it is easy to paint a grim picture of "rapacious Venetians, religious oppression, multiple revolts, and then raids by pirates, followed by a prolonged fight with the Ottomans".[32] The tendency to create a sort of "black legend" of unrelenting awfulness, as with the modern news media, is probably related to the fact that bad news is usually more interesting than good news. It is true that the lives of the peasantry were invariably pretty awful, as they were almost everywhere in Europe at that time. However, as we have seen, after the ending of the rebellions, the Greek archons began to receive grants of land and have access to some government positions, while the urban middle classes grew increasingly prosperous with the expansion of trade. Nowhere was this brighter side of Venetian rule seen more than in the fields of education, culture and the arts.

In the first couple of centuries of Venetian rule, opportunities for education were limited. Some monasteries gave a few classes, while private tutors offered a rudimentary education in Italian, Greek and Latin to children in the cities. Notaries, who had to prepare documents in Greek and Italian, employed specialist private teachers. The general level of education began to improve in the late fourteenth century with the arrival of scholars from Byzantium, as attacks by the Ottomans increased in the empire. The fall of Constantinople hastened this process substantially. These scholars set up schools and contributed enormously to education, literature and intellectual life. From the late fourteenth century, since there were no universities on the island, Cretans started to travel to Italy, especially the University of Padua, to obtain higher education. Many of these went on to successful careers in the Church, politics or the universities all over Europe. Perhaps the most famous of these was Petros Philarges, the first Greek professor at the University of Paris, who later became a cardinal and then, briefly, pope under the name Alexander V. Between 1500 and 1700, more than 1,000 Cretans studied at Padua.

After 1453, Crete became the de facto guardian of Greek intellectual heritage, and the monasteries began to flourish and turn into major centres of learning. The many copyists in monasteries throughout the island played a significant part in disseminating classical Greek texts to the west. The Saint Katherine of Sinai monastery in Candia, in particular, played a central role in the development of the cultural life of Crete between the fifteenth and seventeenth centuries. It built up a substantial library, which was of tremendous importance to the intellectual and artistic renaissance of the island. Its school became a major centre of learning, and it taught Greek classical authors, philosophy, theology, rhetoric and art. Many of its graduates distinguished themselves in literature, while a large number of the greatest icon painters studied there.

At the same time as scholars were returning from European universities to found schools in Crete, there was movement in the opposite direction. Scholars and artists from the island were taking their talents into western Europe, becoming some of Crete's major "exports". The intellectual life of the island was further enhanced during the second half of the sixteenth century, when three academies were founded in Rethymnon, Candia and Chania. These were modelled on similar academies in Italy, and were basically literary societies set up to discuss literature, art and the latest trends in the Italian Renaissance. They were extremely influential, becoming important forums for Italian-Greek cultural interchange.

As previously mentioned, in the early centuries of Venetian rule, there was an impassable barrier between the Latin Venetians and the Greek Cretans. No Cretan could gain feudal rights, and any Venetian who converted to Orthodoxy would lose all such rights. As these barriers began to crumble, a gradual process of Hellenisation of the Venetians took place. Greek became the language of choice, even in court circles; intermarriage became more common; and more and more Venetians became Orthodox. At the end of the sixteenth century, the ultra-conservative proveditore generale Foscarini was bewailing the fact that the Venetians of Crete no longer understood Italian. Even the Catholic Cretans wrote and spoke Greek and felt more in tune with the Greek heritage of their country of birth. In short, apart from the Venetian government itself, Crete had developed into a homogeneous society, with the people of the island no longer Greek, nor Italian, but Cretan. This was to have important repercussions on the development of Cretan poetry and the wider Cretan Renaissance. A line by the Roman poet Horace could now be applied to Venetian Crete: *"Captive Greece captured her uncivilised conqueror, and brought the arts to rustic Latium."*[33]

Literature

From the mid-fourteenth century to the late sixteenth, the foundations were being laid for a distinctive and unique style of Cretan literature, mainly poetry. The literature was mostly satirical or didactic, written in a mixture of late Byzantine vernacular and Cretan dialect, with some elements of more formal, educated Greek. The form used is the so-called political verse, in which each line consists of fifteen syllables.[34] Unfortunately, the poetry of this period has not been given a great deal of attention, and little of it has been translated into English, but a few important figures can be identified. Writing in the second half of the fourteenth century, the poet Stephanos Sachlikis came from a very old and wealthy Candia family. Having dissipated a large part of his inheritance on women and gambling, he spent some time in prison. On his release, he retired to what was left of his property in the countryside. He was eventually given a post as advocate at the Duke's court, but may have fallen from grace and ended up in prison a second time. His poems describe Cretan society, manners and morals, combining sermonising with satire, often in bawdy language. His descriptions of the less salubrious aspects of Candia life are quite vivid and obviously based on personal experience. It is likely that Sachlikis was the first in Crete to use rhyming couplets in his poems.

His contemporary Leonardos Dellaportas is also of interest because, despite being obviously of Venetian origin, he wrote in Greek. His autobiographical poem *Dialogue Between an Unfortunate Man and Truth* is praised for its great beauty and lyrical quality.

I have already mentioned the dramatic poem *The Catastrophe of Crete* by Manolis Sklavos, written in 1508. A year later, the influential poem *Apokopos* (*A Man Cut Off from Life*) was published. The poet, simply known as Bergadis of Rethymnon, used the popular form of a dream poem, describing an imaginary descent into Hades. It contains dramatic descriptions of Hades, and the usual moral exhortations. He decries the ease with which the living forget the dead, the greed of the clergy and the general insensitivity of men. What makes this poem stand out from others of the genre are passages where he praises the joys of life and the beauty of the world. The dead long for light and for the senses they have lost, wondering *"If there are gardens and mountains, if the birds sing,/If the mountains smell fresh, and if the trees blossom"*. The poet himself is attracted by *"The grace of the tree, the enchantment of the place,/And by the melody of the birds"*.[35] This lightness of touch contrasts with another vision of a descent into Hades from the same period. *Complaints in Rhyme on the Bitter and Insatiable Hades* by Ioannis Pikatoros is, as the title suggests, somewhat gloomier and contains macabre and terrifying descriptions of the journey.

Economic and political stability, coupled with the influence of the Italian Renaissance, resulted in what has been called the golden age of Cretan literature. The local Cretan dialect became an important literary language in its own right, characterised by originality and freshness. An anonymous pastoral idyll, *Voskopoula* (*The Shepherdess*), rapidly became popular as a folk song throughout the Aegean, and influenced both Lord Byron and the nineteenth-century Greek poet Solomos. As well as following all the traditions of pastoral poetry, it includes beautiful descriptions of the Cretan countryside. The cave where the shepherdess is found, for example, shows an attention to detail that must be the result of observation rather than imagination:

I turned my eyes to see the cave, beholding
The loveliness there was all round about it;

Outside it, trailed a twining plant like ivy
And she and I interwove it.
Outside, the maid had planted myrtle bushes,
Rosemary and St. John's wort, violets, lilies.[36]

Finely crafted dramas of the late sixteenth century include tragedies such as *Erophili* by Georgios Chortatsis of Rethymnon, and comedies like *Katsourbos* by the same author – certainly the oldest and arguably the finest surviving Cretan comedy. Probably the greatest drama of the period was the early-seventeenth-century play *The Sacrifice of Abraham*, attributed to Vitsentzos Kornaros of Siteia. This was developed from traditional medieval mystery plays, but is written in a fine lyrical style with well-developed and realistic characters.

Kornaros, described by the Greek poet Palamas as "the great immortal poet of the Greek people", went on to write his masterpiece, *Erotokritos*.[37] This verse tale of almost 10,000 lines of fifteen syllables each, written in rhyming couplets, has rarely been out of print and is still read or performed to musical settings today. It is an intensely romantic tale of two young lovers, Erotokritos and Aretousa (daughter of Herakles, the king of Athens). Erotokritos is not of royal blood and is considered unworthy to marry Aretousa, but he serenades her nightly and she falls in love with him. They suffer many ordeals and setbacks in their attempts to be united, but their faith and virtue triumph and they are eventually married. Description, dialogue and action are cleverly interspersed to create a finely woven narrative:

Have you heard of the sad news Aretousa?
Your father has exiled me
He has given me only four more days to stay,
And after that I must go far away abroad alone
And how am I going to be separated from you,
And how am I going to live without you into such exile?[38]

It was largely under the influence of *Erotokritos* that the unique Cretan form of the mantinada became popular. This is a rhyming couplet of fifteen syllables, complete in itself, like an epigram. It played (and still plays) an important part in Cretan cultural life. Often set to music, mantinades cover every aspect of life from politics to love, from betrayal to heroism. What these poems mean for a Cretan is perhaps best expressed in a mantinada: *"A Cretan does not say in plain words what he feels,/With mantinades he weeps or with laughter he peals!"*[39]

Music

The developments in Cretan music during Venetian rule have been less examined but, in both ecclesiastical and secular music, the period seems to have been very rich. The fall of Constantinople brought many exiles to Crete, including many cantors who brought with them the Byzantine chant used in the services of the Orthodox Church. In time, a specifically Cretan style of chant was developed. It was noted for its harmony and, according to some sources, a degree of polyphony influenced by Italian music. A large number of cantors of the highest quality are known to have lived in the main centres of Crete. Upon the capture of Crete by the Ottomans, many of these fled to the Ionian Islands, where the Cretan Chant was still used in churches until recently.

Frangiskos (Francisco) Leontaritis, who lived from 1518 to 1572, is considered to be the father of Greek classical music. He studied in Italy under the great composers of polyphonic music, Palestrina and Lassus, and sang in the choir of Saint Mark's Basilica, Venice. He then moved to Munich, where he was hired as a member of Duke Albrecht's chapel choir. He had already established his name as a composer and singer when he returned to Crete in 1568. He is known to have composed three masses and twenty-one motets, madrigals and other shorter pieces, some of which survive. His music was popular until the seventeenth century, but was then forgotten until its rediscovery in 1980. Several pieces by him can be found on the internet (I am listening to some of them as I write), and all of them demonstrate the subtlety and beauty of his music.

Art and Architecture

Perhaps the most dramatic example of the Cretan Renaissance can be found in painting, specifically icon painting. From the second half of the fourteenth century, émigrés from the Byzantine Empire brought with them the latest styles from Constantinople. A little later, in the early fifteenth century, the influence of the Italian Renaissance began to be felt. Over time, this combination led to a distinctive Cretan School of icon painting. While not straying too far from the stylised and formal Byzantine style, in which beauty was secondary to theological truth, the Cretan School added a richness of colour, and elements of realism and perspective. It could be said that there was a blurring of the distinction between an icon and a painting as the Venetian nobility began to commission religious paintings to display in their houses. The quality of the artists in Crete was such that their icons were disseminated throughout the Mediterranean and northern Europe, and were important exports. By the late sixteenth century, there were over 200 painters in Candia alone, organised into guilds. Most of them seem to have been equally comfortable painting in an Italian or a Byzantine style, or even a combination. It must be admitted that not all the icon painters of Crete were painstaking. There is a record of a transaction in 1499 by which 700 icons of the Virgin Mary were ordered, 500 in the western style and 200 in the Byzantine. The order was to be carried out by just two painters in forty-five days, so it is doubtful that the finished work was of the highest quality.

Among the many painters of the period, five stand out. Angelos Akotantos, who died in 1457, was a conservative who painted in the strictly Byzantine style, and was a major influence on the later Cretan iconographers. He is believed to have been the first to sign his name on the icons he painted, with the phrase "by the hand of Angelos". Andreas Ritzos, active from 1451 to 1492, was a fine example of those painters who were equally skilled in both the Byzantine and Italian styles. Theophanes Sterlitzas-Bathas concentrated mainly on frescoes. So great was his fame that he was commissioned to paint churches in other parts of Greece, including monasteries in Meteora and Mount Athos. As a result, he spread Cretan artistic techniques and style widely.

Painting in the second half of the sixteenth century, Michael Damaskinos was perhaps the greatest of the Cretan School. After a long
stay in Venice, he returned to Crete, where his work epitomised the
blending of Italian and Byzantine styles, showing the influence of
Tintoretto and Veronese while retaining many of the Byzantine traditions. He almost exclusively painted portable icons, many of which
still exist, although he was in such demand that he was commissioned
at one point to paint the frescoes in San Giorgio dei Greci in Venice.[40]
Six of his icons can be seen in the Museum of Saint Katherine, near
Aghios Minas Cathedral, Iraklion.

Domenikos Theotokopoulos, born in 1541 in or near Iraklion, was
the son of a merchant and tax collector. He trained as an icon painter
at the Saint Katherine of Sinai monastery in Candia, possibly under
Damaskinos, and by the age of twenty-two he was already a master in
the guild. In 1566, he sold a panel of *The Passion of Christ* for seventy
ducats, at that time the going rate for a Titian or Tintoretto. Thus, by
the time he left Crete in 1569, he was already established as a highly
talented icon painter. Moving first to Venice and Rome and then to
Toledo in Spain, he became a leading figure in the Spanish Renaissance under his nickname El Greco (The Greek). Although he moved
a long way away from the techniques of icon painting, many aspects of
his unique style are clearly related to his early training. The theological content of his work; the elongated, other-worldly figures; the use
of light which seems to come from inside and transfigures the body
– they all hark back to some of the fundamental aspects of Orthodox
iconography.

A contemporary of Theotokopoulos, Georgios Klontzas, developed
a highly original and inventive style. His icons feature multiple figures
and scenes in miniature, which combine to form a larger narrative on a
particular theme. The detailed work is extraordinary, while the overall
impression is one of harmony. Like the great paintings of Brueghel, his
work elicits deep contemplation even by non-experts. This miniaturist
technique was to have a great influence on later iconographers.

In the field of architecture also, the period of Venetian rule saw major
achievements. In the main cities of Venetian Crete, there were numerous fine buildings based on Venetian architectural styles. In 1632, it
is said that there were ninety-seven palaces in Chania alone, as well

as thirty Orthodox and fifteen Latin churches. Unfortunately, many of the buildings no longer exist, but the Church of Saint Francis in Chania is now the Archaeological Museum. In Rethymnon, the clock tower, the well-known Loggia, a fountain and part of the Porta Guora (Great Gate) are still visible. The Loggia in Candia, sometimes called the most beautiful building in Crete, was restored in the twentieth century and is still in use by the city administration. It was built from 1626 to 1628 by the proveditore Morosini, who also gave his name to the aqueduct and famous fountain at the centre of the city. Interestingly, even some of the Orthodox monasteries built at this time show the influence of Renaissance architecture, including Arkadi and the outstanding Aghia Triada (Holy Trinity) monastery on the Akrotiri peninsula.

11

The Cretan War

1645 to 1669

Background

As we have seen, the late sixteenth and early seventeenth centuries were the high point of Cretan culture in the arts, literature and education. A contributing factor to this Cretan Renaissance and to the prosperity of the island was the long period of peace between 1573 and 1645, perhaps the longest in the recorded history of the eastern Mediterranean. There were several reasons for the peace. On the one hand, the Ottoman Empire was severely weakened by the destruction of its fleet at the Battle of Lepanto, leading to a political crisis and economic and military decline. This, together with a continuing war with Persia, gave the Ottomans little incentive to expand further. On the other hand, Venice itself was going through a phase of economic weakness, and its military capability was substantially reduced. Moreover, in spite of Christian Europe's victory at Lepanto, the bitter conflicts that resulted from the deep religious divides of the Reformation led to a general war-weariness among the Christian nations. This, while not stopping the interminable fighting in northern Europe, resulted in an unwillingness to get involved any further in the eastern Mediterranean. As far as Crete was concerned, the peace treaty signed between Venice and the Ottoman Empire after the fall of Cyprus was the beginning of about seventy years of uneasy but peaceful coexistence.

However, the Ottomans had not forgotten Crete. It was now the last bastion of the Christian East, determining the boundary between two very different cultures. In the early seventeenth century, various events occurred which caused the Ottomans to look again for an excuse to attack Crete. A dynamic and innovative new sultan, Murat IV, who reigned from 1623 to 1640, reorganised the army and carried out substantial economic reforms, bringing stability to the empire. In 1639, the long war with Persia was brought to an end, leaving the sultan to turn his attention westward, encouraged by the increasing strength of a hawk faction in the government which maintained that, since Crete had been part of the Byzantine Empire, it rightfully belonged now to the Ottoman Empire. Moreover, the continuing Thirty Years' War in central Europe meant that there was little likelihood of help for Venice from other countries.

At the same time, the economy of Venice was deteriorating further, with the result that the garrison for the whole island consisted of only 4,000 mercenaries. Even these were often unpaid and forced to moonlight as barbers, tailors and cobblers, clearly not at full battle readiness. The continuing reluctance of the authorities in Venice to arm the Greeks meant that a potential 14,000-strong civil guard was virtually useless. As for the defences, these were in a poor state and deteriorating, but little was done to improve them. This was largely for financial reasons, but the Ottomans also carried out a highly successful diplomatic bluff which convinced the Venetians that any further aggression would be directed against Apulia in southern Italy rather than Crete.

At this time, the Order of the Knights of Saint John, now settled in Malta, was engaged in protecting Christian ships from Barbary pirates. The knights often exceeded this remit by becoming pirates themselves, attacking and plundering Muslim ships. As early as 1639, a proveditore generale warned that such attacks could give the sultan just the excuse he needed for an attack on Crete; when the Venetians captured a pirate ship near Livorno, they freed all the enslaved Muslims as a gesture of goodwill to Constantinople. Nevertheless, in 1644, near the coast of Crete, Maltese pirates captured an Ottoman ship carrying pilgrims to Mecca. It is not clear what happened next. The sultan claimed that the pirates landed at Chania, where they gave some of their prisoners and loot to the Venetian commander, while the Venetians maintained that they had refused entry to any harbour for the Maltese, who merely landed on the unprotected south coast for water and supplies. Whatever the truth, the outraged Ottomans saw the excuse they needed, accusing Venice of collusion in the raid. In spite of several diplomatic negotiations, the Ottoman Empire now had a pretext for war. One hundred warships and 350 transports carrying 50,000 men, under the command of the sultan's son-in-law, set out from Constantinople in the early summer of 1645. The fleet anchored at Navarino in the Peloponnese, under the pretext that it was heading for Malta. Again, the bluff succeeded, and the Venetians were largely unprepared when the fleet actually landed at the western end of the Bay of Chania. There was no resistance, and the army moved quickly towards Chania, supported by the fleet, which set up a continuous bombardment from the sea.

Early Success

The garrison at Chania was small, with only 800 mercenaries and 1,000 armed civil guards, mostly Greek. There were attempts to send help, but these were unsuccessful. A diversionary attack by Cretans from Selino and Sfakia, traditional centres of rebellion, was crushed, while Venice was unsuccessful in its attempt to mobilise a large force from Mani on the Peloponnese. The main Venetian fleet in the Ionian Sea was not strong enough to attempt an attack on the large Ottoman fleet, so the people of Chania were left to their own resources. Nevertheless, their morale was strong and they were determined in their resistance. There are many reports of the heroism of the defenders, including monks, while the women not only kept the soldiers fed and supplied with arms but also fought alongside them on the battlements. The city held out till August but, with the walls badly damaged, defeat was only a matter of time. A final attack led to the loss of 600 defenders, killed and wounded, and the city surrendered almost exactly two months after the siege began. The few remaining soldiers and most of the civilians evacuated the city and fled to the Souda Bay fortress. Those who remained were sold into slavery, while the victorious Ottomans went on a rampage, looting monasteries and churches.

Soon the Ottoman army had subjugated most of western Crete, although they bypassed the Souda Bay fortress, since it was isolated and no longer of strategic significance. Reinforced by a further 40,000

Europa and the Bull.

An unusually tender view of the Minotaur, depicted as a baby with his mother, Pasiphäe.

A section of the Great Gortyn Law Code.

Adoration of the Magi by Michael Damaskinos. A good example of the sixteenth-century Cretan School, showing the fusion of traditional iconography and Cretan Renaissance painting. In icons, only non-saints are depicted facing the viewer. It is therefore believed that the man in the centre looking straight at us is a self-portrait of the artist.

Saint Andrew by El Greco (Doménikos Theotokópoulos). This painting illustrates the artist's unique style, which, to a great extent, derives from his early work as a master iconographer in Crete.

A twelfth-century illustration showing the use of Greek Fire by the Byzantines in the ninth century.

The çinkeli, or gaunche, used to execute rebels.

The Venetian Loggia in Candia (Iraklion), built from 1626 to 1628 by the proveditore Morosini. It is sometimes called the most beautiful building in Crete.

The Morosini Fountain in Candia (Iraklion), built in 1628.

Mehmet Ali, the Egyptian ruler of Crete from 1830 to 1840.

The Arcadian Holocaust by Giuseppe Lorenzo Gatteri, depicting the battle between Ottoman forces and rebels at Arkadi monastery on 8th November 1866.

The flag of the autonomous Cretan state, which existed from 1898 to 1913. The white cross and blue quadrisections represent the Christian population, while the white star on a red field represents the Muslim population.

The flag of Georgos Daskalakis during the 1866 rebellion. It was regarded by many Cretan Christians as a better choice of flag for autonomous Crete. The large initials stand for the words "Crete, Union, Freedom or Death". The inscription in the middle stands for "Jesus Christ Conquers."

Eleftherios Venizelos, an eminent leader of the Greek
national liberation movement, in 1903.

Major-General Bernard Freyberg commanding troops to defend Crete against German invasion in 1941.

SOLDIERS

OF THE

ROYAL BRITISH ARMY, NAVY, AIR FORCE!

There are MANY OF YOU STILL HIDING in the mountains, valleys and villages.

You have to PRESENT yourself AT ONCE TO THE GERMAN TROOPS.

Every OPPOSITION will be completely USELESS!

Every ATTEMPT TO FLEE will be in VAIN.

The COMMING WINTER will force you to leave the mountains.

Only soldiers, who PRESENT themselves AT ONCE, will be sure of a HONOURABLE AND SOLDIERLIKE CAPTIVITY OF WAR. On the contrary who is met in civil-clothes will be treated as a spy.

THE COMMANDER OF KRETA

A German warning to evaders in 1941. A surprising number ignored the warning and escaped to Egypt.

The guerrilla leader Manolis Bandouvas, a charismatic but sometimes erratic leader.

A group of andartes. Resistance to the German occupation was heroic and bitter. Reprisals were ruthless.

The kri-kri, or Cretan wild goat. The species is classified as vulnerable, but the population has recovered slightly in recent years.

The griffon vulture, a species brought back from the brink of extinction – a rare success story in conservation.

troops that landed at Souda Bay in July, the invaders now turned their attention to Rethymnon. The army moved east, plundering and burning villages as they went, although their activities were a little curtailed by orders forbidding acts of violence against Greek Cretans and their property. The aim was to try to get the support of the Cretan peasantry against the Venetians, and this policy met with some success. The invaders also attempted to woo the Orthodox Cretans by offering freedom of religion and, although the restrictions imposed by the Venetians had largely disappeared, this too struck a chord. The Ottomans did in fact appoint a monk from the Arkadi monastery as the Orthodox **metropolitan** bishop of Crete, the first such appointment since the thirteenth century.

By late September 1646, the tiny garrison of Rethymnon was under siege. The commander arranged for a large number of women and children to escape to Candia, but they were refused entry to the city, partly due to fear of the plague, which was again raging. The refugees wandered the countryside unable to find shelter and, starving and disillusioned, many sought the protection of the invading army, giving further propaganda points to the Ottoman government. The "stick and carrot" policy was also apparent in the siege of the city itself. The attackers tried to intimidate the inhabitants by firing arrows with leaflets attached over the walls. The leaflets promised good treatment to the inhabitants if they surrendered, but threatened savage reprisals if they fought on. In spite of a spirited defence and an attempt at help from a small French fleet off the coast, the starving and dispirited citizens surrendered in November. Most of the survivors fled to Candia or the Ionian Islands.

The Siege of Candia

The Ottoman strategy was now to subdue the rest of the island, isolating the formidable fortress of Candia which it could then attack in force. In the spring of 1647, reinforcements arrived to attack and plunder the villages of central and eastern Crete. Venetian forces landed at Mylopotamos and Mirabello to try to hold up the Ottoman advance but, after a few successes, the army was defeated. By the spring of 1648, almost all the Cretan countryside was in the hands of the invaders, with only the fortresses of Gramvousa, Souda and Spinalonga being held by Venetian garrisons. Candia was completely cut off by land, although it still had limited access to the sea. It was time to begin the siege. The sultan had predicted that the conquest of Crete would be easy, and up to this point things had gone smoothly for the Ottoman army. However, the attack on Candia was to prove a very different affair. Over the years, the fortifications had been extended and strengthened to such an extent that the city was often referred to as To Kastro (The Castle).

The Ottomans began a long process of intimidation with daily attacks and continuous bombardment from their cannons. They cut off the main water supply by destroying the aqueduct from the outlying springs. In spite of all this, the defences held and, unbelievably, there was pretty much a stalemate for sixteen years, from 1650 to 1666. Attacks and counter-attacks seemed to resolve nothing, and the siege dragged on and on. If the Ottomans had been able to send massive reinforcements and gain control of the harbour at Candia, no doubt there would have been a different result. However, ongoing wars in the north Balkans kept many of their troops tied up, while the main Venetian fleet still had superiority in the Aegean. Under the command of the talented admiral Francisco Morosini, the Venetian fleet closely monitored the Ottoman fleet and inflicted severe damage on it in 1658. As Europe began to take an interest in the Cretan War, help began to trickle in to Candia, with varying results. In 1650 and 1651, Spain sent a consignment of much-needed grain and eight warships, but a 4,000-strong French force which attempted to recapture Chania in 1660 was defeated and destroyed. A force sent from Venice under a French general also seems to have had little impact.

In 1664, the Balkan wars were ended by a treaty with the Holy Roman Emperor, releasing substantial Turkish forces to be sent to Crete. The sultan decided it was time to bring the war to a conclusion. The current commander-in-chief was recalled to Constantinople and beheaded (the invariable fate of failed military figures in the Ottoman Empire). He was replaced by the experienced and courageous Grand Vizier Köprülü Fazıl Ahmed Pasha. At the same time, the Venetians appointed Admiral Morosini as the new commander of Candia, in an attempt to bring new inspiration to the defence. In the spring of 1667, Köprülü landed with sixty-four galleys and 40,000 soldiers from the Peloponnese, and the siege became even more violent. The aforementioned poem *The Cretan War* describes the horrors of the continuous bombardment in the later stages of the siege:

> *Stones rain down on me, and cannonballs like hail,*
> *Thunder and lightning leave nothing unscathed.*
> *Destroyed my churches, and towers all felled,*
> *As if a whirlwind would snatch me up.*
> *No man went to sleep in his home,*
> *No man could walk the streets without fear.*
> *I am sorely grieved, for I, Candia, am adorned*
> *With the bodies of dead Christians and am bloodstained;*
> *Mute bodies lying in pieces,*
> *Heads, hands and legs scattered all over.*[1]

There were even stories of cannibalism among the starving defenders. When one of the commanders deserted and revealed weaknesses in the fortifications to the Ottomans, it seemed that the end must come soon. More desertions followed, mainly from the galleys, encouraged by bribes from the Ottomans; it is recorded that Köprülü spent 700,000 gold pieces for this purpose. Unpaid mercenaries, quarrelling officers, poor food and disease combined to put morale at its lowest level ever, in spite of all Morosini's efforts.

And yet, still they held. In November 1668, 600 French mercenaries arrived, but were wiped out a month later. Finally, between early February and late June 1669, it seemed that things might be looking up. A total of nearly 17,000 reinforcements arrived, having been sent by the Holy Roman Emperor, Venice, France and various European princes and dukes. The fundamental weakness of many military coalitions came to light when there were continuous disagreements between the foreign commanders over tactics. As a result, such attacks against the Ottomans as occurred led to alarming losses. Eventually, the French commander withdrew his remaining forces from the island, and very little hope remained.

Morosini negotiated for the surrender of the city, and a treaty was signed on 16th September 1669. Under the circumstances, the treaty was fairer than many others at the time, since the victors were conscious of the fact that they would now have to rule the island. Nevertheless, the victory celebrations were spectacular, as described by an eyewitness:

> That night, there were so many thousands of torches and lanterns among the soldiers who lined all the walls of the city, so much pitch and naphtha, tar, oil and wax burning in the arsenals, so many candles, that there was not a single spot on the walls where a light was not burning. Candia glowed like a torch in the night.[2]

The Christian population of Candia were allowed to leave the town unharmed and with whatever possessions they could carry. Morosini led them to the island of Dia, and from there to the Ionian Islands. It is believed that only two priests, three Jews and a few soldiers who converted to Islam remained in Candia. The losses suffered by the Ottomans during the twenty-year siege were appalling. According to their own records, 137,116 Ottoman troops were killed, including 25,000 janissaries (crack troops) and 215 senior officers.

The treaty left the coastal fortresses of Gramvousa, Souda and Spinalonga in Venetian hands, giving Venice protection for its commercial shipping and possible bases for a future return. This forlorn hope also had important ramifications for historians. Morosini included in the treaty a provision that he could take all state archives with him to Italy. Thus, if Venice ever recovered her colony, the archives could be used to quickly re-establish a new administration. In the event, five ships were fully loaded with documents, and although only three reached Venice, the archives have been of enormous value to historians.

12

Ottoman Rule I

1669 to 1821

Administration

Under Ottoman rule, Crete – called Girit in Turkish – was established as an eyalet (province), the primary administrative unit of the
Ottoman Empire. The four territoria of Venetian rule were quickly
reorganised into three districts called pashaliks: Chania, Rethymnon
and Candia (which now included Siteia). Each pashalik was run by a
pasha appointed by the sultan in Constantinople, with the pashas of
Chania and Rethymnon being subordinate to the pasha of Candia.
Candia, known within the empire by its Turkish name Kandiye,
remained the main administrative centre for the island, and its pasha
was the commander-in-chief of Crete and head of the armed forces.
The district of Sfakia was somewhat exceptional. It was first granted
as a fief to the victorious commander of the Ottoman forces, but he
donated it as a vakif (pious endowment) to the holy cities of Mecca
and Medina. This was not good news for the Sfakians as, in addition
to the usual heavy taxes, as described below, the district had to pay a
substantial annual "holy tribute". It was not until 1760 that some relief
from this burden was given.

The pasha of Candia was the supreme civil and military ruler of the
island, being responsible for the collection of revenue and the training
and equipping of the armed forces. Each of the three pashas was assisted
by a divan (council) which met weekly or in emergency session. The
membership of the divan varied over time, but typically it consisted
of the pasha as chairman, the **qadi** (magistrate), the **mufti** (expounder

of Islamic law), the leader of the janissaries and the commander of the military. There was also a secretary, a local Cretan speaker who would communicate between the authorities and the community. At local level, each district had a leader, who represented the Christian community before the Ottoman authorities in matters regarding taxes. They would negotiate the amount and allocation of taxes, and organise their collection and delivery to the authorities or tax farmers. On occasions during the period, but not invariably, a leader would be elected proedros (chairman) of the area.

The power of the pasha often existed on paper only, and his authority could be undermined by the janissaries, an elite force of infantry, originally created to form the sultan's household troops and bodyguards. After the ending of hostilities, the military administration was largely in their hands. They were initially composed of prisoners of war and Christian boys who had been kidnapped and brought up as Muslims, and were characterised by strict discipline and fierce loyalty to the sultan. Over the years, the janissaries grew extremely powerful and wealthy, many becoming senior officers or high state officials, and by the end of the seventeenth century more and more Muslim recruits were joining the force, hoping for rapid advancement. In Crete there were two divisions of janissaries: the imperial janissaries from Constantinople, and the local janissaries recruited from Cretan Muslims – although over time even the imperial janissaries came to be made up largely of local recruits. In Candia, there were five battalions of imperial janissaries, each of 5,000 men, and twenty-eight barracks of local janissaries. A similar force was stationed in Chania to control the west of the island.

Although none of the janissaries in the empire were exactly pussycats, those in Crete seem to have been notorious for their savagery. Their power grew to such an extent that they became a law unto themselves, and were even able to ignore or contravene the sultan's orders. In 1690, the pasha of Chania attempted to curb their powers. He was promptly killed and his body thrown to the dogs. An imperial decree of 1762 sets out the problem:

The brigands and malefactors in the employment of the guard of this fortress, cheating and deceiving their superiors and neglecting their duties, have found the opportunity to openly devote themselves to robbery and crime and, in drunkenness, they tour the neighbourhoods bearing their weapons, and insult the honour of the inhabitants and attack families and their children.[1]

A folk song of the period has a janissary telling a Christian:

This one, you will give me,
That one, I will take,
And this one here, you'll make me a gift of.[2]

In theory, the imperial janissaries were paid by central government, while the others were paid from local taxes. As time went on, payment from the **Sublime Porte** (Constantinople) became more and more irregular and the janissaries sought other sources of income as landowners, tax collectors, tax farmers or even artisans. Thus, they gradually became integrated into the economic life of the island, to the detriment of their military duties. In 1812, there was finally a concerted attempt by the Sublime Porte to crush the janissaries in Crete. Osman Pasha was sent to Crete, and he immediately enlisted Christian warriors from Sfakia to help him implement the policy. He hanged large numbers of janissaries – 500 on a single day, according to some reports. The local Muslims were outraged by this and began the rumour that Osman was a secret Christian, called Yannis. Meanwhile, the Christian Cretans were delighted by Osman's ruthless attack on the janissaries. Osman's anti-janissary policy was continued by his successor, and the power of the janissaries was finally curtailed. In 1826, after a failed janissary revolt against the sultan and the execution of over 6,000 of the rebels, the corps was disbanded by the sultan, and large numbers of the janissaries were imprisoned or exiled. Many, however, were admitted into the new Ottoman army, the Victorious Troops of Muhammad.

The criminal justice system and all cases involving Muslims were based firmly on Islamic law, although sultanic law (qanun) and local customary law were also taken into account by the qadis. The chief qadi was appointed by the Ottoman state and had wide judicial powers. His salary was paid almost entirely from fines. Court procedures were generally simple, based on sworn evidence given by all the participants under binding oaths. First, the accuser was asked to produce two reliable witnesses. If this was done, the trial ended there and the accuser won. If the accuser could not produce witnesses, the defendant was asked to take an oath, which led to acquittal. Oaths were sworn on the Gospel by Christians, on the Qur'an by Muslims and on the Torah by Jews. However, according to Islamic sharia law, greater weight was given to Muslim testimony as non-Muslims were considered inferior in law and, in any case, could not testify against Muslims. This imbalance can be illustrated by the story of Saint Myron, the New Martyr of Crete, a well-known Orthodox saint. Myron was a twenty-year-old tailor and a devout Christian. A group of local Muslims took a dislike to him and began a campaign of harassment designed to provoke him into retaliation, which would bring about immediate punishment. He was of a peaceful disposition and did not react, whereupon they bribed a twelve-year-old Muslim boy to accuse him of sexual molestation, for which the sentence was death. The testimony was taken at face value. Myron was found guilty, and, after unsuccessful attempts to persuade him to convert, he was hanged. Only a few days later, his accuser confessed to perjury and was also punished under Islamic law, although the sentence is not known.

Civil cases in which all participants were Christians or Jews could be dealt with by their own communities, although this did not always happen. These cases were mainly in the realm of family law or disputes between members of the same faith. At various times, there appears to have been some flexibility in jurisdiction between the qadis and the Christian courts administered by the Church authorities. On the one hand, the pashas allowed some extension of ecclesiastical courts into areas outside their strict remit, where this was convenient to the authorities and did not involve Muslims. On the other hand, it was not unknown for a Christian to use the qadi, if he felt that it would be to his advantage. This was particularly so in divorce cases, where Islamic law was much more lenient than Orthodox ecclesiastical law, for example in its acceptance of divorce by mutual consent. The Church was generally totally opposed to such actions, but there is evidence that a more pragmatic approach was occasionally taken. An item in an eighteenth-century collection of canon law warns bishops "to be mild and fair or else run the risk of estranging their flocks, and handing them over to the Muslim unbelievers".[3] In fact, bishops and priests themselves did not hesitate to use the services of the qadi court when they felt that this served their interests.

As in all parts of the Ottoman Empire, the post of dragoman (interpreter of the Sublime Porte) was of immense importance at various times during the period of Ottoman rule. The dragoman was a local who could speak Turkish, and who was nominated for office by the qadi or pasha and appointed by the sultan. His office was in Candia and he was assisted by three Christian secretaries and representatives in Chania and Rethymnon. As the official interpreter, he had considerable influence, and worked closely with the finance director on matters of taxation and employment. Although they were Christian Cretans, the first loyalty of the dragomans was to the Ottoman state, but all too often their loyalty was primarily to themselves. Often oppressive and harsh to their fellow Christians, they were generally disliked by the Cretans, and their irregularities were even commented on in Ottoman state documents.

Almost as soon as the Ottoman army set foot on Cretan soil, tax collection began. The first tax census was carried out in 1650, even before the capture of Candia. Although a tiny amount of land was left in private hands, most of it was nationalised as belonging to Allah and assigned to his representative on earth, the sultan. Certain estates were nominated as religious dependencies, the revenues from which went towards the upkeep of mosques, public works and charitable institutions. The rest of the island was divided into smaller units called timars. These were allotted to Muslims: the larger estates to **aghas** (high-ranking military officials) for service in the Cretan War, and smaller properties to military officers in charge of security. For example, as a reward for his victory at Candia, Köprülü was granted all the land surrounding the city that fell within the range of a cannonball fired from the walls. Within the timars, smaller estates were given to ordinary Muslim subjects. The timar holders did not actually own the land, but had a non-hereditary right to part of the produce in exchange for their administrative or military service to the empire. They also had a right to part of the tax income of the villages within their timar, as well as fines imposed by the courts. The workers, mostly Christians, had a hereditary right to work the land. Legally, they also had a hereditary right to the land itself, through grant of the sultan, who had ownership of the land. They paid no rent but were heavily taxed. From a legal point of view, they were not serfs.

The timar system was already in decline by the time Candia fell and, within a relatively short time, the system was fundamentally changed. The 1670 census and resulting law code introduced, for the first time in Ottoman practice, the concept of private ownership of land. Although the system of land ownership became extremely complicated, in essence the timar holders now became landlords and the agrotes (farmers) tenants. A system of tax farming was introduced, in which the right to collect taxes was auctioned, often to the landlords. Because of the high level of taxation, many of the agrotes were impoverished, their land being seized by the local gentry and converted into private property, leading to a gradual concentration of land into the hands of a few. Thus, the whole system became corrupted, and the resulting erosion of state control led to yet another attempt to regularise the positions of landlords and tenants. Now, and for most of the remainder of Ottoman rule, the landlords provided the land and the agrotes the labour. The landlord was obliged to provide shelter to the labourer and his family, and a small area of land for his use. In return, after production costs and taxes, a portion of the produce was given to the landholder.

Although everyone – Muslims included – had to pay land taxes, the burden on Christians was much heavier, and seems to have been the harshest of any in Greek lands ruled by the Ottoman Empire. Their basic land tax amounted to 20% of the land's revenue, payable annually. This was double the tax of other Greek regions. There was no escape because, from 1685, to prevent people trying to avoid taxation by not cultivating their land, uncultivated farms had to pay a special tax based on the production of previous years. The few Christians who managed to keep their land had to pay a special additional tax. Most hated of all taxes was a poll tax on all Christian Cretans, who were divided into three categories – wealthy, moderate income and poor – and taxed accordingly. On top of all this, there were heavy taxes imposed on the newly re-established Orthodox Church, which in most cases were recouped by the Church from the peasantry.

Heavy as the tax burden was, the story did not stop there. Officials were known to overestimate grain production by as much as three times, by calculating the potential yield rather than measuring the actual harvest. Meanwhile, landowners and officials were able to devise local taxes to extort products of all kinds from the peasants. The most extraordinary was probably the obligation of peasants in the Chania and Rethymnon districts to transport 6,300 loads of snow from the mountains to the towns for producing cold drinks for the pashas and aghas. There were strict orders from the Sublime Porte against such tax abuse, and several offending pashas were in fact beheaded. However, in many other cases, the janissaries simply refused to carry out the orders, and the abuse went unchecked. A more serious development occurred in 1720, when officials were allowed to bid for tax collection rights for life. The vast majority of these contracts were gained by janissaries, and it wasn't long before the tax farming contracts became hereditary. This led to even more ruthless exploitation and vast wealth for the collectors. In turn, this gave them the economic power and strength to largely ignore the central government, a situation that was to have severe consequences.

In spite of heavy taxation and the irregular behaviour of the janissaries, Ottoman rule was not all bad news for the Christian peasantry. The restoration of the Orthodox hierarchy was a major change from Venetian rule, but perhaps a more dramatic improvement for the average Christian was the fact that the Ottomans did not conscript the islanders to work on the galleys, in contrast to many other Greek areas of the empire. While the war with Venice continued, this decision was probably made for tactical and political reasons, as predicted by one of the Venetian generals:

> I think the enemy will behave more prudently [than us]. In order to win the trust of the kingdom's population, he will try not to frighten them, and will ask only that they remain in their village to attend to their fields and their vines for their own account. By enticing them in this way, and with this false pretence of liberty and munificence, the enemy will gain their devotion.[4]

Once the war was over, the motive became more economic. The vastness of the empire gave the Ottomans a virtually unlimited pool of recruits for the galleys, and it made sense to reserve the fertile island of Crete for agricultural production and to ensure it had a thriving rural population.

War and Revolt

Resistance to Ottoman rule began almost immediately. Young men fled to three Venetian fortresses, from which they carried out guerrilla raids. Not for the first (or last) time, many priests could be found among the resistance. The motives for the resistance were often more personal than political – revenge for a particular injustice against a family, for example. Nevertheless, as long as the fortresses existed, there was always the hope that Venice would one day reconquer the island. The guerrillas were known as hains (treacherous ones) by the Ottomans, and they were a thorn in the side of the authorities for many years. Meanwhile, ships from the Venetian fortresses continually harassed Ottoman merchant shipping. The three islands were centres of espionage, especially the fortress at Souda. Several of the Christian secretaries to the divan are believed to have been spies, and there is circumstantial evidence that even some high-ranking Muslims, including aghas, were giving information to Venice, although it is not clear whether this was deliberate or inadvertent.

The Venetian hopes of reconquering Crete lasted fewer than fifty years. During the war between the Holy League and the Ottoman Empire of 1684 to 1699, a Venetian force landed on Crete in 1692, aiming to stir up rebellion and recapture Chania. After forty days, the expeditionary force retreated with many losses, while the fortress at Gramvousa was surrendered to the Ottomans by its commander for a large sum of money. Souda and Spinalonga survived for another twenty-two years as refuges for Cretan families, with about 600 people on each island. During another war from 1715 to 1718, both were finally captured and the inhabitants sold into slavery or enlisted as oarsmen in the Ottoman galleys. Crete, described by one proveditore generale as "the most beautiful crown to adorn the head of the Most Serene Republic", was now totally in Ottoman hands.[5]

From then on, the hains operated from the mountains and remote monasteries, and often acted more as brigands than resistance fighters, as much a danger to the Christian villagers as to the authorities.[6] This led to requests by the villagers for protection and, for a short time, armatoloi (armed Christian militias) were appointed for the purpose. These did something to curb the activities of the hains, but the government was wary of arming Christians, and preferred instead to organise bands of Muslims to hunt them down. Another tactic was to intimidate the villagers into betraying any hains in the area. Christian provincial leaders were held personally responsible for any Muslim taken hostage or for any damage to Muslim property. In some areas, villagers were obliged to act as lookouts or sentries, and any actual help to the hains (or to pirates) was severely punished.

Any hain caught alive suffered torture and a particularly horrible form of execution called the çinkeli. This was a large wooden frame with pulleys at the top and an array of meathooks half way down. The prisoner was hauled up to the top on ropes, which were then released, allowing him to fall onto the hooks below. The rare "lucky" ones would be killed instantly, but usually injuries, not immediately lethal, would condemn the victim to a long and painful death. A French traveller in 1700 described one such execution during which a prisoner, although in great pain, was quietly smoking a pipe.[7] Spasmodic resistance largely died out within a few years, until the major rebellion of Daskalogiannis in 1770.

The authorities had little control over Sfakia, due to its remoteness and difficult terrain. The Sfakians paid their taxes, but were otherwise left largely to their own devices. With access to the sea, a small fleet was established which traded throughout the Mediterranean and even as far as the Black Sea. Not only did this trade bring prosperity to the region, it also brought important contact with the outside world, particularly Russia. Ioannis Vlachos, known as Daskalogiannis (Teacher Ioannis), was a wealthy shipowner and a leading figure in Sfakia. In 1769, Catherine the Great of Russia sent a fleet under her envoy Count Theodore Orloff to the Peloponnese to incite the Greeks into rebellion. Although the rebellion was quashed immediately, Daskalogiannis met Orloff and conceived the idea of a similar liberation movement in Crete, backed by the Russians. He set about fortifying strategic positions in Sfakia and building up stocks of armaments. His plans were not supported by all the locals, and even his uncle, a priest, had severe reservations. A contemporary poem describes his objections:

> *And then the priest shook his head,*
> *Deep in thought, his soul was full of consternation,*
> *"Teacher Yannis," he said, "Come to your senses,*
> *You'll drag the whole of Crete into dire distress,*
> *And you'll bring ruin on Sfakia,*
> *And all the Pashas and the Turk will descend on us,*
> *By the time the ships of Muscovy reach us*
> *The Sfakians won't have a home in Sfakia to rest".*[8]

Nevertheless, the revolt began. The Sfakians refused to pay their poll tax, and drove out the tax collector. A well-armed and well-supplied rebel army of 2,000, together with twenty priests, then moved down from the mountains on Easter Sunday 1770. They spent the next week preparing for war and continuing the Easter celebrations.[9] They then attacked Apokoronas and Aghios Vasileios, forcing the Muslim population to seek refuge in Chania. The Ottoman response was immediate. A force of 15,000 was rushed to Sfakia, causing the leaders to send boatloads of women and children to safety in the southern Peloponnese and the island of Kythera. A major battle on the plateau of Krapi forced the Sfakians to retreat into the high mountains. From there, they successfully defended themselves throughout the summer of 1770, but at a terrible price to the more accessible areas. Villages were destroyed, flocks scattered and many of the inhabitants captured and sent to the slave markets of Candia, among them Daskalogiannis' uncle, wife and daughters. When it became apparent that no help would be forthcoming from the Russians, the situation became hopeless. The pasha offered amnesty to the rebels if they surrendered, which they did, accepting the harsh conditions imposed.

The terms included the requirement that all poll tax be paid, all weapons and stores surrendered and the ringleaders subjected to retribution. There were also tight restrictions on shipping and trade, and on the repair and building of churches. A further tithe to the sultan was to be paid, and all Christian religious ceremonies and the ringing of church bells were forbidden. Daskalogiannis and the leaders gave themselves up, but, in spite of the amnesty, the teacher was flayed to death. The other leaders spent three years in prison, but then escaped back to Sfakia. This rebellion was the first major uprising against the Ottomans in Crete, but also the last for about fifty years.

The Orthodox Church

Even before the Cretan War was over, the Ottomans, as was their normal practice, had begun to re-establish the Orthodox Church hierarchy on the island. Under the millet system of justice, "subordinate" religious groups such as Orthodox Christians, Jews or Armenian Christians were each recognised as a separate community and largely allowed to deal with their own internal affairs. For example, the Orthodox Christians in Crete were considered part of the Orthodox millet, under the leadership of the Patriarch of Constantinople. The island was again divided into twelve dioceses which retained their ancient names, as in Byzantine times. In 1647, the metropolitan bishop of Gortyn was again established as the archbishop of Crete, reporting to the patriarch. He was the head of all the Christians, clergy and laity.

Islamic law allowed the Church several privileges, and in theory the Ottoman authorities had no right to interfere in its work or internal organisation. Anything to do with canon law or family law – such as marriage, divorce or inheritance – was dealt with according to Orthodox Church rules. Orthodox clergy were also protected by order of the sultan and there were strict rules against intimidation of clergy from the authorities.

As can be imagined, this impunity did not stop the janissaries committing acts of violence or murder against the clergy. In one case, in 1779, the bishop of Chania rode his horse through the town gate, an action not permitted to Greeks. The janissaries on guard took this as an insult, and were on the point of burning the bishop and his priests to death, when their anger was diverted by a clever pasha who issued an arbitrary decree that all Greeks of any class must sleep outside the city at night. This seemed to assuage the janissaries' anger, and the rule was rigorously enforced for two months, until the Greeks had raised enough money to bribe the pasha to revoke the decree. It became the practice to rely on bribery rather than decrees from the sultan to ensure safety for the clergy, and it was common for the monasteries to invite a powerful agha to sit on the supervisory committee as protection against janissary raids, for a fee.

With these privileges went certain duties. As well as being expected to keep the Christian population "under control", the patriarchs, metropolitans and bishops also had to act as tax farmers for ecclesiastical taxes. The metropolitan had to pay a tax of 76,000 silver pieces to Constantinople, which he recouped by imposing a tax of twelve silver pieces on each Christian family. The Patriarchate levied a tax of a similar amount on the island, along with various other taxes, including a levy of olive oil for the oil lamps in the churches of Constantinople. In many cases, the patriarch was as harsh as the sultan in enforcing tax collection, and bishops and even the metropolitan could be sacked for non-compliance. In fact, relations between the Cretan Church and the Patriarchate were often strained, and eventually things got so bad that there was a major rift between the two. The Cretan Church declared itself autocephalous (self-governing) and appealed to the sultan, who ratified the decision by imperial decree, forbidding the patriarch from any further involvement in church affairs in Crete. The patriarch acted quickly to get imperial policy reversed, a new metropolitan was installed, the "rebellion" was quashed, and the bishop of Rethymnon, one of the ringleaders, was expelled from Crete. The new metropolitan restored relations with the Patriarchate, and payment of taxes resumed.

Officially, there was freedom of worship for all religions in the Ottoman Empire, but there was still widespread vandalism against Christian churches, as well as occasional attacks on individuals or groups. There were also practical difficulties. In the early days of Ottoman rule, many churches and monasteries were destroyed or converted into mosques, public baths, warehouses or barracks. Unfortunately, among the restrictions imposed on the Christians was that the building of new monasteries or churches was forbidden (although this rule was not always enforced, especially in villages). Even repair and maintenance work required special permits, which were extremely expensive. As a result of this rule, for many years there was no cathedral in Candia. The metropolitan had to tour the area, holding services in any village church or monastery that would allow him. It was not until 1735 that he finally got permission to restore the derelict church of Saint Minas and make it his cathedral.

Sometimes permits for restoration were refused point blank. During the Cretan War, the abbot of Agarathos monastery near Candia had built a fence around the monastery, bearing the heads of decapitated Ottoman soldiers. When, in 1684, the current abbot applied for a permit to restore the monastery, his request was refused brusquely (and perhaps understandably).

Economy and Trade

The war had taken a heavy toll on olive oil and wine production, with many trees and vines cut down or burned. However, the population decline resulted in plentiful grain supplies. For a brief period, Crete was able to export wheat, mainly from Ierapetra and Lassithi. Most of the exports were to North Africa, probably in response to famine, although there were also exports to France during crop failures in 1678. As other forms of farming took over from grain, it again became necessary to import wheat from Constantinople. In the first few years of Ottoman rule, trade in general was very limited, but two years after the conquest a Venetian consulate was established in Candia to oversee what trade with Venice still existed. This was followed in 1674 with a French consulate in Chania. Salt continued to be a major export and, perhaps surprisingly in a Muslim empire, wine production continued. This was primarily for local use or export within the empire; international exports to England and France declined substantially. Grapes were also used to produce raisins, which were highly prized in Constantinople. With the decline of Cretan shipbuilding, described below, international trade was largely in the hands of French merchants using French ships.

The biggest change was probably in olive farming. From a slow start after the war, there was a rapid expansion of olive production, the olives being used primarily for olive oil to make soap. By the early eighteenth century, the French traders were exporting twice as much oil as wine and, between 1720 and 1741, oil exports increased by 50%.

Initially, the oil was shipped to Constantinople and Marseilles, where the soap was manufactured, but a soap production industry soon developed in Crete. This grew from two workshops across Crete in 1717 to over twenty-five in 1732, and then to twenty in Candia alone in 1749. The Ottomans turned over the old cathedral of Chania to soap production, while, in the same town, the Ela Taverna today still shows the structure of its origins as a soap factory. Crete's soap factories were almost entirely owned by Muslims, although, as production increased, Christians became more involved.

Once some sort of normality was restored after the end of the Cretan War, there was a steady increase in trade, still mainly conducted with the French, and involving many new products. Exports now included almonds, chestnuts, honey, wax, cheese, rice, cotton, wool, flax and silk. Medicinal and aromatic herbs were again highly prized, together with laudanum and saffron. Cretan fabrics, especially from the convents, were exported to Europe. Imports were mainly luxury goods like sugar and coffee from Yemen, but salt fish and caviar from Constantinople were still popular, especially during Lent. Interestingly, timber shifted from being an export to an import, largely due to extensive deforestation by the Venetians. In spite of the antagonism between Venice and the Ottoman Empire, trade with Venice continued, and Venetian merchants were still based in Chania. Among the main imports from Venice were metal goods, luxury textiles, leather, paper, glass and books, mainly ecclesiastical.

Shipbuilding continued, although on a much smaller scale. The large state shipyards of Venetian times were gone, but a small fleet was still maintained in Sfakia and there were a number of one-man operations. The latter were mainly used for local coastal trade. For example, the Holy Trinity monastery on the Akrotiri peninsula north of Chania had its own shipyard for boats to bring supplies from the city. The Sfakian ships did range around the Aegean and as far as the Black Sea, but overseas trade was left mainly to French ships, as noted above. The harbour of Candia was completely neglected throughout the eighteenth century. Several travellers report that it was severely silted up and, although big enough for thirty to forty merchant vessels if dredged, could only hold eight or nine in practice. With a de facto depth of only eight or nine feet in the harbour, even those few ships had to be lightened before entering. The procedure was to anchor off the island of Dia, about 11 km north of Candia, where the bulk of the cargo would be unloaded onto small lighters.

Trades and businesses for the most part continued much as before, except that the most profitable were usually carried out by Muslims. In 1685, thirty-one of the thirty-eight bakeries in Candia were owned by Muslims, with similar proportions for butchers' shops. Trades in the larger towns were organised into associations or guilds, under a president recognised by the authorities. Janissaries or their associates played a large part in the guilds, their connections guaranteeing certain judicial privileges and access to the joint funds of janissary regiments. Nevertheless, the guilds in Crete were nowhere near as powerful as under Venetian rule, or indeed in other parts of the Ottoman Empire. In the villages also, Muslims were usually involved in farming, baking, confectionery and knife making, leaving the more "humble" professions to Christians or Ethiopian and Arab immigrants.

Society and Religion

The early years of Ottoman rule saw a steep decline in the Christian rural population due to plague, war, emigration and conversion to Islam. There are no reliable figures, but one estimate in 1687 puts the total population of the island as low as 80,000, of whom 50,000 were Christian. This compares with a total population of just under 300,000 in 1644. A fairly reliable source gives the population of Candia at the end of the seventeenth century as 2,000 Muslims, 800 Christians and 1,000 Jews. So great was the depopulation of Candia that Christians and Jews were allowed to own property within the city, in contrast to the situation in Chania and other cities, where Christians were confined to suburbs outside the walls. In the early eighteenth century, the population began to climb again, and by the end of that century the total figure was 350,000, of whom 200,000 were Christians and 150,000 Muslims. There are varying interpretations of the large number of Muslims in Crete. Some historians assume large-scale immigration from Anatolia, as happened in other Greek areas ruled by the Ottoman Empire, such as the Balkans, but there is actually no evidence for this. Most modern historians now agree that the vast majority of the Muslims were, in fact, Cretans who had converted to Islam. By the same token, it is sometimes forgotten that the invading army and subsequent settlers included Arabs, North Africans and Albanians as well as ethnic Turks.

The extent of the Islamisation of Crete is disputed, and it is still difficult to sort out the exact situation. That there were frequent conversions to Islam is pretty clear, as are the reasons: to reduce the tax burden and harsh treatment, in response to social pressure, or to enjoy legal and financial privileges. It is also likely that some conversions were for genuine religious reasons, but it is impossible to know the extent of this. An English traveller, writing in 1739, even found some examples of people converting in order to take revenge on individual Muslims, since for a Christian to strike a Muslim resulted in severe penalties. Conversion was also the gateway to a military career in the janissaries, and even many of the imperial janissaries were recruited from among Cretan Muslims. Although most of these converts remained in the ranks, there were cases where some rose quickly to becoming high-ranking officers, offering to others the prospect of prestige and wealth. Individual conversion could not be easier: the applicant merely had to recite the Muslim confession of faith and change his name. Often the conversion was recorded in the qadi court, in order to obtain official evidence, but this was not a requirement. Converts were generally adult Orthodox Christians, although a small number of Catholics and Jews are also believed to have converted. If a married man converted, he was expected to take his wife with him into the new faith, although this was not always enforced. If a married woman converted and her husband remained Christian, she was obliged to divorce him, since Islamic law did not allow Muslim women to be put under the authority of non-Muslim men. She retained legal control over any children.

Islamic law allowed marriages between Muslim men and Christian women and, in such cases, the women were allowed to maintain their own religion, as long as the children were brought up Muslim. Mixed marriages were accepted not only by the Islamic courts but, generally, by the local Orthodox clergy as well. A French traveller, writing at the beginning of the eighteenth century, described one such couple:

[They] lived very well and comfortably together, and almost after the Christian Manner, tho' each kept their own Religion, he went to the Mosque, and she to the Church, but the Children were bred as Mahometans; and when she was busied other ways, he did not scruple to light for her the Lamp before the Panagia's [Virgin Mary's] Image.[10]

One result of widespread intermarriage was that relations between Muslim and Christian Cretans were far more complex than straight-forward hostility. The same extended family could contain members of both faiths and, as we have seen, a degree of tolerance even within the nuclear family was not unknown. Many villages had a mixed population of Muslims and Christians who would often share in each other's religious celebrations and would even appear as witnesses in each other's cases. It was not unknown for a Muslim to act as a Christian's koumbaros (best man) at his wedding.

In some cases an entire village, including the priest, would convert. These mass conversions were usually for economic reasons, but in many cases the converts would become fervent, even fanatical, believers, and were looked down on by the local Cretans. On the other hand, some of the converts to Islam were anything but sincere, becoming Muslim in name only but keeping their Christian faith in secret; they were often called crypto-Christians. The Church generally opposed this practice, although there were some bishops who looked on it with sympathy and understanding. In one case, a congregation sought the opinion of the Patriarch of Constantinople on this question, and he rejected the idea totally, but when they appealed to the patriarch of Jerusalem, himself a Cretan, he gave his approval to false conversion on the conditions of "inescapable need" and "pastoral economy" (deviation from the letter of the law in order to adhere to the spirit of the law and charity). Even after converting to Islam, the locals retained their Cretan language and, interestingly, often adapted their new Muslim names to a Greek inflexion. For example, Kemal became Kemalis, or Suleiman became Suleimanis. In many cases, they kept their Greek surnames, so that names like Abdul Kalimerakis were not uncommon. If a Turkish surname was adopted, it was often given a Cretan ending, as in Muladakis.[11]

Although an element of mistrust and animosity always existed between the Muslim and Christian communities, conversion did not automatically create fierce hatred. Some scholars have argued that the two groups were bound by numerous ties including marriage, family links, a common cultural identity (with Greek as the spoken language) and commercial relations between merchants.[12] Even during wartime, relations between merchants of all faiths could be close. Writing of the late nineteenth century in his novel *Captain Michalis*, Kazantzakis gives a detailed and moving description of this ambivalent relationship, which continued throughout Ottoman rule, even during the periods of rebellion. The up-and-down friendship between the captain and his blood brother Nuri Bey is a particularly poignant example. It has been suggested that the more significant divide in Crete was not between Christian and Muslim, but between local communities and the relatively small number of Ottoman officials sent from Constantinople to rule over them. Perhaps not too much should be made of this, though, given that the Muslim Cretans, encouraged by the janissaries, took an active part in the suppression of the Daskalogiannis revolt, which led to a sharp deterioration in relations between the faiths after 1770.

The Muslims in Crete were mainly Sunni, but about 20%, especially among the janissaries, belonged to the Bektashi Order, an offshoot of the Shia branch of Islam. The Bektashi Order was founded in Asia Minor in the thirteenth century and was related to the Dervish Order. It incorporated aspects of Christianity into its basic Islamic beliefs, including a form of baptism, the veneration of saints and icons, drinking of wine and something like a Communion service. There are also elements of Gnosticism, such as belief in reincarnation and even some remnants of paganism. For this reason, the Bektashi Order is viewed with some suspicion by more mainstream Muslims, but it is likely that the "Christian" elements also attracted crypto-Christian converts.

In the towns, Muslims generally led a normal Islamic life, but in the rural areas there was a much more relaxed attitude. Many drank wine on a regular basis, and even the eating of pork was not unknown, while the muezzin's call to prayer was sometimes in Greek rather than Arabic. A traveller in 1795 reported:

The Turks of [the island] are almost completely metamorphosed. They live and eat with Christians without any scruple, almost all drink as much wine as they can get, and their women, instead of being in prison or muffled up, walk about with the same dress and freedom as the Greeks.[13]

This somewhat relaxed attitude to Islam led the pasha of Candia, as early as 1700, to issue two decrees, reminding Muslims of their obligation to pray five times daily and for women not to display their faces in public.

With oppressive taxation, predatory janissaries and authorities largely concerned only with their own comfort, there seems to have been a general decline in moral standards during Ottoman rule. In the countryside, lawlessness was rampant, and theft – particularly rustling – was prevalent. In the towns, prostitution increased. One aspect of the general immorality which the authorities tried to stamp out was the keeping of kapatma, Christian girls taken into Muslim homes as mistresses, a practice strictly against Qur'anic law. Illegitimate children resulting from these liaisons were usually abandoned at the doors of mosques or public baths. In 1763, a pasha issued a decree ordering the leaders of the mosques to find and deal with kapatma:

Search and discover the houses of those who are unlawfully living with an adopted non-Muslim partner within the town, and all those who show a willingness to enter into marriage let them proceed to wed with proper sanctity, whether the partner is a second, third or fourth wife; for those women whom the man refuses to marry and who are in an interesting condition, you must designate a sum for maintenance, and return them to their guardians or relatives. Whichever women do not wish to marry, yet do not wish to stop their relations with the man, or who have nowhere else to go and are wholly helpless, you must hand over to their priests.

This fairly enlightened approach was rare, although several other pashas did arrange limited care and protection of abandoned women and their children if they were the illegitimate offspring of Muslims.

Education and Culture

With the fall of Candia, the Cretan Renaissance came to an abrupt end. Many of the émigrés took their books and manuscripts with them into exile, and those left in the great libraries were largely destroyed. This massive brain drain meant that education among even the elite Christian population was again limited to basic reading and writing being taught in the monasteries. For a long time, even the higher clergy were poorly educated. There were some Muslim madrasas (Islamic schools) in the towns, but since the main subject was Islamic sacred law and theology, and the teaching language was primarily Turkish, the Muslim Cretans fared little better. In short, for the general population, both Christian and Muslim, education was virtually non-existent. Things began to improve from the mid-eighteenth century, when primary schools started to appear in Sfakia; by the end of the century, schools were being founded in the towns. A wider range of subjects was taught, including grammar, logic, poetics and rhetoric and, to a lesser extent, maths, art, music, history and philosophy. At the same time, the libraries in the larger monasteries were restored and expanded, and a few private individuals began to build up their own extensive libraries.

The icon workshops ceased to exist, and most of the artists moved to the Ionian Islands or other Greek areas not under Ottoman rule. Thus, the Cretan School of iconography more or less died out after 1700, with some notable exceptions. In the monastery of Myriokephala, south-west of Rethymnon, there is a superb icon of the Virgin Mary, painted by a monk called Iakovos early in the eighteenth century. Another highly influential painter was Georgios Kastrophylakas (born in 1723), many of whose impressive icons are on display in the Museum of Saint Katherine in Iraklion. Perhaps one of the greatest icons of eighteenth-century Crete, and certainly one of my favourites, is the magnificent *Lord Thou Art Great* by Ioannis Kornaros (born in 1745). This is a composite icon comprising sixty-one scenes from the Old and New Testaments, based on the prayer of the Blessing of the Waters, part of the Theophania (Epiphany) service of 6th January. What makes this piece unique, apart from the sheer quality of the painting, is that, instead of each miniature being separate, the whole picture is unified by streams of water flowing through and between the sections. Intriguingly, it also includes non-Orthodox images – for example, signs of the zodiac and allegorical representations of the four elements. The icon can be seen in Toplou monastery, near Siteia.

In spite of allowing many of the Venetian walls and fortresses to fall into disrepair, the Ottomans were careful to maintain the fountains and aqueducts. Muslims have a religious obligation to wash frequently, and this ensured that, for example, the Lion Fountain in Iraklion is still with us. After the conquest of the island, many churches were converted into mosques, a few of which still survive, especially in Chania and Rethymnon. In the former, the Mosque of the Janissaries is the oldest mosque in Crete, dating from 1645, while the famous Yiali Tzami still dominates the harbour. The church of Aghios Nikolaos on 1821 Square in Chania was built as a church in 1320, converted to a mosque under Ottoman rule and reconsecrated as a church in 1918. Gloriously cross-cultural, it still has an Orthodox bell tower and a minaret, both on a Venetian Catholic building. In Rethymnon, the Neratze Mosque, the Veli Pasha Mosque and the Ibrahim Han Mosque are all worth visiting. Many of the mosques are now used for cultural events or exhibitions.

There were few significant developments in literature during the eighteenth century, but the oral tradition remained strong. Among the urban Muslim literati, poems and other literary forms were written in Ottoman Turkish, and possibly Farsi and Arabic, but so far these have been little studied and are virtually unknown. Some folk songs and poems, both Christian and Muslim, were written down, and in recent years there has been more study of these. Turkish was the official written language for documents, but Cretan Greek was almost universally used for spoken communication. There were also many examples of text written in Greek but using Arabic characters. Both groups continued to compose mantinades, those written by Christians often taking on a revolutionary tone. Rimes (pronounced with two syllables) were longer narrative compositions, usually anonymous and often describing historical events, especially those relating to fighting, but also natural disasters and events of everyday life. *The Ballad of Daskalogiannis* is one such rima, while many others described the exploits, good and bad, of the janissaries. Another, written in Cretan

Greek but using Arabic characters, describes the janissaries' downfall. Unusually, it is signed by the writer, Selim from Chania, and seeks to justify the destruction of the janissaries while showing a little regret for the loss of their colourful and swaggering lifestyle:

> *And where are your treasurers living in comfort,*
> *They who used to wheel and deal with such pompous airs?*
> *Where are your grand benefactors full of good fortune,*
> *The ones all the Turkish dignitaries used to respect so?*
> *Where are your master builders who had their own reserves?*
> *With what a heavy heart they took off their waistcoats and their turbans.*
> *Where are your guards who used to brag?*
> *They used to stroll in the markets and they were like lions.*
> *They are useless idlers, let them cry night and day.[14]*

The bare, matter-of-fact style of the rimes and their descriptions of real events have led to them being sometimes described as "the newspapers of the period".[15]

Muslims and Christians also shared a common musical tradition during this period, but, as with poetry, this was mainly restricted to folk music. The Cretan lyra, originally from Anatolia, was introduced in the eighteenth century, adding to the existing instruments the violin and mandolin, which had been introduced in Venetian times. Immigrants from other parts of the empire also brought with them their own ballads and folk songs. One form of folk music that developed during this period can be described as specifically Cretan. The **rizitika** songs of Sfakia and western Crete probably originated in Byzantine times, and were sung in Venetian times, but they came to much greater prominence during Ottoman rule.[16] Although some were songs of love, they were mainly songs of rebellion and war. The main development during this period was that they were often allegorical in nature to hide their true seditious meaning:

> *—You wild goats and kids, you tamed deer,*
> *Tell me, where do you live, where are you staying in the winter?*
> *—In the precipices we live, the steep peaks are our winter quarters,*
> *The caves in the mountains are our ancestral home.[17]*

Here, the goats are obviously the hains, escaping to the mountains away from the Muslims who mainly lived on the plains. Another rizitiko from Ottoman years is much more direct:

When will the night be starry?
When will it be February?
So I can grab my rifle,
My beautiful cartridge belt,
To descend to Omalos
On the Mousouros road,
To deprive mothers of their sons,
Wives of their husbands,
To deprive new-born babies
Of their mothers,
So they will cry for her breast in the night
And at dawn for milk,
And when the sun rises
They shall cry for their unfortunate motherland.[18]

This song became an anthem of resistance in Crete, and was adapted during the Battle of Crete in 1941, with "Maleme's airport" replacing "Omalos" (see chapter 16).

13

Ottoman Rule II

1821 to 1898

Freedom or Death

In many ways, everything changed in 1821, the year of the mainland Greek uprising against Ottoman rule. For fifty years, since the failure of the Daskalogiannis revolt, Crete had been relatively peaceful, but for most of the nineteenth century repeated uprisings made the island echo to the battle cry of the rebels, Eleftheria i Thanatos (Freedom or Death). This does not mean that there were not periods of peace between the rebellions. Kazantzakis describes the situation succinctly in his novel *Captain Michalis*:

> The cross and crescent side by side, from time to time they were in peace and from time to time a Cretan storm caught them up in a rage, and they attacked one another, and they impaled their teeth to one another's flesh.[1]

The same novel, incidentally, contains excellent descriptions of town and village life in nineteenth-century Ottoman Crete, the ambivalent relationship between Ottoman rulers, Muslim Cretans and Christian Cretans, and the heavy weight of history that lay on the minds of the Cretans, with memories of past failures and expectations of future success.

The events of the period from 1821 to 1898 demonstrate an almost tragic monotony, as the same mistakes are made repeatedly and the shifting tides of international affairs influence Cretan history, both for better and worse. Four themes can be isolated: local politics, Greek independence, Ottoman policy and the involvement of the Great Powers (or protecting powers), primarily Britain, France, Italy and Russia.

Beginning with Crete itself, the inability of the revolutionary leaders to agree among themselves or to submit to an overall military commander, or even to be united on the exact form that a free Crete would take, undoubtedly weakened the various rebellions. At the same time, the Greek revolution began in 1821, leading to the liberation of southern and central Greece and the creation of the Greek state in 1830. From this point on, events on the mainland had a direct impact on events in Crete.

As for the Ottoman Empire, the vacillations in policy of the Sublime Porte sometimes worked in Crete's favour and sometimes disastrously against, but were always disruptive:

> The Ottoman authorities seemed incapable of following a consistent policy, sometimes dangerously compliant and sometimes inappropriately autocratic, as moderation and arrogance succeeded each other with the same frequency that the rulers of the day were sent out – thirty-seven governors succeeded each other in the space of forty-six years, with an average term in office of fifteen months.[2]

There were two causes for these changes in policy. One was the internal politics of the empire, in which a struggle between reformers and conservatives continued for most of the nineteenth century. Perhaps more important from Crete's point of view, however, was the influence of the Great Powers.

To explain the involvement of European countries in the affairs of Crete, it is necessary to take a step back. Since the end of the Napoleonic Wars in 1815, the main aim of the group of countries known as the Concert of Europe had been the maintenance of stability in Europe and the avoidance of another major European war. Britain, France, Prussia (later Germany), Russia, Austria-Hungary and, after unification, Italy "took collective charge of the problems of the continent, while relinquishing nothing of their national sovereignty", and their efforts led to an unusually peaceful century on the continent.[3] Although basically conservative, the Concert did not necessarily oppose all independence movements; as the Ottoman Empire in the Balkans began to break up, it sought to control rather than suppress the new nation states. There were, however, differences of interest between the members of the Concert. While Russia was generally favourably disposed towards its fellow Orthodox peoples of Greece and Crete, Britain and France were suspicious of Russian influence, and for most of the period they tried to maintain the balance of power by supporting the Ottoman Empire. At the same time, self-interest came first, and they were quite prepared to put pressure on the sultan if their interests warranted it.

The First Uprising: 1821 to 1824

Before the outbreak of revolution in Greece, the **Friendly Society** (Filiki Etairia), founded in 1814, was largely responsible for spreading revolutionary ideas. Its members were active in Crete from the beginning, although the network was limited. A rare coded document of initiation exists from that period:

> In the name of the Salvation to come, I confirm Ioannis Birakis, son of George of Sfakia and aged fifty-five, to be a member and supporter of the Friendly Society and ardently to desire the well-being of his nation.[4]

It was taken for granted that the island would take an active part in the uprising when it came, and that Crete would be part of a liberated Greece. From 1816, official representatives from Crete were present on the mainland, and support for the rebellion grew among Cretans, especially the professional class and the clergy. In return, there were expectations that support for Crete would come from the mainland. However, in spite of widespread support for rebellion, Cretans were slow to join the struggle. Their lack of weapons and supplies together with the large Muslim population on the island made them wary of starting something they couldn't finish. Memories of the Daskalogiannis failure were still at the front of their minds. A nineteenth-century Greek observer of the Cretan uprisings wrote:

Unprepared and cut off from the rest of the Greek world, they looked to their own resources and entered the national struggle ... In the beginning, their weaponry amounted to no more than four hundred barrels of gunpowder ... And what about lead and paper? Ecclesiastical books and weights from the steelyards and whatever else could be found were used, to begin with, for making cartridges and rounds. For many months, the Cretans bought at their own expense a barrel of gunpowder for three, four and sometimes five Spanish gold pieces. The number of weapons that were available was extremely limited during the early period of the revolution and those bearing arms probably amounted to no more than about 1200, of whom eight hundred were Sfakians.[5]

Moreover, the Ottoman authorities, as soon as they heard of the insurrection on the mainland, began to take precautions, moving many of Crete's bishops to Candia as hostages.

Nevertheless, following a meeting in Sfakia, in April 1821, the rebels agreed to take up arms. On 14th June, they won their first victory in a battle near Chania. Within a few days, the uprising had spread to the rest of the island, joined by a crypto-Christian janissary, Hussein Agha, who reverted to his Christian name of Michael Kourmoulis and led his whole clan of over sixty men to join the rebellion. Ottoman reprisals were instant and savage. The metropolitan and seven other bishops were hanged. The cathedral in Candia was plundered and burned, while abbots, monks and clerics throughout the island were killed or imprisoned. In some places, the janissaries went on a killing spree against Christians, with 400 victims in Chania and 800 in Candia. Perhaps most horrifying was an attack on a convent in which all the nuns were raped and murdered. The extent of the violence provoked protests from the British and French vice-consuls, which probably prevented a further bloodbath.

In spite of the reprisals, the insurrection continued, with several early successes for the rebels, especially in the Sfakia area, and many of the aghas in the villages being forced to seek refuge in Chania. In a major victory near Kydonia, the pasha of Chania and 5,000 men were defeated and forced to retreat. Meanwhile, a Turkish expeditionary force, attempting to break through from Rethymnon to Sfakia, was annihilated. These victories not only brought an upsurge in morale but, more practically, a large supply of weaponry. In late July, although there was some fighting in the Candia region and the government forces retreated into their fortresses, there was no serious threat from the rebels in that area. Since the rebels in the east of Crete were somewhat isolated from the main forces in the west, the pasha of Candia was now able to direct the bulk of his army, together with troops from Siteia and Rethymnon – 8,000 men in all, plus artillery and cavalry – toward a concerted attack on Sfakia. The rebels were forced back, so that the army from Chania could now join the pasha. Although the rebels checked the Ottoman advance at Theriso, the situation was desperate. Urgent requests for help were dispatched to the Greek navy at Spetses:

> We are in great distress, and no longer have the strength to carry on since the enemy is warring against us both by land and sea, certain that the absence of Greek ships will mean the destruction of the Christians.[6]

No assistance materialised, and the Ottoman army broke through into Sfakia at the end of August. All resistance was crushed, and the whole district was devastated as in 1770. The Ottoman troops returned to their fortresses, and the revolution seemed to have been suppressed.

Not so. In the autumn of 1821, the rebels regrouped and succeeded in expelling the Ottomans from Apokoronas and Kydonia. In spite of this, a problem was emerging that had been seen before in several other eras. It was becoming clear that personal ambition and disputes between the chieftains were weakening the revolution. The Sfakians had set up the Chancellery of Sfakia to plan and co-ordinate the revolution, organise the supply of arms and provisions, protect the civilian population and manage fundraising. However, the chancellery did not have the strength or legitimacy to control local disputes between chieftains, so they appealed to the new Greek government to appoint a commander-in-chief for Crete. Michael Afendoulis was duly given the job and he arrived in Crete in November 1821.

On the whole, the appointment of Afendoulis was not a great success. He did put the revolution on a firmer foundation and was instrumental in spreading the insurrection to the rest of the island. He also attempted to give shape to the struggle for freedom by planning a form of political organisation. However, the Cretans were generally suspicious of the "outsider", and his weak physique did little to inspire confidence among the tough Sfakians. Moreover, his obvious ambition and arrogance made him unpopular with many, resulting in constant arguments with the chieftains and the creation of more divisions than before, some of which ended in violence and murder. The failure of a siege of Rethymnon and defeat in a major battle were blamed on him, and he became even more unpopular.

In May 1822, assisted by his friend Petros Skylitsis, he summoned a general assembly at Armeni, near Apokoronas, to vote for an interim revolutionary government for the island. The assembly was chaired by Skylitsis, a much more flexible and diplomatic character, who worked hard for reconciliation between the factions. The forty representatives from all regions of Crete agreed a declaration of freedom, based on the Greek Constitution of 1822, and approved a plan for a caretaker administration. The island would be divided into four prefectures, subdivided into provinces and communities (an arrangement pretty much the same as that which later existed in Crete for most of the twentieth century, until the recent reforms of 2011). Central power rested with a general eparch (provincial governor), supported by a General Chancellery composed of a general secretary and secretaries for the economy, the police, war, the sea and justice. Representation in the Greek parliament was outlined, and a new Cretan flag designed. Afendoulis was appointed general eparch, but Skylitsis fled the island when news of the landing of an Egyptian army reached him.

Even as the assembly was still debating the future, events were taking a turn for the worse. The main Ottoman army was occupied in mainland Greece, and the continuing insurrection in Crete was of some concern to the sultan, who sought the aid of Mehmet Ali, the somewhat rebellious governor of Egypt. With the hope of eventually ruling over Crete and expanding into Sudan and Syria, he sent a large army under the command of his brother-in-law, Hassan Pasha. Hassan landed at Souda at the end of May and immediately set out to crush the rebels. His first attack on a fortified position at Malaxa, south of Chania, succeeded in driving out the rebels, but this was followed by a major defeat at Krousonas, south of Candia. Realising that tough battles lay ahead, Hassan turned to diplomacy. He released the bishop of Kydonia and "persuaded" him to issue a pastoral encyclical commanding the rebels to lay down their arms. At the same time, he published declarations calling on the people of Crete to submit to the "beneficent" ruler of Egypt, Mehmet Ali, and promising a just and honest administration. Both stratagems failed completely, and Hassan resumed military operations in August.

He met with some initial success, but suffered losses, culminating in a long and bloody battle near Tylissos, west of Candia. He decided to concentrate on the Lassithi plateau, the centre of resistance in the east and a major source of food supplies for the rebels. He withdrew to an area near Candia, regrouped his forces and attempted to break through into the plateau. Finding all the passes held securely by the rebels, he set out on a long outflanking movement to the south through Viannos, circling round past Ierapetra, through Kroustas and Kritsa to the Katharo plateau. From this less-protected area, he was able to sweep into Lassithi. He laid waste to the plateau, destroying most of the resistance, and then wintered in the bay of Mirabello.

It was during a battle near Kritsa that the extraordinary Cretan heroine Rhodanthe was killed. The daughter of a priest, she had been abducted by a drunken Ottoman officer, who had killed her mother. She managed to escape by cutting the officer's throat, and, disguised as a young man, she joined the rebellion, fighting with great courage among the men. It was only after she was shot that her comrades discovered who she really was. Rhodanthe, "The Girl from Kritsa", is still commemorated in songs and poems, and is highly honoured in her native village.[7]

After the defeat on Lassithi, a few armed rebels and around 2,000 civilians took refuge in a cave near Milatos. In February 1823, the Egyptians laid siege, bombarding the cave with cannon fire for two weeks. The rebels eventually surrendered, and most were slaughtered, the rest being sold into slavery.[8] As Hassan moved his army towards Messara for the next stage of the war, he fell from his bolting horse and was killed, in what the Cretans believed to be an act of divine retribution.

On the political front, Afendoulis finally fell out with the Cretan chieftains, who had him arrested and accused of negligence, inertia, excessive ambition and treasonable inclinations. He was thrown out of Crete, leaving the revolution leaderless. Although Emmanuel Tombazis was now appointed governor-general, he did not arrive in Crete until May 1823. He brought with him five warships, 600 volunteers and, most importantly, new hope for the revolution. After an early success with the surrender of the town of Kastelli Kissamos in the west, he headed towards Chania and the janissary base at Selino. In early June, Hassan's replacement, Hussein Bey, landed with 3,000 extra men. He decided to continue with Hassan's strategy of suppressing the east first, and led an army of 12,000 men (plus cavalry and artillery) to meet Tombazis, now near Candia. On 20th August, a battle near Amourgelles resulted in defeat and retreat for the Cretans, leaving the Ottoman army in control of the whole Messara plain.

Hussein continued to move west towards Rethymnon, and the Cretans now faced a critical situation. After the failure of a belated attempt to capture Gramvousa, and with renewed tensions between the revolutionary factions, Tombazis sought help from Greece:

> Sir, hard-pressed Crete is now breathing its last. A little military help and the arrival of ships could relieve the island of the threat of annihilation. It is a rich land and could repay the cost many times over; it needs only to be saved from the enemy and the plunderers who squander the national wealth. Sir, if the Greek nation loses Crete, it will lose its right eye and independence will not amount to much. May the honourable Commission therefore hasten to secure the salvation of the island while the enemy still leaves us time to do so; otherwise all will have been in vain.[9]

Unfortunately, Greece was itself embroiled in a political and economic crisis, and the revolutionary war was facing setbacks, so no help was available from that quarter.

Hussein continued his advance, plundering the area of Apokoronas and attacking Sfakia, where many of the chieftains finally capitulated. When his army reached the harbour of Loutro, the Greek fleet was forced to evacuate over 10,000 refugees, in Crete's own version of the Dunkirk evacuation. In all, it is believed that about 60,000 Cretans fled the island in early 1824. There was, from then on, a permanent and influential Cretan lobby in Greece. Tombazis himself left, and the revolution was virtually over. With some wisdom and a view to the future, Hussein granted a general amnesty and Crete now became an invaluable supply base for the Ottoman army on the mainland. The rebellion was now reduced to night-time raids, sabotage and guerrilla warfare between the Cretan Kalisperides (Good Evenings, so called because they usually attacked at dusk) and bands of janissaries called Zourides (Cretan Weasels, fierce nocturnal carnivores).

Gramvousa and Renewed Hopes: 1825 to 1830

It was not long before rebellion flared up again. In the middle of 1825, a small group captured the island fortress of Gramvousa, while a second force took the fortress at Kissamos. This was of serious concern to the new Egyptian governor, Mustafa Naili Pasha, who immediately dispatched a large army to recapture the fortresses. Although his efforts failed, he was able to prevent the revolt spreading in the west, and Gramvousa and Kissamos remained isolated. With no way of breaking out from the island, the rebels on Gramvousa turned to piracy and harassed shipping operations, both Ottoman and European, along the coast. They also began to establish a community on the island, building a school and a church dedicated to Panagia Kleftrina (Our Lady of the Pirates), still existent but in a ruined state. A new Cretan Council was established on the island as the official revolutionary authority, but was slow to spark any interest in the rest of Crete, until international events changed the situation.

The 1827 Treaty of London sought to bring to an end the Greek War of Independence by establishing an independent Greek state as a dependency of the sultan, under the protection of the Great Powers. Tombazis believed, perhaps wrongly, that only areas of Greece actively involved in revolt against the Ottomans would be included within the borders of the new state. He urged the Cretans to revive and extend the rebellion to ensure Crete's inclusion in Greece. Reinforcements landed at Aghios Nikolaos in eastern Crete. The rebels quickly gained control of a large part of the east – but, with no overall command and a lack of discipline among the troops, the revolt quickly became fragmented, leading to retreat. Some of the rebels fled to the mountains and some to Gramvousa, while the rest left Crete. By this stage, even the Greek government was losing patience with the piracy on Gramvousa. Early in 1828, the Greek head of state, Governor Ioannis Kapodistrias, asked Britain and France to send fleets to destroy the pirate ships and hand over the fortress to Britain.

Just before the British intervention, in January 1828, Hadji-Michalis Dalianis, a famous revolutionary from Epiros, had landed at Gramvousa with a small force, intending to bring the revolution to life again. By early March, he had captured the great fortress at Frangokastelli and set up a base for further advances. The surrounding area had been so thoroughly intimidated by Mustafa's threats of reprisals that Dalianis was unable to stir up other districts. Lacking supplies and support, the Sfakian chieftains advised retreat to the mountains and a continuation of the guerrilla war. In spite of this, Dalianis insisted on battle. On 18th May 1828, 600 Cretans with 100 cavalry faced Mustafa's army of 8,000 men and 300 cavalry. The result was a foregone conclusion: Dalianis and over half his men were killed in a decisive victory for the Egyptian army. It did not all go Mustafa's way, however, for as he returned towards Chania he was harried by repeated ambushes and attacks, and he reached Chania with his army in disarray.

Over the years, there have been sightings of ghostly figures moving towards the fortress at Frangokastelli at dawn on the anniversary of the battle. There has never been any logical explanation for this phenomenon, but these so-called Drosoulites (Dew Shadows) have been reported on several occasions. In 1890, for example, a small group of Ottoman soldiers thought they were being attacked by rebels, and fled in panic. During the Second World War, even a German patrol found the shadows so convincing that they opened fire, unfortunately giving away their position to a nearby resistance group.

Having been somewhat equivocal in its support of the Greek revolution, the British government was determined to exclude Crete from the new state. Its reasons were a mixture of wanting to keep the balance of power between the Ottoman Empire and Russia, and fear of an expansion of Russian influence in the Mediterranean. The result was that, under British influence, Governor Kapodistrias sent representatives to the island, calling for a halt to hostilities. This request was ignored, the Cretan Council was revived and the revolt spread east again towards Siteia. The Ottoman response was extremely violent: in the summer of 1828, fierce fighting broke out in Messara, followed by a second massacre of Christians in Candia, in which 800 were killed. Similar attacks took place in Rethymnon and other towns. There was an outcry in Europe about the massacres, and a swing in sentiment towards the rebels.

In October 1828, British and French fleets arrived in Souda Bay, and the British admiral was charged with negotiating a ceasefire. While this was going on, Tombazis seized the opportunity to return to Crete with a view to taking control of Siteia region, the only area still entirely in Ottoman hands. Whether he was seeking to strengthen the negotiating hand of the rebels or to continue to work for total independence is not known. He captured Siteia and managed to drive the Ottoman troops into their fortresses, including Ierapetra and Spinalonga. However, an Egyptian army quickly recaptured Siteia, and the revolution again became indecisive. Nearly all of the rural areas were now in the hands of the revolutionaries, and the Ottomans were confined mainly to the large cities and a few fortresses.

All this became academic when the London Protocol of 1830 finally set out the limits of the new Greek state. Crete was not included. The bitterly disappointed Cretans appealed passionately to the Greek government:

> Crete has always been and will remain to be an inalienable part of Greece, having fought and still fighting with the rest of the revolutionary parts of the country since the beginning of the struggle for freedom, and no one can understand how, with the various manoeuvres of the representatives of respected monarchies, these same powers can simply neglect to take Crete into account while a violent war is still raging on its land and the Turks have been pushed back by the Greeks into their strongholds ... We can find no other salvation than in our arms and in honourable death; and if Christendom wishes to abandon us to the ferocity of the Turks, having seen our women, children and parents slaughtered, let us then too become victims – but noble victims of constancy of spirit and belief in our inalienable rights.[10]

A final attempt to retake the island of Gramvousa failed. In June 1830, ships of the Great Powers landed west of Candia to enforce the cease-fire and impose order on the island.

Egyptian Rule: 1830 to 1840

Mehmet Ali was granted rule over Crete, and Mustafa Naili Pasha was confirmed as governor. Mehmet Ali was looking towards per-manent control of the island and a minimum of intervention by the Great Powers, both of which gave him an incentive to present the new administration as fair and impartial. At the same time, in Egypt he had shown himself to be a moderniser and an enlightened, if ruth-less, ruler. Mustafa Pasha's first act was to declare a general amnesty and the laying down of all arms. The ceasefire held, although many of those opposed to it left the island, the Muslims emigrating to Asia Minor and the Christians to Greece. He then initiated an ambitious programme of public works, largely ignored by the earlier Ottoman governments. Roads were built, bridges and aqueducts repaired and the harbours dredged. At the same time, he began a whole schedule of welfare policies, issuing a decree claiming that:

> The sole object of their master, Mehmet Ali Pasha, was to establish the tranquillity and to cause the prosperity of Crete, and to deliver the Christians from the vexations to which they were formerly exposed.[11]

To this end, land confiscated from émigré Christian families was returned, destroyed olive presses were restored and schools for Muslims and Christians were built. There were also improvements to the justice system and, perhaps most significantly, the public health system (described below). However, some of Mustafa's policies were not at all popular with the Muslim community. The janissaries, disbanded and suppressed in 1826, were replaced by Albanian and Egyptian forces that did not show particular favour to the Muslim Cretans, who were also replaced by Albanians in administrative posts. It was now ruled that Muslims had no right of entry to Christian homes without permission, and could not settle in rural areas unless they already had property there, thus initiating further migration to the cities.

Unfortunately, all Mustafa's reforms required a great deal of money, and now the administration showed the ruthless side of its modernising. An oppressive new tax on agricultural products was established, which caused great hardship to both Christian and Muslim farmers, and the curtailing of the power of upper-class Muslims now made the two communities equal in discontent. There was opposition throughout Crete. Eventually, in September 1833, 7,000 Christians, with the tacit or open support of many Muslims, gathered to protest at Mournies near Kydonia. They also agreed on a petition to be sent to the Great Powers, seeking protection from arbitrary military and political power. The arbitrary military power responded immediately. Although all arms were forbidden at the protest and many armed chieftains had been turned away, Mustafa ordered his cavalry to charge the protesters and disperse them. The ringleaders were arrested and hanged, as were many other Christians and Muslims suspected of complicity. The Egyptian administration was strong enough to prevent intervention by the Great Powers, and the protest collapsed. It became clear that there was no hope of freedom without help from outside, and a group of exiled Cretans twice proposed that the British should invade Crete and declare it a protectorate. They received no response to either proposal.

Meanwhile, the ever-ambitious Mehmet Ali had attacked the Ottoman Empire in Syria, but, in spite of a major victory, he had been forced to withdraw to Egypt by the intervention of the Great Powers. France and Britain, still anxious to keep the Ottoman Empire intact, overcame Russian objections and, at the 1840 Treaty of London, placed Crete back under direct rule from Constantinople. In central and northern Greece, revolts in Thessaly and Macedonia were seeking to join these regions to Greece and, in 1841, simultaneous revolts in east and west Crete sought to achieve the same aim. This time, many chieftains were reluctant to join the uprisings, and there was no support from Greece. In addition, the Great Powers maintained constant pressure to end the rebellion. After fierce battles in Apokoronas and near Chersonisos, the revolt ended.

A chance for peace: 1841 to 1866

In spite of the change of rule, Mustafa Pasha remained in Crete as general commissioner until 1850 and began to initiate further reforms. For his long service on the island, he was given the honorary name Mustafa Naili Pasha Giritli (his new epithet meaning "The Cretan"). The capital was moved to Chania and the island divided into twenty-three provinces, each administered by a councillor supported by one Muslim and one Christian sergeant-at arms. The bulk of the tax-collecting rights were removed from the aghas and given to the provincial councillors, who were now responsible for administration, tax collecting, the police and the judiciary. The gendarmerie remained in the hands of the Albanians, who continued to be protective of the Christians and to intervene in their support on many occasions. Mustafa himself seems to have been quite favourably disposed towards the Cretans. He spoke Greek fluently, although he could not write it, and most of the women in his harem were Greek. His first wife was the daughter of a priest and was allowed to remain a Christian, even maintaining a small church in the garden of the pasha's home.[12] Mustafa's successor was a fair governor, who continued the reforms and was generally looked on favourably by the Cretans, but when Veliyüddin Pasha became governor in 1855, there was a return to a harsher regime.

As part of the 1856 Treaty of Paris, which ended the Crimean War, France and Britain influenced the sultan to issue the famous Imperial Reform Edict, the **Hatt-i Hümayun**. This clarified and extended the Edict of Gülhane of 1839, which had first officially declared that, contrary to the principles of Islamic Law, Muslims and non-Muslims would thenceforth be legally equal subjects of the sultan. The 1856 text, virtually dictated by the Allied ambassadors to the Sublime Porte, granted religious toleration to Christians throughout the empire, and guaranteed the safety of all subjects without distinction of class or religion. There was no discrimination regarding entry into public services or into civil and military schools. Joint courts were to be set up, and there was to be equal taxation for all religious groups. Under Veliyüddin Pasha, the decree was almost completely ignored, leading to further uprisings. Although these were unsuccessful, the edict had created a clear focus and a forward path for the revolutionary movement. The imposition of new taxes and a general curfew brought renewed protests and, in 1858, 5,000 people assembled near Chania. They elected a committee to send appeals to the Great Powers and to the sultan. The result was somewhat different from that of the deadly protest of 1833. When Veliyüddin ordered an attack on the protesters, his military commander refused to carry out the order and, shortly after, envoys arrived from the sultan, agreeing to satisfy the demands. Veliyüddin was removed from office and his successor, Sami Pasha, began negotiations. An imperial decree was issued, granting religious, tax, administrative and judicial privileges to the Cretans, as well as the right to bear arms.

A small development, but one of great importance for future events, was the creation of Demogerontia (Councils of Elders) in Chania, Rethymnon and Candia. There were separate councils for Muslims and Christians, each composed of six to seven members. The councils were responsible for social welfare, education and family and inheritance law. One member of each council was a clergyman appointed by the Church or Muslim scholars, and the rest were elected by members of guilds, merchants and other well-to-do subjects of the sultan.

The Great Cretan Revolution: 1866 to 1869

After twenty-five years of uneasy peace, 1866 saw perhaps the greatest uprising of the Ottoman years. Underlying this eruption was the Cretan Christians' continuing dissatisfaction with their inferior status and despair that they would ever attain freedom or union with Greece. As is often the case, the immediate sparks that ignited the rebellion were almost trivial. Ismael Pasha, the governor appointed in 1861, was initially a just and mild ruler, to the extent that the Cretans had petitioned that he stay in post after the end of his term. Then, after a short period, he changed tactics. In spite of the terms of the 1856 edict, he instituted harsh new taxation measures, mainly on agricultural produce. When he began to interfere in Church affairs, involving himself in a dispute between the Councils of Elders and the monasteries, the Cretans felt he had overstepped the mark.

In May 1866, representatives from all over Crete gathered near

Chania and composed a petition to the sultan, asking him to intervene. At the same time, they again petitioned the Great Powers to
support them in achieving union with Greece. The sultan firmly
rejected their demands, and after a meeting near Apokoronas the representatives formed themselves into a revolutionary General Assembly and declared revolution. Support from outside was mixed. Britain
and France were still determined to keep the Ottoman Empire intact,
while the former also had its own reasons for supporting the status
quo. After the rebellion of 1857 to 1859 in India and the continuing
troubles in Ireland, the last thing the British government wanted was
to be seen to support a nationalistic religious group fighting against an
imperial master. Russia, on the other hand, after being outvoted at the
Treaty of Paris, supported the idea of an independent Crete.

Within Greece itself, opinion was divided. The government, dependent on the support of Britain and France, was definitely opposed to the
revolution. A communiqué from the minister of foreign affairs was
unequivocal:

> Under the present state of affairs in Europe and the East, any impru-
> dent move in Crete would certainly be disastrous. The Cretans must
> be extremely cautious and not be drawn into any kind of insurgency,
> whether from a poor estimation of the political situation in Europe
> or from the irresponsible exhortations and incitements of hasty and
> reckless persons.[13]

However, this was not the opinion of all in parliament, and popular
opinion in Greece was firmly on the side of the rebels. A Central
Committee for the Support of the Cretans was set up, and supplies
including money and food were collected in mainland Greece and on
the islands. Some areas also sent volunteers and weapons.

The Cretans made a touching appeal to the president of the United
States, asking for help in turning the heads of the Great Powers:

> Mr. President, if injustice in your mother land was set right by the
> sacred struggle which through Divine blessing was conducted to
> triumph by the ever-to-be remembered WASHINGTON, how is
> ours justified? We should be happy if we had only the shadow of the

benefits which your country gained in that epoch. Being in such a condition, we, the respectfully undersigned representatives of the Cretan people dare to ask, Mr. President, the intercession of the great democracy, one in which you happily reside, in order that our matters may obtain attention from the cabinets of the great European Powers. Blessing the highest for the prospects and strength of the glorious democracy of the United States of America, we take the liberty of subscribing ourselves the humble servants of your Excellency, the representatives of the Cretan People.[14]

The appeal brought little practical help, partly because of the **Monroe Doctrine,** which limited American influence outside its own continent, and partly because of the economic and political crisis the United States was facing in the aftermath of its civil war. Nevertheless, the Cretans received considerable moral and financial support from the American people, together with a small number of volunteer fighters.

Within Crete, there was a great imbalance between the two sides. Ottoman and Egyptian troops numbered some 45,000, together with about 10,000 Cretan Muslims under arms. The army was well equipped, with up-to-date equipment and the full financial support of the empire. Since the reorganisation of the imperial army, the troops were loyal and well disciplined, with experienced officers and a clear line of command. The rebels had about 25,000 men under arms – including volunteers from Greece itself, other parts of Europe and the United States – but, although most of them were experienced and courageous fighters, the old problem of a command structure, or lack of one, remained a fundamental weakness. Power was in the hands of the General Assembly, but this body varied in its composition and frequently moved its base. Each of the leaders in Chania, Rethymnon and the eastern region had the title "commander", but there was no overall commander-in-chief.

As news of the uprising spread, there was a general flight of Muslims from the villages to the larger towns, and Christians to the mountains. Early successes by the rebels led the sultan to recall the veteran Mustafa Naili Pasha Giritli. His first step was diplomatic, offering satisfaction of all just demands and an amnesty in return for the rebels laying down their arms. This was rejected immediately by the assembly, which by now would not be satisfied by anything less than freedom. For many, even that was not enough, and the battle cry now became Enosis i Thanatos (Union or Death). Early victories by Mustafa in the area of Theriso were balanced by surprise attacks and defeats on the march, in which he lost many men. The defeat of one of the rebel commanders with heavy losses at Vafes, south-east of Chania, was a tremendous blow to the rebels' morale, and led to another offer by Mustafa of amnesty and safe passage out of Crete for the Greek volunteers. This time, many villages across the island accepted, and it seemed that the revolution might die before it had really begun.

Mustafa now turned his attention to the Rethymnon area, and led 15,000 men to Arkadi monastery, where the revolutionary commanders had their headquarters. About 300 armed men and 600 women and children took refuge in the heavily fortified monastery, which was surrounded by the Ottoman forces. Having agreed safe passage for the few who wanted to leave, the abbot, Gabriel Marinakis, and the commander, Ioannis Dimakopoulos, rejected the terms of surrender offered by Mustafa. Although the rebels held out for a day, Marinakis being killed fighting on the walls, the Ottomans brought up huge cannons and set up a continuous bombardment, eventually smashing the west gate. As they broke in at dawn on 8th November, the rebels blew up the powder magazine, killing most of the Cretans but also inflicting massive damage on the Ottoman army. Hundreds were killed, but the ramifications of this tragedy went far beyond the immediate battle. The sacrifice became a great moral victory for the rebels, and support for the revolution spread throughout Europe and the United States, bringing fresh volunteers from Serbia, Hungary and Italy, as well as Greece.[15]

Moving further east, Mustafa had mixed fortunes, defeating the rebels in several battles but suffering heavy losses. Leaving the east unresolved for now, he turned back towards the west. Here there were the usual cases of bickering between the leaders and shortages of weapons, and he met little resistance. Much of Sfakia now capitulated, although Mustafa again suffered extensive losses of men, arms and supplies in ambushes as he withdrew for the winter. European (especially French) opinion was now shifting in favour of Crete, and with the war in something of a stalemate, the sultan again tried diplomacy. He issued a decree calling for the election of representatives, one Muslim and one Christian for each province, to meet in Constantinople for a resolution of the problems. When he received no response from the revolutionaries, he turned back to the military option, replacing Mustafa with a very able general, Ömer Pasha.

Ömer's strategy was two-pronged. First he attacked Sfakia but, failing to make much progress, he left his second in command to hold his positions in the Apokoronas and Kydonia areas and turned east to Lassithi. All the main passes were held by the rebels, but Ömer joined with forces from western Crete at Kastelli and then, in a clever and courageous flanking manoeuvre, took the army over the mountains, sweeping down on Lassithi to defeat the rebel army on the plain. However, no sooner had he turned back west to resume his attack on Sfakia than the rebels and villagers returned to the Lassithi plateau. Although Ömer again succeeded in subduing Sfakia, the pattern of the war was becoming clear: the Ottoman army was usually able to defeat the rebels in open battle, but was unable to impose a permanent and stable rule in the more remote areas. This stalemate caused the sultan again to consider diplomacy and to adopt a more conciliatory policy.

In September 1867, Ömer was recalled, and a five-week ceasefire and general amnesty were declared. The sultan sent his grand vizier, the reformist but authoritarian Mehmed Emin Aali Pasha, to Crete, with a remit to accept almost any form of government short of union with Greece. He initially offered administrative concessions and various privileges for the Christians, together with a basic form of autonomy for Crete. In spite of a largely negative response from the General Assembly, he went ahead and announced elections in the Ottoman-held areas. An assembly of thirty Muslims and twenty Christians was duly convened in Chania. Although the assembly had little legitimacy on the island as a whole, it did have the support of the British and the anti-revolutionary faction, and pointed the way towards a possible future for Crete.

An imperial decree, the **Organic Act**, was issued in January 1868, and consolidated the reforms outlined by Aali Pasha. Crete was to become an administrative province of the empire under a governor-general appointed by the sultan. The island was divided into five councils and twenty-five provinces, each governed by both Christians and Muslims, according to a fixed ratio. Turkish and Greek were both recognised as official languages. Some tax concessions were granted, and a Commercial Bank was established. Arrangements were also made for the election of a General Assembly, which would meet for forty days each year and would be responsible for legislation of a strictly local nature, such as transport, public works, trade, farming and education. At the same time, to solve the problem of permanent control, the new governor had a series of heavily fortified towers built at strategic points in all the provinces. Each was manned by a permanent garrison, which could maintain surveillance in all parts of the island.

The revolution was by now rapidly losing steam and, although guerrilla warfare and lightning strikes continued, supplies were much reduced and morale was low. Few Greek ships were able to get past the Ottoman fleet. In any case, as European diplomacy switched back to support of the empire, the Great Powers forbade Greece from setting up volunteer forces to help rebellions in any Ottoman areas and from sending provisions. When the revolutionary government was besieged near Kissamos and most of its representatives killed, the few remaining leaders in the east gave up the struggle, some accepting amnesty, some becoming outlaws. By January 1869, the great revolution was over.

Stumbling Towards Freedom: 1869 to 1898

The Organic Act was undoubtedly a step forward, and was seen by the Ottoman government as a major concession to the Christians of Crete. Nevertheless, it had fundamental flaws and remained uneven in its treatment of Muslims and Christians. It was never likely to gain acceptance by the Christians, who now had broader aims. The new General Assembly was of mixed membership, but the Christian population (constituting 74% of the Cretan whole) was only allowed a majority of two, later just one. Moreover, the assembly was indirectly elected by the local committees of elders, which left great scope for fraud and intimidation. The debates of the assembly were chaired by the governor-general, who, together with the sultan, had to ratify all decisions.

In the event, there were continual violations even of these limited terms, while much of the decree was never fully implemented at all. Very few decisions were ever ratified, and the governor-general frequently dissolved the assembly before its forty days were up. Protests to the Sublime Porte were ignored and the protesters either exiled or imprisoned. For ten years following the end of the revolution, the island was administered by military leaders who were generally anti-Christian and despotic. The **beys**, wealthy Muslim landowners who now exercised most of the power on the island, were opposed to even the limited rights granted by the Organic Act. In general, after the hope and excitement of the Great Revolution, Crete now entered a period of stagnation. Planned public works were abandoned, and social welfare became virtually non-existent. Even the Orphans' Fund, set up in 1858 as part of Sami Pasha's reforms, was riddled with corruption and served mainly as a source of pocket money for the beys who administered it.

In 1875, rebellion against Ottoman rule broke out in Bosnia-Herzegovina, reigniting the revolutionary spirit in Crete. There were discussions in both Crete and Greece on the way forward and, although there was little support for an uprising, the idea of Crete as a British protectorate gained new impetus. The General Assembly petitioned the Sublime Porte to implement the terms of the Organic Act fully and to issue an imperial decree to safeguard its provisions. This was ignored, and when a further petition was sent to the governor-general asking that Crete be considered a self-administered province, he responded by dissolving the assembly and ordering the arrest of the Christian representatives, who fled to Apokoronas. In 1876, the sultan granted the first constitution to his empire, which allowed Crete to send two representatives, one from each faith, to the parliament in Constantinople. It was a measure of the distrust felt towards the empire that the Cretan Christians regarded this as a step backwards that returned the island to the status of a province. In the first election of March 1877, only five Christians voted, and the representative elected refused office, as did his replacement.

The Bosnian-Herzegovinian rebellion had now escalated into a war between the Ottoman Empire and Russia and, by the spring of 1877, new opportunities for uprising were opening up. The likely victory of

Russia and the weakness of the empire also led to renewed support from Greece, including help in returning exiled leaders to Crete. With no prospect of reinforcements from the Sublime Porte, the administration again tried negotiations, supported by the British. In no mood for compromise, a Pan-Cretan Revolutionary Assembly was called in Fres, Apokoronas, which demanded that Crete be immediately declared an autonomous principality, paying tribute to the sultan, and that the governor should be a Christian, his election being guaranteed by the Great Powers. When no reply was received, rebellion broke out across the island in January 1878. The Muslims again fled to the cities and, within a short time, the whole island was in rebel hands except for the three main cities, plus the fortresses at Ierapetra, Spinalonga, Izzeddin, Kissamos and Gramvousa.

Within a month, the war between Russia and the Ottoman Empire was ended by the Treaty of San Stefano, which obliged the empire to comply with all the provisions of the Organic Act. By now, the rebels expected more, and the Great Powers promised that the Cretan question would be fully considered at the Congress of Berlin which had been called to revise the Treaty of San Stefano. The consuls of the Great Powers ordered a ceasefire but, when the Congress added nothing to the treaty, the armed struggle continued. The British now proposed new concessions to the rebels and, after further negotiations, the **Halepa Charter** was signed by all parties and ratified by imperial decree.

The charter, while not meeting all the aspirations of the assembly, was a substantial improvement on the Organic Act. The governor-general *could* be a Christian, although that would not necessarily be the case. He would be appointed for a five-year term, which could be renewable. If the governor-general were a Christian, he would be assisted by a Muslim councillor, and vice versa. The General Assembly would consist of eighty deputies, forty-nine of them Christian and thirty-one Muslim. A Cretan gendarmerie of both faiths was to be set up. Greek would become the official language of the island, although official documents would be issued in both Greek and Turkish. There was to be a general amnesty and temporary tax exemptions. There was even provision for the setting up of literary associations and a free press. The charter ushered in another decade of relative peace, and under Ioannis Fotiadis (governor from 1880 to 1885) there was some progress in social and economic affairs, with new schools being established and the first attempts to protect Cretan antiquities. Nevertheless, there were weaknesses in the implementation of some of the terms of the charter. The first governor was replaced after only fourteen days, and Fotiadis was the only one to serve his full term. The historian Leonidas Kallivretakis makes a pertinent comment:

> It is notable that the Sublime Porte appeared more prepared to appoint governors of Christian origin (which was only envisaged as a possibility in the Halepa Pact) than to keep them in post for five years (which was an express obligation).[16]

This was also a decade of considerable political activity within the assembly. The representatives fell broadly into two parties, conservative and liberal, but the political groupings in the assembly were, in fact, far more complex. The Organic Act had resulted in a number of administrative posts, most of which were filled by members of old Cretan families, very conscious of their social standing and often on good terms with the Ottoman administration. These represented the conservative wing of the assembly. Although they included popular leaders like Hadji-Michalis Yannaris, there was a general feeling that they regarded the assembly as a meal ticket, and they were nicknamed the Karavanades. This term is almost impossible to translate directly, but it includes the ideas of greed, self-interest and social snobbery. The Karavanades were often politically revolutionary but socially conservative, and would sometimes form alliances with powerful Muslim beys to oppose even limited reform measures instituted by the Sublime Porte. Most of the senior clergy were within the group.

The liberals, known as xypoliti (barefoots), were generally more progressive, and included almost all the scholars and many lower clergy. Their aim was to reform the system and, although they were in the majority, they were often persecuted by the more powerful Karavanades as well as by the authorities. There was a similar division on the Muslim side, but the exact composition of all groups tended to fluctuate depending on the exact issue. During this period, the political world was quite anarchic, and disputes often degenerated into violence, vandalism and even murder. The assembly also acted as an electoral court, which meant that much of the forty-day session was often wasted in challenges to the results and attempts to invalidate them. Since the Halepa Charter also called for the majority of public offices to be filled by election, the political volatility spilled over into the administration as well.

The 1888 election was won by the xypoliti and, in spite of continual objections, they managed to pass several useful reforms relating to the organisation of the municipalities and the gendarmerie, and the foundation of a bank. Probably the most significant reform was a new electoral law which, for the first time, introduced secret suffrage for all men. The 1889 election was also won by the xypoliti, with a substantial majority of forty to eleven among the Christian members. The Karavanades immediately tabled a motion calling for union with Greece, an illegal act at the time and probably designed to disrupt the working of the assembly. With the reluctant support of the majority, the resolution was passed, together with a number of economic demands. The governor-general offered to discuss solutions to the economic problems, but rejected the independence movement. He dissolved the assembly and issued an arrest warrant for the leading members, who fled to the mountains and declared revolution. There were armed clashes between Christians and Muslims and amongst rival Christian groups. When the Greek government declared its intention to intervene to protect the Christian population, the Sublime Porte replaced the governor-general with a hard-line military commander, Sakir Pasha.

The new governor declared martial law, instituted courts martial and enforced the death penalty on a regular basis. He restricted the activities of the Muslims and drove the armed Christians into the mountains, while the majority of the Christian members of the assembly fled to Greece. Using the revolt as an excuse, he revoked the Halepa Charter without informing the Great Powers, and returned Crete to direct Ottoman rule. The five-year term for the governor was abolished, judges and public prosecutors were appointed for life, and preference was given to Turkish speakers in appointments to the civil service. The General Assembly was reduced to fifty-seven members, thirty-five of them Christian and twenty-two Muslim, again elected indirectly. All political and religious privileges were revoked, heavy taxation was imposed and it seemed as though Crete had gone back to square one.

Over the next five years, there was much discussion of rebellion but little action, and the Christian Cretans were coming to terms with the fact that union with Greece was not a realistic aim, at least in the short term. The mood was swinging towards the creation of an autonomous or semi-autonomous state under the protection of the Great Powers. From that position, union could be reconsidered when the circumstances were more favourable.

In 1895, a massacre of Armenians in the Ottoman Empire caused European opinion to turn against the Sublime Porte, and again a weak Ottoman government reversed its policy. The governor-general was replaced by a Christian, Alexander Karatheodoris, and Christians again began to participate both in the General Assembly and in public office. This time, it was the Muslim population that objected to the new governor, and bands of Muslims began to commit acts of violence in an attempt to provoke a state of emergency. Their efforts were matched by Christian guerrilla groups, and the general anarchy led to Karatheodoris dissolving the assembly. An able Sfakian politician, Manousos Koundouros, organised a secret action committee, which approved a note to be sent to the consulates of the Great Powers, calling for Crete to be declared autonomous and for the full terms of the Halepa Charter to be restored with improvements. This was considered seditious, and arrests were ordered, without success. A new governor-general decreed a general amnesty, but this was rejected by the revolutionaries, who successfully besieged the Ottoman garrison at Vamos, south-east of Chania. Volunteers again headed for Crete, and violence escalated across the island. The massacre of monks at the monastery of Saint John in Anopoli shocked the Great Powers into intervening. They pressurised the Sublime Porte into making concessions, and new terms were agreed by their consuls and accepted by the rebels. Crete was to have full economic and judicial independence, with the Great Powers as guarantors, and the terms of the Halepa Charter were to be restored. The consuls formed themselves into a consular commission to oversee the reform process.

The "Last" Revolution: 1897 to 1898

It was becoming clear that, while the Christians of Crete were inching towards their aim of full autonomy, it was now the Muslim population that was afraid of losing its privileged position. Communal violence increased, and both sides burned olive plantations, causing disruption to agricultural production. In the summer of 1896, many mosques and Muslim settlements were burned down, and in September 1896 the situation deteriorated further with the murder of a Christian public prosecutor in Chania. Under pressure from the Great Powers, the Ottoman Empire implemented some of the rulings of the constitution of 1878, agreed in the Halepa Charter. A Cretan gendarmerie was set up under a British major, but this never got off the ground before the fighting broke out in earnest. The violence spread, and included the burning of the bishop's residence and the Christian areas of Chania. Four hundred sailors and marines from Britain, France and Austria-Hungary landed at Chania to protect European lives and property. These were later followed by Italian and German contingents. It is estimated that, during this period, over 3,000 Christian families and over 5,000 Muslim families were left homeless, the latter mainly taking refuge in the cities, putting great pressure on the infrastructure and creating public health problems.

At this point, the Greek government intervened, sending warships under the command of Prince George, second son of the king of Greece, to blockade transports from the Ottoman Empire. Cretan officers in the Greek army were ordered to resign and set up a volunteer force to send to Crete and, in February 1897, 1,500 men landed under the command of Colonel Timoleon Vassos, a representative of the king. Vassos proclaimed that he had come to occupy the island in the name of the king of the Hellenes. The expeditionary force was greeted with jubilation by the Christians, and the rebellion quickly spread, with some initial successes. Meanwhile, the governor-general, Berovic Pasha, took refuge on a Russian ship and fled to Trieste. With the arrival of Prince George and Vassos, the international troops in Chania now turned their attention to trying to stop the revolution getting out of control. Before long, a larger force of regular troops landed, and a 6 km exclusion zone was established around Candia.

At one point, the rebel army violated the exclusion zone; the response was swift and severe. European warships bombarded the revolutionary military camp on the Akrotiri peninsula, leading to widespread outrage across Europe. Similar bombardments occurred at Malaxa and Kissamos in support of Ottoman forces under attack from Greek and Cretan Christian forces. To co-ordinate their actions, the Great Powers set up the Council of Admirals, formed from the commanders of each of the fleets.

The Great Powers now controlled all the principal coastal towns and had complete control of the sea, but their military position was not brilliant. They were faced with the opposition of 1,500 Greek troops plus an unknown number of armed Christian rebels, not to mention a potentially violent reaction from several thousand Ottoman troops and armed Muslim irregulars. In this context, they continued their attempts to persuade the insurgents to accept a ceasefire and limit their demands to autonomy, which was now becoming almost a certainty. In a memorandum, the Powers made their intentions explicit:

> Europe has decided that Crete is to be no longer governed by the Turks, but to be autonomous and governed by its own people; any aggressive acts by Cretan Christians therefore only prejudice the case before Europe.[17]

Nevertheless, both the Cretan rebels and the Greek government still refused to agree to anything short of union and the war raged on in all parts of the island, especially the Candia area.

In April and May 1897, in response to the Greek intervention in Crete and Greek attacks over what was then its northern border into Ottoman territory, the empire declared war on Greece: Greece lost the war within 30 days. As a result, Greece was forced to withdraw its troops from Crete, and the Cretan leaders were no longer in a position to hold out for union. In a unanimous vote, the General Assembly accepted autonomy. The Cretans requested a governor from among the Great Powers, believing that this would add legitimacy to the island and ensure it received the support of Europe. Since there was total disagreement among the Great Powers over who should be selected, Prince George of Greece was finally appointed as high commissioner, against the wishes of the Sublime Porte, which did not want a Greek. An executive council of five men took over the internal administration until his arrival. The council included a young politician who we will see much more of later: Eleftherios Venizelos.

On 18th July 1898, the General Assembly issued a statement:

> The Assembly of the Cretans, working with exemplary order and unanimity of purpose, has decided to accept the plan for a caretaker administration of the island proposed by the commanders of the fleets in accordance with the decision of the Protecting Powers.[18]

Germany had for some time been drawing closer to the Ottoman Empire, and had finally withdrawn from the Cretan Concert late in 1897, followed in 1898 by Austria-Hungary. The protecting powers were therefore Britain, Italy, Russia and France. Oversight of the island was provided by the Council of Admirals, whose main duty was the maintenance of order. One of its actions, however, ended up creating considerable disorder. In order to raise funds to begin establishing the new administration, the Council of Admirals decided to take over the customs houses at the beginning of September 1898, replacing the Muslim staff with Christians. Reservations were expressed by the British admiral and by the Russian, Italian and British consuls, but these were ignored. Many of the Muslims were, of course, outraged. Not only had the customs officials lost their jobs, at a time when the towns were packed with refugees, but they felt that they were being unfairly targeted for tax collection anyway. While this might not have been the intention of the admirals, it was effectively true. At that time, the Christians in the countryside were largely out of reach of the tax collectors, so that any taxes collected came from the predominantly Muslim cities. In short, as the historian Mick McTiernan has written, "The Muslims considered themselves as being asked to pay for the introduction of a Christian dominated regime, intent on removing existing Muslim privileges."[19]

While Muslims in Chania and Rethymnon generally accepted the takeover of the customs houses by the admirals, it was a very different matter in Candia. After meeting some opposition, the British consul and the commander of the British troops managed to reach a compromise, which defused the situation, but were immediately ordered by the admirals to "take possession at once even by force".[20] When a small group of British soldiers attempted to seize the customs house, they were met by angry Muslim demonstrators. It is not known whether the British or the Muslims fired first, but very soon there was an exchange of fire, leading to a full-scale battle in which the British troops were forced to retreat. Meanwhile, the protesters continued to attack Christian areas, burning shops and offices, and killing hundreds. The governor declared martial law on 9th September, which was sufficient to restore order until reinforcements could be brought in. About 800 Christians – including the British vice-consul, who was a Cretan, and two British subjects – died in the riots, as did twenty-nine Muslims. Seventeen British servicemen were killed, and thirty-nine seriously wounded. A Victoria Cross was awarded to Royal Naval Surgeon William Maillard. Having reached the relative safety of the customs house, he saw a sailor fall wounded and, according to the official citation:

> Returning through a perfect deluge of bullets into the boat ... [he] endeavoured to bring into safety Arthur Stroud, Ordinary Seaman, who had fallen back wounded into the boat as the other men jumped ashore. Surgeon Maillard failed to bring Stroud in only through the boat being adrift, and it being beyond his strength to lift the man (who was almost dead) out of so unstable a platform. Surgeon Maillard returned to his post with his clothes riddled with bullets, though he himself was unhurt.[21]

After order had been restored, the British authorities set up courts martial to try the riot leaders and those believed to be guilty of the murders of British servicemen, although many in Britain regarded the institution of courts martial in the circumstances as being of dubious legality. It was argued that the British military did not have the authority to try Ottoman citizens for crimes committed against British troops, when those troops were in Crete with the consent of the Ottoman government. In any event, courts martial were set up in Candia to try those accused of killing British soldiers, and a separate tribunal was established to try those involved in the murder of British civilians. Although the latter was organised entirely by the British, it was designated an International Military Tribunal. At the two courts martial held, twelve people were sentenced to death, four to twenty years of penal servitude and one acquitted, while the International Military Tribunal resulted in a further five executions. Although public executions had been abolished in the United Kingdom thirty years before, all the executions were public hangings from the ramparts above Candia. Even contemporary observers considered this to be somewhat unusual, but justified it as a way of intimidating other potential rioters, as one observer noted in his diary:

> Upon the wall ... rose ... a giant box-like hut ... In England a public execution is unthinkable; as an example to the fanatical hordes in the East it is often imperative for the common safety. The gallows was of a design set up on the highest point of the city where none could fail to see it.[22]

A British sailor was even blunter in his appraisal:

> Each nationality had its own way of punishing the blood-thirsty native. The Italian shot them on sight; the French chopped their heads off; the Russian whipped them to death – all without a vestige of a trial. But the British – good old solid British – brought them on board the battleships, imprisoned them in cages composed of torpedo nets on the mess-deck and solemnly tried them by Court-Martial. Afterwards we hanged them – solemnly, and in the face of all men; and I don't think there was a man among us who felt sorry for these degraded beasts whose murders had been so fearful.[23]

Sixty further cases were referred to the Italian Military Commission in Chania, of whom two were executed by firing squad for the murder of Cretan Christians.

There had been an agreement that small garrisons of Ottoman troops be left in the fortresses as symbols of the continuing sovereignty of the sultan, but it was decided that the admirals would be unable to restore order as long as the troops remained. Some 10,000 Ottoman troops and officials were therefore forced to leave the island, and the

Ottoman fleet was banned from Cretan waters. The evacuation proceeded peacefully for the most part, although it was subject to delaying tactics by the Sublime Porte. One elderly Ottoman colonel refused to leave voluntarily and had to be taken to the boat by an armed escort, thus preserving his honour. By the evening of 6th November, the last member of the Ottoman administration had left the island.

The Council of Admirals now issued a proclamation that all Cretans should give up their arms, and that Muslims would be under their protection. They should return to their villages and their lives and property should be respected. Throughout the island, the troops of the Great Powers set up temporary administrations, and were successful in the collection of arms from both Muslim and Christian civilians. Communal violence became extremely rare, although a potential flashpoint involved the way in which the new high commissioner was to arrive on the island. The proposal that Prince George should land from the Greek royal yacht was quickly vetoed by the Great Powers, and so he arrived in Crete in the French flagship, escorted by warships of the other three Great Powers.

Prince George landed on 21st December 1898, and on 26th December the Council of Admirals was dissolved. Although Crete was still legally under Ottoman sovereignty, in reality it was now able to govern itself for the first time in about 3,000 years.

Economy and Trade

The fighting of the nineteenth century resulted in large fluctuations in the population, due to both death and emigration. For example, the total population of Crete virtually halved between 1821 and 1830. Although the figures are approximate, there were about 213,000 people across Crete before the rebellion, but only 129,000 by 1832, according to that year's census. By 1858, the population had recovered to about 279,000, but then another 30,000 are believed to have died or emigrated during the revolution of 1866 to 1869. The reasonably accurate census of 1881 shows another recovery taking the population back to over 276,000. This period shows a gradual but significant increase in the proportion of Cretan land owned by Christians, from 20% at the beginning of the century to 60% in 1866. This caused one governor to comment wryly that, if the trend continued, the Christians would ultimately buy Crete from the Ottomans without the need for revolution. There was also a change in the proportions of the Muslim and Christian populations. The 1881 census includes a breakdown of the population by religion, and shows it to have been 73% Orthodox Christians and 26% Muslims (with the other 1% accounted for by a handful of Jews, Catholics, Protestants and Armenians). This is very different from before 1821, when the population was about half-and-half Muslim and Christian. The same census also shows that over 82% of the rural population was Christian, while 70% of the urban population was Muslim.

Not surprisingly, there was little development in the economy, and Crete remained almost exclusively agricultural. For much of the period, the land was under-cultivated and there were few developments in farming. As much as two thirds of the available land was left for grazing by sheep and goats, while the lack of a good road system restricted the amount of trade both locally and through the ports. During the revolutions, many Muslim landowners abandoned the countryside and sold their land to Christians. This generally led to the break-up of large estates into smallholdings, which tended to be less efficient. The farmers and their labourers shared harsh conditions and heavy taxation. Since there was no agricultural bank, loans against next year's crop could only be obtained from passing traders at exorbitant rates, sometimes as much as 25–39%.

The most important crop remained olive oil, which accounted for just under 50% of total agricultural production.[24] However, during the rebellion of 1821, there was large-scale destruction of olive trees, both by the Ottoman troops (for use as fuel) and by the Christians (as reprisals against the Muslims). This led to a decline in supply until the situation improved in the 1830s. Due to harvesting practices, lack of pruning and poor storage, Cretan olive oil was, at this time, of poor quality, and most of the production went to supply the soap industry, or was used for engine lubrication and lamp oil. Any surplus oil was sold to merchants who had the facilities to store it and then sell it on when prices peaked. Soap manufacture in Crete continued to prosper until the 1870s, when a number of poor olive harvests led to a fall in olive oil supply. At the same time, after the 1860s, Cretan soap began to suffer competition from the poorer-quality but cheaper soap from Rhodes and Mytilene. Markets in Anatolia were lost and, by the 1880s, some Cretan producers were desperate enough to add soapstone to the product, increasing the weight but reducing the quality. The only result was a further decline in demand for Cretan soap, and by 1893 there were just five factories left in operation, serving the domestic market only. This was in sharp contrast to 1881, when there were fifteen factories in Candia and ten in Chania. This collapse was one of many examples of the de-industrialising of Crete during the late nineteenth century.

The vineyards, like the olive groves, had been largely destroyed in the 1821 rebellion, and were mostly abandoned by their owners. For a long time there was little growth, but massive destruction of French vineyards by disease in the 1870s led to increased demand for grapes, raisins, wine and raki from Crete, which in turn led to higher prices and the planting of new vines. The government encouraged the expansion of vineyards by various measures, including a thirteen-year exemption from some taxes if the new cultivation was on previously abandoned or unused land. By the mid-1880s, demand dropped again as the vine disease in France came under control, and the French immediately imposed a high tariff on wine imports. Much of Crete's wine industry was now devoted to the production of brandy and, by the 1890s, there were already two distilleries operating in Iraklion, in a rare case of exceptions to the general trend towards de-industrialisation.

Otherwise, carob and citrus tree production increased to meet overseas demand, and levels of exports remained relatively steady for most of the period. In contrast, textile production was extremely volatile and was largely controlled by external factors. Cotton, for example, was in limited supply and of poor quality, but during the American Civil War Britain encouraged cotton farming in Crete to compensate for the loss of United States supplies. After the end of the American Civil War, demand for Cretan cotton plummeted, and this, together with the disruption of the 1866 Great Cretan Revolution, saw the virtual extinction of cotton production in Crete. Silk farming also had fluctuating fortunes. A silkworm disease in France in 1853 led to increased demand, and the price of Cretan silk in 1856 was double the price of

1836. The silk was of a high quality, and silk-spinning mills were set up in Chania and Candia. Then, in the 1860s, it was the turn of Crete to suffer losses, which were due to disease and damage caused by its 1866 revolution, leaving the silk farmers in no position to compete with silk being imported to Europe from the Far East. Prices plummeted, the farmers began to export the raw silk cocoons for spinning elsewhere, and another industry died.

From the middle of the century, a cottage industry of weaving developed, working mainly with wool but also with flax, cotton and silk. However, the cloth produced was chiefly for personal use within the household, with any surplus being sold in the domestic market. There were growing imports of European fabrics, mainly from England. Another disturbing trend in the balance of trade was the increasing import of flour rather than grain, implying that even the industry of milling was in decline. Before 1857, there had been no flour imports. By the 1880s, flour represented 9% of all imports, while in the early years of the twentieth century this percentage had climbed to 18.5%. All in all, in spite of occasional successes, the Cretan economy was fairly stagnant during the nineteenth century. Overseas trade was frequently interrupted by naval blockades by one or the other side during rebellions, and what industry existed was either small in scale or in decline. Imports exceeded exports for most of the period, and the trade gap widened.

Health

There were some improvements in infrastructure and social welfare during the Egyptian rule of Mehmet Ali, among which were significant public health reforms.[25] An Austrian doctor and botanist had visited Crete in 1817 and reported a pretty grim picture. There were very few doctors in the towns and a total lack of medical care for the majority of the population. The plague and smallpox were rampant, and yet there was a complete absence of hospitals and a total disregard of hygiene. Once Egyptian rule was established, Mehmet Ali set out to emulate in Crete the major improvements he had already begun in the Egyptian health system. His aim was to protect and improve the health of the occupying army and administration, but this, of course, had the bonus of also protecting the local population from disease. Italian and French doctors and pharmacists were brought to the island, and an ambitious programme of building was begun. Sanitary stations, lazarettos, dispensaries and hospitals were built, and generous funding was allocated for the purpose. The lazarettos and sanitary stations actually ended up making a profit from the issuing of certificates of health for travellers and goods. Most importantly, the smallpox vaccine was imported from France for the free vaccination of all children, regardless of religion.

The government also took steps to eradicate, or at least control, the social causes of ill health. Vagrancy was reduced by giving a small pension to all soldiers retired on medical grounds, while some financial support was given to the very poor – in return for which they had to cultivate some idle land. Even prostitution was controlled and restricted to specified areas. Street cleaning was carried out more thoroughly, both for hygienic reasons and in response to the great importance placed on cleanliness in the Qur'an. Quarantine rules were enforced, in spite of various medical theories of the time that the plague was not communicable and that quarantine was an unacceptable interference with trade, communication and the free movement of people. Although the rules were not always followed, it is noticeable that there were no outbreaks of the plague in Crete during the 1830s. Health and social reforms were not always welcomed by the Cretans, who regarded them with suspicion as being yet another means of control by the government. They probably had a point, as the reforms primarily served military needs and helped to legitimise Egyptian rule in the eyes of the Great Powers, with promotion of social welfare being a secondary consideration. Nevertheless, the reforms did help to improve the health of Cretans during the decade of Egyptian rule, and, to a lesser extent, in the years after.

Education

As with almost every other aspect of society between 1821 and 1898, the education system waxed and waned. By the end of the eighteenth century, elementary schools had begun to appear in the towns. But, after the rebellion of 1821, the Ottoman authorities became suspicious of Christian schools as offering opportunities to teach sedition. All schools were closed, and their teachers either fled or were imprisoned. Apart from the school established by the rebels on Gramvousa in 1826, there was little formal education on the island for several years.

This is perhaps a good point at which to tackle the thorny issue of "secret schools". Throughout Greece, it was widely believed that, under oppressive Ottoman rule, children were forced to have lessons in secret, usually in monasteries. Although most historians, including Greeks, have found no evidence for the existence of these schools, the story refuses to die out completely. It seems possible that, although there was never any widespread use of or even need for secret schools, they may have existed as a temporary measure during periods of oppression such as between 1821 and 1830. It is also conceivable that the Ottoman authorities were correct in their suspicions, and secret revolutionary training may have taken place.

During the period of Egyptian rule, the situation improved, and the administration allowed the schools to open again. On a visit to Crete in 1833, Mehmet Ali gave his somewhat supercilious blessing to the establishment of schools:

> It is only right that the government should save the people of the island from ignorance and perdition and that they should be enlightened by knowledge and education.[26]

In 1837, an American school was founded in Chania with 400 boys, 150 girls, four male teachers and two female teachers. It quickly gained a considerable reputation, but was viewed with suspicion by the Patriarch of Constantinople, who regarded it as a den of Lutheran and Calvinist ideas. He made several attempts to have the school shut down, but without success. In the event, the school was closed by the sultan in 1843, along with all American schools in the Ottoman Empire.

Outside the main towns, education was still largely in the hands of the Church, which ran small schools in the monasteries and villages. In 1842, an interesting development occurred in Rethymnon, where the school began a process of training the best twenty-four pupils to be elementary teachers. They were provided with teaching aids, given a small salary and sent to establish elementary schools in villages around the island. After the Hatt-i Hümayun of 1856, the number of schools of all types increased and, by 1866, there were boys' and girls' schools in all the major towns.

These promising improvements in educational standards were completely disrupted by the rebellion of 1866 to 1869, but recovery was relatively quick, aided by the Organic Act's establishment of Greek as the official language. Greek was now taught in both Christian and Muslim schools and, by 1872, education was again in a healthy situation. The Halepa Charter made provision for education associations to be founded, and this resulted in renewed cultural activity including the publishing of newspapers and the founding of public libraries. After years of spasmodic and unco-ordinated education in Crete, the General Assembly passed the 1881 Education Act, which made elementary schooling compulsory for all boys and girls, and established secondary schools in Chania, Candia, Rethymnon and Neapolis.

Sadly, in spite of this progress, illiteracy remained a problem, especially in rural areas. Some wealthier families were able to send their children to schools in Athens or Constantinople, but the vast majority were unable to read a newspaper. According to the 1881 census, the illiteracy rate for Christian men was 82% and for Christian women it was 97%. The situation was marginally better for the mainly town-dwelling Muslims, with illiteracy rates of 81% and 88% for Muslim men and women respectively. After the Education Act, the situation began to improve, but there can be no doubt that the nineteenth century was the nadir of education in Crete.

The Church and Religious Relations

Throughout the period of revolutions, the Church played an important role in the struggle for freedom. From the beginning, prominent Church leaders were involved in the Friendly Society, and Church wealth was often put at the disposal of the rebels. As we have seen, clerics were regularly on the front line as hostages or victims of reprisals, but many went further and gave up their religious vocations in order to fight beside the insurgents. Others offered their education to the revolutionary assemblies by acting as secretaries or diplomats. In general, the Orthodox Church does not canonise warriors, so, although they are revered by the people of Crete, the abbot and monks of Arkadi are not regarded as saints. The story of the New Martyr, Saint George of Alikianos, is different. During the 1866 uprising, he acted as a courier, carrying messages and proclamations between the revolutionary leaders in the Apokoronas region. Captured in possession of documents, he was executed in February 1867. Because he did not bear arms but showed tremendous courage in his work for the revolution, he was declared a saint, representative of many others who undertook similar feats.

As for the organisation of the Church, there were few significant developments. Pastoral care was limited for much of the time, especially in the years after 1821, when so many bishops were executed and the island was without a metropolitan for two years. Due to the drastic decline in the population, the patriarch merged the existing dioceses into five in 1831 but, by 1862, the number of dioceses had been restored almost to the status quo. In 1877, the General Assembly abandoned the system of paying the bishops from a special tax, a procedure that had been wide open to corruption and abuse, and began paying them a salary from the state treasury.

In 1859, there was an intriguing attempt to restore the fortunes of the Roman Catholic Church in Crete, which had been almost non-existent since the Venetians departed. A rumour began that France would step in and act as a protecting power if Crete converted to Catholicism and recognised the pope as head of the Church. Whether this originated from the Catholic Church or was subtle French diplomacy, there were 30,000 converts by the end of the year. The Church of Crete and the Patriarchate responded forcefully, supported by the Church of Greece and the Greek government. High-ranking clerics were sent to Crete to preach against the conversions, while the Greek government also supported the Orthodox cause. When the other Great Powers expressed alarm at the potential threat of excessive French influence, the movement quickly folded.

The policy of the Ottoman administration towards church buildings became somewhat milder in the nineteenth century, especially under Egyptian rule. Permission was granted more often for the repair and restoration of churches and, under the terms of the Hatt-i Hümayun, the ban on building new churches was finally lifted in 1856. In 1862, work began on the construction of Aghios Minas in Candia, which was finished and consecrated in 1895. During the same period, belfries were allowed, and church bells could be rung for the first time since 1669. The general relaxing of restrictions led to many crypto-Christians returning to the fold.

Earlier in the period of Ottoman rule, there had been severe penalties attached to converting from Islam to Christianity. It was for such an offence that the only other major Cretan saints of the period met their deaths. The two brothers Angelis and Manuel and their cousins George and Nicholas were prosperous young farmers, living near Rethymnon. They were crypto-Christians but, after taking part in the 1821 revolutionary war on the mainland, they decided the time was right to declare their Christianity. In spite of the certainty of a death sentence, they joined the other Christians to pay their taxes and were arrested as apostates from Islam. Refusing to fully embrace Islam, they were beheaded in October 1824.

Relations between Muslims and Christians generally deteriorated during the period of revolutions, and religious intolerance on both sides increased dramatically. Desecration of places of worship and graves and attacks on the religious symbols of both faiths became more frequent. After the 1821 revolution, the number of mixed marriages decreased, partly as a result of a ban on conversions or mixed marriages by the Egyptian rulers, and partly because of the increasing alienation between the two communities. As noted above, there was a substantial decline in the proportion of Muslims on the island, which cannot be explained by purely demographic causes such as birth rate or emigration. There seems to have also been a great increase in reconversion to Christianity, due to reasons such as fear of the growing power of the Christian community and, in some cases, desire to recover ancestral property that was now in the hands of Christians. The converts were generally looked down on by the Christians, given nicknames such as "Turko-Maria" or "Turko-Manolis". The sultan's Hatt-i Hümayun of 1856 proclaimed:

All forms of religion are and shall be freely professed in my domin-
ions, no subject of my Empire shall be hindered in the exercise of
the religion he professes, nor shall be in any way annoyed on this
account. No one shall be compelled to change their religion.[27]

This admirable statement of religious tolerance had the unfortunate
effect of making the Muslim community feel increasingly under threat
and, especially after the bitter fighting of 1866, there was a substantial increase in religious fanaticism among the Muslims, mainly in the
cities. On the other hand, Muslims in the villages often felt themselves
vulnerable and could expect little protection outside the towns. As
one Muslim of the time described it, they risked their lives even travelling to the local mill. The guarantees of safe passage given by the government and by the Great Powers were generally not trusted, and the
second half of the century saw the beginnings of large-scale emigration
of Muslims to Anatolia.

In spite of the general distrust between the two communities and
the level of violence on both sides, there were instances of humanitarian acts. There are stories of Muslims protecting local Christian families from attack, and vice versa. For example, the courageous actions of
two groups of sympathetic Christians are known to have saved some
Muslims' lives in February 1897, when a serious outbreak of violence by
Christians in and around Siteia – previously a relatively peaceful area
– led to over 800 Muslim deaths. The British consul, Sir Alfred Biliotti, reported afterwards that one group rescued forty-five Muslims,
including thirty-two women and children, from a cave where they
had taken refuge, "declaring that they would be killed before allowing
the Mussulmans whom they had taken under their protection to be
molested".[28] Biliotti also reported on another case:

Four Christians of the village of Sfaka ... undertook to convey to the
sea-shore twenty-five Mussulmans living in their village, and that
having met a band of about seventy armed Christians who wanted
to kill them, the four Christians mentioned above stood in front
of the Mussulmans, and declared to their co-religionists that they
would have to pass their corpses to reach the women and children
whom they had promised to rescue. This resolute attitude saved the

twenty-five Mussulmans. These are the only two cases which have been mentioned to me by the Mussulmans I met but there may have been many more as praiseworthy.[29]

14

Autonomy

1898 to 1913

Prince George, High Commissioner 1898 to 1906

The arrival of Prince George signalled a new beginning for Crete. Special services were held throughout the island, and the Ottoman flag was hauled down everywhere except above the fortress at Souda. There was widespread enthusiasm for the new arrangement. The politician Manousos Koundouros illustrated the general feeling of euphoria by writing in his diary, "The national dream was at last fulfilled. Prince George of Greece landed here today bearing the title of High Commissioner of the Great Powers, but in essence he was prince regent."[1] Even a minority of Muslims welcomed autonomy as bringing a real chance of peace and stability. Amidst all the rejoicing, however, there were signs that many Cretans regarded autonomy as only a prelude to union with Greece, as hinted at in Koundouros' final comment. The story was not yet over.

There were several immediate changes. Candia was renamed Iraklion, the drachma was established as the Cretan currency and a new flag was designed for the Cretan state. The flag had a white cross which divided it into four parts. Three of these were blue, while the top-left segment was red and contained a white star. This design was highly symbolic, the cross and the three blue segments paying homage to the Greek flag, and the white star on the red background representing the Muslim community. However, the flag was not entirely popular among the mostly Christian population. Many wanted a variation on the flag raised by Georgos Daskalakis at Arkadi in 1866. This had four blue segments and included the initials of the words "Kriti, Enosis, Eleftheria i Thanatos" ("Crete, Union, Freedom or Death"). It also included an abbreviation of the words "Jesus Christ Conquers".

The four protecting powers maintained oversight of the island, and stationed troops in each region: the Italians in Chania, the Russians in Rethymnon, the British in Iraklion and the French in Lassithi. Prince George was based in Chania, which remained the administrative capital of the island. The role of the troops of the protecting powers was ostensibly peacekeeping and security. On the whole, they fulfilled these duties satisfactorily but, as often happens in such situations, they sometimes acted more like occupiers. The military authorities occasionally used the need for security to justify some fairly arbitrary decisions. For example, they insisted that the General Assembly only meet in Chania, where it would be easier to control due to the presence of the foreign consulates and most of the western fleets. The British forces in Iraklion made themselves unpopular by refusing access for civilians to the Venetian walls, the traditional location for an evening volta (stroll). However, there were attempts to provide entertainment for the locals with frequent parades, military band concerts and, to the bemusement of many, cricket matches.

On his arrival in Crete, Prince George made a speech pledging to ensure good government and urging his subjects to pursue social harmony:

> I shall work to the utmost of my abilities for your prosperity; I shall make every effort to govern well, justly and impartially, so that you may obtain true security, which will be guaranteed solely by the rule of law and benevolent institutions. I know that you will be prudent and that you will obey the authorities ... You must now forget your old differences and, regardless of race or religion, you must now live in harmony together, under a common and benign state.[2]

This was a promising start, and within a few weeks efforts were made to set up institutions for the new state. A committee of twelve Christians and four Muslims was appointed to draw up a constitution, and January 1899 saw the holding of elections to the Cretan Assembly, open to all male Cretans over the age of twenty-five. However,

Muslims and Christians could only vote for members of their own faith. The first meeting of the assembly took place in February, consisting of 138 Christian and 50 Muslim deputies.

By April, the new constitution was published and approved by the Great Powers, including significant stipulations on freedom of religion, laid out in several articles:

Article 7: All Cretans are equal before the law and have the same rights, regardless of religion;

Article 8: Public posts are open to all Cretans, regardless of religion, according to their skills and qualifications; ...

Article 10: Freedom of religion is protected and proselytism is prohibited though not against the personal will of citizens who have henceforth the right to publicly declare their religious beliefs. Religious differences, or change of religion, have nothing to do with property rights, real rights, and legal obligations;

Article 11: Public worship of all officially recognized religions is free and protected by the state as long as it does not violate the law or police regulations.[3]

A government was formed, including Eleftherios Venizelos as Minister of Justice, the Muslim Hussein Yenitsarakis as Minister of Public Order and Manousos Koundouros as Foreign Minister, although in practice foreign affairs were largely determined by representatives of the protecting powers. The Bank of Crete was established with the help of the Bank of Greece, and the Great Powers granted the new state a loan of 4 million French francs to start it off. A new gendarmerie was set up, based on the Italian carabinieri and with Italian officers. All in all, the first few years of autonomy boded well for the future. According to Koundouros' diary, they "proved to be happy years for Crete from the point of view of public order, and civil and organisational projects".[4]

Unfortunately, Koundouros may have been a little optimistic, as there were already three sources of potential conflict. Firstly, the constitution, largely influenced by the Great Powers, was inherently conservative and put too much power in the hands of the high commissioner. The latter had wide – almost complete – executive, legislative and judicial powers, and was not subject to the decisions of the General Assembly, only to the wishes of the protecting powers. A quarter of the assembly was directly nominated by the high commissioner, and its function was almost entirely deliberative. It has been argued that, in essence, the early days of autonomy merely replaced direct Ottoman rule with direct international supervision.[5] The constitution explicitly stated that the high commissioner would "actively participate in and supervise all the authorities, and in general govern and represent the State."[6]

Secondly, this imbalance of power was exacerbated by the character of the prince himself. He was authoritarian and somewhat arrogant, and had a strong sense of his royal status. He also believed strongly that the interests of the country would be best served by his own centralist rule, and not by the assembly – beliefs that not only contradicted the essence of autonomy, but reversed the consultative processes implicit in settlements like the Halepa Charter. These personality traits and beliefs were encouraged by his advisors, most of whom he brought with him from Athens. The advisors themselves also caused bad feeling among the Cretans by grabbing many of the more important administrative posts. Hadji-Michalis Yannaris and a group of deputies wrote a letter of protest to the prince in July 1905, but with little result.

Thirdly, there was the old question of enosis, union with Greece. At this time, Prince George was firmly in support of autonomy, but believed that evolution towards union would happen gradually through representations and petitions to the Great Powers. The latter, on the other hand, were convinced that autonomy had solved the Cretan question once and for all, and insisted on maintaining the status quo. Far from being settled, however, the Cretan question was about to re-emerge, if it had ever truly gone away. While George was visiting European capitals in a futile attempt to canvass support for enosis, a growing number of people (led by Venizelos) were looking for immediate improvements. Venizelos was prepared to postpone demands for union in order to concentrate on achieving true autonomy and reduce the influence of the protecting powers. He proposed, as a first step, the removal of all foreign forces and their gradual replacement by the local civil guard, led by Greek officers. In order to achieve this, he needed the prince to be willing to share power with the assembly and ultimately to become accountable to it. There was, of course, no support for this idea from either the prince or his advisory council, and the argument quickly turned into an open rift. Referring to the prince's frequent trips to Europe to discuss the possibility of union, Venizelos said:

> Speaking as one of the three hundred thousand Cretans, I do not surrender to you the right to negotiate, without reference to others, the national interests of my homeland.[7]

This was too much for the prince, and he had Venizelos removed from office in March 1901, following this with a ban on freedom of the press and the detention of leading supporters of Venizelos.

A strong opposition to the high commissioner now gathered around Venizelos, and the acrimony between the two sides festered for several years, in spite of some attempts to bring them to the negotiating table. Elections in 1903 brought a majority for the supporters of the Prince, and Venizelos was imprisoned for a short time. An American journalist visiting Crete in 1905 summed up the situation concisely:

> A provisional arrangement which involved a mild but decidedly illiberal despotism, on the one hand, and economic stagnation on the other, could not be popular; and its failure only reinforced the hereditary instinct of the Cretans in favour of union with Greece. The more they manifested their discontent, the more the administration exaggerated its original tendency to arbitrary personal rule.[8]

The situation could not continue indefinitely. Things finally came to a head in February 1905, when Venizelos issued a declaration containing three alternative proposals: immediate union with Greece, active pursuit of union or, at the very least, a less authoritarian constitution. The declaration set the stage for action, with Venizelos threatening, "We will pursue the realisation of this plan even by means of popular insurrection."

The Theriso Rebellion, 1905

On 23rd March, 300 armed men gathered in the village of Theriso, south of Chania. The following day, they were joined by Venizelos, Konstantinos Manos and Konstantinos Foumis. The rebels formally raised the Greek flag and announced the creation of a Revolutionary Assembly and a provisional government. What came to be known as the Theriso Rebellion had begun. In the words of Venizelos, "When authority takes the people's liberties away by force, this opens the path to legitimate revolution and once this path is taken the victor will always be the people."[9]

A small force of gendarmes attempted to break up the meeting, but was fired on, and one gendarme was killed. Within a very short time, the number of rebels at Theriso had risen to 3,000. The protecting powers then dispatched an international force of French, Russian and Italian troops, together with more Cretan gendarmes, to subdue the rebellion. However, in spite of two interviews with Venizelos, the commander of the troops failed to persuade the rebels to disperse. Choosing not to use force, he withdrew his men to await further orders. In fact, most of the protecting powers held back from further action at this stage, preferring to wait and see how things developed, although the British landed an extra 300 soldiers to ensure the safety of the Muslims in Iraklion. Only the Russians, who supported Prince George, took any military action; a Russian warship bombarded the rebel positions near the coast.

The revolt spread quickly, gaining the support of powerful local leaders, military officers and several bishops, and the rebels rapidly gained control throughout the west and centre of the island. The determination of the insurgents was demonstrated when they set up a caretaker government in Theriso; created departments to deal with economics, transport and internal affairs; collected their own taxes; and issued a total of 100,000 drachmas of bonds to create a "war chest". They published a newspaper and even issued their own postage stamps, some of which featured the head of King George of Greece, implying that union had already been achieved. The gendarmerie was still under the control of the high commissioner and, although their loyalty could not be guaranteed, the prince now declared martial law. Crete was on the verge of civil war but, apart from a few minor encounters in the Chania region, there was no further bloodshed.

The Great Powers now intervened to attempt to reach a political solution. They accepted that Prince George had lost all credibility and public support as high commissioner, and that Venizelos and his supporters might be the solution rather than part of the problem. In spite of protests from the prince, the four consuls met with Venizelos in November 1905. Enosis was not on the table, but it was agreed that an International Reform Commission would be set up to determine the future of Crete. New municipal elections would be held under international supervision, and there would be an amnesty for all the rebels except for deserters from the gendarmerie. Venizelos for his part agreed to bring the rebellion to an end. The following February, the International Reform Commission proposed a new settlement for Crete. There was to be a new and more democratic constitution, giving King George I of Greece the right to appoint the high commissioner. A new Cretan civil guard was to be established, headed by Cretan officers from the Greek army. Once order had been restored, all foreign troops would be withdrawn.

Although Prince George no longer had the support of the protecting powers, his involvement in Cretan history was not yet over. He still had widespread support across the island and, in the first assembly elections after the revolt, the royalists and the Venizelists gained an equal number of seats, with both parties needing the Muslim deputies to gain a majority. At the end of August 1906, a large number of armed supporters of the prince arrived in Chania, intending to prevent him leaving Crete. A few days later, Prince George called a meeting of the assembly, which could have resulted in a defeat for the Venizelists and almost certain violence. The European consuls sent troops to occupy the building and close the assembly, thus undermining the prince's authority and effectively usurping his powers. On 22nd September, Prince George announced that he would leave the island. Violence broke out in Chania, but the unrest was suppressed by the international troops, reinforced by British sailors and marines. George's hopes of a ceremonial departure were dashed when further violence broke out, resulting in the death of one of the Russian consul's bodyguards. The prince was smuggled onto a Greek warship and, bitter and disillusioned, he left Crete on 26th September.

Alexander Zaimis, High Commissioner 1906 to 1908

Immediately after Prince George left, King George I appointed as high commissioner Alexander Zaimis, who was formerly prime minister of Greece (and would become its president in future). A new draft constitution was submitted at the end of 1906, and was accepted, meaning Zaimis was able to form a new government. By July of 1907, the new civil guard had been set up, and most of the Great Powers' forces were withdrawn, the remainder following within a year after guarantees of safety for the Muslim population had been given.

It wasn't long before the question of enosis again arose, sparked off by three events. The Young Turk Revolution in **Istanbul** led to considerable political instability within the Ottoman Empire. Bosnia-Herzegovina and Bulgaria, like Crete, were nominally under Ottoman sovereignty but, in 1908, Austria-Hungary annexed the former, while Bulgaria unilaterally declared complete independence from Ottoman rule. Apart from causing an international incident and possibly laying the foundations of the First World War, both actions were eventually accepted as faits accomplis by the European powers, leading to new Cretan demands for union with Greece. In what amounted to a bloodless revolution, while Zaimis was away on holiday in Aegina, there were popular votes throughout Crete in favour of enosis. A resolution was published and ratified by the Cretan Assembly in September 1908, stating, "The government of the State of Crete, having accepted the unalterable will of the Cretan people, hereby declares the independence of Crete and its union with Greece, that it may now comprise an inalienable part of the Greek State."[10]

The assembly then abolished the post of high commissioner, annulled the Cretan constitution, adopted the Greek constitution and recognised King George I of Greece as head of state. An all-party caretaker government was formed and, for the next few years, the government was entrusted to a series of three-member committees, appointed by the assembly. In the spring of 1910, a general election saw the Venizelist party win a substantial majority of seats. The Greek government held back from formal recognition of the Cretan constitution, and took no action apart from advising Zaimis not to return to Crete. Despite protests from Turkey, the Great Powers also decided not to intervene, except on one occasion.

When the last foreign troops had left Crete on 25th July 1909, ships of the protecting powers remained on station in Cretan waters. Called stationnaires, their duties included intervention to prevent disturbances, and the maintenance of Ottoman sovereignty, represented by the flag at Souda Bay. Their orders were:

> The stationnaires will protect the Turkish Flag and the flags of the four Powers on the Island at Souda bay. In case of disturbances which the local authorities are unable to suppress, the Commanders of the stationnaires will take the necessary steps to restore tranquillity in accordance with the recommendations of the Consuls General ... The foregoing instructions include authority for the Commanding officer of the British Stationnaire to join his colleagues in the use of force in case of need without special instructions in an emergency.[11]

Almost immediately following the departure of the European troops, Greek flags were raised at the fortress of Souda and in Iraklion, causing outrage to Istanbul and the threat of an Ottoman fleet returning to Crete. Diplomatic efforts to persuade the Cretan government to have the flags removed were unsuccessful, and a small force of local gendarmes in Chania withdrew in the face of armed Cretan Christian opposition. On 18th August, an international force of marines and sailors landed at Chania and, with the co-operation of the gendarme commander, removed the flag and flagpole. The Greek flag remained flying in Iraklion until the British commander of the force made it clear to the Assembly that he was prepared to use force to remove it if necessary.

Enosis

In a strange development, after a military coup in Athens, Venizelos was invited to act as mediator between the king, the government, the parliament, the troops and the people, in order to break the stalemate between the various factions. After fresh elections in Greece, Venizelos became prime minister of Greece in October 1910. There followed a period of impasse in Crete, with the Cretans regarding themselves as part of Greece, but the Greek government still not accepting union. Cretan deputies to the Greek parliament were elected but, nervous of further problems with the Great Powers and Turkey, the Greek government – ironically including Venizelos – several times refused them admittance to parliament. Again, talk of rebellion was in the air and a revolutionary assembly was set up in 1912. External events, however, pre-empted a further revolution.

In October 1912, the First Balkan War broke out, with Bulgaria, Serbia, Greece and Montenegro allied against the Ottoman Empire. The victory of the Balkan allies was to see the end of Ottoman rule in Europe, but from the Cretan point of view the war had another significant outcome. In an effort to build support and present a united front for the war, the Greek parliament finally opened its doors to the Cretan deputies, the speaker reading the resolution that "Greece recognizes that there is just one parliament common to both the free kingdom (of Greece) and the island of Crete". Venizelos still held back from formal recognition of enosis, and appointed a new high commissioner, but it was clear that de facto union was in place.

As one of the victorious allies, Greece was in a strong negotiating position, and, in May 1913, the Treaty of London forced the sultan to resign all rights over Crete to the Great Powers. This was confirmed in a separate treaty between Greece and Turkey. The Great Powers now ceded all rights over the island to Greece, and the flags of Italy, France, Russia, Britain and Turkey were lowered from the castle at Souda. On 1st December 1913, a formal declaration of union was made by King Constantine I (who had succeeded George I in March that year) and Venizelos at Chania.

Economy

As for the economy, at the best it could be described as struggling. Agriculture, the main source of income, suffered severely in the early years of this period. During the revolution of 1896 to 1898, over 13% of all the trees in Crete – about 1.5 million – were destroyed, including olives, oaks, carobs and citrus. These would take a minimum of five years to recover. There was a general decline in the number of sheep and goats, while arable land remained largely uncultivated. With a serious shortage of labour caused by war and emigration, the situation was desperate. Furthermore, the general economic crisis in Europe, together with disastrous harvests in 1900 and 1901, led to a sharp recession. This meant that the essential modernisation of agriculture could not be carried out. Nor could work begin on many vital infrastructure projects. Among these were the necessary massive improvements to the road network, and port improvements and extensions; due to the neglect of the ports during most of the Ottoman period, apart from Souda, ships still had to anchor offshore and be served by lighters. All these projects needed vast sums of money. For example, restoring the port at Iraklion required about 10 million drachmas, while a proposed rail link between Iraklion and Messara would cost about 9 million – but the budget for the whole island was 450,000 drachmas!

One of the problems for the government was a lack of revenue. Under the terms of autonomy, many taxes still had to be paid to Istanbul, while import and export duties were largely fixed by the protecting powers, often in favour of the trade of their respective countries. Even the substantial church revenues were under the control of the Patriarchate, which meant they were not always used for the benefit of the Cretan public. There was the possibility, at one time, of foreign investment in the island, including French capital to develop the vineyards and the development of a railway by a German syndicate. Unfortunately, the inherent instability of the economy deterred these investors, and nothing came of the projects.

Another factor making life extremely difficult for those in rural areas was a shortage of cash in the economy as a whole, leading to a major debt crisis among farmers. A 1901 law on debt provided a two-year grace period for those financially ruined and one year for the rest, but there was no cancellation of debt as there had been in a similar attempt at debt relief in 1879. As a result, the situation quickly deteriorated again, and prosecution and forced sale of defaulters' land at low prices continued. From 1900 to 1901, there was hope of a cure for the problem of debt. The old Public Benefit Foundation, also known as the Agricultural Bank, together with the new Bank of Crete, began to offer low-interest loans to farmers. Unfortunately, neither institution could keep up with the demand, and both ran out of funds to finance farming loans almost immediately. Unregulated high-interest loans from private lenders continued. What funds were available from the two banks tended to go to richer and larger landowners. Since the government was responsible for selecting members of the commission that elected the lending committees of both institutions, there was also a tendency to give preferential treatment to the governing party's supporters. The few people who could gain access to bank lending were thus able to lend privately to small landowners at higher interest rates.[12]

From 1906 onward, the economy began to strengthen. The measures enacted in the early years of autonomy bore fruit, as woodland was reinstated and agricultural improvements were initiated. Weather conditions improved, and better harvests led to increased tax revenues. Meanwhile, both banking institutions rationalised their procedures, became more efficient and increased their business. This meant that the supply of money improved, and low interest rates became available to more farmers. The extent of the improvement is illustrated by the fact that the government imposed a 13% tax on exported olive oil. In fact, it was olive oil that led to an improvement in the balance of trade. Total trade – exports plus imports – increased from about 25 million drachmas at the beginning of the century to 40 million in 1912. Another factor was a massive increase in remittances from emigrants living abroad, which improved the finances of families on the island and, together with the less oppressive interest rates, led to increased purchases of property.

The situation regarding property was somewhat chaotic. Even with economic hardship and excessive interest rates, there was still a great desire for land as a protection and security for the future. Squatting was not uncommon on land that belonged to the state, Muslim religious foundations or absent Muslim owners. Although Muslims who had emigrated retained their property rights, the state had only six months to take legal action to regain land occupied by squatters, and most of the time it went to the squatters by default. In any case, land was cheap. Many Muslim landowners panicked after the expulsion of the Ottoman troops, and began selling off their land at knockdown prices. The British consul reported in 1899 that "those who own land covered with barley or wheat abandon or sell it as if it had no value and depart in haste, as if their life were in danger. This kind of panic has engulfed the whole Muslim population."[13] This led to a depression in land prices that lasted for much of the period of autonomy. On the other hand, the consul was perhaps overstating the case. Many Muslims did stay, and, under the relatively successful protection of the government, they felt secure for the future and continued to invest locally in land and other businesses throughout the period and after union with Greece. Indeed, the Cretan Archives of the Ottoman Bank reveal a rather sad story of one Hüseyin Haniotakis, who leased some fertile fields for four years in August 1922. In July 1923, under the Convention Concerning the Exchange of Greek and Turkish Populations, he was among the remaining Cretan Muslims to be expelled to Asia Minor (see chapter 15).[14]

Society

After the granting of autonomy, there was a substantial decline in the number of Muslim Cretans, mainly caused by continuing emigration to Istanbul and Asia Minor. Initially at least, the Great Powers, in particular the British, did what they could to discourage Muslim emigration, although Prince George was suspected of working to encourage it. Nevertheless, between 1881 and 1900, the Muslim population nearly halved to about 35,000, while the number of Christians increased by about 30% to 270,000. From 1898 to 1899 alone, over 50,000 Muslims emigrated, mainly from rural areas, reducing the Muslim proportion of the rural population to just 3%. In Sfakia, the Muslim population declined by 97%. Generally, under the autonomous government, the exodus was orderly, with assistance given by the state. It is worth noting that poverty and insecurity also led to a smaller-scale but significant emigration of Cretan Christians, looking for a better life in Europe and the United States. Again, these Christian emigrants were mainly from rural areas and were to play a significant part in the Cretan economy in later years. About 7,500 Christians are estimated to have left between 1900 and 1910.[15]

As for the Muslims who stayed, their lives seem to have been relatively comfortable, certainly when compared with the previous few decades. To demonstrate its legitimacy, the government took seriously its responsibility to protect the Muslim community, while the decline in the Muslim population meant that the Christians no longer felt under threat. There was thus little further communal violence, and the Muslims who remained gradually came to be viewed as a cultural minority with their own place in the community. Although the Ottoman government kept an eye on events on the island and was prepared to act against manifestations of aggressive Greek nationalism, as in the case of the raising of the Greek flag, links with the Sublime Porte became tenuous and restricted to humanitarian support or legal details. For example, Muslim judges and interpreters of Islamic law continued to be licensed by the supreme Ottoman Islamic authority. In short, Cretan Islam came to be identified with localised communities in the cities, which were moderately prosperous and active in religious and charitable institutions.

Aside from the strict Islamic rules about personal cleanliness, the Ottoman authorities had not been scrupulous in ensuring public health, and sanitation in the towns was in a pretty bad state. In 1897, a lieutenant in the Royal Army Medical Corps described Candia as being in a repellent condition:

> An overpowering stench [arising] from its streets, which were almost impassable, being full of decaying offal, in which crowds of flies rested. Pariah dogs were the only scavengers, and many of these were unsightly objects, covered with sores and dying of disease ... The ditches outside the ramparts [below the British tents] were in so bad a state that it was a most unpleasant experience to venture through the town gates, as they were made the receptacle of all kinds of filth, as well as being the favourite place to drive animals about to die, where they were left to rot or be devoured by the dogs.[16]

As with the Egyptians in the 1830s, the protecting powers' concerns for the health of their soldiers led to improvements in sanitation and medical care, which benefited the population as a whole. In spite of the political uncertainty, the government also instigated major improvements in public health, including a concerted attempt to control leprosy, which was at this time endemic in Crete. Although it is now known that leprosy is not very contagious, horror of the disease meant that, for most of human history, the only response to it was isolation. In Crete, people with leprosy were usually confined to small colonies outside the main towns, where they lived in total poverty, dependent on the charity of passers-by. In 1903, the island of Spinalonga was selected as a single isolation area for all people on the island diagnosed with leprosy. The segregation was compulsory, immediate and rigorously enforced, with no appeal. The following year, the first group of these people was settled on Spinalonga. This group numbered 148 men and 103 women, and the colony's average population remained between 200 and 400, although at times it was much higher. The Muslim residents of the island were evicted and offered compensation of 120,000 gold drachmas, but they refused to accept it as too little.

Initially, things were chaotic. There had been no preparations to receive the new inhabitants and they merely moved into abandoned Muslim houses or slept in the open, relying on relatives to send them food and supplies. Disillusioned and bored, the inhabitants felt completely abandoned by society. Drunkenness and violence were endemic. In 1905, there was a revolt over the lack of facilities and the inhuman treatment, which only brought marginal changes. Real improvements in conditions would not be seen until much later.

One benefit brought to Crete by the protecting powers was a more efficient postal service, although this, like the public health improvements, was largely for the powers' own convenience. Under the Ottomans, the most reliable postal service had been provided by three post offices operated by the Austro-Hungarian Empire in Chania, Iraklion and Rethymnon. The various protecting powers now established post offices in their respective sectors: France's post offices operated from 1902 to 1903, Russia's in 1899 only, Britain's from 1898 to 1899, and Italy's from 1900 to 1912. The Austrians continued to operate their post offices from 1903 until 1914. As the postal system developed, the Cretan state also began to issue stamps and provided a postal service from 1900, which continued until union with Greece.[17]

There was also continuing progress in education. The 1899 constitution guaranteed free compulsory education for boys and girls:

Article 21: Education is free, but it has to be provided by individuals scientifically and morally qualified according to the criteria established by law, and under the supervision of the relevant authority, with regard to morality, public order, and respect of governmental law. Primary education is compulsory and free.[18]

Within two years, there were over 500 elementary schools throughout Crete, increasing to 656 by 1910. Grammar schools were also established, and in 1903 a teacher-training college was established in Iraklion and a seminary was founded in Aghia Triada monastery, on the Akrotiri peninsula.

Culture

Although the frenetic political atmosphere of the Cretan state left little time for leisurely pursuits, there were important cultural developments which were to continue to be a feature of the island even after union. Many libraries were established, both public and private, and the period saw the foundation of a number of literary societies. People began to take a great interest in Cretan culture and history, and one of the most popular writers of the period, Ioannis Kondylakis (who lived from 1861 to 1920), wrote stories of Cretan village life in the later years of Ottoman rule, such as *Patouchas* and *When I Was a Teacher*. The combination of katharevousa (formal Greek), Cretan dialect and demotiki (the spoken Greek language) gives his writing richness and depth that, unfortunately, lose a lot in translation. As part of this renewed interest in Cretan culture, the first full critical edition of *Erotokritos* (see chapter 10) was published. It is worth noting that Nikos Kazantzakis (who lived from 1883 to 1957) was fifteen years old when the autonomous state was created; although his main literary work came much later, his first novel, *Serpent and Lily*, was published in 1905.

One of the most important cultural developments during this period was in the field of archaeology. From about 1900, with the discovery of the Minoan civilisation, Crete became the centre of world attention. There was a general feeling that the new archaeological finds, which appeared to reveal the origins of Greek culture, fitted in with the waves of Cretan nationalism and the desire for enosis. The general poverty on the island also meant a steady supply of cheap and willing labourers to work on the digs. With the Cretan State Antiquities Law of 1899, amended in 1903, the new government established a framework of regulation governing the excavation and disposal of Cretan antiquities. Proposed sites were divided between French, Italian and British teams, roughly according to the areas of influence of those countries. The government undertook to requisition the land, although the archaeologists were required to pay compensation for any damage. All antiquities remained the property of the Cretan state, but duplicates or other unwanted items could be exported. In fact, there seem to have been large numbers of exemptions allowed.

To ensure the correct running of the sites, supervision of all the projects was in the hands of two very talented Cretan scholars and self-taught archaeologists, Joseph Hatzidakis and Stefanos Xanthoudidis.[19] In 1869, the Imperial Museum in Constantinople had been established and had begun collecting antiquities from around the empire. Hatzidakis founded the Cretan Philological Committee in 1875, with the aim of collecting any antiquities found on the island and keeping them in Crete. They were reasonably successful in this, and founded the Cretan Museum, which became the Heraklion Archaeological Museum, in 1904. Hatzidakis and Xanthoudidis were also instrumental in putting the Minoan legacy at the heart of education in Crete, organising school trips to sites and arranging for local students to work with foreign archaeologists. Visits to the Heraklion Archaeological Museum and the site at Knossos became essential for high-ranking visitors to Iraklion and, as early as 1904, people were incorporating "Minoan" columns into their houses.

The archaeological exploration was not without controversy. Although there was considerable rapport between the British archaeologist Sir Arthur Evans and the two Cretan scholars, this did not stop Evans refusing to allow school parties to enter Knossos if they were carrying the Greek flag, or prevent him flying a British flag from the top of his house, to the annoyance of many locals. This was fairly typical of the disdain showed by the foreign archaeologists towards their Cretan counterparts. At one point, Xanthoudidis discovered several prehistoric tombs 2 km from Phaistos, which was part of an Italian dig. The

Italians immediately and successfully claimed that it was within their jurisdiction and took it over. Such high-handed actions have led to the situation in Crete being called "archaeological colonisation".[20] Athens attempted to establish some authority over Cretan archaeology, but it was usually the foreign schools that dominated, and, in spite of the legal framework, it was less a case of co-operation with the authorities than of occupation of the sites. Another source of conflict was between the Cretan authorities and archaeologists on the one side and the local farmers on the other. Not all of the latter were willing to lease their land, especially in the difficult economic conditions of the time. There was also the perennial problem of unauthorised collection of antiquities, leading Hatzidakis to lament:

> Many times the plough or the pick of the farmer strike by chance upon some monuments of the past, lying under the soil, thus forcing them to come out in the light, and then either ignorance and lack of taste wears and mutilates them into being used for various needs of everyday life, or, even worse, the (inclination to) exploitation and greed, sacrilegiously interferes and manages to export them out of the island for trade.[21]

15

Union with Greece

1913 to 1941

Administration

Under the terms of the union, Crete became an administrative province of Greece, with its capital in Chania. It was divided into four nomoi (prefectures) along the lines already established in the period of autonomy: Chania, Rethymnon, Iraklion and Lassithi. Prefects were directly appointed by the government. A secretary of state for Crete was also appointed by the government, and had general oversight of the island. In the early days, Crete was staunchly Venizelist, and there was some instability in the administration, resulting in the post of secretary of state twice being abolished for a short time, in 1915 and 1925. Crete was allocated 16 out of the 300 members of the Greek parliament.

Politics

For the greater part of the twentieth century, Crete tended to have a liberal or left-wing orientation, and in the early years of union most Cretans were firmly Venizelist. In 1916, Prime Minister Venizelos rebelled against King Constantine I (who reigned twice, from 1913 to 1917 and 1920 to 1922). The king favoured Germany, and insisted on neutrality during the First World War. Venizelos set up a rival government in Thessaloniki in order to take Greece into the war on the side of the Allies. In this, he had the firm support of the Cretan population and of the Army Division of Crete. Indeed, Crete became part of the "provisional state" along with northern Greece and the Aegean Islands. After the abdication of Constantine I under pressure from the Allies, Venizelos again became prime minister of the whole of Greece.

The turbulence of Greek politics continued after the First World War. Between 1924, when a republic was declared, and 1935, when King George II was restored (he too reigned twice, from 1922 to 1924 and 1935 to 1947), there were twenty-three changes of government, a dictatorship and thirteen coups. King George II appointed a former general, Ioannis Metaxas, as minister of war and then prime minister in April 1936. The appointment was met with strikes and riots, giving Metaxas the opportunity to suspend parliament and establish a dictatorship. Major parts of the constitution were suspended, and political parties were outlawed. Censorship was imposed, and all strikes were declared illegal. After an attempt on Metaxas' life, there was further repression and the arrest of many deputies and ex-ministers. The prison on the island of Gavdos to the south of Crete held up to 250 political prisoners during this period.

In spite of the harsh regime and the unpopularity of Metaxas, there was little organised resistance until 1938, when a group based in Chania staged a coup attempt. The political leader was Aristomenis Mitsotakis, a former minister and nephew of Venizelos, and the military commander was the former general Manolis Mantakas. On 28th July, about 400 or 500 men seized the Chania radio station. They broadcast a declaration calling on the king and the armed forces to overthrow the dictator's regime and restore democracy:

> To His Majesty the King, the armed forces and to the Greek people.
>
> Both Army and people in brotherhood, have abolished the odious and tyrannous rule represented by General Metaxas.
>
> Having regained their freedom, they appeal to the King and request the immediate removal of the tyrannical Government of Metaxas, the restoration of the nation, the law and the freedom of the people, and the formation of a Government of National Salvation composed of the best Greeks, regardless of any political factions, to confront immediately any internal and external danger, which our country incurs, and for the creation of a new Greece,

that shall be truly spiritually united and able to face with courage and prudence all the difficult times, that humanity passes through.

With fraternal greetings to the armed forces and the whole nation.

Long live the King, long live Hellas.

The Revolutionary Committee: Mitsotakis, Voloudakis, Mountakis, Paizis, Mantakas, military commander.[1]

This was part of a wider national movement organised in Athens by Emmanuel Tsouderos, governor of the Bank of Greece, and involving the Communist Party of Greece (**KKE**). However, the planning for the coup was very poor. There was a lack of co-ordination, and there were far too few people involved in the plot for it to have a hope of succeeding. A naval force was dispatched to Crete and a squadron of seaplanes to Milos and, aside from some minor clashes, the attempted coup quickly collapsed within a few hours.

Metaxas declared martial law, and a military court was set up in Chania to try the organisers of the coup. On the whole, the plotters were treated with relative lenience. Some, including Mitsotakis, escaped to Cyprus but were sentenced to death in absentia, the sentences never being carried out. Another sixty, including Tsouderos, were convicted and deported but were amnestied the following year. General Mantakas was arrested and sentenced to life imprisonment, but he was freed by an armed group from his village and he took to the mountains. He remained in hiding in the Samaria Gorge until the occupation by the Axis Powers, against which he fought with the **andartes** (resistance fighters) of the National Liberation Front/Greek People's Liberation Army (**EAM/ELAS**).

Economy

The Cretan economy remained rooted in tradition, based mainly on olive cultivation, but, with the support of the Greek government, it slowly became better organised and more efficient. Exports came to include whole olives as well as olive oil and soap, while raisins from the Iraklion area and good quality wine from Chania were also exported.

Tobacco and silk were produced in large quantities, as were cereal crops, citrus fruits, almonds, chestnuts and carobs. Standardisation of dairies was carried out and strict quality control introduced, leading to an increase in the production of high-quality cheese. Apart from the old soap factories, there was still very little industry, apart from a raisin-processing plant in Iraklion, followed by a lemon-processing factory in 1930. The balance of trade remained healthy, and the Cretan economy was generally strong compared with many other parts of Greece, although there was still much poverty in rural areas.

At last, the Cretan government was in a position to do something about cleaning up and improving the harbours. A new large harbour was built in Iraklion with a 600 m jetty giving mooring for large ships. Although passenger railway travel never came to Crete, between 1922 and 1937 an industrial railway ran between the Koules fortress in Iraklion and the village of Xiropotamos, to help with the construction of the harbour. Of immense significance for the future, airfields were built in the 1930s at Maleme, near Chania, and at Iraklion.

From 1928 to 1939, Imperial Airways seaplanes used Crete as a refuelling stop on flights from London to Egypt and India. A fuel depot was built on the coast near Elounda, where the planes could moor and take on fuel. The use of a seaplane could cut the journey time from England to India from thirty days (by sea) to ten. The exact route varied, but a typical course was London, Trieste, Faliro, Elounda, Alexandria, Aden, Bombay. The planes could hold fifteen passengers (increasing to twenty-eight by 1937), together with mail. Both Churchill and Gandhi are reputed to have stopped over in Elounda at some time, but there is no evidence for this, and it may well be a local myth. From 1932 to 1939, the *MV Imperia* was the ship used to transfer passengers and crew from the seaplane to the shore. Its captain, Francis Grant Pool, joined the Special Operations Executive (**SOE**) at the outbreak of the war and was instrumental in helping several hundred Allied soldiers escape the island after defeat in the Battle of Crete in 1941. He received the Distinguished Service Order and Distinguished Service Cross for his efforts.[2]

Spinalonga

After the union with Greece, the situation on the leprosy colony of Spinalonga deteriorated as more people diagnosed with leprosy were brought in from all over Greece. The disillusioned islanders decided to live their own lives as best they could, more or less ignoring the authorities. The island became a centre for the smuggling of alcohol and cigarettes, and offered safe landing places for smugglers right up to the 1920s. Fighting was still common, and the police were often summoned from the nearby village of Plaka by the ringing of the church bell. Order was usually restored quickly, but in extreme cases a small prison on the island could be used. This rarely happened, and the prison was eventually abandoned.

At last, between 1926 and 1933, the government supervised a range of improvements on Spinalonga initiated largely by Venizelos. These included the installation of an electric generator and the building of separate hospitals, one dealing with leprosy symptoms and the other with other illnesses. After 1930, the inhabitants of the colony were given a small pension. Perhaps the greatest improvement in their lives, however, was less tangible. In 1936, a law student from Athens University called Epameinoudas Remountakis was exiled to the island. This charismatic young man set out consciously to transform the morale of the islanders and to give a little joy to the "Island of Tears". He set up the Aghios Panteleimon Fraternity of Spinalonga Patients and, by involving the inhabitants in various projects, he gradually created a true community. Under his guidance, streets were cleaned, houses were whitewashed, and a library, a school and two churches were built. Spinalonga even had its own cinema, many years before any of the nearby villages. Remountakis encouraged the celebration of the Orthodox festivals, and classical music played over loudspeakers helped to bring comfort to the sufferers:

> We celebrated Easter differently; a group of us visited all houses to give our wishes. We gave treats to all the [disabled]. It was a beautiful and unforgettable Easter, we all became brothers and all our differences vanished and we all shook hands, as the day called for.[3]

Although Spinalonga remained a place of pain and sorrow, the work of Remountakis at least gave the islanders a degree of dignity and a little normality.

The improvements, both practical and spiritual, were supported by the Orthodox Church. From the late 1920s, there was a resident priest on Spinalonga. Without exception, each priest was a man of true spirituality and compassion. Besides serving the religious needs of the patients, the priests identified themselves with the community, sharing their griefs and joys, just like any parish priest. In general, all healthy people on the island left at dusk, and the gates were locked. Doctors, nurses, civil servants and police all returned to the mainland – but the priests remained. The Church hierarchy in the area also allowed compassion to bend the rules. It was illegal for people with leprosy to marry, but the local bishop refused to implement the law on Spinalonga, allowing the full rites of Christian marriage and baptism to take place there. This alone helped to normalise life for the patients and, as Remountakis remarked, "the ceremony was followed by celebrations that lasted all night long, as was the case among the healthy population".[4] The Church also allowed divorce for patients who were permanently separated from their spouses. The tragedy of the Spinalonga marriages, however, was that any healthy children born were removed immediately and sent to orphanages.

Exchange of Populations

On 30th January 1923, as part of the negotiations leading up to the Treaty of Lausanne in July that year, the Convention Concerning the Exchange of Greek and Turkish Populations was signed by Venizelos and Kemal Ataturk. This agreement addressed the chaotic events of the previous few years, in which Greek refugees had joined the retreating Greek army after its defeat in the Greco-Turkish War from 1919 to 1922. In Crete, most of these refugees came from around Smyrna. About 20,000 were resettled in the area of Iraklion, and 7,000 in other parts of the island. With the formal exchange of populations under the new agreement, a further 7,000 came to Crete. At the same time, the relatively few Muslims remaining in Crete – about 30,000 – were relocated to Anatolia and other locations, and their property and homes were allocated to the refugees. The Muslim congregations of Crete worked hard to ease the hardship of the emigration, arranging the transport of moveable property and the sale of houses and land. They also used their funds to pay the transport expenses of orphans and impoverished families. The initial influx of Christian refugees to Crete caused tremendous logistical problems for the secretary of state, and the provision of shelter and medical care became a major problem.

In a slightly odd decision reminiscent of the old Ottoman millet system (see chapter 12), the exchange of populations was based entirely on religion. This caused much heartache to people of both sides. By this time, most Muslims in Crete were natives of the island and Cretan Greek speakers. They were now displaced from their homes and "returned" to countries they had never seen – mainly the Anatolian coast of Turkey, but also Syria, Lebanon and Egypt. Similarly, Greek Orthodox residents of Asia Minor were uprooted from their familiar surroundings and resettled in a country with which they had no connection other than a shared religion.

Personal stories of the refugees from a 2014 documentary by Maria Iliou, *From Both Sides of the Aegean,* bring to life the bare historical facts. Meni Atsikbasi, the daughter of Greek Orthodox refugees from Turkey, was brought up in a village on Lesvos inhabited exclusively by refugees:

> I met many refugees and saw how their souls wept. And they always smiled wanly when they spoke of Asia Minor, their homeland, their houses, their lives there ... This conversation took place every day. They'd finish work and then start talking about their homeland, what they did there, what it was like ... And I can honestly say that from what they told me, I am familiar with every square inch of their homes ... where the gardens lay ... the pomegranate trees, the jasmine bushes where the bakery was located ... everything about their life as though I was there.[5]

From the other side, Husnu Karaman's Muslim family left Crete for Turkey, but in their new home in Çeşme, the conversation was always about Crete:

No evening went by without Crete. It was always Crete. What did Crete mean to my family? It was their homeland. My father always said they lived there 300 years ... We sprouted roots there. We grew up there. But we were uprooted. Nothing you tell a refugee is of any value; all he seeks is his homeland.[6]

Although the population exchange had its tragic aspects, it did have a positive side. The refugees on both sides took with them to their new homes a whole range of distinctive cultural features including dialects, customs and cuisine. For example, it is probable that the use of horta (wild greens) was almost unknown in Turkey until the Muslim Cretans (or Cretan Turks as they were commonly called) introduced their use to the local population. On the whole, the Christians who settled in Crete were fairly easily assimilated into the general population. On the other hand, many of the Cretan Turks remained in tightly knit communities, retaining their unique culture and the Cretan dialect. Some of these communities still exist as Giritli (the Turkish word for "Cretan"). An interesting sidelight to the story is that Bülent Arinç, the deputy prime minister of Turkey from 2009 to 2015, is a Cretan Turk and speaks fluent Cretan Greek. Unfortunately, this did not stop him being an enthusiastic proponent of the idea to turn Aghia Sophia in Istanbul back into a mosque.

16

The Battle of Crete and Occupation

1941 to 1945

There are innumerable books in existence dealing with one or other aspect of the Battle of Crete, with between 200 and 300 currently being sold online. Of necessity, this chapter can only give a general outline of the main events, while focusing mainly on the people of Crete. For those who want to explore more deeply, my highly recommended sources for further reading are listed in the notes section of this book.[1]

Background

On 28th October 1940, an Italian army invaded Greece from Albania, but, poorly equipped and badly led, the Italians suffered a major defeat, being pushed back into Albania by the Greek army. This was, in fact, the first Allied victory against an Axis power in the war, prompting Churchill to comment, "Hence, we will not say that Greeks fight like heroes, but that heroes fight like Greeks." A counteroffensive by the Italians failed, and by spring 1941 the Albanian front had reached a stalemate. With the arrival of British Empire troops in Greece, Hitler was forced to assist Italy by invading Greece on 6th April 1941. The Germans attacked from Bulgaria, creating a second front, which left the Greek forces on the Albanian border outflanked and isolated. The British Empire troops had to retreat southwards and, despite a heroic stand at the ancient battlefield of Thermopylae, they were ultimately forced to evacuate. By 27th April the swastika was flying from the

Acropolis, and by 30th April the whole of mainland Greece was in German hands. Hitler now turned his attention to the island of Crete, its strategic position making it an ideal "aircraft carrier" and base for attacks on Egypt, Cyprus and Palestine. British naval superiority meant that an attack from the air was the only solution, and General Kurt Student, creator of an elite force of airborne troops, eventually convinced Hitler that such an operation was feasible. The final plan of attack for this Operation Mercury was to capture the three airfields at Maleme, Rethymnon and Iraklion, together with the city of Chania and the harbour at Souda Bay. From these points, the rest of the island could be subdued.

Out of the 58,000 British Empire troops sent to Greece, 2,000 were killed or wounded and 14,000 captured during the entire campaign.[2] Nevertheless, the delay at Thermopylae had provided valuable time to organise a largely successful evacuation. The king of Greece, George II, and his government escaped to Crete, along with about 27,000 Allied troops – Britons, Australians, New Zealanders, Cypriots and Greeks. A similar number were evacuated to Alexandria. While Greece was now a lost cause, holding Crete became of paramount importance. Not only did its harbours provide refuelling bases for Britain's Royal Navy, but bombing raids on Hitler's Romanian oilfields could be launched from its airfields.

The commander-in-chief of the forces in Crete was the New Zealander Major-General Bernard Freyberg. His orders were to "maintain defence of Crete to the utmost", but he was faced with several problems.[3] The garrison, established in 1940, consisted of an infantry brigade plus signals and medical teams, but had done little to prepare for a possible invasion. Before Freyberg, there had been five commanders in six months, which had not helped the situation. The reinforcements evacuated from the mainland were now added to the defence forces, but were not as effective as they might have been. Although they were mainly in still-intact military units, most of them were exhausted and had left behind everything except their personal weapons. Indeed, many had lost even these. In a signal to General Wavell, commander-in-chief of the Eastern Mediterranean, Freyberg said:

Forces at my disposal are totally inadequate to meet attack envisaged. Unless fighter aircraft are greatly increased and naval forces made available to deal with seaborne attack, I cannot hope to hold out with land forces alone, which as a result of campaign in Greece are now devoid of any artillery, have insufficient tools for digging, very little transport, and inadequate war reserves of equipment and ammunition.[4]

The local Cretans were ready to fight and, as we shall see, did so with great courage, but they had few weapons, as most had been confiscated by Metaxas after the failed 1938 coup. Antique Turkish rifles, swords and hunting rifles were all pressed into service. Resident Greek troops in Crete normally consisted of the 7,000 tough and experienced soldiers of the 5th Cretan Division, an equal number of reservists and about 1,000 paramilitary police. Such a force would have been a considerable asset, but all except 1,000 had been deployed on the Albanian front, where they fought valiantly before final defeat most of them being either captured or stranded on the mainland.[5] Including evacuees, there were fewer than 4,000 Greek soldiers in Crete, less than 20% of them armed.

Theoretically, Freyberg had one great advantage. British intelligence was able to break the codes used by the German **Enigma machine** and thus had access to top-secret German signals. The intelligence gathered was code-named "Ultra". Freyberg therefore knew that the main German attack would be on the airfield at Maleme, which was inadequately defended, especially to the west. The irony was that he could not redeploy his troops in case it became obvious that Britain was decoding Enigma signals. He was limited to actions which could have stemmed from more normal intelligence sources, and Maleme remained vulnerable.[6] There is a lot of argument about the extent to which Freyberg's hands were tied by the secrecy of Ultra, some military historians arguing that some of his odder decisions were prompted by his conviction that Maleme was a diversion and that the main invasion would be by sea.

The Battle Begins

While General Student was in command of the parachute troops and the invasion overall, the Luftwaffe air corps responsible for bombing raids was under the command of General Wolfram von Richthofen (a cousin of the Red Baron). He had previously been in command of the blanket-bombing raids on Guernica and Belgrade, which didn't bode well for Crete. From 1st May, the Germans carried out heavy aerial bombardments of Maleme and Iraklion airfields, as well as Souda Bay and Chania. The unrelenting horror of this was recalled vividly by an eyewitness:

> The piercing whistle of a bomb being dropped was enough to nail you to the ground. Once there, you waited for death. Then you heard the blast and the earth's tremor rocking you. The closer the bomb fell, the louder and shriller the whistle. You consoled yourself with the fact that another one had gone. When they threw a bunch of them, however, which was normally about six, you lost count and concentration and left yourself at God's mercy. We were then told that during the bombings, we should keep our mouths open to avoid bursting our eardrums.[7]

On 20th May, after nearly three weeks of "softening up", further "earthquake bombardment" and low-level machine-gun attacks preceded glider and paratroop landings. What Churchill called "a head-on collision with the very spear-point of the Nazi lance" had begun.[8] In spite of the preliminary attacks on defensive positions, there were heavy casualties among the parachutists and the troops landed by glider, and the number of casualties suffered by the 7th Parachute Division was higher than the total for the German army in the war to date. Helmut Wenzel describes his jump under fire:

> Crete is in sight. Stand by! We are still about 180 metres above ground; we'll be dangling from our 'chutes too bloody long! A splattering against the fuselage and the fellow behind me collapses unconscious – or dead? No time to think about it. Now's the moment ... Here I go, the first to jump. As the 'chute opens, I hear whistling in the air, all around me. It's bullets! The British are ready for us and greet us. In no time I become aware of floating over a British position. Six Tommies are standing firing at me. Bloody bastards! Wait till I touch down![9]

The historian Antony Beevor points out the effect of such landings on the morale of the paratroopers:

> For most parachutists, the idea of jumping from the air and then floating down to attack their enemy gave a sensation of invincibility. To find themselves so vulnerable instead was the most disorientating shock of all. That the defenders should shoot at them when helpless struck many of them as an outrageous violation of the rules of war.[10]

Estimates vary, but it is believed that on the first day of the attack about 2,000 parachutists were killed.

It was not only Allied guns that killed the paratroopers. In other parts of Europe, underground movements only really developed a year or so after German occupation, but the Cretan resistance began with the landing of the first parachutist. The courage of the Cretan civilians – including boys, old men and women – was breathtaking. Many observers on both sides were astounded at the sight of women carrying sickles or wearing cartridge belts, or priests leading their parishioners into battle. One woman who became a Cretan heroine was the 22-year-old Georgina Anyfantis, who had fled from the mainland after her parents were killed in an air raid. She asked for a chance to fight and was issued with a uniform. She was assigned to a machine gun defending a landing field. After the rest of her group were killed in a bombing raid, she remained on duty. When German troop transports flew in low, she opened fire at point-blank range, bringing down two planes, each carrying twenty men. She escaped before the airfield fell, and was evacuated to Egypt, where she served as a volunteer in the South African Women's Air Force. The German troops, shocked as they were by the civilian resistance, seemed particularly horrified by women fighting. They would examine the shoulder of a female suspect, and if they saw a bruise that could be from the recoil of a rifle, or if she had been caught with a knife, she would be shot immediately.

Although there were pockets of German troops in and around Maleme, their position was not strong, and they were vulnerable to counter-attack. Meanwhile, events at the Rethymnon and Iraklion drop zones had favoured the Allies. In the former, the defenders,

including the Cretan gendarmerie, were disciplined, and after a somewhat chaotic attack the Germans were contained. A counter-attack
saw the capture of many prisoners and much-needed weapons. In Iraklion, there were heavy losses of German planes and troops, thanks to
quick and decisive action by the Allied officers. A fierce defence of the
Chania Gate by a mixed force of Greek soldiers, gendarmes and civilians was eventually overwhelmed and forced to surrender, but British
reinforcements counter-attacked and the Germans withdrew.

General Student was shocked by the strength of the resistance.
German intelligence had grossly underestimated the strength of the
Allied garrison in Crete, and had predicted that the local Cretans
would accept the invaders or even welcome them. By nightfall on
the first day, Student's commanders were convinced they had lost the
battle, and expected a strong counter-attack. After horrendous losses
and the deaths of many of his senior officers, Student was under pressure to abort the mission. Instead, he was more certain than ever that
the key to success was the Maleme airfield, and decided to send the
next wave of paratroopers there rather than Iraklion. Meanwhile, still
convinced that the main invasion would come from the sea, Freyberg
ordered the bulk of the troops guarding Maleme to withdraw to the
south-east. This decision was coupled with a tragic failure of communications which led to the New Zealand battalion, which held Hill
107 overlooking the airfield, to also withdraw. This essentially gave the
high ground to the Germans, allowing them to bring in further reinforcements with fewer losses.[11]

The Battle Continues: 21st to 27th May

With no counteroffensive by the Allies, Student was able to reinforce
Maleme, and by late afternoon the Germans were in control of the
airfield. They were now able to land troops directly, although not
without continuing heavy losses. Freyberg's conviction that Maleme
was a diversion led him to assign his largest and best-equipped battalion to Chania in defence of the port. He did, however, assign a small
force to an attack on Maleme, which was too small to be effective
now that German reinforcements were arriving continuously. A small

German flotilla of transports bringing low-priority supplies and rein-forcements to Crete was intercepted by the Royal Navy and destroyed, so that only one caique reached the island. Because poor communica-tions meant that Freyberg was unaware of the full picture at Maleme, he believed that the main battle, the sea invasion, had been won.

On 22nd May, German troop carriers continued to reinforce Maleme. New Zealand and Australian forces finally counter-attacked at Maleme, but were forced to withdraw towards Souda Bay under heavy bombard-ment, enabling the Germans to bring in about 12,000 reinforcements. Meanwhile, the Royal Air Force carried out several bombing raids on Maleme, but with heavy losses of planes. At this point, a concerted attack on the airfield might still have succeeded, but continuing com-munications problems and lack of co-ordination between the senior officers led to inaction. Instead, there were further withdrawals.

The situation at Rethymnon had reached a virtual stalemate, with the airfield and port still held by the Allies. At Iraklion, a platoon was completely annihilated by Cretan civilians, but, after the previ-ous day's withdrawal by the Germans, the city suffered heavy bombing raids. Here too there was stalemate. At this point, it was decided that King George II, Crown Prince Paul and the prime minister should be evacuated to Egypt. After a tense three-day journey over the moun-tains, at one point passing within 1 km of the German front line, they were taken off by ship from Aghia Roumeli.

Even on the Maleme front there were some successes, among them the defence of a vital hill by Greek "irregulars". A charismatic and some-what eccentric British officer, Captain Michael Forrester, had been training a group of 200 Greek soldiers using a series of whistle signals to solve the language problem. Many of the villagers had also watched his training sessions. An eyewitness reported what happened when the Germans attacked the hill, before the reserves could be deployed:

> Out of an olive grove on the adjoining hill, came Captain Forrester, clad in shorts, a long yellow army jersey, brass polished and gleam-ing, web belt in place and waving his revolver in his right hand ... He was at the head of a crowd of disorderly Greeks, including women; one Greek had a shotgun with a serrated-edge bread knife tied on like a bayonet.[12]

The account of a commander of the reserves continues the story:

> Over an open space came running, bounding and yelling ... Greeks
> and villagers including women and children, led by Michael For-
> rester twenty yards ahead. It was too much for the Germans. They
> turned and ran without hesitation.[13]

A second German flotilla was turned back by the Royal Navy, but air
attacks led to heavy losses of ships and men. Such was the intensity of
the bombing, mainly by Stuka dive-bombers, that shell shock, nicknamed "stukaritis", became almost endemic among the ships' crews.
One survivor called this "the blackest week for the Royal Navy in the
whole of World War Two ... perhaps even of all time".[14] A total of eleven
warships were lost and over 2,000 naval personnel killed or missing.
The British warships were forced to withdraw to Alexandria, but by
this time the defence of Crete was pretty well a lost cause anyway.

The next day, preparations were made to withdraw west from
Maleme to Galatas, on the way to Chania. A German motorcycle battalion was also advancing on Palaiochora on the south coast, to prevent
reinforcements from landing. At Kandanos, the charismatic priest
Father Stylianos Frantzekakis led a group of villagers and a handful
of gendarmes in attacking the battalion, successfully delaying it for
two days before withdrawing. Tragically, after the island was occupied,
General Student ordered reprisals. Kandanos and several nearby villages were burned to the ground, 180 residents killed and all livestock
slaughtered. The area was declared a "dead zone", and the surviving
residents were forbidden to return or attempt to rebuild the village. A
notice posted by the Germans read:

> On the 3rd of June 1941, the village of Kandanos was razed to the
> ground never to be built again. This was an act of reprisal for the
> brutal murders of German parachutists, mountain forces and engi-
> neer corps by the men, women and priests who dared stand in the
> way of the Great Reich.[15]

Over the next few days, the battle continued, with the Germans beginning to get the upper hand at Maleme. Ruthless carpet bombing of

Chania was reminiscent of Guernica and resulted in the destruction of thirteen Venetian palaces. The new positions at Galatas were under attack from the west and south, and the village fell, but a courageous counter-attack by New Zealanders and miscellaneous stragglers forced the Germans back, giving valuable time for a further orderly withdrawal to Daratsos. It was during the battle for Galatas that the women of Crete again showed the sort of courage that would earn a regular soldier a medal, as the historian Takis Akritas recounted in 1949:

> A group of girls led by a mother of four, Mrs. Katsoulis, ran and brought in the wounded. They took care of them and prepared their food, ignoring the enormous risks they were running ... Many of them sacrificed their dowries. They tore new sheets to use as bandages. When asked why they were destroying these useful things, they replied in true Greek fashion, "What's the point of having a dowry if we become slaves"?[16]

It was rapidly becoming clear that Crete could no longer be defended, and on Tuesday 26th May Freyberg sent a cable to Wavell:

> I regret to have to report that, in my opinion, the limit of endurance has been reached by the troops under my command. From a military point of view, our position is hopeless. Provided a decision is reached at once, a certain proportion of the force might be embarked.[17]

The next day, agreement was given for withdrawal south over the White Mountains towards Sfakia, from where the Allied troops could be evacuated.

Retreat and Evacuation

The retreat of the Allied troops was characterised by great courage but also ineptitude and a degree of chaos. A rearguard formed of exhausted New Zealand and Australian units was supplemented by a recently landed force of 500 British commandos. The intelligence officer for the commandos was the writer Evelyn Waugh, who provides some of the most dramatic descriptions of the withdrawal in both his diary and his 1955 novel *Officers and Gentlemen*. The role of the rearguard was to protect the rear of the retreating army and hold back the Germans as long as possible. They were aided in this by the mistaken German belief that the main retreat would be towards Rethymnon and Iraklion. As a result, the Germans only sent one regiment south against what they thought was a secondary group.

Nevertheless, the retreat became a horror story. During the day, the rearguard was subjected to artillery shelling and constant air attacks from machine guns and dive-bombers, but was still able to cover the withdrawal, allowing the main body of the retreating army to reach the south coast. The bombardment, which must have been a nightmare of terror, was described by Waugh with typical dry understatement as "like German opera – too long and too loud".[18] The troops retreated in varying degrees of order. While some infantry troops maintained discipline and continued to march in formation, there were many stragglers who lost all sense of discipline and became little more than a rabble. With scant food or water and with disintegrating boots, even the better disciplined suffered intensely as they threaded their way across the mountain tracks. A young Greek medical officer wrote:

> I knew that I was taking part in a retreat; in fact, I wondered if it should not be called more correctly a rout as, on all sides, men were hurrying along in disorder. Most of them had thrown away their rifles, and a number had even discarded their tunics as it was a hot day ... Nearly every yard of the road and the ditches on either side were strewn with abandoned arms and accoutrements, blankets, gas masks, packs, kitbags, sun-helmets, cases and containers of all shapes and sizes, tinned provisions and boxes of cartridges and hand grenades.[19]

In Iraklion, the Royal Navy organised a direct evacuation by night, and, after handing over as many guns and supplies as possible to the local Cretans, nearly 3,500 embarked. Although the evacuation orders did not include Greeks, it was later reported that twelve Greek soldiers, six male civilians and five women managed to get aboard ship. Unfortunately, various delays meant that the ships were still in the Aegean at dawn. Heavy bombing attacks led to the loss of over 20% of the evacuees. The garrison in Rethymnon was overwhelmingly outnumbered, and there was no way it could be safely evacuated. The commander decided to surrender in order to prevent needless loss of life, but allowed his second in command to lead anybody who wanted to join him into the hills. After several months in the mountains, thirteen officers and thirty-nine other ranks escaped to Egypt by submarine.

On the south coast, German air superiority meant that only the fastest Allied warships could hope to approach the coast, and only at night. Moreover, they would only be able to take a relatively small number of evacuees at a time. It was therefore decided that only organised units would be allowed to embark, and stragglers with no equipment were to be abandoned. However, the priority process was chaotic, and there has been much criticism of some of the decisions taken. In spite of the lack of organisation, the evacuation was relatively successful.

From 28th May to 1st June, varying numbers were successfully taken off the island, until the decision was taken to abandon the evacuation. In total, about 12,000 men were rescued. Estimates of the number left behind vary, but it was somewhere between 3,000 and 6,500. Of these, most surrendered as instructed, but some collected what arms they could and headed for the mountains. Even some of the wounded managed to escape from the coast to find sanctuary with Cretan families in remote areas. Others managed to find fishing boats, or commandeered damaged landing craft, which they made seaworthy, and attempted their own escape by sea. Over 300 reached Egypt in this way. Those who surrendered were taken prisoner and marched back over the mountains, ironically following the same route as their retreat. The twenty or so Cretans found with them were all shot.

The reasons for the loss of the Battle of Crete have been argued over at length, many putting the blame on General Freyberg. He undoubtedly made mistakes, including the delay in the counter-attack on Maleme and his conviction that the main invasion would come from the sea. Other causes, however, were outside his control. Lack of the air support he had requested was certainly a factor, as was the poor condition of many of his troops. Moreover, indecision on the ground and poor communications in the chain of command turned a potentially difficult situation into a disaster.

It has been claimed that the Battle of Crete, although a defeat for the Allies, had positive results in that it caused a delay to the start of Operation Barbarossa, the German invasion of Russia. This claim has now been shown to be incorrect. However, the invasion did have some indirect positive results. The incredible losses by the Germans – nearly 4,000 killed or missing, about 2,500 wounded and 350 aircraft destroyed – deterred Hitler from ever again attempting such tactics. Hermann Goering had proposed just such an airborne attack on England, but after Crete this proposal never again saw the light of day. Although many of the surviving paratroopers received the Iron Cross, they were stood down as airborne troops and sent to Russia as elite infantry. General Student himself was reassigned. Ironically, he was in command at Arnhem in 1944, when the Allies' own airborne operation failed.

Occupation

After the evacuations at Sfakia, the Germans moved quickly to establish control over the island. Their headquarters was at Chania, where the commander of what they called "Fortress Crete" was based. Once Student had left in June 1941, the commander was General Alexander Andrae, responsible for some of the early reprisals, but he was replaced a year later by the relatively more enlightened General Bruno Bräuer. The second in command, the divisional general, was based in Iraklion, with his residence at the Villa Ariadne at Knossos, built by Sir Arthur Evans. The first divisional general was Friedrich-Wilhelm Müller, who had a reputation for brutality. In spring 1944, he was promoted to commander and was succeeded by General Heinrich Kreipe. The eastern end of the island was controlled by an Italian division under the command of General Angelo Carta, who had his headquarters at Neapolis. The Italians had landed at Siteia on 28th May and there is conflicting evidence of whether they were opposed or not. In general their rule was more liberal and relaxed than that in the German zone, but there are some reports of executions in the early days.

The German garrison ranged from 75,000 men at its maximum in 1943 to just over 10,000 at the time of surrender in 1945. The south coast of the island was a prohibited zone, with regular patrols to deter landings of Allied operatives and weapons or smuggling out of evaders, but there was a general reluctance to patrol in the highland areas. On the whole, the Germans, like the Ottoman Turks, had almost complete control over the towns, while carrying out ruthless reprisals to deter attacks from the andartes (Cretan guerrillas) in the mountains.

The German authorities moved quickly to enforce their rule. An amnesty was declared for all weapons, with the warning that for each gun found after the expiry of the amnesty, ten people would be shot. The Cretans responded by handing in all hunting rifles, which would be listed in the register in Chania, together with useless, rusted old guns. They carefully hid the remaining working guns for future use. All mules were requisitioned, and motor vehicles had to be registered with the German authorities. In Chania, the German headquarters, there was a curfew and complete blackout from sunset to sunrise. All public meetings were banned, and printing presses could only be operated with a special permit. Newspapers were, of course, censored, and people could only listen to Greek or German radio, with severe penalties for those caught listening to the BBC.

While the Germans were able to recruit some collaborators and informers, they were relatively unsuccessful in this, and were more likely to be the subject of informing to the resistance. The ordinary Cretan gendarmerie and police were, as in all occupied countries, expected to work alongside the Germans, but would often pass information or warnings to the andartes, and in some cases they actively worked for the resistance.

In 1943, a Greek-speaking German non-commissioned officer, Friedrich Schubert, managed to gather a group of 100 Cretans who, wearing German uniforms, acted as paramilitary terror squads. They mainly operated in the east of the island, concentrating on finding and killing supposed communists. Their activities were too sadistic and ruthless even for most of the Germans, and within a few months many had deserted. An ambush by ELAS guerrillas killed and captured many more, and Schubert and the remnant of his group were transferred to Macedonia, where they continued their terror. On the mainland, the Germans were able to recruit a "security battalion" from among anti-communist Greeks, specifically to fight ELAS. In Crete, on the other hand, they had no success, but did set up a lightly armed "special gen-darmerie" of about 200 men. This also failed to take off, and after con-tinual attacks by the andartes, most of them deserted. So ineffective were they that, in the trials of collaborators after the war, none of the rank and file were even charged. The commander was found not guilty, but was later shot by an unknown assassin.

Life under occupation was grim. There was widespread starvation, but no famine as there was in mainland Greece. George Psychounda-kis, the famed "Cretan Runner" who helped the British agents in Crete, described how the Cretan ingenuity in finding food helped, with snails and horta (wild vegetables) becoming staples of the diet:

> Everybody suffered from hunger during the Occupation, but 1942 was the worst, especially the winter, when we nearly starved. It was then that the snail kingdom suffered the fiercest inroads. Every night, armed with oil dips and torches, the villagers would set out in hundreds in search of the priceless treasure which was the most luxurious fare to be found in house or inn.[20]

Even the traditional Cretan hobby of sheep stealing could bring an occasional supplement to the diet. Fishing was difficult due to the confiscation of all caiques, but was nevertheless carried out. A few fishing boats were also used illicitly to trade with the mainland, to take escapees and evaders off the island and to bring home members of the 5th Cretan Division who were still stranded. Leather was unob-tainable, but the locals found that cutting up old car tyres provided serviceable rubber soles. It became the custom for any British opera-tives or andartes being taken off the island by launch or submarine to leave behind their boots as well as their weapons. The shortages were worsened by the requisition of food by the occupying forces. If they paid at all for the food they took, the rates were pathetic – 120 drach-mas for a cow, for example, which was enough to buy two cigarettes. Forced labour was used to dig trenches, build fortifications and roads, and load and unload cargo in the harbour. This too could be paid or unpaid according to the whim of the officer, but the rates were 700 drachmas for a day's work, which would buy two eggs. Needless to say, Cretan labourers rarely worked their hardest for the Germans.

The inhabitants of the colony on Spinalonga suffered particular hardship. Isolated because of their leprosy on an island where little food could be grown, they were dependent on food supplies from the mainland. In the chaotic circumstances of the occupation, they were largely forgotten, and for some time the Italian occupation forces were not even aware that the island was inhabited. It is estimated that 100 patients died of starvation during the occupation. Eventually, a priest appealed to the Italians to send troops to the island, pointing out the conditions under which they were living, as one of the inhabitants recalled:

> The Italians and all the civil servants were crying ... The officer in charge told us, "I will accompany the priest to Neapolis and talk to General Carta and we will do our best for you." Then they all left, the Italians, the civil servants and the priest. On the following day, the miracle happened. A boat brought us twenty kilos of flour per patient.[21]

The use of reprisals against civilians, including women and children, was without doubt the worst aspect of the occupation. General Student had been shocked by the attacks on soldiers by poorly armed civilians, and immediately after the Battle of Crete he set up a judicial inquiry into the activities of the Cretans during the battle. However, stirred up by widespread rumours that German soldiers had been mutilated, reprisals began even before the inquiry started. In fact, the inquiry could only account for about twenty-five mutilations in the whole of Crete, almost all of them certainly inflicted after death. The highest number was about six out of a complete detachment almost entirely wiped out at Kastelli Kissamou. Some 200 civilian men were executed for this. From the beginning of the invasion to September 1941, a total of 1,135 Cretans were executed, only 224 of them sentenced by the military tribunal. A tribute to the bravery of Cretan civilians comes from a rather unexpected source. The brutal General Andrae, responsible for many of the executions, wrote:

The courage of the Cretan facing the firing squads is legendary. Cretans turn into mythical figures ... Nowhere have I witnessed such love of freedom and defiance of death as I did on Crete.[22]

The Jews of Crete did not escape the Holocaust. By 1941, there were only about 300 Jews on the island, almost all of them concentrated in Chania. As soon as German control of the island was established, the ageing rabbi of the city was forced to submit a list of the members of his community. Nothing much came of this, however, until May 1944 when, almost as an afterthought, all the Jews in Crete were arrested and imprisoned in Aghia Prison in reportedly atrocious conditions. Along with Greek and Italian prisoners, they were then put aboard a ship bound for Piraeus, where they would join Jews from Corfu and Zakynthos for transportation to Auschwitz. Tragically – or, it could be argued, mercifully – the ship was torpedoed by a British submarine and sank within fifteen minutes. None of the prisoners survived. About twenty-five Cretan Jews survived the war. A few escaped the initial round-up preceding the deportations; the others were members of the 5th Cretan Division who did not return to the island at the end of the Albanian campaign.

Evasion

For a handful of Allied troops and for the Cretans themselves, the Battle of Crete may have been over, but the battle *for* Crete had only just begun. Of the troops left behind at Sfakia, a number decided to evade capture and hide until they could find a way to escape from the island. Together with men who had escaped from the loosely guarded prison camp at Galatas, there were probably about 1,000 Allied troops scattered around the island.[23] At one point, the relatively safe village of Theriso held fifty Allied soldiers and was described by one evader as an overcrowded **Anzac** club. In another village, Vafes, there was a large house that gave food and shelter to so many stragglers that it became known locally as The British Consulate. Within a very short time, the Cretans had set up a sophisticated resistance network, which included organising escape routes to lead evaders to safe havens. Filoxenia, the traditional hospitality of the Cretans, was expanded in time of war to providing false papers, medical assistance and hiding places. Regarding the Allied troops as palikaria (brave warriors), even the ordinary villagers took the soldiers to their hearts and gave them protection, food and supplies. The literature is full of tributes from evaders and escapees, all of them variations on the same sentiment: "[The Cretan people] would go to any lengths to protect us with complete disregard for their own personal safety."[24]

Central to the escape of the evaders was the monastery of Preveli, which, because of its location, was an ideal spot for rescue by submarine or escape by boat. The operation was organised largely under the influence of the extraordinary abbot Agathangelos Lagouvardos, who set up a committee to organise the monks and local people into units for guard duty and for the protection and care of Allied evaders hidden in the surrounding mountains. The abbot wrote later:

> We held a conference in the monastery and we decided to give food to the British troops who were hiding near the monastery and at the same time to the Germans who were in a guard post, so as to avoid suspicion by the Germans that we were hiding British troops near the monastery. This plan succeeded and the Germans did not suspect that British troops were being hidden within three kilometres of the monastery; on the contrary they reported to their HQ that they were being well treated.[25]

When the monastery was raided by SS troops, Agathangelos was forced into hiding. The monastery was ransacked, furniture and vestments destroyed, buildings damaged and precious relics removed to Rethymnon. The monks were interrogated harshly to reveal details of the escape activities and the whereabouts of Agathangelos, but they pleaded ignorance, claiming wrongly that the abbot was a tyrant who never consulted the ordinary monks. Where he was now they had no idea. As for themselves, they merely followed monastic tradition and the teaching of Jesus by providing shelter to any visitor, without enquiring who they were or where they came from. It was just possible that they might have fed a foreigner or resistance worker by mistake. After the intervention of the local bishop, they were released, and continued their activities of caring for Allied soldiers trapped on the island and giving information and support to the guerrillas. Meanwhile, Agathangelos escaped to Egypt, where he became chaplain to the Greek army. He died in Cairo in 1942.

Even in the grim, sometimes tragic lives of the men on the run, there were moments of comedy:

> An Australian private, seeking the south coast of Crete during an evasion which had started well – he was already in plain clothes of a ramshackle sort – found out that he had to cross a main road under constant German watch. He had no time to wait for dark. The only hope of cover seemed to be a shepherd. He came upon a dozen sheep in the charge of a shaggy biped bundle of rags, before whose face he crackled his only inducement, a white five-pound note. The bundle at first said nothing, but repeatedly lifted his head sharply, in the Greek sign for "no". When an hour's attempt to chaffer had produced no more result, the bundle remarked in broad Glasgow Scotch, "Gae and find yer own bluidy sheep. I've spent half a day getting this damn lot."[26]

The Germans were obviously aware of the activities around Preveli and other escape points, but had little success in preventing them. They tried sending out spies in British battle dress to discover where the escape routes were and which villages were involved. They rarely found out anything, as the villagers quickly became quite skilled at spotting imposters. The usual technique was for the Cretans to beat up the "British" spy, while proclaiming loudly their loyalty to the German Reich. They would then drag him to the nearest garrison for arrest, receiving less-than-heartfelt thanks from the senior officer. In spite of the dangers and difficulties, between June 1941 and May 1943 it is believed that nearly 900 Allied troops successfully escaped from Crete and safely reached Cairo.

Resistance

Back in May 1940, John Pendlebury, formerly the curator of the

Knossos archaeological site, returned to Iraklion, ostensibly as British vice-consul. His real purpose was to start organising a resistance network among the Cretan leaders in preparation for a possible German invasion. He was ideally suited to the task; in the words of a Cretan colleague at Knossos, "He knew the whole island like his own hand, spoke Greek like a true Cretan, could make up mantinades all night long, and could drink any Cretan under the table."[27] Although he was shot by the Germans in the early days of the Battle of Crete, by that time he had already helped the Cretans to form the basis of an effective resistance. The SOE, a British force formed in 1940 to conduct espionage, sabotage and reconnaissance in occupied Europe, sent several agents into Crete to help the resistance network. They included, among others, the flamboyant Patrick Leigh Fermor, described by a friend as "the Byron of our times",[28] Tom Dunbabin, Sandy Rendel, Xan Fielding and Bill Stanley Moss. Often regarded as daring but eccentric amateurs, between them they managed to collate an impressive amount of information from intelligence provided, at great risk, by the Cretans.

On the Cretan side, there were many groups of andartes throughout the island whose reckless courage sometimes infuriated the more strategic-minded SOE operatives. Nevertheless, British and Cretan generally worked well together and developed respect and admiration for each other's qualities. The main problem was the already developing opposition between the two political groupings in the resistance. ELAS was a mainly communist group led by General Mantakas, a survivor of the 1938 attempted coup. **EOK**, the National Organisation of Crete, was a loose alliance of non-communist groups, predominantly Venizelist, led by Colonel Andreas Papadakis. It was set up with the support of Tom Dunbabin as a counterweight to the communists. One of the largest guerrilla groups was led by Manolis Bandouvas. Describing him, Leigh Fermor wrote, "Massive and heavily whiskered, he had a very forceful personality and wielded immense influence on the simpler mountaineers. He was quite fearless, but also headstrong and domineering and prone to rash acts."[29] Although a republican and nominally part of EOK, Bandouvas tended to act independently of any political grouping.

The operatives and andartes were given logistical support from landings on the south coast, usually by armed caiques or submarines at the beginning, but by mid-1942, when it became too dangerous for submarines, fast motor launches were used. A two-way traffic developed: agents and supplies were landed, and evaders taken off. For all concerned, it was a dangerous and extremely uncomfortable life. The agents and wireless operators lived mainly in caves in the mountains, often with little food, enduring the blazing heat of the Cretan summer and the freezing cold of the winter. Parachute drops of food supplies, weapons and clothes helped a little, but all too often the drops went astray or were stolen by desperate locals. The operatives were given outstanding support by many Cretan women working as secretaries and interpreters for the Germans and secretly passing on vital information to the resistance, and by guides and runners, who were usually shepherds. Leigh Fermor wrote about their work:

> The job of a war-time runner in the Resistance Movement was the most exhausting and one of the most consistently dangerous of all. It entailed immense journeys on foot at full speed over some of the most precipitous country in Europe, carrying messages between the towns and the larger villages and the secret wireless stations in the mountains; humping batteries and driving camouflaged explosives and arms and, occasionally, a British straggler in disguise, on the backs of mules through heavily garrisoned areas ... None of them were paid and there was no incentive but a sense of duty to their country and their allies.[30]

Perhaps the most famous of the runners was George Psychoundakis, whose book about the war is a great read. Born in 1920, the young man had already helped guide the retreating Allied troops to the south coast when he became a runner in 1942, carrying messages between resistance groups and guiding people unfamiliar with the area. On one occasion, he ran from Kastelli Kissamou in the north to Palaiochora in the south in the course of a single night – a distance of 70 km by the modern main road, but probably twice as far over the rugged landscape he would have traversed. After the war, he was awarded the British Empire Medal. For some years he and another former andarte were caretakers at the German War Cemetery above Maleme.

As in previous centuries, the Cretan monasteries played an important role in the resistance. As well as the help given by Preveli to the escapees, Toplou monastery, east of Siteia, was able to use its remote location to act as a refuge for guerrillas and agents. The monks also set up a wireless base to communicate with Allied headquarters in Cairo. In 1944, their activities were discovered, and the abbot and three monks were executed. The wireless operators and several civilians were also arrested, tortured and transferred to Aghia Prison. One of the survivors, the sister of an operator, movingly describes the part played by a rizitiko song [see chapter 12] on their ride to the harbour for transportation to Germany:

> The day came for us to leave for Germany. We said goodbye to our fellow prisoners with tears in our eyes and got in the cars that would take us to Souda, from where the ship was to depart. As we drove through the city's centre, we all began to sing simultaneously the Rizitiko song, *"When will the sky be clear? When will it be February?"* This song had become Crete's National Anthem for all of us, myself included. The Germans were seething and screamed at us to stop. We carried on singing. The [people of Chania] stared at us in amazement. People opened their windows and gazed at us thunderstruck. Some took handkerchiefs from their pockets and secretly wiped the tears from their eyes, others blew kisses at us, making sure not to be seen by the Germans, while others gave us the Victory sign. We, the youth of Crete, took to our feet and raised our voices defiantly, *"Where is the starry night?"*[31]

Throughout the occupation period, there were numerous ambushes and attacks by andartes and commando operations by Britain's Special Boat Service (SBS) and Special Air Service (SAS). In fact, it is to the Germans that Crete owes some of the improved roads on the island, which they built in open areas away from popular ambush locations. In the spring of 1942, the Germans began to use Cretan airfields as staging posts for reinforcements to Rommel's Afrika Korps in Libya, and the resistance attempted to step up its activity. The SOE launched SAS and SBS attacks on Kastelli Pediados and Iraklion airfields, causing substantial damage but also resulting in fifty Cretan hostages being executed. By early 1943, as the war in North Africa was going the Allies' way, the Germans feared a counter-invasion of either Crete or mainland Greece. Defences were improved, and 45,000 reinforcements, desperately needed on the Russian front, were brought in.

The repeated attacks and ambushes, combined with rumours of invasion, caused morale among the occupying forces to slump, and this process was sped up by an SOE leaflet campaign. One melodramatic offering written by Leigh Fermor had quite a poetic turn of phrase:

> Germans! You have now been two years in our island and your rule has been the blackest stain on the pages of your already besmirched history. You have proved yourselves unfit to be considered as a civilised race, and infinitely worse than the Turks, who were noble enemies and men of honour.
>
> You have proved yourselves savages, and as such you will be treated.
>
> But not yet.
>
> Wherever you go, Cretan eyes follow you. Unseen watchers dog your footsteps. When you eat and when you drink, when you wake and when you sleep, we are watching you.
>
> Remember!
>
> The long Cretan knife makes no sound when it strikes between the shoulder blades. Your time is running out. The hour of vengeance is drawing near.
>
> Very near.
>
> Black Dimitri.[32]

Spot searches for arms were increased using detachments of 200 or 500 men. A village would be surrounded at night, and the soldiers would move in at dawn. The entire population would be locked in a church or school while a thorough search was made. These operations were usually based on tip-offs by spies but, since there were probably more spies on the Cretan side, they were often unsuccessful.

Things did not always run smoothly for the SOE agents. On the one hand, the SOE organisation in Cairo was bureaucratic, characterised by departmental rivalries and personal infighting. This often resulted in poor communication and contradictory orders. At the same time, jealousy and personality clashes among the andartes were accentuated by political differences. The communist andartes of ELAS lost a lot of support by propagating the policy of Communist International that North Epiros, Thrace and parts of Macedonia were not ethnically Greek – a view that was anathema to the majority of Cretans. Nevertheless, they were still a powerful force and, unlike on the mainland, the British officers in Crete remained on reasonable terms with the ELAS leadership. Xan Fielding, realising that working together was essential, organised a meeting at Theriso between Nikolaos Skoulas, the mayor of Chania, representing EOK, and General Mantakas, representing ELAS. The meeting included the young Konstantinos Mitsotakis, who would later become a prominent politician and the prime minister of Greece. They agreed on a non-aggression pact, and a committee of three from each side under Mantakas was set up to co-ordinate their activities.

In the east of the island, Italian rule was generally light and humane under General Carta. Many Cretans sentenced to death in Lassithi and Siteia were smuggled away to the Dodecanese, or had their executions faked. With the armistice between the Italian government and the Allies in September 1943, the situation became confusing, which was not helped by Carta's indecision. His counter-espionage officer proposed that the Italians ally themselves with the andartes and hold the east of the island, and Leigh Fermor secretly negotiated with Carta in Neapolis. This idea came to nothing. Two Italian battalions did take to the hills above Siteia, but shortage of food forced them to return to their units. In the end, the Italian troops were given three options by the Germans: put themselves under German command, lay down their arms and work in labour gangs, or be interned as prisoners of war. Those who chose the third option were later embarked on the same ship as the Chania Jews, which was sunk by an Allied submarine. General Carta escaped from the island by launch, with the help of Leigh Fermor.

The Italian armistice led to increased guerrilla attacks, sometimes by over 100 andartes, the raids being designed to convince the Germans that the Allied invasion of Europe would be through south-eastern Greece via Crete. SBS raids successfully destroyed a large fuel dump at

Peza and many planes on the airfield at Kastelli Pediados. Meanwhile, the guerrilla leader Bandouvas, convinced that the British would soon be landing on Crete, carried out a large-scale attack on a German column on the Viannos plateau without authorisation, killing over 100. The response from General Müller was immediate and savage. He swept through the plateau, burning six villages and executing 500 civilians, putting Bandouvas' force to flight and scattering it. Bandouvas and the remnant of his group were evacuated to Egypt. More successful was an ambush at Koustogerako, a small mountain village in western Crete. Knowing a German platoon was approaching in search of ten andartes from the village, the men hid in the hills above. When the women and children of the village were lined up for the inevitable execution by machine gun, the andartes fired on the execution squad, killing ten and causing the rest of the patrol to flee. The first shot, which killed the machine gunner, was from a staggering 400 m. The women and children then joined their menfolk in the mountains. When the Germans returned the next day, they found the village deserted, and blew up all the houses. Shortly after, there was another successful ambush on a patrol at Achlada, where nineteen Germans and three Italians were killed.

Perhaps the best-known guerrilla operation was the abduction of the divisional general, Heinrich Kreipe, made famous by the film *Ill Met by Moonlight*, starring Dirk Bogarde.[33] The kidnap was organised by Leigh Fermor and Bill Stanley Moss of the SOE, with the eager help of a group of eleven andartes. After the daring and audacious capture of the general near his residence at the Villa Ariadne, he was taken south across Mount Ida to the coast. Unrelated German activity in the area caused some delay in getting away, and the party had to hide up. At one point, seeing the large number of armed guerrillas moving freely about the area, General Kreipe reportedly commented wryly, "I am beginning to wonder who is occupying the island – us or the English."[34] In a bizarre but rather moving example of camaraderie, Kreipe and Leigh Fermor spent some of the time quoting the Roman poet Horace to each other. Finally, on 14th May 1944, with an SBS covering force, Leigh Fermor, another SOE agent, two andartes and the prisoner were evacuated by motor launch. The escapade was of little military value, but it left the Germans rattled by a tremendous blow to their morale. On the other hand, it was an equally enormous boost to the morale of the Cretans. One of the andarte leaders joked:

> Everybody felt taller by two centimetres the next day ... Out of 450,000 Cretans, 449,000 claimed to have taken part in the Kreipe operation.[35]

To try and prevent the usual reprisals, Kreipe's car was dumped close to the sea, indicating that he had been taken off by submarine. On the front seat, Leigh Fermor left a sealed letter to the German commander, stating that the operation was a purely British affair, organised from Cairo and carried out by SOE operatives with no Cretan involvement, and that no action against the local population would be justified. There is some argument about whether the ruse worked. An order for the destruction of the village of Anogeia mentions that the kidnappers passed through it, but this was three months after the event, and that fact could have been added simply to give legitimacy to reprisals based on other resistance activity.

By the autumn of 1944, it was becoming clear that the Germans were preparing to retreat to the northern coastal cities. Attacks on fuel reserves by the SBS and on German outposts by the andartes escalated, but so did reprisals. A small group of Germans were shot at Anogeia, and a further group of thirty who came to punish the village were ambushed and killed when they arrived. A larger force returned, executed forty-five villagers and burned down the whole village. The order reads as follows:

> Since the town of Anogeia is the centre of English espionage on Crete, since the people of Anogeia committed the murder of the Sergeant Commander of the Yeni-Gave, as well as of the garrison under his command, since the people of Anogeia carried out the sabotage of Damasta, since in Anogeia the guerrillas of the various resistance bands take refuge and find protection and since the abductors of General Kreipe passed through Anogeia using it as a transit camp, we order its complete destruction and the execution of every male who is found in the village and around it within a distance of one kilometre. 13th August, 1944.[36]

In an attempt to thoroughly intimidate the guerrillas prior to their retreat, the Germans launched an assault on the Amari valley. In eight days, nine villages were looted and burned and 164 inhabitants were shot. Orders from Cairo prohibited any further attacks to avoid reprisals, now that the Germans were in retreat. Nevertheless, ambushes continued, most notably a major battle near Apostoli, 25 km south-east of Rethymnon, and an ambush near Mount Psiloritis. German troops were now becoming severely demoralised, and the rate of desertions became alarming. This trend was encouraged by undercover agents and propaganda newspapers printed by the SOE.

The Germans finally evacuated Iraklion on 11th October and Rethymnon two days later, consolidating their troops in Chania. They destroyed bridges as they retreated, including a Venetian bridge near Rethymnon. In the liberated areas there were attacks on collaborators, leading to the declaration of martial law. Civil war was in the air, but for the time being this conflict was limited to some incidents between rival groups of andartes. The Cretan resistance forces and all British agents were now technically under the command of officers from the regular Greek and British armies, although unauthorised actions continued to happen. There were ongoing attempts to prevent open warfare between ELAS and EOK, which were largely successful, apart from a few minor skirmishes.

Liberation

The last few months of the war were mainly ones of stalemate, with the Germans firmly entrenched in the area around Chania and the andartes and regular troops unwilling to cause unnecessary bloodshed before the inevitable surrender. On two occasions, the Germans launched attacks: once on the ELAS headquarters at Panagia, and once on the British headquarters at Vaphe. Both were beaten off by andartes. The Royal Navy was now able to operate by day, and regular deliveries of supplies were made by launch at Palaiochora, the return journeys being used to take off prisoners. Among these were an entire battalion of Italians who had deserted with their colonel, under the encouragement and assistance of British agents.

As could be expected, in the liberated areas collaborators were dealt with ruthlessly. In some cases, courts were held, sentencing some to execution and some to imprisonment according to the severity of their crime. Even those sentenced to prison, however, were usually killed by andartes. There was also a rash of individual attacks on Germans. One such was somewhat tragic and caused outrage among Cretans, since the victim was a German doctor who had treated Cretan patients whenever possible and had actually become loved by the villagers.

On 7th May 1945, the stalemate finally ended with the unconditional surrender of the remaining German forces. Fearful of reprisals, they refused to capitulate to the Greek army, and eventually a surrender was secretly negotiated with the British who, much to the disgust of the Cretans, guarded the Germans as they were shipped out from Souda Bay.

In 1946, war crimes trials were held in Athens for the notorious General Müller, "The Butcher of Crete," as well as for General Bräuer, who had generally behaved with decency. Both were sentenced to death, but the execution of General Bräuer caused international shock. Ironically, General Andrae and other senior officers who were far guiltier escaped with prison sentences. Many years later, General Bräuer's body was brought from Athens and reinterred in the German military cemetery at Maleme. The man who carried out the burial was George Psychoundakis, the Cretan runner. Friedrich Schubert was found guilty of 271 murders and many cases of arson, rape and theft. He was sentenced to death and executed in Thessaloniki in October 1947. All surviving members of his group were arrested on sight and tried for murder in Athens or Iraklion. All were executed. A special court was set up in Chania to try those accused of collaboration. About sixty were found guilty, of whom four were sentenced to death, four to life imprisonment and the rest to prison for periods ranging from eight months to twenty years.

In spite of the horrors of the Battle of Crete and the occupation, past bitterness has now largely, if not totally, disappeared. Adolf Strauch, one of the many former German soldiers who returned to the island, wrote:

I know that Cretans are now very proud of their fight for freedom waged against us. I respect their attitude and understand the sacrifices made by them ... However, as I see it, that was a senseless shedding of blood. After remembering those days, I am happy that we now understand one another, that we respect each other and that we can forgive.[37]

If that seems a little idealistic, perhaps the last words in this chapter should go to a group of old Cretan women encountered by the historian Costas Hadjipateras at the German military cemetery. When he asked them why they were lighting candles on the graves of past enemies, one replied, "They, too, have a mother, and she is far away or dead. We also lost our sons, killed or executed by the Germans. We know how a mother feels. Now, we are their mothers."[38]

17

Civil War

1945 to 1949

During the final months of the German occupation, there was much jockeying for position between the rival groups of andartes. As the Germans gradually withdrew towards the west, eastern Crete was largely under ELAS control, but the early enthusiasm for ELAS rapidly disappeared. By February 1945, many members and most leaders had abandoned the organisation, and ELAS ceased to have any significant influence in the east. Meanwhile, in January 1945, ELAS forces had taken up positions around Rethymnon and blockaded entry into the city, but after three days and twenty-seven deaths they were dispersed by EOK andartes. In Iraklion, the end of the month brought more clashes, in which six ELAS fighters and two British soldiers were killed. Further skirmishes in the Chania area led to hostages being seized on both sides, leading to fears of an all-out civil war. A meeting between the leaders of the main groups led to the release of all hostages and a treaty guaranteeing freedom of movement between the Chania and Rethymnon prefectures. To enforce this, a joint ELAS/EOK garrison was set up at Klima on a pass between the two areas. In March, the ELAS commander ordered his guerrillas to disband in all liberated areas, except for the regiment in Chania, which would remain fully armed until the German surrender. EOK also disbanded in 1945, although former members retained their anti-communist politics. Tensions continued and there was some fighting, but party politics was forgotten in the midst of celebrations of the end of the war in May.

However, in 1946, various factors led to a resumption of civil war in Greece. Although the tragedy of events in Crete should not be

underestimated, the fighting there never reached the scale and intensity of that on the mainland. There were many reasons for this, some
positive and some negative. In the first place, the Cretans' legendary
independence of mind meant that they tended to reject any centralist
doctrine, whether monarchist or fascist, and whether imposed by the
Russian communist party or even the central government in Athens.
Indeed, in the referendum of September 1946, Crete voted by 70% for
a republic, in contrast to the national vote of 70% in favour of restoring the monarchy. On a more practical level, the numbers involved
in the rival groupings were much smaller in Crete, since many of the
most active young resistance fighters on both sides had been drafted to
fight in the civil war on the mainland.

In many respects, the communists of Crete differed from their comrades on the mainland. ELAS groups in Greece, perhaps justifiably, felt
betrayed by the British, who had sided with the monarchists. In Crete,
the ELAS andartes had less cause for bitterness, and on the whole
had got on quite well with the British agents. Similarly, EOK guerrillas had fought bravely alongside the communists, and there was no
way they could be accused of collaboration, as was the case with some
nationalist groups on the mainland. The result of the referendum also
showed that Crete was no hotbed of monarchists. It has been argued
that sometimes allegiance to one or the other side was more related to
long-standing vendettas than to politics, such as in the case of an entire
family joining ELAS because their ancient enemies had joined EOK.

Nevertheless, the civil war in Crete did exist and needs to be
described, at least in outline.[1] On 28th October 1946, the anniversary of the outbreak of war between Italy and Greece, the Democratic
Army was formed from the remnants of the ELAS andartes. However,
apart from a few murders, usually driven by personal motives, fighting
did not really start until April 1947, a whole year after the civil war on
the mainland began. The first serious action of the war was a successful
raid on Maleme airfield, in which members of the Democratic Army
seized weapons and all the military equipment they could find. For
the next few months, there were several skirmishes between former
ELAS guerrillas and government troops, usually instigated by attacks
on gendarmerie posts. "Civilian" hostages were frequently taken, but
were in most cases released unharmed, and at this stage of the war even

captured gendarmes were often released after being stripped of their outer clothes and boots. Those who were executed were usually known collaborators. In the east, a resurgent rebel group, aided by fifty-five deserters from the military base at Aghios Nikolaos, actually held the town of Ierapetra for a few hours, but withdrew after seizing all the supplies they could carry. There was a quick response from the gendarmes, the military and some nationalist bands, and the guerrillas were forced to split into small groups. These were gradually destroyed, and after the leader of the eastern rebels was killed the few survivors fled west to link up with the stronger guerrilla groups there.

It can be argued that the civil war in Crete should be more accurately described as a rebellion. It was less of a war between two rival groups seeking power than an insurrection against the generally accepted government, although the latter did receive support from armed former EOK nationalists. The military governor of the Chania prefecture, Pavlos Gyparis, was determined to defeat the communist rebels completely, and created a battalion of gendarmes specifically for that purpose. The guerrillas continued to attack gendarmerie posts and carry out raids on the villages of nationalist supporters. Nevertheless, continued harrying by Gyparis, coupled with revenge killings and attacks by nationalists, forced the guerrillas to split up into smaller groups and scatter. One of the guerrilla leaders was killed in June 1947, and when another was killed in battle in September, they decided to change their strategy.

The plan was for the Democratic Army to set up base on the Omalos plateau, from which they would continue to make raids but would avoid open battles. If attacked, instead of fighting it out, they would retreat higher up into the mountains, or into the Samaria Gorge. Meanwhile, government forces increased their patrols and continued to arrest communist sympathisers in the villages. An amnesty was offered by the Greek government, and a large number of the guerrillas and people who had helped them surrendered. Those who gave themselves up were released after signing a declaration of future good behaviour. Morale was now very low, and the size of the Democratic Army was shrinking daily. The remaining guerrillas were forced to go on the offensive to get food and money, but raids on farms and shepherds led to a decline in support for the communists and an increase in the number of informers. Continued individual murders of gendarmes and nationalists made it easy for Gyparis to find volunteers for small defence units in the villages.

As the deadline for the end of the amnesty approached, Gyparis published open letters in the newspapers, appealing to senior members of the guerrilla army to give themselves up. None were successful. On a more personal level, he also encouraged relatives of the guerrillas to send them letters urging them to surrender. Among these were a widowed mother who threatened to disown her son, a father who urged his son to surrender or be expelled from the family, and – most poignantly – a young woman who told her fiancé she would break off the engagement if he did not give himself up. Given the way Cretans feel about family, a few of these appeals may have been successful (although, in the latter case, the man refused and later married someone else). In one tragic case, a father persuaded his younger son to surrender, but when he and the boy's godfather tried the same thing with his elder son, Christos, the son murdered both men as "traitors". The case became front-page news and even shocked many of Christos' communist friends.

Although a recruitment campaign by the KKE brought membership of the Democratic Army back up to about 300, this put even more pressure on food supplies, and early 1948 saw increased raids on villages and theft of sheep and goats. This in turn lost the guerrillas more support, even among those villagers and shepherds who had previously helped them, leading to further desertions. After the attempted assassination of Sophokles Venizelos, a government minister and the son of Eleftherios, the military command was passed to Lieutenant Colonel George Vardoulakis, who reinforced the gendarmerie and declared all-out war on the Democratic Army. After a few skirmishes and a steady flow of surrenders, most of the hard-pressed remaining guerrillas established camp in Samaria Gorge. Vardoulakis used 1,000 men to block all the six known paths through the mountains and keep the guerrillas bottled up. The communists retreated to higher ground in the area of Prinias, where a fierce battle took place and about seventeen guerrillas were killed. There are no reports of any prisoners. About ninety guerrillas escaped by using an unmarked route known only to local shepherds, climbing over precipitous and extremely dangerous mountains. The route was difficult enough by day, but the escapees had to climb by night. Nevertheless, only one person fell. A further twenty escaped by hiding among the rocks to the north-east for a few days until it was safe to move.

The defeat in the Samaria Gorge marked the end of the Democratic Army, and, in effect, the civil war in Crete was over. From this time, the remaining guerrillas were fugitives, only moving at night and with little support in the villages. Increasingly desperate and isolated groups carried out a few raids on villages and attacks on buses, mainly for food and weapons. They also took to assassinating those who had previously surrendered and given information to the authorities, although they did no harm to those who had kept quiet. The final "action" took place in November 1949, when two gendarmes at a guard post on the outskirts of Chania were murdered in a night attack. As for the government forces, Vardoulakis began the grisly practice of exhibiting the dead bodies or heads of important guerrilla leaders killed in battle. This was mainly to prove that these (often well known) andartes really were dead, but also to create an element of terror among the remaining supporters. The hunt continued for the remaining few, and by April 1956 there were only eight still at liberty. Six of these escaped to Italy and then to exile in Tashkent, but two remained in hiding.

The extraordinary story of George Tzobanakis and Spiro Blazakis has become something of a legend. This pair continued to hide in remote caves, mainly in the Apokoronas area where they had grown up, living on wild vegetables and what they were given by a few loyal comrades in the villages. They were at risk of death many times from the dangerous locations of the caves, but apart from occasional illnesses they seemed to have stayed in excellent health, considering their living conditions. Both of them suffered from boredom, and Tzobanakis certainly suffered from bouts of depression. In 1964, an amnesty was granted to most of the remaining communists in prison, but not to the two fugitives, because not all of their crimes were considered to be political. For example, in November 1949 they killed a hunter who had spotted them, but since the civil war had officially ended that summer this was not classed as a political crime.

Under the Greek military dictatorship (which lasted from 1967 to 1974), they were twice offered amnesty, but they refused – partly because they believed that it would be a betrayal of their communist principles, and partly because they distrusted the military junta. They had good reason for this, as all the communists amnestied in 1964 had been rounded up by the junta in 1967 and returned to prison. By this time, Tzobanakis and Blazakis had become almost heroic figures, nicknamed the Eagles of Crete. Finally, with the fall of the junta and the restoration of democracy under the government of Konstantinos Karamanlis, all political prisoners were released, and the KKE was legalised. At first, the government refused to grant an amnesty to the two fugitives, for the same reason as in 1964, but after a favourable interview published in the *Guardian* newspaper gained some international sympathy for the pair, an offer of unconditional amnesty was made in February 1975. After twenty-six years in hiding, Tzobanakis and Blazakis now felt able to return to society.

18

Post-War Crete

1949 to the Present

Administration

In 1971 the administrative capital of Crete was moved from Chania to Iraklion, and in 1994 the prefects were elected for the first time. The national Kallikratis Programme reforms of 2011 then abolished the prefectures and replaced them with regional units. Crete now became an administrative region of Greece (its title being Periphereia Kritis), containing four regional units virtually identical to the previous prefectures. The reforms also saw the amalgamation of many dimoi (municipalities) into larger units.

Perhaps this is a good place to dispel another Cretan myth. Sometime around 2010, news articles began to claim that there was a growing movement for Crete to become independent from Greece. It was further asserted that, as part of the 1913 treaty which united Crete with Greece, the people of the island would have the opportunity to decide by a referendum in 2013 whether they wanted to leave Greece. Nobody seems to know where these rumours originated, or whether they were a hoax or a genuine ambition from some disenchanted quarters in the island. What is certain, as has been pointed out by several academics, is that there is no mention of such a referendum in the 1913 constitution. Nor is there any great desire for independence among the Cretans. Certainly, the people of the island often refer to themselves as Cretans first and Greeks second, but this is evidence of local pride rather than any desire to secede, in the same way that people who are proud of being from Yorkshire do not wish to leave the UK.

Indeed, the opposite may be the case. As a perceptive American Cret-
ophile wrote in 1905:

> The Cretans have an intense enthusiasm for "Hellenism" in the
> abstract, and desire a union with Greece; but they have no exagger-
> ated respect for the Greeks of the mainland ... Indeed, I often used
> to suspect that the true Cretan, in his secret mind, imagines that
> union means the annexation of Greece to Crete.[1]

Politics

After the end of the war, Greek politics was noted for its instability.
Between 1945 and 1967, there were thirty-three changes of prime minister, including nine caretaker governments when no parliamentary
majority could be formed. Against this background, Cretan politics
was relatively stable. As noted in chapter 15, after unification with
Greece, Crete remained staunchly Venizelist, and this trend continued after the war. The island generally voted for the Liberal Party of
Sophokles Venizelos or, later, the Centre Union party of Georgios
Papandreou. After the fall of the Greek junta and the restoration of
democracy in 1974, the Greek parliament more or less settled down
into a two-party system, with governments alternating between the
conservative New Democracy (ND), founded by Konstantinos
Karamanlis, and the left-of-centre Panhellenic Socialist Movement
(PASOK), founded by Andreas Papandreou. From 1974 until 1990,
Crete was a PASOK stronghold, with that party on occasions polling
twice as many votes as ND.[2] This trend continued into the 1990s, and
in most elections the island returned a majority of PASOK members
amongst its sixteen MPs, often against the national trend.

In the somewhat chaotic elections since 2012, Crete has generally
swung behind the left-wing Coalition of the Radical Left (Syriza)
party, although what the future now holds is anybody's guess.[3] Perhaps
unsurprisingly, the right-wing Popular Orthodox Rally party has made
little headway in Crete. In some parts of Greece, especially the islands
most affected by the immigration crisis, the ultranationalist Golden
Dawn party has seen a surge in support, giving it about eighteen seats

in parliament. In Crete, on the other hand, there has been very little support, largely due to the perception of Golden Dawn as a neo-Nazi party. Although the party denies this, its reputation was enough for twenty-six villages in Crete to give no votes at all to Golden Dawn in the two elections of 2015. One of these villages was Anogeia, the scene of one of the worst of the massacres during the Second World War. Interviewed for Greek television, one old man there said, "With so many dead, so many homes razed, we all decided with the blood which our families shed, we would not vote for this barbaric ideology, which is a blot on humanity."[4] Another created a spontaneous mantinada: *"The Anogeian carries great pride/Because he didn't vote for the party that kills."*[5]

From 1967 to 1974, Greece was ruled by a military junta, which was characterised by strict curtailment of political liberties and civil rights, imprisonment or exile of opponents and intense (and enforced) patriotism. At the same time, the period saw high rates of economic growth, low inflation and low unemployment. There is little published information about the impact of military rule on Crete, but limited anecdotal evidence gained from personal interviews indicates that the junta was regarded mainly with indifference among the usually volatile islanders. Perhaps because of its relative isolation, and perhaps because one of the top three organisers of the coup, Stylianos Pattakos, was a Cretan, military rule on the island seems to have been relatively light. Even the requirement for all houses to display the Greek flag on national holidays was no problem for the inherently patriotic Cretans. For the rest, while accepting the road improvements, hospital building and debt relief for farmers initiated by the government, Cretans were generally prepared to wait patiently until the "aberration" disappeared. A common adjective used by mainland Greeks to describe Cretans is kouzoulos, which can be translated as "dotty" but also means not taking things too seriously. This characteristic was apparent during the junta years.

In spite of limitations on entertainment and a curfew on discos and nightclubs, tourism began to prosper, and, despite the inherent puritanism of the regime, a hippie colony at Matala was left largely undisturbed. The writings of a young Englishman travelling and working in Crete from 1968 to 1975 illustrate the laid-back attitude of the Cretans towards the strict laws of the junta. He described an evening in a taverna in Iraklion:

> These tunes went on for a while, forty or fifty minutes with the women dancing then the mood changed and the next tune was much slower but more majestic. Four men stepped up onto the stage to dance and I was amazed to see that one of these men was the chief of police who had given me my work permit. He was not in uniform now, of course. The law laid down by the new military junta did not allow more than about five or six people to be together in a public place, but this is Crete, of course, here there were nearly five hundred people all enjoying themselves and not giving a damn about the government. Not least the chief of police. I smiled, what could I say. He certainly knew how to dance.[6]

Demographics

During the post-war period, there has been an increase in population from about 440,000 in 1940 to over 600,000 in 2011. A slowdown in the 1950s – followed by a drop of 2.9% in the 1960s – may have been due to emigration, but has been more than compensated for by large increases from the 1970s onwards. The rural population peaked at 350,000 in 1951 (75% of the population of Crete), but then began to decline until, by the time of the 2011 census, 42% of the population lived in the main cities.[7] There has been a general movement from inland villages to coastal tourist resorts, resulting in some of the more remote villages becoming almost deserted. As in the rest of Greece, the 2008 financial crisis led to emigration from Crete, especially among the young and better educated, but the still-thriving tourist industry has moderated the worst effects. Ironically, the recession also led to a slowdown in the rural decline, as unemployed youngsters moved back to the villages to live with their parents or grandparents.

The effects of emigration have been more than counteracted by immigration. The recession has led to an increase in young people moving to Crete from other parts of Greece, to seek work in the tourist industry. This is mainly seasonal. There are also many immigrants from more affluent European Union (EU) countries, who come to seek a more relaxed lifestyle, and work in tourism, property, teaching and trades. Most of these immigrants gravitate towards the coastal resorts or towns, but another group has migrated to all parts of the island. These are the retirees from northern Europe – mainly the UK, France, Germany and the Netherlands – looking for a place in the sun where they can live either permanently or for part of the year. This group has had a significant effect on the economy, and in some cases these expats have helped to bring deserted villages back to life.

Originally, economic immigrants to Crete came mainly from Albania, but later they increasingly hailed from fellow EU members such as Romania and Bulgaria, and more recently from Pakistan and various African countries. These immigrants generally work in less-skilled, lower-income jobs (usually in agriculture in rural areas, and in tourism or construction in towns), and in the context of a booming economy they pose little threat to Greek workers. After the crisis of 2008, however, there was a collapse in the property market and an 80% fall in activity in the construction sector. This has led to immigrants now competing with locals for low-paid jobs, although the flourishing tourist sector helps to mitigate the effects. In the 2001 census (the first to collect such information), non-Greeks represented 7.6% of the population of Crete, and it is forecast that this will increase to 10% by 2021, leading to a 4.8% increase in the total population of the island, at a time when the figures for Greece as a whole will remain static or fall.

To date, the European refugee crisis has not caused problems in Crete, as the majority of refugees tend to head for the mainland or the more northerly Greek islands. Recently, however, rumours of plans to rehouse substantial numbers of refugees in Crete have caused some rumbles of discontent.

Economy and Infrastructure

In the immediate post-war period, the Cretan economy remained primarily agricultural. In spite of the move towards service industries – mainly tourism – which began in the 1970s, agriculture still accounted for about 38% of the economic activity on the island in 2016. Partly

because of the landscape, there are few large-scale agricultural enter-
prises and most production comes from small farms, often still using
traditional methods. From the 1950s, there was a rapid increase in the
use of plastic greenhouses for cultivation of tomatoes and bananas,
especially in the areas around Ierapetra and Malia. Unfortunately, this
was accompanied by increasing use of pesticides and chemical fertilis-
ers. In recent years, this trend has been counterbalanced by a growing
interest in organic farming on the island. Greece joined the EU in
1980 and, in general, Crete has benefitted from Common Agricultural
Policy subsidies for Cretan olive and sheep farmers.

The main exports continue to follow the traditional pattern: raisins,
wine, olives, olive oil, fresh fruit, fresh vegetables, honey and herbs
(both culinary and medicinal). Since interest in natural products and
health foods is increasing, the latter four items are seeing something
of a surge in demand. Cretan sheep and goat cheeses continue to be
of high quality, especially local feta, anthotiros, mizithra and graviera.
All types of Cretan cheese are finding an increasing export market.
There is scope for better marketing of Cretan olive oil, which is of
excellent quality, but much of which is exported to Italy to be blended
with poorer-quality oil and re-exported, sometimes back to Greece.
In an interesting development, Zaro's natural mineral water, bottled
from sources at the foot of Mount Psiloritis, was recently judged to
be the best bottled water in the world. Zaro's was awarded gold at the
Berkley Springs International Water Tasting, in competition with over
600 bottled waters from around the world. It beat the £80-a-bottle
Svalbarði Polar Iceberg Water into third place. Given the popularity
of bottled water and the relative cheapness of Zaro's, there must surely
be an export opportunity here.[8]

Whether for wool, meat, milk or cheese, sheep and goats still play
an important part in the economy. Herds are still grazed in the traditional way on higher pastures in summer, moving to lower valleys in
winter. Much of this movement is now carried out by transporting the
animals by lorry in autumn to industrial farming areas. In some parts
of the island, however, the animals are moved in the traditional way by
a herder and one or two dogs, and it is quite common, even on major
trunk roads, to have to stop one's car to allow a herd of sheep or goats
to cross. Often, the only nod to modernity is that the shepherd follows

his herd in a 4×4 rather than on foot. Fishing remains important on the coast, and is almost entirely carried out by individual fishermen in small caiques. The fish caught are relatively limited in quantity, but are of very good quality.

Due to the continuing strength of its agricultural sector and its strong tourism base, Crete has suffered less than many parts of Greece during the recession. The two sectors are, indeed, complementary, as the winter olive-picking season falls outside the main summer tourist season. For this reason, it is unlikely that attempts to extend the tourist season into the winter will be successful in Crete, although a later finish and earlier start are possible.

The major development in infrastructure has been the improvement of the road network. With assistance from an EU structural fund, the roads along the north coast between Chania and Siteia have been considerably improved over the last few years, the ultimate aim being a major trunk road for the entire length of the island. There have also been significant improvements to road access to the remoter areas, including the Lassithi plateau. In 2000, a study investigated the feasibility for two tram lines in Iraklion, one linking the stadium to the airport, and the other travelling between the centre of Iraklion and Knossos. No approval has yet been given for this proposal.

Disappointingly, the idea of a north coast railway remains a dream, in spite of support from the Green Party and detailed studies and plans published in 2007 and 2012. More feasible is the planned new airport at Kastelli, north-east of Iraklion, to replace the overstretched Nikos Kazantzakis Airport in Iraklion. Although the airport was originally set to be operational by 2018, the submissions process has been continuously postponed. Finally, in October 2016, a bid for the financing, construction and operation of the airport was made by a consortium comprising a local construction company and a major Indian group. There is no information yet on the next step, although major road improvements between Iraklion and Kastelli are continuing.

High and increasing demand for electricity in Crete, particularly during the tourist season, has put tremendous strain on the island's power supply. Fortunately, its climate provides opportunities for expanding renewable energy sources. Although there is limited potential for wave power and agricultural biomass units, there have been developments in wind and solar power. Crete is an extremely windy island, and by 2014 thirty wind farms were producing 18.3% of Crete's electricity. Over the last few years, solar power has also increased dramatically. Installations range from large solar thermal power plants to small solar panels on individual houses. Many hotels are installing large photovoltaic systems, and two have pointed the way to massive future savings in power demand by using solar-powered air conditioning plants.

Wildlife

Unfortunately, the post-war period has seen an increase in the number of bird and mammal species becoming endangered. The spiny mouse (*Acomys minous*) and Cretan shrew (*Crocidura caneae*) are unique to Crete and predate human occupation of the island. Both have been forced further and further into the mountainous highlands by habitat loss, and are now only to be found above 1,200 m. The Cretan shrew has also suffered by being displaced by the common shrew, and is classified as vulnerable. The spiny mouse is now very rare, but there is insufficient data to classify its status, which is probably somewhere between vulnerable and critically endangered.

The best-known Cretan mammal is the kri-kri, the Cretan wild goat (*Capra aegagrus cretica*), known since Minoan times and possibly introduced from Persia. Classified as vulnerable, its situation has improved a little. During the war, it was hunted almost to extinction by andartes hiding in the mountains, and in 1960 there were fewer than 200 surviving. After it was made a protected species, the population recovered somewhat, but it remains vulnerable both through human disturbance and by interbreeding with domestic goats. There have been successful attempts at repopulation by isolating groups of kri-kri on uninhabited islands like Thodorou, near Chania; Dia, north of Iraklion; and Aghioi Pandes, near Aghios Nikolaos. The total population is now about 2,000, mainly on these islands, the peaks of the Lefka Ori (White Mountains), and the remoter parts of the Samaria Gorge.

The loggerhead sea turtle (*Caretta caretta*), as in many parts of the world, is extremely vulnerable to environmental change. There is major danger from rubbish washed into the sea, particularly plastic bags, which the turtles mistake for edible jellyfish. In Crete, three important turtle nesting sites in Rethymnon, Chania and Messara Bay have been affected by the pressure of tourism, although there have been partially successful efforts to protect the sites by local volunteers and by the Sea Turtle Protection Society of Greece. Nevertheless, there have been many sightings of dead turtles at various locations on the island, and constant vigilance is needed at the nesting sites.

The magnificent golden eagle (*Aquila chrysaetos*) is now extremely rare in Crete, with only a few breeding pairs remaining in remote areas. The smaller Bonelli's eagle (*Aquila fasciatus*) has fared better and, although the population has declined, it is not endangered. The bearded vulture (*Gypaetus barbatus*), one of the rarest **raptors** in Europe, can now be found only above the tree line, and at one point the population was reduced to twenty-five individuals and four breeding pairs. A conservation project from 1998 to 2002 helped to reverse the decline by providing feeding stations in the mountains. An education project set up at the same time has brought the use of poisons and the shooting of raptors under control. In 2014, there were seven breeding pairs successfully producing five young. There were also six solitary adults, and it was hoped that they would breed with the young birds. The species is still extremely vulnerable, however, and in 2016 it was estimated that there were only nine or ten breeding pairs. The education programme also helped with the declining population of griffon vultures (*Gyps fulvus*), which had reduced from 200 breeding pairs in the 1980s to 140 in 2010. The process has been reversed, and griffon vultures are now fairly common in large numbers in all areas of the island.

Spinalonga

In 1948, new forms of treatment for leprosy were developed, with impressive results. Over the subsequent few years, many patients were cured and allowed to return home. By 1957, only twenty patients remained on the island, and they were transferred to the Aghia

Varvara Hospital in Athens, after which the Spinalonga colony was closed. The resident priest at the time, Father Chrysanthos, opted to stay on Spinalonga so that he could conduct memorial services for the dead on the first, third and fifth anniversaries of their deaths. He left after the final fifth anniversary in 1962. After this, Spinalonga was left derelict, with building materials and anything else useful being taken by local villagers.

That is not the end of the story, however. From the 1980s, restoration work began on the settlement buildings and the Venetian walls, and boats began to take tourists to the island. Many books were written about the leprosy colony, but it was probably *The Island* by Victoria Hislop, published in 2005, which put Spinalonga on the map.[9] Since a television adaptation on a Greek channel in 2010, it has become a major tourist attraction for foreigners and Greeks alike, the second most popular archaeological site in Crete after Knossos. In an ironic twist, the Island of Tears has thus become a major source of income for the surrounding area.

Culture

In some respects, Crete is still a very traditional society, and even in the twenty-first century the Cretan dialect is widely spoken. Traditional costumes can still be seen in the countryside, not least because, for mountainous areas, they remain extremely practical. Like most Greeks, the vast majority of Cretans are baptised into the Orthodox Church. Although devoutness is definitely not what it was, especially among the young, and attendance is declining, the Church still plays an important role in the lives of most Cretans. This role is as much cultural as religious; the traditions of the Church provide continuity with the past which, to some extent, helps to counteract the influences of globalism and materialism. The art of iconography endures too: not only is there a host of highly skilled icon painters throughout Crete painting icons using traditional methods, but a number of original painters have added modern touches to the ancient themes and techniques. Like the icon painters of the Cretan Renaissance, some of these have taken their talents far and wide, working in churches on

Mount Athos, and in Russia and the United States. On a more secular level, food in Crete also has a cultural aspect. In spite of the ubiquitous Coca-Cola and burgers, there are still few homes where you cannot find traditional dishes served regularly.

Notwithstanding the growing influence of American and European music, especially among young people, Cretan dances and music are still widely performed, and not just for the tourists. There are many local variations, but they are generally based on the old "warrior" dances representing heroism, dynamism and rebelliousness. Dances mostly for men – such as the Kastrinos from Iraklion, or the Pento-zalis, which was reputedly invented by Daskalogiannis (see chapter 12) – are fast, with complicated steps and energetic leaps. In contrast, the Siganos, dating from Ottoman times, is a slower communal dance representing unity and freedom, while the Sousta, for both men and women, is a story of love and seduction. There are few wedding receptions that do not begin with a version of the Siganos in which the bride and groom are gradually joined by the best man or woman, the parents and eventually the whole extended family. During the heat of summer, when Athens virtually closes down, popular and famous Greek music groups travel around the country, performing in even the smallest villages.

As for poetry, the classic *Erotokritos* is still frequently recited or sung, either as a whole or in extracts. Not long back, I was present at a spontaneous performance of verses from the poem by a famous Cretan singer. Well-known mantinades and rizitika are also often sung informally at parties and celebrations. The great lyra player and composer Nikos Xylouris from Anogeia (who lived from 1936 to 1980) did much to popularise rizitika (and Cretan music generally) in the cities, before his early death at the age of forty-four. He was nicknamed the Archangel of Crete.

Rizitika and mantinades are not merely repetitions of archaic songs and poems, but living art forms. The great song of rebellion *"When will the night be starry? When will it be February?"*, mentioned in chapter 12, received a new lease of life under the military dictatorship in Greece when students sang it during their occupation of the polytechnic university in Athens in 1973. The line *"to descend to Omalos"* was changed to the words *"to walk down to the Faculty of Law"*. Mantinades are also still being composed. A delightful modern example comes from Aristides Chairetis, a shepherd from central Crete widely acknowledged as the greatest mantinada composer of today: *"My thought goes out to my true love a million times a day./No wonder it is tired out and can no longer stray."*[10] Moreover, as throughout their history, mantinades have remained relevant and up to date: *"In the sheepcote I set up a modem to use,/For to sell on the Net the milk from my ewes."*[11]

Alongside these natural links with the past, tourism has played a part in restoring some of the traditional festivals and events that were in danger of dying out. For example, the village of Kritsa holds a traditional wedding every so often, when a young couple volunteer to follow all the old wedding customs for the benefit of visitors. Other villages have revived the old raki celebrations, when the first distillation of the year's raki is sampled, or fish nights, when locally caught fish are barbecued to the accompaniment of music and dancing. Meanwhile, the EU has provided funds to aid the restoration of historical sites. There has also been an attempt to re-establish the famous windmills of Lassithi, which once covered the plateau but have since largely fallen into disuse and been replaced by diesel pumps.

One final aspect of Cretan culture that is worth mentioning is the increasing interest taken by Cretans in their own history and traditions. In 1953, the Historical Museum of Crete was founded, with exhibits ranging from the Byzantine era up to and including the Second World War. Since 1980, the Natural History Museum of Crete has helped to illustrate the flora and fauna of the island from prehistoric times to the present. At the same time, there has been a growth in the number of folk museums around the island, ranging from a few exhibits displayed in one room to the magnificent Lychnostatis open-air museum near Chersonisos. The latter promotes understanding and awareness of Cretan folk heritage not only through exhibitions of old artefacts but also with gardens containing examples of indigenous Cretan plants, fruit trees and herbs, as well as a comprehensive collection of rocks and fossils found on the island. Even the building of the museum (from 1986 to 1992) was carried out using traditional manual methods of construction, with no mechanical aids.

As we have seen, archaeological excavations continue to reveal new insights into the ancient world, although financial constraints have curtailed some of the activity in recent years. All archaeological work takes place under the supervision of the Ministry of Culture and the University of Crete, often in co-operation with foreign universities (mainly British, American, French and Italian). It is also worth mentioning that recent refurbishments to the Heraklion Archaeological Museum and the Historical Museum of Crete have made them a joy to visit.

Children of Crete

As well as maintaining its own cultural traditions, Crete has continued, as in previous eras, to export its talent to the wider Greek artistic scene. The great writer Nikos Kazantzakis produced his most famous novels in the 1940s and 1950s. Although he has been described as more of a philosopher than a novelist, it is his novels that have spread his fame worldwide, including *Zorba the Greek* (1946), *Christ Recrucified* (1948), *Captain Michalis* (1950, its UK title being *Freedom and Death*), *The Last Temptation of Christ* (1955) and *Saint Francis* (1956, its UK title being *God's Pauper*). His *Report to Greco*, published posthumously in 1961, was a mixture of autobiography and fiction, and gave deep insights into his philosophy. *The Last Temptation of Christ* fell foul of the Roman Catholic Church and was included in the Vatican's Index of Prohibited Books, a decision to which Kazantzakis responded with a letter to the Vatican quoting the third-century Christian philosopher Tertullian: "Ad tuum, Domine, tribunal appello" ("At Your court, Lord, I make my appeal"). The Greek Orthodox Church also accused him of heresy, blasphemy and irreverence – charges which he refuted in a letter to the Holy Synod:

> You have execrated me, Holy Fathers; I bless you. I pray that your conscience may be as clean as mine and that you may be as moral and as religious as I am.[12]

In spite of continuing rumours to the contrary, and although he came close to it, Kazantzakis was never actually excommunicated by the Orthodox Church. Indeed, after his death, his coffin was laid in the

Cathedral of Saint Minas in Iraklion for people to pay their respects, after which he was given an Orthodox funeral by the Archbishop of Crete. He was buried on the Martinengo Bastion, the highest point of the Venetian walls of Iraklion. On his tombstone, at his request, are the words, "I fear nothing, I hope for nothing, I am free." In 1968, the Patriarch of Constantinople Athinagoras stated that "Kazantzakis's books adorn the Patriarchal Library".

One of the greatest Greek literary figures of modern times, Odysseas Elytis (who lived from 1911 to 1996), was born in Iraklion, although his family moved to Athens during his school years.[13] His poetry, often described as "romantic modernism", is complex and richly textured, with references to Ancient Greece and Byzantium mingled with a sort of twentieth-century mythology. The citation for his receipt of the Nobel Prize for Literature, which he won in 1979, declared:

> [His poetry] depicts with sensual strength and intellectual clear sightedness, modern man's struggle for freedom and creativity ... [In] its combination of fresh, sensuous flexibility and strictly disciplined implacability in the face of all compulsion, Elytis' poetry gives shape to its distinctiveness, which is not only very personal but also represents the traditions of the Greek people.[14]

One of his most famous creations is *To Axion Esti* (*Worthy it is*), written in 1959 and set to music in 1964 by Mikis Theodorakis (who himself has a Cretan father, although he was born in Chios). It is a long and intricate cycle of poetry and prose exploring his own life, the richness of Greek culture and tradition and the human condition. The language is difficult and, as acknowledged by translators, not easy to do justice to in English. The following is a tiny sample, and the powerful music for the oratorio by Theodorakis is well worth seeking out:

> *The blood of love has robed me in purple*
> *And joys never seen before have covered me in shade.*
> *I've become corroded in the south wind of humankind,*
> *Oh distant mother, my rose unfading.*

On the open sea they lay in wait for me,
With triple-masted men-of-war they bombarded me,
My sin that I too had a love of my own,
Oh distant mother, my rose unfading.

Once in July her large eyes
Half-opened, deep down in my bowels,
For a moment to light up the pure life,
Oh distant mother, my rose unfading.

And since that day the wrath of ages
Has turned on me, shouting out the curse:
"He who saw you, let him live in blood and stone,"
Oh distant mother, my rose unfading.

Once again I took the shape of my native country,
I grew and flowered among the stones.
And the blood of killers I redeem with light,
Oh distant mother, my rose unfading.[15]

Also born in Iraklion, in 1939, the great Greek composer Giannis Markopoulos moved to Athens to complete his musical studies at the age of seventeen. He moved again to England in 1967 when the junta came to power, and studied under several eminent British composers, including Elisabeth Lutyens. Returning to Athens in 1969, he organised performances of his work, which not only revolutionised Greek music but acted as thinly veiled criticisms of the junta and support for those protesting against it. Working alongside Nikos Xylouris, he developed music which combined Cretan instruments with standard western orchestras (for example, the beautiful *Concerto Rhapsody* for lyra and orchestra). Among his enormous output, it is worth mentioning two other pieces: the large-scale choral work *Liturgy of Orpheus*, and *Re-Naissance: Crete – Between Venice and Constantinople*, a massive symphony dealing with the Cretan influence on the empires that invaded and ruled the island. Like many Greek composers, Markopoulos does not see any distinction between high art and popular music, and his composition most familiar to English listeners is almost certainly the music for the 1977 BBC series *Who Pays the Ferryman?*, which is set in Crete.

Other children of Crete, like Elytis, only have a tenuous link to the island but are nevertheless claimed by Cretans as their own. Nana Mouskouri, one of the bestselling singers of all time – and, to many people, "the voice of Greece" – was born in Chania in 1934, but moved with her family to Athens when she was three years old. In July 2008, just before her final concert in Athens, she gave an emotional farewell performance in Chania. Less famous is Giannis Anastasakis, born in Chania, whose parents emigrated to the United States in 1935 when he was two years old. Under his anglicised name of John Aniston, he appeared in many American television films and series, including *Days of Our Lives*. He is the father of the actress Jennifer Aniston, star of the sitcom *Friends*.

Crete on Film

The landscape and culture of Crete have been spread around the world by film and television.[16] Perhaps the most famous example is the 1964 film *Zorba the Greek* starring Anthony Quinn, Alan Bates and Irene Papas, based on the Kazantzakis book. Filming locations used included the town of Chania, the Apokoronas region and the Akrotiri peninsula. The famous Sirtaki dance scene, with music by Theodorakis, was filmed on the beach of the village of Stavros. In the same year, Disney's *The Moon-Spinners*, starring Hayley Mills, was released. It was far from being such a classic as *Zorba*, but included some interesting location shots of the countryside around Elounda. In 1968, the German director Werner Herzog made the short film *Letzte Worte* (*Last Words*). Set on the island of Spinalonga, it tells the story of the last man to leave the island after the leprosy colony was closed. Depending on your point of view, it could be described as unconventional, avant-garde, thought-provoking or just weird.

In the 1970s, two BBC drama series written by Michael J. Bird helped to put one part of Crete on the map. *The Lotus Eaters* was filmed in and around Aghios Nikolaos and broadcast from 1972 to 1973. Starring Ian Hendry and Wanda Ventham, it now looks somewhat dated, but contains some interesting location shots. Michael J. Bird's subsequent Cretan series has worn much better. Set and largely filmed in Elounda, *Who Pays the Ferryman?* stars Jack Hedley and was broadcast in 1977. The theme tune by Markopoulos became a hit in the UK in 1978. These two series were largely responsible for an upsurge in tourism in the area from the late 1970s onwards.

The Final Invasion

And so we come to the last – to date – invaders of Crete: the tourists. No battles were involved this time, but it is possible that the long-term effects of tourism could be as far-reaching as previous military invasions.

Until the post-war period, Crete was virtually unknown as a holiday destination, except by individuals or small groups of intrepid travellers, some of whose experiences are quoted in previous chapters. There was little change in the 1960s and early 1970s, when Crete was "discovered" by backpackers and hippies. Many of them settled in the caves at Matala on the south coast, a place made famous in Joni Mitchell's song *Carey*, the lyrics of which can be found on her website.[17] Apart from the hippies, of whom the government strongly disapproved, tourism was actively encouraged by the junta, and by 1973 the number of tourists to Crete had risen to about 31,000 annually, dropping to 24,700 after the restoration of democracy in 1974.

For the next fifteen years, there was a slow but steady increase in the number of visitors to the island, but it wasn't until the 1990s that the real boom occurred. Available statistics are only for international arrivals to Crete by air, and do not include internal flights from other parts of Greece or arrivals by sea. Nevertheless, the figures are impressive: 1.5 million visitors in 1990, 2.5 million in 1997 and 2.8 million in 2007. Due to the recession, tourism then stagnated a little for a few years, but began to recover in 2012, reaching 3.5 million in 2014. In 2008, tourism accounted for 40% of the island's income and 36% of employment, while many other sectors, especially services, are heavily dependent on tourism. Most tourists come from Europe – mainly the United Kingdom, Germany, France, the Netherlands and Scandinavia. There is also a big influx of Italians during their annual holiday period in July. In recent years, increasing numbers of Russians have visited Crete, which has in turn led to a rise in investment from Russia, including in new hotels. In 2017, *Time* magazine chose Crete as the third most important place in the world to visit, while it was placed sixth in the world and fourth in Europe in TripAdvisor's Travellers' Choice awards.

The 20% increase in the population of Crete during the holiday season has, of course, put considerable strain on public services, but on the whole, transport, rubbish collection, water supply, electricity supply and availability of parking are just about holding their own. The exception is Iraklion airport, which can be a nightmare in peak season. The increase in flights to the small airports at Chania and Siteia has done little to improve the situation, but the new airport at Kastelli should solve the problem, if the project ever comes to fruition.

There has also been pressure on the environment due to new hotels and holiday complexes springing up at an alarming rate. To date, however, development has been regulated and hotels are limited to three floors, to avoid the rows of skyscrapers that mar the beauty of some Spanish resorts. In 2014, a bill was presented in the Greek parliament allowing hotels and other businesses to claim stretches of coastline for the exclusive use of their customers, but a massive outcry forced its withdrawal. Currently, all beaches in Crete remain open to the public and free to use, except for charges for sunbeds and umbrellas. The biggest environmental impact has undoubtedly been an increase in sea pollution. Although most Cretan beaches are kept clean and many have been awarded Blue Flags, rubbish and waste washed into the sea has had an impact on sea life, particularly the loggerhead sea turtle.

The rise in all-inclusive holiday packages has had a negative impact on local village tavernas, bars and shops in parts of Crete, but so far there has been little attempt to counteract this damage. Most of the resorts are foreign owned, and contribute almost nothing to the local economy. It is unlikely that the situation will improve without government intervention. Restriction of licences could halt the steadily increasing number of all-inclusive resorts, while aggressive marketing of the joys of participating in the authentic Greek experience could help.[18]

Many cruise ships now include Chania, Iraklion and Aghios Nikolaos in their schedules, and this has had a generally positive effect on the economies of these towns. There are concerns about the potential for environmental damage from waste and oil spillage, but, according to the coastguard, there is little evidence of this to date.

Into the Future

In one sense, the only certainty about Crete is that its future will be very different from its past. The cultural influences of globalisation, the Internet and immigration from northern Europe are already visible in ways that are subtle but significant. Three examples will illustrate this point – two relatively trivial, and the third extremely dangerous.

Firstly, about fifteen years ago, Crete discovered the joys of northern European Christmas decorations, including lights, trees and Father Christmas figures. These, however, supplemented the traditional Cretan celebration of Christmas, rather than replacing it.

Secondly, twenty years ago, dogs were only kept for hunting or guarding property, but now – possibly under the influence of UK and German immigrants – an increasing number of Cretan families own a pet dog.

Thirdly, the healthy aspects of the Cretan diet are taking a severe beating from the encroachment of junk food and fizzy drinks, and child obesity is fast becoming as big a problem in Crete as it is in the UK.

On the other hand, as noted above, the people of Crete still show their historic resilience in retaining those aspects of their culture that are most important to them, such as the Orthodox faith, Cretan music and dancing, and, up to a point, their food. It is always dangerous to generalise, especially about a whole group of people, but social scientist Diana Conyers has made a convincing argument about Crete's adaptability:

> Over the centuries, the Cretans developed the capacity to take what they wanted from the invaders and ignore what was of no benefit to them, to tolerate them if they did not cause too much trouble and to revolt against them if they did.[19]

It seems that most of Conyers' statements remain true in relation to the explosion of tourism, while there is even an occasional glimpse of her latter point about revolting. When Spinalonga first became a popular excursion site, the tourist coaches would drop visitors at the boats and pick them up as soon as they returned from the island. This meant that, apart from the boat owners, local businesses gained no benefit from the visits to Spinalonga. The businessmen of Elounda therefore blockaded the only road into the village until the coach companies agreed to give the visitors at least an hour in the village for shopping and eating. The rebellious spirit still lives!

To sum up, in spite of all difficulties, it is likely that the spirit of Crete will survive. It is appropriate that the final words of this history should go to a Cretan in the form of a mantinada:

Οσο θα στέκει να κτυπά ήλιος στον Ψηλορείτη,
Θα στέκει και θα πολεμά και θα γλεντίζει η Κρήτη

As long as the sun rises over Mount Psiloriti,
So long will we stand up to fight and to party in Kriti.[20]

Glossary

agha
A civil or military officer in the Ottoman Empire. Later used as a general term of respect for upper-class Muslims in Crete.

andarte
pl. andartes
Greek guerrilla resistance fighters during the Second World War.

Anzac
An acronym for Australia and New Zealand Army Corps.

apetairos
pl. apetairoi
Without political rights. Non-Dorian, free inhabitants of Crete.

archon
A leader. Applied to the Greek-speaking Cretan nobility under Venetian rule.

archontopoula
Young leaders, specifically the twelve original Byzantine nobles allegedly sent to Crete by the emperor Alexios I. They later formed the Greek-speaking Cretan aristocracy.

atrium
pl. atria
An open central courtyard in Roman houses.

Berbers
Indigenous people of North Africa, from Libya to Morocco. The Muslim invaders of the Iberian peninsula were largely Berbers.

bey
Used loosely to describe a wealthy Muslim landowner in Ottoman Crete.

Byzantine Empire
The date of the transition from the Roman Empire to the Byzantine Empire has been the subject of much argument. Various options include:
285 – The first division of the empire into east and west by Diocletian
330 – Emperor Constantine moves the capital of the empire from Rome to Byzantium, renaming it Constantinople
395 – the final split between a Greek eastern empire and a Latin western empire
827 – the Arab conquest of Crete

Calvinism
A major branch of Protestantism that follows the teachings of the Swiss theologian John Calvin.

Carthage
A city state in what is now Tunisia which rivalled Rome for supremacy in the Mediterranean. At one point, Rome was very close to defeat at the hands of Hannibal but, after three wars, Carthage was completely crushed by an army led by Scipio Africanus.

chrysovoulo
A binding document sealed with gold and issued by the Byzantine emperor.

doge
The chief magistrate and leader of the Republic of Venice from 697 to 1797. Elected for life by the aristocracy of the city state.

EAM/ELAS
The National Liberation Front (Ethnikó Apeleftherotikó Métopo) was the main resistance movement in Greece and Crete during the Second World War. Affiliated to the Communist Party, it also included other republican and left-wing groups. Its military wing was the Greek People's Liberation Army (Ellinikós Laïkós Apeleftherotikós Stratós).

emir
Ruler of an Arab country, roughly equivalent to a prince.

Enigma machine
German mechanical cipher machine used during the Second World War to encrypt secret messages. A team at Bletchley Park was successful in cracking the codes and producing vast quantities of German military intelligence known as Ultra. The 2014 film *The Imitation Game* tells the story of Alan Turing and his codebreaker team.

EOK
The National Organisation of Crete (Ethnikí Orgánosi Krítis), the non-communist, largely Venizelist resistance movement in Crete during the Second World War.

fiefs/fiefdoms
Under the feudal system, a fief or fiefdom was inheritable property or rights granted by an overlord to a vassal who held it in return for allegiance and service.

Friendly Society
The Friendly Society or Society of Friends was a secret nineteenth-century organisation whose purpose was to overthrow Ottoman rule in Greece and establish an independent Greek state.

genome
The complete set of genes or genetic material present in a cell or organism.

Greek Fire
Incendiary weapon, a bit like a flame thrower, used by the Byzantine army and navy. It was particularly effective at sea, since the fire would continue to burn on water. The composition of Greek Fire is still unknown.

hagiography
The writing of the lives of saints, usually written in a reverential style, with the emphasis on spiritual lessons rather than strict biographical facts.

Halepa Charter
An agreement made in 1878 between the Ottoman Empire and the representatives of the Pan-Cretan Revolutionary Assembly, and formulated by Britain. It set out a variety of reforms which virtually amounted to autonomy for Crete. It was revoked by the Ottoman governor in 1889, leading to further rebellions.

Hatt-i Hümayun
The Imperial Reform Edict imposed on the Ottoman Empire by Britain and France in 1856. It declared that Muslims and non-Muslims would henceforth be legally equal subjects of the sultan, granted religious toleration to Christians throughout the empire and guaranteed the safety of all subjects without distinction of class or religion.

hominins
A group of primates comprising those species regarded as humans, direct ancestors of humans or very closely related to humans.

Istanbul
After the fall of Constantinople, the Ottomans called the city both Istanbul and, more formally, Konstantiniyye. Western Europe, however, continued to call it Constantinople until the twentieth century. To prevent confusion, I have chosen to follow the western European approach in this book. It is interesting to note that the

name Constantinople is still used within the Greek Orthodox
Church and by many Greeks.

jurists
Highly respected and influential experts in Islamic jurisprudence and
law.

KKE
The Communist Party of Greece (Kommounistikó Kómma Elládas).

koinon
A league or federation. The Koinon of the Cretans (loosely meaning
the Cretan League) was a sort of assembly of representatives from all
the cities of Dorian Crete.

Levant
The coastal countries of the eastern Mediterranean, comprising
Lebanon, Syria, Israel, Palestine and Jordan.

Mesolithic era
see Stone Age

metropolitan
The senior bishop of a province in the Orthodox Church. Usually the
bishop of the main town in the province, the metropolitan has higher
status and greater responsibilities than other bishops.

Monroe Doctrine
Set out in 1823, the Monroe Doctrine was the long-standing United
States policy of opposing further European colonialism in North and
South America. As a corollary, the United States also undertook not
to interfere in the internal concerns of European countries.

mufti
An Islamic scholar who interprets and expounds Islamic law. Muftis
are jurists qualified to give authoritative legal opinions known as
fatwas, and they rank above qadis.

Neolithic era
see Stone Age

Organic Act
An imperial decree issued in January 1868 which made some concessions to Cretan demands for reform. It included joint Muslim and Christian local government, recognition of Turkish and Greek as official languages and a General Assembly for local legislation.

Palaeolithic era
see Stone Age

pasha
A high-ranking Ottoman military or civil commander. In Crete it refers to the governors of the three provinces or pashaliks.

patriarch
In this context, the term refers to the heads of the ancient bishoprics of Alexandria, Antioch, Jerusalem, Constantinople and, before the Great Schism of 1054, Rome. From 1589 to 1721 and from 1917 to date, Moscow has also been a patriarchate. The patriarchs have authority over all bishops within their patriarchate. The Patriarch of Constantinople, also known as the Ecumenical Patriarch, is accepted as the highest dignitary of the Greek Orthodox Church with great spiritual authority but, unlike the Pope, is "first among equals" rather than a ruler.

Pax Romana
A long period of *relative* peace within the Roman Empire, lasting from 27 BC to AD 180.

Peak sanctuaries
Sacred places, usually in the open air, found at or near the top of mountains in Crete. They were an important feature of religious rites in Minoan times.

Pentecost
The event described in the Bible in Acts 2:1–41, in which the Holy
Spirit descended on the apostles.

pithos
pl. pithoi
Large storage pots used in the Bronze Age for oil, grain, dried fish,
beans and olives. They were also used at times for burial.

Pontus
Kingdom to the south and east of the Black Sea. King Mithridates VI
waged several wars on Rome until he was finally defeated in 64 BC,
whereupon Pontus became a Roman province.

proconsul
An official of ancient Rome, acting on behalf of a consul. Often, he
was a former consul. Under the Roman Empire, the title was held by
a civil governor of a province, e.g. Crete.

protopapas
pl. protopapades
Literally "first priest". Under Venetian rule, this was a Greek
Orthodox priest paid by Venice and recognising the supremacy of the
pope. More generally, the title is still used in the Orthodox Church to
signify a senior non-monastic priest.

proveditore generale
pl. proveditori
Governor-general. Under Venetian rule, a proveditore generale with
absolute military powers could be appointed in times of great danger.
After 1569, the post became permanently established in Crete.

raptor
Bird of prey, such as an eagle, hawk or vulture.

rizitiko
pl. rizitika
Folk song originating from Sfakia and western Crete in Byzantine times, becoming popular in the Ottoman period and remaining in favour to the present day.

qadi
A Muslim magistrate.

rectore
pl. rectores
Governor of one of the main towns in Venetian Crete.

serf
In the feudal system of medieval Europe, a serf was an agricultural labourer bound to his lord's land. The serf was required to work for the lord of the manor, who owned the land. In return, he was entitled to protection, justice and the right to cultivate certain fields within the manor for his own needs.

SOE
The Special Operations Executive, a British force formed in 1940 to conduct espionage, sabotage and reconnaissance in occupied Europe.

Stone Age
The Stone Age is broken down into the Palaeolithic, Mesolithic and Neolithic eras, a rough categorisation based on the types of tools and communities found. The dating is approximate and varies according to location.

Sublime Porte
A common term to describe the imperial government in Constantinople. It derives from the Great Gate of the Topkapi Palace, from which the sultan's decrees were often read.

Uniate

The Eastern Rite Catholic Churches, developed after the Council of Florence in 1439, kept the organisation and liturgy of the Orthodox Church while accepting the supremacy of the pope. The term "Uniate" to describe these Churches is regarded as somewhat disparaging by the Roman Catholic Church, but is commonly used in the Orthodox Church, and would certainly have been in common circulation in Venetian Crete.

vassal

In the feudal system, a vassal was granted the use of land in return for his allegiance and usually military service to his feudal lord.

Acknowledgements

I would like to thank the many friends and family who helped in checking the manuscript for errors and readability; their suggestions and criticisms played an essential role in the creation of this book. Too many to name them all, I must nevertheless mention two in particular who have been of inestimable help and support: Rosemary Copsey, who can spot a repetition at 100 yards and Ralph "the Comma King" Lane.

Thanks also to Manolis Sfyrakis for help with translations, and to Aspassia Moulakaki, who sought out some extremely useful Greek statistics websites.

I am not a professional historian, and this book would be considerably poorer without the assistance of experts on the various periods, who checked for accuracy and, in some cases, offered valuable insights into the latest research. I was moved by the willingness of extremely busy academics to spend time helping me:

Antonis Anastasopoulos, University of Crete (Ottoman rule)
Mohamad Ballan, University of Chicago (Arab rule)
Dr. Matthew Buell, Concordia University (Bronze Age)
Professor Vassilios Christides, Institute of Graeco-Oriental and African Studies (Arab rule)
Dr. Theocharis Detorakis, University of Rethymnon (Byzantine period)
Dr. David Holton, University of Cambridge (Venetian rule)
Colin Janes, author of *The Eagles of Crete* (Civil War)
Dr. Anna Kouremenos, American School of Classical Studies (Roman rule)
Dr. David Lewis, University of Edinburgh (Dorian period)

Mick McTiernan (Autonomous Crete)

Georgios Markakis and Yiannis Markakis, Lychnostatis Museum
(Post-war period)

Major (Retd) John Netherwood (Second World War)

Dr. Monique O'Connell, Wake Forest University (Venetian rule)

Peter Rogers (Venetian rule)

Dr. Thomas Strasser, Providence College (Prehistoric period)

I must include a word of thanks to the wonderful websites Academia.edu and JSTOR, which contain enormous collections of academic theses and articles, and to Project Gutenberg, the source of most of the quotations from classical historians in this book.

Thank you to the Museum of Christian Art, Iraklion for its assistance in sourcing Plate 3, and to the Historical Museum of Crete for its assistance in sourcing Plates 9 (top), 12, 13 and 14–15.

Finally, a big thank you to Harry Hall of Haus Publishing, who had faith in my book, and to Jo Stimpson for the thorough work she has done on editing my original draft. Her efforts certainly improved clarity and readability.

Image Credits

Notes

Preface

1. Theocharis E. Detorakis, *History of Crete,* John C. Davis trans. (Iraklion, 1994).
2. Diodorus Sikeliotes, quoted in Detorakis, *History of Crete.*

1 **Introduction**

1. Nikos Kazantzakis, *Freedom and Death,* Jonathan Griffin trans. (London: Faber and Faber, 1956).
2. Robert Pashley, *Travels in Crete* (London: J. Murray, 1837).

2 **Mythological Crete**

1. According to mythology, the Greek word for Crete, "Kriti", derives from this early race.

3 **Prehistoric Crete**

1. August 2017 saw the publication of the discovery in 2010 of fossilised footprints west of Kissamos. They appear to be hominin and date from 5.6 million years ago, during the late Miocene epoch, at a time when Crete was attached to the mainland. The discovery raises the possibility that hominin ancestors of man, most likely *Graecopithecus*, were present in the area at a much earlier date than previously believed. The findings are, however, speculative and somewhat controversial; both the dating and the fact that they are hominin footprints have been questioned.
2. Quoted in John Noble Wilford, "On Crete, New Evidence of Very Ancient Mariners", *The New York Times*, 15th February 2010.
3. See: Thomas F. Strasser et al., "Stone Age Seafaring in the Mediterranean: Evidence from the Plakias Region for Lower

Palaeolithic and Mesolithic Habitation of Crete", *Hesperia*, vol. 79, no.2, April–June 2010, pp. 145–190; Thomas Strasser, "Dating Palaeolithic sites in southwestern Crete, Greece", *Journal of Quaternary Studies*, vol. 26, no. 5, July 2011, pp. 553–560; John Noble Wilford, "On Crete, New Evidence". For up-to-date information on the site, see: *The Plakias Stone Age Project*, http://plakiasstoneageproject.com, accessed 26th February 2019. The site includes fascinating 3D images of three of the stone axes, which you can examine from all sides.

4. Curtis Runnels, "Early Palaeolithic on the Greek Islands?", *Journal of Mediterranean Archaeology*, vol. 27, no. 2, 2014, pp. 211–230.

5. Runnels, "Early Palaeolithic".

6. Cyprian Broodbank and Thomas F. Strasser, "Migrant Farmers and the Neolithic Colonization of Crete", *Antiquity*, vol. 65, no. 247, June 1991, pp. 233–245.

7. "Fact Sheet", *The Plakias Stone Age Project*, http://plakiasstoneageproject.com/fact-sheet, accessed 26th February 2019.

8. For more detail on Stone Age Greece in general, see: "Stone Age", *Foundation of the Hellenic World*, http://www.ime.gr/chronos/01/en, accessed 26th February 2019.

9. Jeffery R. Hughey et al., "A European population in Minoan Bronze Age Crete", *Nature Communications*, vol. 4, 2013.

10. Broodbank and Strasser, "Migrant Farmers".

11. For a detailed study of the early fauna, see: Alexandra van der Geer, Michael Dermitzakis and John de Vos, "Crete Before the Cretans: The Reign of Dwarfs", *Pharos*, vol. 13, pp. 121–132.

4   The Bronze Age

1. For the full study, see: Hughey et al., "A European population". For a briefer report, see: Stephanie Seiler, "DNA analysis unearths origins of Minoans, the first major European civilization", *University of Washington*, 14th May 2013, http://www.washington.edu/news/2013/05/14/dna-analysis-unearths-origins-of-minoans-the-first-major-european-civilization, accessed 26th February 2019.

2. Iosif Lazaridis et al., "Genetic origins of the Minoans and Mycenaeans", *Nature*, vol. 548, no. 7666, 10 August 2017.

3. For a relatively clear summary of the main periods, see: *Minoan Crete*, http://www.minoancrete.com, accessed 26th February 2019.

4. Jarrett A. Lobell, "The Minoans of Crete", *Archaeology*, May/June 2015.

5. For a fascinating animation of the Knossos palace as it might have looked, see: Make Greek language a world language, "Ancient Greece - Crete - Minoan palace" [video], *Facebook*, https://www. facebook.com/mglawl/videos/1029623517112275, accessed 26th February 2019.

6. For, excellent descriptions of all the archaeological sites, see: *Minoan Crete*, http://www.minoancrete.com, accessed 26th February 2019.

7. Arthur Evans, *Cretan Pictographs and Prae-Phoenician Script* (New York: G. P. Putnam's Sons, 1895).

8. This phenomenon is by no means unknown. Chinese ideograms are an example, while the development of the Cyrillic alphabet from the Greek alphabet is an even closer parallel.

9. Richard Vallance Janke and Alexandre Solcà, *High Correlation Linear A–Linear B vocabulary, grammar and orthography in Linear A* (Ottawa and Athens: Les Éditions KONOSO Press, 2018).

10. Quoted in Lobell, "The Minoans of Crete". For more details on the Gournia excavations, see: *Gournia Excavation Project*, http://www.gournia.org, accessed 26th February 2019.

11. Quoted in Andreas N. Angelakis and Joan B. Rose eds., *Evolution of Sanitation and Wastewater Technologies Through the Centuries* (London: IWA Publishing, 2014)

12. For full details of the studies carried out in this field by the University of Uppsala, see: Mary Blomberg, *Minoan Astronomy*, http://minoanastronomy.mikrob.com, accessed 26th February 2019.

13. Gretchen E. Leonhardt, "Pax Minoica and the Okinawan Peace", *Konosos*, 13th April 2012, https://konosos.net/2012/04/13/pax-minoica-and-the-okinawan-peace, accessed 26th February 2019.

14. Plato, *Laws,* Robert Gregg Bury trans. (Cambridge: Harvard University Press; London: William Heinemann Ltd, 1967–1968), Book 4, 706b.

15. Homer, *The Iliad*, Martin Hammond trans. (London: Penguin Classics, 1987), Book 2, 646–652.

16. For a fascinating and very readable description of the process written by Ventris' colleague, see: John Chadwick, *The Decipherment of Linear B* (Cambridge University Press, 2008).

17. The Bible, Titus, 1:12.

5   Dorian Crete

1. Homer, *The Odyssey*, E.V. Rieu trans. (London: Penguin Classics, 1991), Book 19, 175–177.

2. Alicia McDermott, "Knossos Thrived Well into the Iron Age and Was Much Larger than Once Believed", *Ancient Origins*, 10th January 2016, https://www.ancient-origins.net/news-history-archaeology/knossos-thrived-well-iron-age-and-was-much-larger-once-believed-005137, accessed 19th March 2019.

3. Plato, *Laws* (Urbana: Project Gutenburg, 2013), Book 1, paragraph 11, retrieved 19th March 2019 from http://www.gutenberg.org/files/1750/1750-h/1750-h.htm.

4. "Diodorus Siculus, Book 37", *Attalus*, http://www.attalus.org/translate/diodorus37.html#18, accessed 19th March 2019.

5. For a detailed study of the prosperity of the cities during the Hellenistic period, see: Philip de Souza, "Late Hellenistic Crete and the Roman Conquest", *British School of Athens Studies*, vol. 2, 1998.

6. "Diodorus Siculus, Book 33", *Attalus*, http://attalus.org/translate/diodorus33.html#10, accessed 19th March 2019.

7. Polybius, *The Histories of Polybius*, Evelyn Shirley Shuckburgh trans. (Urbana: Project Gutenburg, 2013), IV, 54. retrieved 19th March 2019 from http://www.gutenberg.org/files/44125/44125-h/44125-h.htm.

8. Plutarch, *Plutarch's Morals*, William W. Goodwin trans. (Boston: Little, Brown, and Co., 1878), vol. 3, p. 62, retrieved 19th March 2019 from https://oll.libertyfund.org/titles/1213.

9. Paula Perlman, "Imagining Crete", in Mogens Herman Hansen ed., *The Imaginary Polis*, Acts of the Copenhagen Polis Centre, vol. 7, p. 302.

10. Attributed to Hybrias the Cretan, 4th century, quoted in "Skolion (drinking song) attributed to Hybrias the Cretan", *Fairfield*, http://faculty.fairfield.edu/rosivach/c1115/hybrias.htm, accessed 19th March 2019.

11. I am grateful to David Lewis for help with the paragraphs on slavery.

12. For an excellent analysis of the reasons for slave revolts, see: Paul Cartledge, "Rebels and 'Sambos' in Classical Greece", *History of Political Thought*, vol. 6, no. 16, 1985.

13. Angelos Chaniotis, "The Great Inscription, Its Political and Social Institutions and the Common Institutions of the Cretans", in *The Great Inscription of Gortyna. One hundred and twenty years after discovery. Proceedings of the 1st International Conference of Studies on Messara*, 2005.

14. This was the term used in Gortyn, Lyttos and several other cities. In others, including Olous and Kydonia, they were called demiourgoi, and in Itanos and Praisos archontes.

15. For the full text, see: Ronald F. Willetts ed., *The Law Code of Gortyn* (Berlin: Walter De Gruyter & Co., 1967). For a summary, see: "Ancient History Sourcebook: The Law Code of Gortyn (Crete), c. 450 BCE", *Fordham University*, https://sourcebooks.fordham.edu/ancient/450-gortyn.asp, accessed 19th March 2019.

16. This inscription implies that 1 stater is equal to 2 drachmas, but the exact relationship varied by location and time.

17. Aristotle, quoted in Detorakis, *History of Crete*, p. 52.

18. Quoted in Detorakis, *History of Crete*, p. 53.

19. Claudius Aelianus, quoted in Detorakis, *History of Crete*, p. 54.

20. Strabo, *Geographies* (Urbana: Project Gutenburg, 2014), book 10, chap. 4, 16, retrieved 19th March 2019 from http://www.gutenberg.org/ebooks/44885.

21. "Plato: HIPPIAS (major)", *Elpenor*, https://www.ellopos.net/elpenor/greek-texts/ancient-greece/plato/plato-hippias-major.asp?pg=8, accessed 19th March 2019.

22. Quoted in John Guyton, "Epimenides, Prophet from Crete", *Searching for GSOT*, 22nd August 2016, https://johnguyton. wordpress.com/2016/08/22/epimenides-prophet-from-crete/, accessed 19th March 2019.

23. Aristotle, *The History of Animals,* D'Arcy Wentworth Thompson trans. (ebooks@Adelaide, 2015), III, 2, retrieved 19th March 2019 from https://ebooks.adelaide.edu.au/a/aristotle/history/index. html.

24. Quoted in Robin Waterfield, *The First Philosophers: The Presocratics and Sophists* (Oxford University Press, 2000). One type of meteorite, the diogenite meteorite, is named after Diogenes.

25. Plutarch, *Life of Lycurgus*, Bernadotte Perrin trans. (Cambridge: Harvard University Press, 1914), pp. 214–215, retrieved 19th March 2019 from http://penelope.uchicago.edu/Thayer/E/ Roman/Texts/Plutarch/Lives/Lycurgus*.html.

26. For a detailed and interesting discussion of the sanctuaries in Dorian Crete, see: Angelos Chaniotis, "Extra-urban Sanctuaries in Classical and Hellenistic Crete", in Georgios Deligiannakis and Ioannis Galanakis eds., *The Aegean and its Cultures* (Oxford: Archaeopress, 2009).

6   Roman Rule

1. "Pompey by Plutarch", *The Internet Classics Archive*, http:// classics.mit.edu/Plutarch/pompey.html, accessed 19th March 2019.

2. Lucius Annaeus Florus, *Epitome of Roman History*, E. S. Forster trans. (Cambridge: Harvard University Press, 1929), book 1, section XLII, chap. III, 7, retrieved 19th March 2019 from http://penelope.uchicago.edu/Thayer/E/Roman/Texts/Florus/ Epitome/1L*.html#XLII.

3. In spite of his incompetence in military affairs, Marcus Antonius Creticus was described by Plutarch as "not very famous or distinguished in public life, but a worthy good man, and particularly remarkable for his liberality." See: "Antony by Plutarch", *The Internet Classics Archive*, http://classics.mit.edu/ Plutarch/antony.html, accessed 19th March 2019.

4. "Diodorus Siculus, Book 40", *Attalus*, http://www.attalus.org/translate/diodorus40.html#1, accessed 19th March 2019.

5. Cassius Dio, *Rome*, Earnest Cary trans. (Cambridge: Harvard University Press, 1914), p. 30, retrieved 19th March 2019 from http://penelope.uchicago.edu/Thayer/E/Roman/Texts/Cassius_Dio/36*.html.

6. "Pompey by Plutarch", *The Internet Classics Archive*, http://classics.mit.edu/Plutarch/pompey.html, accessed 19th March 2019. 400 furlongs is about 80 km, or three days' march.

7. Angelos Chaniotis, "What Difference did Rome make? The Cretans and the Roman Empire", in Björn Forsén and Giovanni Salmeri (eds.), *The Province Strikes Back. Imperial Dynamics in the Eastern Mediterranean* (Helsinki: The Finnish Institute at Athens, 2008), pp. 83–105.

8. Apollonia, the port of Cyrene, was only 300 km from Gortyn, compared with 800 km from Alexandria and 900 km across desert from Leptis Magna.

9. Edward Gibbon, *The History of the Decline and Fall of the Roman Empire* (Urbana: Project Gutenburg, 2008), vol. 1, chap. 6, part III, retrieved 19th March 2019 from http://www.gutenberg.org/ebooks/25717.

10. Cornelius Tacitus, *Complete Works of Tacitus*, Alfred John Church and William Jackson Brodribb trans. (New York: Modern Library, 1942), 15.20, retrieved 19th March 2019 from http://mcadams.posc.mu.edu/txt/ah/Tacitus/TacitusAnnals15.html.

11. Angelos Chaniotis, "Hadrian, Diktynna, the Cretan Koinon, and the Roads of Crete", in W. Eck, B. Fehér, and P. Kovác eds., *Studia Epigraphica in memoriam Géza Alföldy* (Bonn: Habelt 2013), pp. 59–68.

12. This deforestation was continued twelve centuries later by the Venetians, leading to the extensive denuding of Cretan uplands that we see today.

13. Production of whetstones has continued in Elounda to the present day, although the quarry is nowadays only opened on request.

14. See Anna Kouremenos, "A Tale of Two Cretan Cities: The Building of Roman Kissamos and the Persistence of Polyrrhenia

in the Wake of Shifting Identities", in Brita Alroth and Charlotte Scheffer eds., *Attitudes toward the Past in Antiquity: Creating Identities* (Stockholm University, 2014), pp. 129–39.

15. See: Anna Kouremenos, *Houses and Identity in Roman Knossos and Kissamos* (unpublished, 2013), lent to me by Ms. Kouremenos with permission to quote. The figures are estimates by archaeologists.

City	Area	Estimated population
Gortyn	150 ha	22,500
Hierapytna	150 ha	22,500
Kydonia	85 ha	12,750
Kissamos	71 ha	8,875
Phaistos	62 ha	7,750
Knossos	50–60 ha	6,250–7,500
Aptera	42 ha	5,250
Polyrrhenia	30 ha	3,750

16. Martha W. Baldwin Bowsky, "Colonia Iulia Nobilis Cnosus, the first 100 years: the evidence of Italian sigillata stamps", in Rebecca J. Sweetman ed., *Roman Colonies in the First Century of Their Foundation* (Oxford: Oxbow Books, 2011).

17. Dianne Skafte, "Creativity as an Archetypal Calling", in Dennis Patrick Slattery and Lionel Corbett eds., *Depth Psychology – Meditations in the Field* (Einsiedeln: Daimon, 2004).

18. Ewen Bowie, "Greek Poetry in the Antonine Age", in Donald A. Russell ed., *Antonine Literature* (Oxford: Clarendon Press, 1990).

19. The Bible, Acts 27:7–13.

20. Quoted in Philip Schaff and Henry Wace eds., *Nicene and Post-Nicene Fathers, Second Series, Vol. 1* (Buffalo: Christian Literature Publishing Co., 1890), retrieved 19th March 2019 from http://www.newadvent.org/fathers/250104.htm.

21. The martyrs still commemorated include twelve unnamed soldiers, Theophilos and his family, and Cyril, bishop of Gortyna, who was martyred at the age of ninety-three in about AD 300. There is a chapel dedicated to Saint Cyril in Stavion, at the top of the Asterousia Mountains. In the reign of Emperor Decius (AD 249 to AD 251), of the ten martyrs of Crete, two are known

to have come from Knossos and Iraklion, the rest from western Crete.

22. Kouremenos, *Houses and Identity*.

23. Philostratus, *Life of Apollonius,* F.C. Conybeare trans. (Cambridge: Harvard University Press, 1912), 4.34, retrieved 19th March 2019 from https://www.livius. org/sources/content/philostratus-life-of-apollonius/ philostratus-life-of-apollonius-4.31–35.

24. Ammianus Marcellinus, *Roman History*, C.D. Yonge trans. (London: Bohn, 1862), book 26, 10.16–19, retrieved 19th March 2019 from http://www.tertullian.org/fathers/ammianus_26_ book26.htm.

7   The First Byzantine Period

1. Nicetas Patricius, "Saint: Andrew Of Crete", *Nektarios*, http:// users.uoa.gr/~nektar/orthodoxy/agiologion/saints_08th-10th_ centuries/102.htm, accessed 19th March 2019.

2. Procopius, *History of the Wars,* H.B. Dewing trans. (Urbana: Project Gutenburg, 2005), book I, XXII, retrieved 19th March 2019 from http://www.gutenberg.org/ebooks/16764.

3. For the full description, see: Procopius, *History of the Wars*.

4. "The Great Canon of St Andrew of Crete", *Азбука веры* [*Alphabet of Faith*], https://azbyka.ru/molitvoslov/the-great- canon-of-st-andrew-of-crete.html, accessed 7th March 2019.

5. For a brief life of Saint Andrew and several of the other saints mentioned in this book, see: Christopher Moorey, *Traveling Companions* (Chesterton: Ancient Faith Publishing, 2012).

6. Socrates Scholasticus, "Church History (Book VII): Chapter 38. Many of the Jews in Crete embrace the Christian Faith", *New Advent*, http://www.newadvent.org/fathers/26017.htm, accessed 28th February 2019.

7. Titus M Sylligardakis, *Cretan Saints*, Timothy Andrews trans. (Saint Smaragdos Group, 1988).

8   The Arab Emirate of Crete

1. Although, for simplicity, I have followed common practice in referring to the conquerors of Crete as Arabs, they were in fact a combination of Arabs, Berbers and non-Arab Muslims.

2. Gibbon may have confused the leader of the Arab invaders, Abu Hafs, with a leader of the attack on Sicily, Abu Caab.

3. Gibbon, *The History of the Decline and Fall*, vol. 5, chap. 52 part 4.

4. In a better-documented incident that was recorded in 828, the Arab commander of the invasion of Sicily gave orders to burn the ships to keep them out of Roman hands. It is possible that Gibbon, not for the first time, confused the sources.

5. Iosephus Genesius, *On the Reign of the Emperors* (Canberra: Australian Association for Byzantine Studies, 1998), pp. 39–41.

6. Quoted in Detorakis, *History of Crete*, p. 123.

7. Leo the Deacon, *The History of Leo the Deacon: Byzantine military expansion in the tenth century*, Alice-Mary Talbot and Denis F. Sullivan trans. (Washington, D.C.: Dumbarton Oaks Research Library and Collection, 2005), book II, section 8.

8. Quoted in Detorakis, *History of Crete*, p. 124.

9. Ibn Hazm, quoted in Mohamad Ballan, "Andalusi Crete (827–961) and the Arab-Byzantine Frontier in the Early Medieval Mediterranean", *Ballandalus*, 9th April 2015, https://ballandalus.wordpress.com/2015/04/09/andalusi-crete-827–961-and-the-arab-byzantine-frontier-in-the-early-medieval-mediterranean-2, accessed 28th February 2019.

10. Nicholas Mystikos, quoted in Julian Chrysostomides, "Byzantine Concepts of War and Peace", in Anja V. Hartmann and Beatrice Heuser eds., *War, Peace and World Orders in European History* (London: Routledge, 2001).

11. For details, see: Ballan, "Andalusi Crete".

12. Yāqūt, quoted in Mohamad Ballan, "Andalusi Crete (827–961) and the Arab-Byzantine Frontier in the Early Medieval Mediterranean", *Ballandalus*, 9th April 2015, https://ballandalus.wordpress.com/2015/04/09/andalusi-crete-827–961-and-the-arab-byzantine-frontier-in-the-early-medieval-mediterranean-2, accessed 8th March 2019.

13. Quoted in Vassilios Christides, *The Conquest of Crete by the Arabs (ca. 824). A Turning Point in the Struggle between Byzantium and Islam* (Athens: Akademia Athenon, 1984), p. 121.

14. Sophia Oikonomou, *The Life of Ioannes Xenos: critical edition and commentary* [PhD thesis] (University of London, 1999), https://kclpure.kcl.ac.uk/portal/files/2930492/DX214561.pdf, accessed 28th February 2019.

15. Quoted in George C. Miles, "Byzantium and the Arabs: Relations in Crete and the Aegean Area", *Dumbarton Oaks Papers*, vol. 18, 1964, p. 15.

9 The Second Byzantine Period

1. George Dalidakis, "Cretan Nobility and the Legend of the 12 Young Rulers", *Explore Crete*, http://www.explorecrete.com/history/crete-byzantium-rulers.htm, accessed 1 February 2019.

2. Leo the Deacon, *The History of Leo the Deacon,* Alice-Mary Talbot and Denis F. Sullivan trans. (Cambridge: Harvard University Press, 2005), book II, para. 6.

3. Denis F. Sullivan ed. and trans., *The Life of Saint Nikon* (Massachusetts: Hellenic College Press, 1987).

4. Sullivan, *The Life of Saint Nikon.*

5. Oikonomou, *The Life of Ioannes Xenos.*

6. The full story of the Fourth Crusade is extremely complex but absolutely fascinating. For further reading, many excellent books are available, including Volume 3 of Steven Runciman's *A History of the Crusades,* still relevant and readable after fifty years.

7. The official title of the city state of Venice was The Most Serene Republic of Venice (Serenissima Repubblica di Venezia), sometimes just referred to as the Serenissima.

8. As I write, the amount paid for the island would buy a four-bedroom villa with a pool and a sea view in Elounda. The Venetians got quite a bargain!

10 Venetian Rule

1. For the sake of clarity, from here on, I shall only use "Candia" to describe the city, unless quoting from contemporary sources.

2. Monique O'Connell, *Men of Empire: Power and Negotiation in Venice's Maritime State* (Baltimore: Johns Hopkins University Press, 2009), p. 133.

3. O'Connell, *Men of Empire.*

4. For a detailed account of the revolts, see: Detorakis, *History of Crete.*

5. Lorenzo de Monacis, quoted in Sally McKee, "The Revolt of St. Tito in fourteenth-century Venetian Crete: A reassessment", *Mediterranean Historical Review*, vol. 9, no. 2, 1994.

6. Detorakis, *History of Crete*, p. 201.

7. This is another name for the ducat, about £42,000 at today's gold prices.

8. Will of Markos Papadopoulos, quoted in Detorakis, *History of Crete*, p. 206.

9. Detorakis, *History of Crete*, p. 176.

10. William Lithgow, quoted in John Tomkinson ed., *Travels in Crete* (Athens: Anagnosis, 2013).

11. Quoted in David Holton ed., *Literature and Society in Renaissance Crete* (Cambridge University Press, 1991).

12. See: "The History of the Jews of Crete", *Etz Hayyim Synagogue*, www.etz-hayyim-hania.org/the-jews-of-crete/the-history-of-the-jews-of-crete, accessed 28th February 2019.

13. Molly Greene, *A Shared World: Christians and Muslims in the Early Modern Mediterranean* (Princeton University Press, 1959).

14. Quoted in Chryssa Maltezou, "The Historical Context", in Holton, *Literature and Society.*

15. Quoted in Maltezou, "The Historical Context".

16. Quoted in Greene, *A Shared World.*

17. Quoted in Greene, *A Shared World.*

18. Sally McKee, "Women under Venetian Colonial Rule in the Early Renaissance", *Renaissance Quarterly*, vol. 51, no. 1, spring 1998.

19. McKee, "Women under Venetian Colonial Rule".

20. It was in a barrel of malmsey that Richard III is alleged to have had his rival for the throne, George Plantagenet, Duke of Clarence, drowned.

21. Canon Pietro Casola, quoted in Tomkinson, *Travels in Crete.*

22. Quoted in Detorakis, *History of Crete*, p. 201.

23. See: David Jacoby, "Cretan Cheese: A Neglected Aspect of Venetian Mediterranean Trade", in Ellen E. Kittell and Thomas F. Madden ed., *Medieval and Renaissance Venice* (University of Illinois Press, 1999).

24. Canon Pietro Casola, quoted in Tomkinson, *Travels in Crete*.

25. Quoted in Holton, *Literature and Society*, p. 70.

26. Quoted in Detorakis, *History of Crete*, p. 198.

27. Quoted in Detorakis, *History of Crete*, p. 198.

28. Quoted in Detorakis, *History of Crete*, p. 199.

29. Fynes Moryson, quoted in Tomkinson, *Travels in Crete*.

30. Quoted in Detorakis, *History of Crete*, p. 200.

31. For much of this detail about the plague of 1592, see: Costas Tsiamis et al., "The Venetian Lazarettos of Candia and the Great Plague (1592–1595)", *Le Infezioni in Medicina*, vol. 22, no. 1, March 2014.

32. Personal correspondence with the author, August 2016.

33. Horace "Horace: The Epistles", *Poetry in Translation*, A. S. Kline trans., 2005, https://www.poetryintranslation.com/PITBR/Latin/HoraceEpistlesBkIIEpI.php#anchor_Toc98154295, accessed 19th March 2019.

34. The term "political verse" has nothing to do with politics, but is a literal translation of the Greek word politikos, meaning "civil", and thus relates to secular as opposed to religious poetry.

35. Konstantinos Demaras, *A History of Modern Greek Literature* (State University of New York Press, 1972).

36. Quoted in Rosemary Bancroft-Marcus, "The Pastoral Mode", in Holton, *Literature and Society*.

37. Quoted in Detorakis, *History of Crete*, p. 219.

38. For this translation and the original Greek set to music, see: Cobone, "Erotokritos Ερωτόκριτος Excrept 1614" [video], *YouTube*, 24th May 2016, https://www.youtube.com/watch?v=Q_03zbslDKc, accessed 19th March 2019.

39. Quoted in Yannis Samatas, "Mantinades in Crete", *Explore Crete*, http://www.explorecrete.com/cretan-music/mantinades.html, accessed 28th February 2019.

40. San Giorgio dei Greci is Saint George of the Greeks, an Orthodox church built in Venice in 1548.

11 The Cretan War

1. Quoted in Detorakis, *History of Crete*, p. 240.
2. Quoted in Greene, *A Shared World*.

12 Ottoman Rule I

1. Quoted in Detorakis, *History of Crete*, p. 272.
2. Quoted in Yorgo Dedes, "Blame it on the Turko-Romnioi (Turkish Rums): A Muslim Cretan song on the abolition of the Janissaries" in Evangelia Balta and Mehmet Ölmez eds., *Between Religion and Language* (Istanbul: Eren, 2011).
3. Antonis Anastasopoulos, "Non-Muslims and Ottoman Justice(s?)", in Jeroen Duindam et al. eds., *Law and Empire: Ideas, Practices, Actors* (Leiden & Boston: Brill, 2013).
4. Quoted in Greene, *A Shared World*.
5. Quoted in Greene, *A Shared World*.
6. Chainospilios (Cave of the Hains) near Iraklion was one such hideout, used many years later by British agents and Cretan resistance fighters during the German occupation.
7. Joseph Pitton de Tournefort, quoted in Tomkinson, *Travels in Crete*.
8. Barba-Pandzelios, quoted in Detorakis, *History of Crete*.
9. The week after Easter is known as Bright Week in the Orthodox Church and includes several important feast days.
10. Aubry de la Motraye, quoted in Tomkinson, *Travels in Crete*.
11. There is a widespread belief that the diminutive "-akis" ending on Cretan names was a derogatory usage by the Turks, but the fact that Muslim Cretans also used the suffix is evidence that this is a myth. Although the suffix can mean "little", as in "neraki" (a little water), it was also used to denote "son of", and seems to have predated Ottoman rule.
12. In particular, see: Greene, *A Shared World*.
13. John Bacon Sawry Morritt, quoted in Tomkinson, *Travels in Crete*.
14. Quoted in Dedes, "Blame it on the Turko-Romnioi".
15. Quoted in Dedes, "Blame it on the Turko-Romnioi".
16. Some scholars have, in fact, traced their origins back to the warlike songs of Dorian times.

17. Translated by Hasse Petersen, quoted with his permission. See his website at www.kretakultur.dk.

18. Translated by Hasse Petersen, revised by Manolis Sfyrakis. For the original Greek version of this mantinada, *Πότες θα κάμει ξαστεριά, ποτες θα φλεβαρίσει*, sung by the great Cretan singer Nikos Xylouris, see: SmileLikeYouMeanIt88, "Νίκος Ξυλούρης - Πότε θα Κάνει Ξαστεριά" [video], *YouTube*, 23rd February 2009, https://www.youtube.com/watch?v=nzSjGLAVQpY, accessed 19th March 2019.

13 Ottoman Rule II

1. Kazantzakis, *Freedom and Death*.

2. Leonidas Kallivretakis, "A Century of Revolutions: The Cretan Question between European and Near East Politics", in Paschalis Kitromilides, *Eleftherios Venizelos: The Trials of Statesmanship* (Edinburgh University Press, 2006)

3. Quoted in Mick McTiernan, *A Very Bad Place Indeed for a Soldier: The British involvement in the early stages of the European Intervention in Crete, 1897–1898* [dissertation] (King's College London, 2014).

4. Quoted in Detorakis, *History of Crete*, p. 292.

5. Kallinikos Kritovoulidis, quoted in Detorakis, *History of Crete*.

6. Quoted in Detorakis, *History of Crete*, p. 299.

7. For a fictionalised telling of the story of Rhodanthe, see: Yvonne Payne, *Kritsotopoula* (Bristol: SilverWood Books, 2015).

8. Although not a major battle of the war, this event is interesting because the cave, still accessible, contains a small chapel containing an ossuary with the bones of many of the victims. A service of remembrance is held in the cave on Saint Thomas Sunday (the Sunday after Orthodox Easter).

9. Quoted in Detorakis, *History of Crete*, p. 311.

10. Quoted in Detorakis, *History of Crete*, p. 319.

11. Robert Pashley, *Travels in Crete*, 1837.

12. Quoted in David Barchard, "The Clash of Religions in Nineteenth Century Crete", in David Shankland ed., *Archaeology, Anthropology And Heritage In The Balkans And Anatolia* (Istanbul: Isis Press, 2004).

13. Quoted in Detorakis, *History of Crete*, p. 332.

14. "The Insurrection in Crete. Appeal to the United States", *The New York Times*, 29th September 1866.

15. To this day, Arkadi monastery remains one of the most sacred sites in Crete. A service of commemoration is held every 8th November, on the Feast of Saint Michael and All Archangels, the date of the battle.

16. Kallivretakis, "A Century of Revolutions".

17. Quoted in Pinar Senisik, *The Transformation of Ottoman Crete* (London: I.B. Tauris, 2011).

18. Quoted in Detorakis, *History of Crete*, p. 366.

19. For this and most of the detail given about the Candia riots, see: Mick McTiernan, *A Very Bad Place*. Used with the permission of the author.

20. Quoted in McTiernan, *A Very Bad Place*, p. 31.

21. Quoted in McTiernan, *A Very Bad Place*, p. 32.

22. Quoted in McTiernan, *A Very Bad Place*, p. 42.

23. Quoted in McTiernan, *A Very Bad Place*, p. 42.

24. For a detailed analysis of the Cretan economy in the nineteenth century, see: Manos Perakis, "An Eastern Mediterranean Economy Under Transformation: Crete in the late Ottoman era (1840–98)", *Journal of European Economic History*, vol. 40, no. 3, December 2011.

25. For a thorough analysis of these reforms, see: Panagiotis Krokidas and Athanasios Gekas, "Public Health in Crete under the rule of Mehmed Ali in the 1830s", *Égypte/Monde arabe*, vol. 3, no. 4, 2007.

26. Quoted in Detorakis, *History of Crete*, p. 375.

27. Quoted in Anna Kouvarakis, *Historical and Cultural Dimensions of the Muslim Cretans in Turkey* [Master's thesis] (Istanbul Bilgi University, 2014), http://openaccess.bilgi.edu.tr:8080/xmlui/bitstream/handle/11411/718/anna%20kouvaraki.pdf, accessed 8th March 2019.

28. Quoted in David Barchard, "The Fearless and Self-Reliant Servant: The Life and Career of Sir Alfred Biliotti (1833–1915), an Italian Levantine in British Service", *Studi Micenei ed*

Egeo-Anatolici [*Mycenaean and Aegean-Anatolian Studies*], no. 48, 2006, pp. 5–53.

29. Quoted by Mick McTiernan in personal correspondence with the author, 2019.

14 Autonomy

1. Quoted in Detorakis, *History of Crete*, p. 405.
2. Quoted in Detorakis, *History of Crete*, p. 406.
3. Quoted in Elektra Kostopoulou, "The Island that Wasn't: Autonomous Crete (1898–1912) and Experiments of Federalization", *Journal of Balkan and Near Eastern Studies*, vol. 18, 2016.
4. Quoted in Detorakis, *History of Crete*, p. 407.
5. Kostopoulou, "The Island that Wasn't".
6. Quoted in Detorakis, *History of Crete*, p. 407.
7. Quoted in Detorakis, *History of Crete*, p. 408.
8. H.N. Brailsford, "The Future of Crete", *The North American Review*, vol. 181, no. 585, August 1905.
9. Quoted in Philip Carabott, "A Country in a 'State of Destitution' Labouring under an 'Unfortunate Regime': Crete at the Turn of the 20th century (1898–1906)", *Creta Antica*, no. 7, 2006.
10. Quoted in Detorakis, *History of Crete*, p. 418.
11. The Admiralty, quoted in "August 18 1909, the Powers return", *The British in Crete, 1896 to 1913*, https://britishinterventionincrete.wordpress.com, accessed 18 February 2019. Courtesy of Mick McTiernan.
12. For much of the information given on the economy of this period, see: Manos Perakis, "Muslim exodus and land redistribution in Autonomous Crete (1898–1913)", *Mediterranean Historical Review*, vol. 26, no. 2, 2011.
13. Quoted in Perakis, "Muslim exodus and land redistribution".
14. Elektra Kostopoulou, "The Art of Being Replaced: The Last of the Cretan Muslims Between the Empire and the Nation-State", in Jørgen S. Nielsen ed., *Religion, Ethnicity and Contested Nationhood in the Former Ottoman Space* (Leiden: Brill Publishers, 2012).

15. The sources for these statistics include: Perakis, "Muslim exodus and land redistribution"; Carabott, "A Country in a 'State of Destitution'"; Detorakis, *History of Crete*.

16. Quoted in McTiernan, *A Very Bad Place*.

17. For philatelists, the stamps of the European post offices and the Cretan State are an interesting study.

18. Quoted in Kostopoulou, "The Island that Wasn't".

19. It is possible that the character of the archaeologist Hatzisavvas in Kazantzakis' novel *Captain Michalis* was based on Joseph Hatzidakis.

20. Vasilis Varouhakis, *Ignorant Peasants, Patriot Antiquarians and National Benefactors from the West* [seminar], University College London, 30th April 2014. Seminar paper available at https://www.academia.edu/7149398/ Ignorant_peasants_patriot_antiquarians_and_national_ benefactors_from_the_West_Crypto-colonial_and_national_ archaeologies_as_identity_politics_in_the_Cretan_state.

21. Quoted in Varouhakis, *Ignorant Peasants*.

15 Union with Greece

1. "Το Κίνημα των Χανίων κατά της Μεταξικής Δικτατορίας" ["The Movement of Chania against the Metaxic Dictatorship"], *Ριζοσπάστης* [*Rizospastis*], 29th July 2007, https://www. rizospastis.gr/story.do?id=4144432 , accessed 8th March 2019. Translated by Manolis Sfyrakis.

2. Information from Dave Davis, author of an unpublished booklet on Imperial Airways and Elounda.

3. Quoted in Georgios Mamakis, *Spinalonga, The Island of Suffering, Faith and Hope* (Neapolis: Holy Metropolis of Petra and Cherronisos, 2011).

4. Quoted in Mamakis, *Spinalonga*.

5. Maria Iliou, *From Both Sides of the Aegean: Expulsion and Exchange of Populations, Turkey-Greece: 1922–1924* [film], 2014.

6. Iliou, *From Both Sides of the Aegean*.

16 The Battle of Crete and Occupation

1. My main sources of research were: George Forty, *Battle of Crete* (Hersham: Ian Allan Publishing, 2001); Seán Damer and Ian Frazer, *On the Run* (London: Penguin, 2006); Antony Beevor, *Crete: The Battle and the Resistance* (London: John Murray, 2011); Costas Hadjipateras and Maria Fafalios, *Crete 1941 Eyewitnessed* (Athens: Efstathiadis Group, 2007); George Psychoundakis, *The Cretan Runner*, Patrick Leigh Fermor trans. (London: Penguin, 2009).

2. See: Beevor, *Crete: The Battle and the Resistance*.

3. Quoted in Forty, *Battle of Crete*.

4. Quoted in Beevor, *Crete: The Battle and the Resistance*.

5. In one action, a single regiment of the Cretans put a whole Italian division to flight.

6. So accurate was the information Freyberg received that, as he watched the German planes approaching, he said to one of his officers, "H'mph. They're dead on time" (quoted in Beevor, *Crete: The Battle and the Resistance*).

7. Hadjipateras and Fafalios, *Crete 1941 Eyewitnessed*.

8. Quoted in Beevor, *Crete: The Battle and the Resistance*.

9. Hadjipateras and Fafalios, *Crete 1941 Eyewitnessed*.

10. Beevor, *Crete: The Battle and the Resistance*.

11. Hill 107 is now the site of the German War Cemetery at Maleme.

12. Quoted in Beevor, *Crete: The Battle and the Resistance*.

13. Quoted in Beevor, *Crete: The Battle and the Resistance*.

14. Hadjipateras and Fafalios, *Crete 1941 Eyewitnessed*.

15. Hadjipateras and Fafalios, *Crete 1941 Eyewitnessed*.

16. Takis Akritas, quoted in Hadjipateras and Fafalios, *Crete 1941 Eyewitnessed*.

17. Quoted in Hadjipateras and Fafalios, *Crete 1941 Eyewitnessed*.

18. Quoted in Philip Eade, *Evelyn Waugh: A Life Revisited* (London: Hachette, 2016).

19. Quoted in Beevor, *Crete: The Battle and the Resistance*.

20. Psychoundakis, *The Cretan Runner*.

21. Quoted in Mamakis, *Spinalonga*.

22. Hadjipateras and Fafalios, *Crete 1941 Eyewitnessed*.

23. There were so many escapes from the Galatas prison camp that all prisoners were moved to the mainland in February 1942.

24. Bruce Johnston, quoted in Damer and Frazer, *On the Run*.

25. Quoted in Chris Moorey, *Crowns of Barbed Wire: Orthodox Christian Martyrs of the Twentieth Century* (self-published, 2015).

26. Quoted in Damer and Frazer, *On the Run*.

27. Quoted in Beevor, *Crete: The Battle and the Resistance*.

28. Jeffrey Myers, "My Meeting with the Byron of Our Times", *Patrick Leigh Fermor*, 21st February 2015, https://patrickleighfermor.org/2015/02/21/my-meeting-with-the-byron-of-our-times, accessed 8th March 2019.

29. Psychoundakis, *The Cretan Runner*.

30. Patrick Leigh Fermor, "Introduction", in Psychoundakis, *The Cretan Runner*.

31. Katina Eleftheraki in Hadjipateras and Fafalios, *Crete 1941 Eyewitnessed*.

32. Quoted in Beevor, *Crete: The Battle and the Resistance*.

33. The film was based on the book of the same name (W. Stanley Moss, *Ill Met By Moonlight*, London: Cassell Military, 2014). Patrick Leigh Fermor also wrote an account of the kidnap (Patrick Leigh Fermor, *Abducting a General: The Kreipe Operation and SOE in Crete,* London: John Murray, 2014).

34. Quoted in Moss, *Ill Met By Moonlight*.

35. Quoted in Beevor, *Crete: The Battle and the Resistance*.

36. Quoted in Beevor, *Crete: The Battle and the Resistance*.

37. Quoted in Hadjipateras and Fafalios, *Crete 1941 Eyewitnessed*.

38. Quoted in Hadjipateras and Fafalios, *Crete 1941 Eyewitnessed*.

17 Civil War

1. I am indebted to Colin Janes for his book *The Eagles of Crete: An Untold Story of Civil War* (self-published, 2013). Before his book was published, there was almost no information in English on the civil war in Crete.

18 Post-War Crete

1. Brailsford, "The Future of Crete".

2. We arrived in Crete during the lead-up to an election, and nearly every road had the word "PASOK" painted on it in large letters. Knowing almost no Greek and nothing about Greek politics, we thought for a long time that these were road signs meaning something like "slow".

3. See: "Parliamentary Elections September 2015", *Ministry of Interior*, http://ekloges.ypes.gr/current/v/public/index.html?lang=en#%7B%22cls%22:%22main%22,%22params%22:%7B%7D%7D, accessed 19th March 2019; and "Elections Results", *Ministry of Interior*, http://www.ypes.gr/en/Elections/NationalElections/Results, accessed 19th March 2019.

4. Petros Drygiannakis, "Τα Ανωγεια Φτυνουν Την Χρυση Αυγη Και Δεν Την Ψηφιζουν..." [video], *YouTube*, 27th January 2015, https://www.youtube.com/watch?v=leFiYXugsL8, accessed 8th March 2019.

5. Drygiannakis, "Τα Ανωγεια Φτυνουν Την Χρυση Αυγη".

6. Ray, "Junta Days Chapter 06", *Crete: The Island in the Wine Dark Sea*, https://crete.wordpress.com/junta-days/junta-days-chapter-06, accessed 28th February 2019.

7. All statistics are from the Greek website *e-Demography* which, among many other things, analyses census results. Unfortunately, the site is entirely in Greek. See: *e-Demography*, http://www.e-demography.gr/ElstatPublications/censuses/index.cfm?year=2001, accessed 19th March 2019.

8. "Zaro's Named Best Bottled Water in the World", *Greek Reporter*, 28th February 2017, https://greece.greekreporter.com/2017/02/28/zaros-named-best-bottled-water-in-the-world, accessed 19th March 2019.

9. Although this is probably the best-known novel based on Spinalonga, there are several other excellent books, including Beryl Darby's Cretan Saga series of novels, beginning with *Yannis* (Brighton: JACH Publishing, 2006).

10. "Aristides Chairetis, the mantinades composer of Love", *Explore Crete*, http://www.explorecrete.com/cretan-music/mantinades_Chairetis.html, accessed 28th February 2019.

11. Yannis Samatas, "Mantinades in Crete", *Explore Crete*, http://www.explorecrete.com/cretan-music/mantinades.html, accessed 28th February 2019.

12. Quoted in Niki P. Stavrou, "A Glance upon his Life", *Kazantzakis Publications*, http://www.kazantzakispublications.org/en/kazantzakis.php, accessed 8th March 2019.

13. He used a pen name, having been born Odysseas Alepoudellis.

14. "Odysseus Elytis", *Poetry Foundation*, https://www.poetryfoundation.org/poets/odysseus-elytis, accessed 8th March 2019.

15. Odysseus Elytis, *The axion esti*, Edmund Keeley and George Savidis trans. (London: Anvil Press Poetry, 2007). The Keeley and Savidis translation is widely acknowledged to be the one that does most justice to the original.

16. However, the film about the wartime abduction of General Kreipe, *Ill Met by Moonlight,* was filmed not in Crete but at Pinewood Studios in England, with location shooting in the Alpes-Maritimes in France and Italy, and on the Côte d'Azur in France.

17. "Carey", *Joni Mitchell*, http://jonimitchell.com/music/song.cfm?id=88, accessed 21st March 2019.

18. In November 2017, I heard that many of the larger hotels in Crete have agreed to offer more half-board or bed and breakfast holidays. I have been unable to verify this – but, if true, it is a positive move.

19. Diana Conyers, *Uncaptured Crete* (Iraklion: Mystis Editions, 2015).

20. Mantinada by Yiorgis Karatzis, carved on a sculpture by Franz Herman Polgar in the Lychnostatis Museum. The sculpture contains wood carvings depicting the history of Crete.

Index